Edited by Alex Johnson

ART DAY BY DAY

366
BRUSHES
WITH
HISTORY

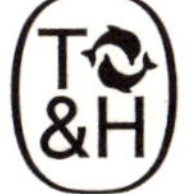

To Wilma, Robert, Edward and Thomas

First published in the United Kingdom in 2021 by
Thames & Hudson Ltd, 181A High Holborn,
London WC1V 7QX

First published in the United States of America in 2021 by
Thames & Hudson Inc., 500 Fifth Avenue, New York,
New York 10110

Art Day by Day: 366 Brushes with History

Page design by Lisa Ifsits

British Library Cataloguing-in-Publication Data
A catalogue record for this book is available from
the British Library

Library of Congress Control Number 2021934158

ISBN 978-0-500-02364-8

Printed and bound in the UK by CPI (UK) Ltd

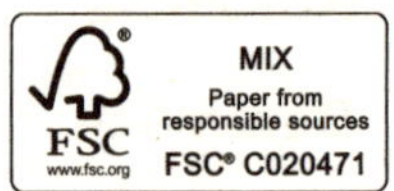

Be the first to know about our new releases,
exclusive content and author events by visiting
thamesandhudson.com
thamesandhudsonusa.com
thamesandhudson.com.au

Contents

Introduction

Historians tend to take the long view. They examine the growth of movements, the developments of trends, ongoing phases, long sweeps of time, decline and fall. There is nothing wrong with this, except for the danger that it can relegate the individual act or the moment of revelation to a position of less importance.

The 366 snapshots in time from around the world and throughout history featured in this book aim to redress that balance, whether that is the first work of art made in space (18 March) or dinner inside a giant dinosaur sculpture (31 December). Using diaries, posters, letters, catalogues, autobiographies, advertisements, television listings, speeches, transcripts, cartoons, song lyrics and interviews, it offers an important event that happened on that day in the history of art. Here are famous paintings, comic strips, photographs, ancient sculptures, murals, manifestos, births, marriages and deaths, from the genius of the old to *The Shock of the New*, and terracotta soldiers to a self-shredding Banksy.

Each entry begins with a quote, giving artists, critics and commentators their voice to speak directly to us, followed by a note of explanation to illuminate its importance and a brief round-up of other events on that day. Not every entry is momentous, but all are significant. Yes, there are thefts, murders and eureka moments, but there are also President Theodore Roosevelt's doodles and Michelangelo's kidney stones. Every day has a story to tell.

So here is the moment when the ancient statue of *Laocoön and His Sons* is dug out of the ground fifteen hundred years after it is described by Pliny the Elder. We sight the Easter Island statues and Tsar Alexander III opens the first Fabergé egg. Edward Hopper finishes *Nighthawks*. Apollinaire records his thoughts on seeing sketches by Picasso for *Les Demoiselles d'Avignon*. The Etch A Sketch goes on sale. *The Rebel* starring Tony Hancock premieres and Brian Ward takes the album cover photo for *The Rise and Fall of Ziggy Stardust and the Spiders from Mars*. Judy Chicago opens *The Dinner Party*. Saddam Hussein's statue is toppled in Baghdad.

Each entry can be read entirely on its own although I hope the accounts will also be signposts to longer journeys. Van Gogh's diaries are fascinating and freely available online. The full story behind Théodore Géricault's *Raft of the Medusa* (glimpsed on 2 July) is remarkable. There is only room to touch on Rembrandt's inventory of possessions, but a longer investigation is certainly worth the effort.

However you read it – methodically day by day, randomly as it falls open, by your family's birthdays – I hope you find plenty to enjoy and much food for thought.

January

The first iron bridge
opens to the public, 1781

Of the iron bridge over the Severn, which we crossed and where we stop'd for half an hour, what shall I say? That it must be the admiration, as it is one of the wonders, of the world. It was cast in 1778, the arch is 100 feet wide, and 55 feet from the top of the water, and the whole length is 100 yards; the country agreed with the founder to finish it for £6,000 and have meanly made him suffer for his noble undertaking. After this survey, we entered Mr Bank's iron furnace (on the hillside) and were most civilly shown by him all the astonishing progress of such (hellish hot) manufactories; he employs 700 workmen and said there were seven other neighbouring furnaces of the same size; judge then of the flourishing state of this branch of trade, and how it must enrich this vicinage and the kingdom! Every cart belonging to this trade is made of iron and even the ruts in the road are shod with iron!

John Byng, diary entry, July 1784

The world's first cast-iron bridge made a lasting impression on English traveller and diarist John Byng (1743–1813) when he first visited it in Shropshire. Designed by local Shrewsbury architect Thomas Pritchard (1723–1777) working with iron manufacturer Abraham Darby III (1678–1717), who owned the ironworks where the bridge was cast, it enabled goods to be transported easily across the river as the area forged the Industrial Revolution. Scaffolding and a wooden framework were used during construction and about three-quarters of the bridge's components were made individually and fitted together using carpentry joining techniques, such as dovetail joints.

From its opening on New Year's Day, 1781, tolls were collected on the bridge until 1950 – the sign outside the tollhouse specifically states there is no exemption for serving soldiers, mail wagons and members of the royal family. Although it became a scheduled monument in 1934, the iron bridge came close to being demolished and replaced in the 1950s but has now been recognized as a UNESCO World Heritage Site.

Its picturesque gorge setting has attracted many artists, including English painter Michael Angelo Rooker, whose 1782 engraving so entranced US president Thomas Jefferson that he hung a copy of it in the dining room of his

Monticello home in Virginia. In 1979, as part of its bicentenary celebrations, the Royal Academy of Arts in London held an exhibition of art depicting the bridge from its construction to the present day called 'A View from the Iron Bridge'.

While it entranced Byng, topographical writer the Reverend Richard Warner was not so sure when he visited the area in 1801, describing it as:

> A scene in which the beauties of nature and processes of art are blended together in curious combination. The valley...would be exceedingly picturesque, were it not for the huge foundries, which, volcano-like, send up volumes of smoke into the air, discolouring nature and robbing the trees of their beauty; and the cast heaps of red-hot iron ore and coke, that give the bottom 'ever burning with solid fire' more the appearance of Milton's hell than of his paradise.

ALSO ON THIS DAY 1944: Death of English architect Sir Edwin Lutyens (*see* 11 November) · **1999:** *Girl with a Pearl Earring* by Tracy Chevalier is published · **2001:** In Magnuson Park, Seattle art group Some People anonymously erect a replica of the monolith in *2001: A Space Odyssey*

2 JANUARY

A game inspires the oldest painting of a football match, 1895

I have had a chat with Mr T. M. Hemy, the distinguished artist who was born at Newcastle, but who is practically a Sunderland man by sympathy, as his many fine pictures of portions of this town show. And I am glad to find that my friend is marching on from one big achievement to another. His world-famous works *And Every Soul Was Saved*, *The Wreck of the 'Birkenhead'* and others which have won him the proud title of 'The Clark Russell of the Brush' are to be followed by one which I believe will be the finest and most striking of a soul-stirring series. The theme is the fight between HMS *Shannon* (38 guns) and the United States frigate *Chessapeake* [*sic*] (50 guns) in 1813.

By the way, Mr Hemy has also earned fame as a football painter.

'Echoes of the Week' column,
***Sunderland Echo*, 7 January 1895**

Sunderland v. Aston Villa 1895 by English painter Thomas Hemy (1852–1937), although not the world's oldest-known football painting (local artist Jos Curry painted the Sunderland AFC team in what has become the accepted official squad pose in 1892), it is the oldest showing a match in progress. Also known as *A Corner Kick* and *The Last Minute – Now or Never*, the moment portrayed between the two top sides is a corner in the 2 January game at Sunderland's Newcastle Road ground. It ended in a 4–4 draw.

Hemy had been a sailor in his youth and, like his famous brother artist Charles Napier Hemy, he usually focused on marine paintings, hence the *Sunderland Echo*'s comparison with nautical novelist William Clark Russell. However, he also depicted more urban local scenes and this 2.5 × 3.7 metre (8 × 12 foot) painting shows a greatly packed old-fashioned penalty area, a pitch in a truly terrible condition and piles of straw by the touchline, which was used to cover pitches to protect them from frost in winter.

After a chequered history of ownership, the painting is now appropriately on permanent show at Sunderland's Stadium of Light football ground.

ALSO ON THIS DAY **1462:** Italian painter Piero di Cosimo born · **1777:** German sculptor Christian Rauch born · **1938:** English photographer David Bailey born

3 JANUARY

John Ruskin meets Rose La Touche for the first time, 1858

...the drawing room door opened, and Rosie came in, quietly taking stock of me with her blue eyes as she walked across the room; gave me her hand, as a good dog gives its paw, and then stood a little back. Nine years old, on 3 January 1858, thus now rising towards ten; neither tall nor short for her age; a little stiff in her way of standing. The eyes rather deep blue at that time, and fuller and softer than afterwards. Lips perfectly lovely in profile; a little too wide, and hard in edge, seen in front; the rest of the features what a fair, well-bred Irish girl's usually are; the hair, perhaps, more graceful in short curl around the forehead, and softer than one sees often, in the close-bound tresses above the neck.

John Ruskin, *Praeterita*, 1885

In his memoir *Praeterita*, English art critic and polymath John Ruskin (1819–1900; *see also* 13 May) recounts his first impressions of Rose La Touche, who became his pupil, muse and object of his affection, even after her death in 1875. Their relationship is alluded to in the novel *Lolita* by Russian-American author Vladimir Nabokov.

Ruskin was taken with her immediately and, after a lengthy correspondence, proposed to her when she was eighteen. However, the match was opposed by her family (and indeed Ruskin's ex-wife Scottish painter Effie Gray) and the two only met intermittently. After several years of consideration, Rose turned down the proposal of the man she called St Crumpet. Her death, probably of anorexia, caused Ruskin much mental anguish and in his later years he sought comfort in spiritualism, trying to contact her in the afterlife and calling out for his 'Rosie-Posie'.

Praeterita also includes Rose La Touche's first letter to Ruskin in which she describes a trip to Nice. 'Some wise, and prettily mannered people have told me I shouldn't say anything about Rosie at all. But I am too old now to take advice,' he wrote, 'and I won't have this following letter – the first she ever wrote me – moulder away.'

ALSO ON THIS DAY 1027: Death of Japanese calligrapher Fujiwara no Yukinari · **1795**: Death of English pottery entrepreneur Josiah Wedgwood (*see* 15 May) · **2000**: Final daily edition of the comic strip *Peanuts* by Charles M. Schulz (*see* 2 October 1950)

4 JANUARY

On Kawara begins
his Date Paintings, 1966

Kawara said very little about his art and preferred to leave much about it unexplained. He did, however, identify one central theme: human consciousness, an individual's heightened awareness of his or her existence in the world. Kawara also said that a Date Painting represents a paradox – that each painting forever signifies the present by bearing the name and date of the day it was made, yet once the day is over, that present belongs only to the past.

**Press release for the 'On Kawara – Silence' exhibition
at the Guggenheim Museum, New York, 22 December 2014**

Famously silent about his life and work, Japanese artist On Kawara (1933–2014) worked on his 'Today' series, or Date Paintings, for forty-eight years, producing thousands of works that consisted of the date painted in white on a colour-block background. Starting with *JAN. 4, 1966*, each date was hand-drawn in a kind of Gill Sans or Futura sans-serif typeface and in the language and dating system of the country of the 112 in which he was working, so *26. ÁG. 1995* when he was in Reykjavik, Iceland. If the language did not use the Roman alphabet, he used Esperanto instead. If he had not finished the painting by midnight, he discarded it.

Intended as a comment on the very meaning of existence, and the concepts of place and time, every painting was accompanied by a homemade cardboard box that included information about Kawara's experiences that day, especially snippets from newspapers such as obituaries or weather forecasts, mostly from the *New York Times*. The collection also contained a smudge of the paint used. Although integral to his work, these boxes are not usually exhibited alongside the paintings.

The paintings were made in Liquitex on canvas, were all horizontal, except for three days around the moon landings in 1969, varied in size from A4 up to 3.5 metres (11½ feet) and used red, blue or dark grey backgrounds behind the centred text. Kawara, who worked without an easel, applied four coats of paint, rubbing each coat down when dry in preparation for the next.

Other work reflects a similar fixation with date and time. Between 1968 and 1979 he sent daily postcards to friends and colleagues stamped with the time he woke up, while his two-volume book work *One Million Years* lists consecutive dates a million years into the past and another million into the future to celebrate everybody who has lived and died as well as the last survivor. Live readings of this are performed by two readers, one male and one female, reciting alternately.

Indeed, rather than provide a biography for exhibition catalogues, he only offered the number of days from his birth to the opening of the exhibition. He died at 29,771.

The exhibition catalogue
without an exhibition, 1969

40 KHZ ultrasonic soundwave installation, January 4, 1969, 8.25 mm ultrasonic soundwave. Collection Mr. Seth Siegelaub, N.Y.

Robert Barry artwork entry,
January 5–31, 1969 **exhibition catalogue**

American art dealer and curator Seth Siegelaub (1941–2013) was one of the leading promoters of conceptual and unconventional art in the USA in the 1960s and was also responsible for the 1971 Artist's Reserved Rights Transfer and Sale Agreement, which stated 'that should there ever be a question about artists' rights in reference to their art, the artist is more right than anyone else'. Among the group exhibitions that he organized was 'January 5–31, 1969', for which he took an intriguingly conceptual route rather than the conventional approach in that the exhibition catalogue was the only actual object on display. There were no paintings, no sculptures and no objects. The catalogue *was* the exhibition, containing works such as the one by American artist Robert Barry (b. 1936) above.

As well as Barry, the other artists taking part were Douglas Huebler (1924–1997), Joseph Kosuth (b. 1945) and Lawrence Weiner (b. 1942), each of whom included a statement about their work. The unpaginated, spiral-bound, twenty-eight-page catalogue measured 18 × 21 cm (7 × 8¼ inches) and was printed in black and white. The exhibition ran for a month in a temporary space at 44 East 52nd Street in Manhattan, New York.

ALSO ON THIS DAY 1477: German painter Hans Memling is wounded at the Battle of Nancy · **1892:** In Finland, German astronomer Otto Brendel takes the first photograph of the aurora borealis · **1917:** Death of English painter and stained-glass window designer Isobel Gloag

The hero of the Battle of Jersey dies, 1781

A body of French Troops having invaded the Island of Jersey in the year 1781, and having possessed themselves of the Town of St. Heiller's [*sic*], and taken the Lieutenant-Governor prisoner, obliged him in that situation, to sign a capitulation to surrender the Island; Major Peirson, a gallant young officer, under the age of twenty-four years, sensible of the invalidity of the capitulation made by the Lieutenant-Governor, whilst he was a prisoner, with great valour and prudence, attacked and totally defeated the French Troops, and thereby rescued the Island, and gloriously maintained the honour of the British arms; but unfortunately for his country, this brave officer fell in the moment of Victory, not by chance shot, but by a ball levelled at him, with a design by his death to check the ardour of the British Troops. The Major's death was instantly retaliated by his black servant on the man that shot the Major.

Extract from a brochure given to visitors at the first public showing in 1784 of John Singleton Copley's *The Death of Major Peirson, 6 January 1781*

Anglo-American painter John Singleton Copley (1738–1815) lived and worked successfully in England for forty years, making his name as a portraitist and with several large history paintings, including his 1783 depiction of the death of Major Francis Peirson (sometimes also spelled Pierson).

The Major's death came at the final efforts by the French army to take the island of Jersey from the British in 1781. French troops invaded on the morning of 6 January, but Peirson – the young commander of the two-thousand-strong British garrison – refused to surrender, went on the attack and was killed by a French shot in St Helier's Royal Square. This is the moment portrayed by Copley in *The Death of Major Peirson, 6 January 1781*, with Peirson leading the charge and his servant (sometimes referred to as 'Pompey' and modelled on the servant of the auctioneer James Christie) shooting Peirson's killer. After his death, the French were comprehensively defeated.

Peirson was acclaimed a national hero and Copley was immediately commissioned by publisher and future Lord Mayor of London John Boydell to mark his service to the country. When Copley first exhibited the painting in

May 1784 in rooms at 28 Haymarket, London – controversially done privately rather than at the Royal Academy – it attracted immense public crowds who each paid a shilling admission. It now belongs to the Tate and featured on the Jersey £10 and £1 notes between 1989 and 2010, and in a series of 7p, 10p, 15p and 17p stamps in 1981.

ALSO ON THIS DAY 1832: French painter and sculptor Gustave Doré born · **1902:** Death of Norwegian painter Lars Hertervig · **1998:** *Little Mermaid* statue in Copenhagen is decapitated by vandals (*see* 9 January 1998)

7 JANUARY

Tate Britain in London floods, 1928

Whole Country Swept by Gale.

- Trail of wreckage and Large Number of Casualties.
- THAMES EMBANKMENT FLOODED.
- Midnight Refugees from South Side Houses Camp Out in Waterloo.

Remarkable scenes were witnessed all along the Embankment. At the Houses of Parliament the water 'cataracted' over the parapet into the open space at the foot of Big Ben. The floods penetrated into Old Palace Yard, which shortly after one o'clock was about a foot under water in parts.

Flooding was worst at Charing Cross and Waterloo bridges, where the river sweeps round. Water poured over the Embankment, and the road was covered in a depth of several inches.

At intervals along the Embankment stood tramcars derelict and deserted. Later attempts were made to tow them through the floods by means of motor-lorries. Taxicabs and motor-cars splashed along the far side of the road. The public subway, Westminster Bridge, was flooded to a depth of four feet. There were miniature waterfalls at Cleopatra's Needle and the Royal Airforce Memorial, and the training ship President floated at street level.

The only spectators of the strange scenes were policemen, belated theatregoers and the usual Embankment stragglers.

Manchester Guardian, **7 January 1928**

A potent meteorological cocktail of heavy snow, sudden thaw and a colossal storm brought floodwater from the Thames surging into the Tate Gallery (now Tate Britain) in London in the early hours of 7 January 1928, reaching depths of up to 2.5 metres (8 feet). Fourteen people died in the city floods and around four thousand were made homeless.

Tate director Charles Aitken had major problems reaching the gallery (and at one point needed to be rescued when he fell into a flooded manhole), where he and Tate staff worked with volunteers – including many from London's other major galleries and museums – to pump the waters away from the nine basement galleries, which were all submerged.

Although eighteen paintings were ruined and nearly three hundred more damaged, the overall damage was not catastrophic. The newly finished murals by Rex Whistler on the restaurant walls emerged almost undamaged despite being entirely underwater for some time and covered in mud, and the colour on the Turner watercolours somehow had not run. There was also a happy ending for John Martin's enormous 1822 painting *The Destruction of Pompeii and Herculaneum*. Initially regarded as unsavable, it was rediscovered forty-five years later rolled up inside French artist Paul Delaroche's painting *The Execution of Lady Jane Grey* (1833), which itself had been considered lost. About a fifth of Martin's painting, including the volcano, needed major restoration but after careful work it went on display in an exhibition of Martin's work at Tate Britain in 2011.

Further floods in 1953 and 1967 came dangerously close to causing more damage to the Tate but a combination of a new storage area and the construction of the Thames Barrier now provides fully secure protection against flooding. Hopefully.

ALSO ON THIS DAY 1619: Death of English goldsmith and portrait miniaturist Nicholas Hilliard · **1830:** Death of English painter Thomas Lawrence · **1990:** Leaning Tower of Pisa is closed after leaning worsens (*see* 9 August)

Art forger Eric Hebborn sustains a fatal head injury, 1996

On the whole, critics, connoisseurs and art historians, when obliged to go beyond statements of fact – such as authorship, subject matter, measurement and medium – and speak of the quality of the drawing, tend to do so in the vaguest of terms…. To imagine that one can learn about drawings simply by looking at them is presumptuous, not unlike imagining that one can learn how aeroplanes work simply by flying in them.

Eric Hebborn, 'The Language of Line', unpublished manual

English painter Eric Hebborn (1934–1996) was arguably the 20th century's greatest art forger. After a troubled childhood, he studied at Chelmsford and Walthamstow art schools and then went on successfully to the Royal Academy of Arts in London and won a scholarship to the British School at Rome.

Working as an art restorer, he learned about the history of paper and moved on to making full-scale forgeries and paintings in the style of Old Masters, including Van Dyck, Rubens and Piranesi. These were sold through major art auction houses and Hebborn claimed his work found homes in many of the world's famous galleries, a claim they deny.

Hebborn openly admitted his forging career in 1984 and went on to attack what he saw as the pomposity, hypocrisy and general worthlessness of the mainstream art world in a series of books, including his autobiography *Drawn to Trouble*, *The Art Forger's Handbook* and his unpublished 'The Language of Line'.

Hebborn lived in Italy for many years and his death in Rome three days after sustaining a mysterious head injury following a night out with friends remains unexplained, with theories ranging from a stroke to a personal vendetta and even a mafia killing.

ALSO ON THIS DAY 1037: Chinese painter and calligrapher Su Shi born · **1638:** Italian painter Elisabetta Sirani born · **1775:** Death of English typeface designer John Baskerville

'Monuments of idolatry and superstition' are destroyed, 1643

Sudbury, Suffolk. Peter's parish. Jan. the 9th 1643. We brake down a picture of God the Father, 2 crucifixes, & pictures of Christ, about an hundred in all; and gave order to take down a cross off the steeple; and diverse angells, 20 at least, on the roof of the church.... Gregory parish. We brake down 10 mighty great angels in glass, in all, 80.... Allhallows. We brake about 20 superstitious pictures; and took up 30 brazen superstitious inscriptions, *ora pro nobis* and *pray for the soul.*

William Dowsing, journal entry,
9 January 1643

During the English Civil War, Puritan commissioner William Dowsing (1596–1679) was not unusual for focusing on destroying what government ordinances of the day described as 'monuments of idolatry and superstition', but he was unique in that he kept a meticulous diary about his brutal work in Suffolk, Cambridgeshire and Norfolk between 1643 and 1644.

During the 'second Reformation' of the 1640s, he roamed hundreds of parishes – and Cambridge colleges – in the region, shattering stained glass, removing monumental brasses, pulling down altar rails and confiscating crucifixes, stone crosses and statues. Angels and cherubim were his particular bête noires. He undertook the work personally and with apparent genuine religious zeal, but also had a team of assistants, some of whom were members of his family, to support his iconoclasm, for which he charged the churches themselves in addition to issuing fines for any non-compliance.

'Basher' Dowsing, as he was sometimes called, ended his course of destruction at the close of 1644 and returned to obscurity after Edward Montagu, 2nd Earl of Manchester, who had appointed him, quarrelled with the leader of the parliamentary forces, Oliver Cromwell. What is believed to be his portrait is on display at the Wolsey Art Gallery in Ipswich, Suffolk.

ALSO ON THIS DAY **1875:** Gertrude Vanderbilt Whitney, founder of the Whitney Museum of American Art, born · **1908:** Death of German illustrator and painter Wilhelm Busch · **1998:** Decapitated head of the *Little Mermaid* is returned (*see* 6 January 1998)

Darwin is intrigued by drawings of Galápagos finches, 1837

Mr Gould exhibited from Mr Darwin's collection of birds a series of Ground Finches, so peculiar in form that he was induced to regard them constituting an entirely new group, containing 14 species, and appearing to be strictly confined to the Galápagos Islands. Mr Gould believed the whole of these birds to be undescribed, and remarked that their principal peculiarity consisted in the bill presenting several distinct modifications of form, while the general contour of the species closely assimilated. He proposed to characterize them under the separate generic appellations of *Geospiza*, *Camarhynchus*, *Cactornis* and *Certhidea*.

Proceedings of the Zoological Society of London, 1837

When English naturalist Charles Darwin (1809–1882; *see also* 27 May) returned to London from his voyages aboard the HMS *Beagle*, he showed his bird specimens to ornithologist and illustrator John Gould (1804–1881). Gould examined them and in great excitement arranged a meeting with Darwin on 10 January 1837 at which he pointed out that among them was an entirely new grouping and at least a dozen new species. It was a key moment in Darwin's theory of evolution.

When Darwin's five-volume write-up of the voyage appeared as *The Zoology of the Voyage of the H. M. S. Beagle* (1838–43), it was richly illustrated and the plaudits for the illustration work went to Gould. It was not J. Gould who had done the major creative work, however, but E. Gould, his wife Elizabeth (1804–1841).

Although her work has been compared to that of American painter John James Audubon (*see* 27 January), Elizabeth Gould's name is noticeably absent from the title pages of the books that she worked on with her husband (whose name is front and centre). However, it was Elizabeth who lithographed the fifty plates (as she had the eighty for the monumental *A Century of Birds from the Himalaya Mountains*). In truth, the sketches, drawings and designs were Elizabeth's – done while looking after their half a dozen children – and John made minor changes or none at all.

11 JANUARY

Art detective Charles Koczka
makes his finest haul, 1985

Perhaps the best day of my professional career came on 11 January 1985, when, in less than eight hours, I recovered three stolen objects: a Roman head of Socrates, worth $50,000; a 19th-century French painting, worth $12,000; and an Italian masterpiece painted by Bernado Bellotto in the 18th century, worth over $400,000. I went out by myself, in a little hatchback car, and seized the goods from three separate locations. It was pure joy, like hitting three home runs.

Charles Koczka, *Arts & Antiques* magazine, November 1986

As long as there has been art there has been stolen or looted art. The Egyptian Pharaohs' graves were plundered hundreds of years before Christ's birth, Rome has been sacked regularly and the Aztecs lost their gold to greedy conquistadores. In modern times, the size of the stolen art market has been estimated at US$6 billion a year.

Perhaps the most organized theft of art was committed by Nazi Germany during the 1930s and Second World War, but a counter-attack came in 1943 when the Allied Forces set up the Monuments, Fine Arts, and Archives Program to initially protect irreplaceable cultural works in battle areas (*see* 4 May) and, after the war ended, to search for and return those that had been stolen or concealed. Their work was celebrated in American actor and film director George Clooney's 2014 film, *The Monuments Men*.

US Customs Service special agent Charles Koczka – dubbed 'Raider of the Lost Art' by *Customs Today* magazine – was among the modern art detectives who track down stolen masterpieces, alongside Charles Hill (who helped recover Edvard Munch's *The Scream* stolen in 1994; *see* 12 February), Chris Marinello (founder of Art Recovery International, which has recovered art worth more than $500 million) and Arthur Brand (also known as the 'Indiana Jones of the art world', with Salvador Dalí, Tamara de Lempicka and Pablo Picasso recoveries under his belt).

ALSO ON THIS DAY 1494: Death of Italian painter Domenico Ghirlandaio · **1762:** Death of French sculptor Louis-François Roubiliac · **1966:** Death of Swiss sculptor Alberto Giacometti

12 JANUARY

Matthew Paris enters the Abbey of St Albans, 1217

About this same time [1255], too, an elephant was sent to England by the French king as a present to the king of England. We believe that this was the only elephant ever seen in England, or even in the countries on this side the Alps; wherefore the people flocked together to see the novel sight.

Matthew Paris, *Chronica Majora*, 1235–59

Any list of 13th-century English artists would feature cartographer and illuminator Matthew Paris (1200–1259) at its head. After becoming a monk in early 1217 at the famous Abbey of St Albans in Hertfordshire, he wrote and illustrated a number of key histories of England. His two major works are the *Chronica Majora* and *Historia Anglorum*, which he constantly updated and that attracted the attention of Henry III, who was a regular visitor to the abbey.

Paris probably contributed most of the illustrations, including the thirty-two 'tinted drawings' of English kings that open the *Chronica Majora*, with coloured washes outlined in dark ink, a style formerly known as the School of St Albans. The most famous part of the book is Paris's remarkably accurate large map of Britain, which includes a bridge joining Scotland to England, crenellations along the Antonine and Hadrian Walls, Mount Snowdon ('Snaudun'), and numerous towns and cities from Pontefract to Dover.

Among his many illustrations – which range from half pages to small works in the margins – is one of an elephant with its keeper. The pachyderm was a present from Louis IX of France to Henry III and was painted from first-hand observation since it includes knee joints at a time when most people believed elephants somehow managed without them.

Digitized manuscripts of Paris's work, including the elephant and map, are available to view at the British Library's website www.bl.uk/manuscripts.

ALSO ON THIS DAY 1773: The Charleston Museum is the first museum to open in the USA · **1856:** American painter John Singer Sargent born · **1895:** National Trust is founded in the UK

13 JANUARY

Brian Ward takes the
Ziggy Stardust album photo, 1972

It's strange that I used to be chased out of the street with my felt-tip pen for scrawling 'Ziggy Woz Here' and now I'm unveiling a plaque. I guess the Ziggy Stardust generation has really come of age....

Ziggy appeared from the shadows of a much darker London than the one we know now, certainly no pedestrian walkways and alfresco dining; a much poorer, less glamorous London, still in the shadow of the Second World War. And that's the important context.

He was the ultimate messianic rock star, and with him David Bowie successfully blurred the lines not just between boys and girls, but himself and his creation. Bowie was Ziggy come to save us – and I bought him hook, eyeliner and haircut.

Looking back to what we can now call the Golden Age of Rock, this was a cultural highpoint of some significance. The album *The Rise and Fall of Ziggy Stardust and the Spiders from Mars* not only changed Bowie's life forever, it also changed mine, allowing a generation of adolescents to find an escape from the ennui of existence and the hard times of the early seventies.

As a teenager any visit to the West End would have to involve a pilgrimage to here. We'd stare at the phone box that Ziggy had obviously teleported himself into, and then try to fathom the meaning behind the K. West sign. K. West? Yes, Quest! It all made sense back then.

I believe that Ziggy is now one of London's great fictional characters and stands alongside the likes of Dorian Gray and the Artful Dodger, as well as antiheroes such as Steerpike and of course *Clockwork Orange*'s Alex.

**Gary Kemp, speech at the unveiling of a plaque
to mark the album cover shoot, 27 March 2012**

Ziggy Stardust was the most famous incarnation of the English musician and actor David Bowie (1947–2016), immortalized on his iconic album *The Rise and Fall of Ziggy Stardust and the Spiders from Mars*. The shot for the front cover was taken by photographer Brian Ward on Heddon Street, just off Regent Street, in London. Originally on Royal-X-Pan Black & White film, it was colourized by artist Terry Pastor.

The album's interior sleeve photos were taken in Ward's studio at 29 Heddon Street where he had also photographed the artwork for Bowie's album *Hunky Dory*. When he suggested trying some exterior shots, Bowie was the only band member who was happy to venture outside into the drizzle – in his jumpsuit designed by Freddie Burretti (Bowie wore this the following month on the TV music show *The Old Grey Whistle Test*), Yamamoto platforms and Gibson Les Paul guitar. Ward later said that Bowie wanted the image to look like an alien in a kind of 'Brooklyn alley scene' atmosphere.

Key elements of the shoot included a red K2-series public telephone box (since removed and then reinstated), used on the back cover, and a sign for local furriers K. West who initially complained through their lawyers that the photo was damaging to their business. The sign was auctioned off as fan memorabilia and in its place a plaque erected by The Crown Estate, which owns the street, marks the spot of the shoot, but an ornamental gas light above the doorway remains.

In 2010, the cover was chosen by Royal Mail to appear in its Classic Album Cover stamp set.

ALSO ON THIS DAY **1625:** Death of Flemish painter Jan Brueghel the Elder · **1911:** Rembrandt's *The Night Watch* is attacked in the Rijksmuseum, Amsterdam (*see* 14 September) · **1938:** French cartoonist Cabu (Jean Cabut) born

14 JANUARY

The statue *Laocoön and His Sons* is dug up, 1506

There are not many sculptors of high repute; for, in the case of several works of very great excellence, the number of artists that have been engaged upon them has proved a considerable obstacle to the fame of each, no individual being able to engross the whole of the credit, and it being impossible to award it in due proportion to the names of the several artists combined. Such is the case with the Laocoon, for example, in the palace of the Emperor Titus, a work that may be looked upon as preferable to any other production of the art of painting or of statuary. It is sculptured from a single block, both the main figure as well as the children, and the serpents with their marvellous folds. This group was made in concert by three most eminent artists, Agesander, Polydorus and Athenodorus, natives of Rhodes.

Pliny the Elder, *Natural History,*
1st century AD

The statue that Roman author Pliny the Elder (AD 23/24–79) describes in Emperor Titus's palace is almost certainly the one that today stands in the Vatican Museums. Commissioned by a wealthy Roman, perhaps from the imperial family, it is variously dated to *c.* 30 BC–AD 70 and the almost life-size figures show Trojan priest Laocoön and his sons Antiphantes and Thymbraeus as they are attacked by sea serpents. Laocoön also makes a memorable appearance in Virgil's *Aeneid* where he tries to alert the Trojans to the truth behind the Trojan horse: 'Do not trust the Horse, Trojans / Whatever it is, I fear the Greeks bearing gifts.'

The statue was disinterred from the vineyard of Felice de Fredis on the Oppian Hill on 14 January 1506, to the immediate delight of Pope Julius II and Michelangelo, who used Laocoön as the basis for some of the faces in the Sistine Chapel (*see* 1 November). Though well preserved, Laocoön's right arm had disappeared, as had parts of the serpents and one of the children's right hands. The larger son had also become detached from the group. Various suggestions about the position of Laocoön's arm included Michelangelo's that it should be bent back over his shoulder, while later centuries opted for a straighter, outstretched position.

The sculpture was looted by Napoleon after his 1799 invasion of Italy (*see* 25 May) and only returned in 1816 after his fall from power.

ALSO ON THIS DAY **1836:** French painter and lithographer Henri Fantin-Latour born · **1883:** Italian-born French fashion designer Nina Ricci born · **1928:** American photographer Garry Winogrand born

The British Museum
opens to the public, 1759

From my youth I have been a great observer and admirer of the wonderful power, wisdom and contrivance of the Almighty God, appearing in the works of his Creation; and have gathered together many things in my own travels or voyages, or had them from others, especially my ever honoured, late friend William Courten, Esq, who spent the greatest part of his life and estate in collecting such things, in and from most parts of the earth, which he left me at his death...and his collections kept entire; and whereas I have made great additions of late years as well to my books, both printed as manuscript, and to my collections of natural and artificial curiosities, precious stones, books of dried samples of plants, miniatures, drawings, prints, medals and the like, with some paintings concerning them, now placed in my house and gardens, amounting in the whole to a very great sum of money, reckoning them at the first costs to at least £50,000. Now desiring very much that these things tending many ways to the manifestation of the glory of God, the confutation of atheism and its consequences, the use and improvement of physic, and other arts and sciences, and benefit of mankind, may remain together and not be separated, and that chiefly in and about the city of London, where I have acquired most of my estates, and where they may by the great confluence of people be of most use.

Will of Sir Hans Sloane, 1739

When the doors of the British Museum first opened to the public at Montagu House on Great Russell Street in London, the holdings were largely formed from the legacy left specifically for such a purpose by Sir Hans Sloane (1660–1753), an Anglo-Irish doctor, businessman, botanist and collector.

Further to the conventional details of bequests and burial details, Sloane left thousands of objects to the nation, from coins and medals to books and plant specimens. In addition to his own flotsam and jetsam, his collection was enhanced by acquiring other people's collections, in particular his friend William Courten's extensive 'cabinet of curiosities', which ranged from crocodile testicles and mammoth teeth to paintings on vellum by embroiderer

Guillaume Toulouze from Montpellier in France. Sloane's ability to build up his collections relied at least partly on the profits received from the Jamaican sugar plantations owned by his wife Elizabeth's family, and that were made from the exploitation of enslaved Africans.

Today, the British Museum has around eight million objects in its collection.

ALSO ON THIS DAY 1955: Death of French-American painter Yves Tanguy · **1962:** Europe's oldest manuscript the Derveni papyrus (*c.* 340 BC) is found in Greece · **2012:** Death of Danish illustrator Ib Spang Olsen

16 JANUARY

Superman becomes a daily newspaper strip, 1939

Jerry Siegel stinks. Poor American youth who must live in such a polluted atmosphere and fail to notice the poison they swallow every day.

Das Schwarze Korps, 25 April 1940

Along with Zatara Master Magician, Sticky-Mitt Stimson and Scoop Scanlon, Five Star Reporter, Superman was introduced to the reading public in the first issue of *Action Comics* magazine in June 1938. Daily newspaper syndication soon followed in January 1939, with a Sunday strip from November. *Superman* eventually appeared in more than three hundred daily newspapers and ninety Sunday papers, reaching a readership of more than 20 million. A copy of that first comic in excellent condition fetched $3,207,852 at auction in 2014.

Comic book writers and artists Jerome Siegel (1914–1996) and Joseph Shuster (1914–1992) came up with the idea of the Man of Steel in the early 1930s but their creation received numerous rejections before being picked up by the McClure Syndicate. *Superman* was also pencilled in later years by Wayne Boring and Curt Swan, who introduced elements such as the telephone box quick change and eclectic storylines, including saving Santa Claus from Hitler. Indeed, in 1940, so annoyed by *Superman* were the Nazis that the SS's weekly newspaper, quoted above, published an appalling full-page anti-Semitic rant about Siegel and his creation.

Architectural interest in the comic strip is provided by the *Daily Planet* building where Kal-El/Superman/Clark Kent works as a journalist. Shuster insisted that it was partly modelled on the Old Toronto Star Building in his Canadian hometown (which he said also provided inspiration for the fictional city of Metropolis where it stands), but arguments have also been made for Cleveland's AT&T Huron Road Building and Paramount Pictures' old headquarters in Manhattan.

ALSO ON THIS DAY 1477: German cartographer Johannes Schöner born (and died 1547) · **1691:** Flemish sculptor Peter Scheemakers born · **2013:** Death of André Cassagnes, French inventor of the Etch A Sketch (*see* 12 July 1960)

17 JANUARY

Feast day of Anthony the Great

...the devil, who hates and envies what is good, could not endure to see such a resolution in a youth, but endeavoured to carry out against him what he had been wont to effect against others. First of all he tried to lead him away from the discipline, whispering to him the remembrance of his wealth, care for his sister, claims of kindred, love of money, love of glory, the various pleasures of the table and the other relaxations of life, and at last the difficulty of virtue and the labour of it; he suggested also the infirmity of the body and the length of the time. In a word he raised in his mind a great dust of debate, wishing to debar him from his settled purpose.

Athanasius of Alexandria, *Life of Antony*, **356–362**

The story of the battle with demons experienced by one of the earliest Christian monks St Anthony the Great (251–356) in his self-imposed wanderings in the Egyptian desert was first documented by his contemporary and bishop of Alexandria, Athanasius of Alexandria (c. 293–373). The account has provided inspiration for many artists, including German engraver Martin Schongauer, Michelangelo and French painter Paul Cézanne.

The triptych of *The Temptation of St Anthony*, Dutch painter Hieronymus Bosch's oil painting on wood from about 1501, is full of the painter's characteristic fanciful imagery. The left panel shows St Anthony flying before demons force him back to Earth where, among many other unusual characters, a bird is ice skating. The middle panel shows St Anthony resisting the demonic happenings around him, including various examples of witchcraft and heresy, featuring a devil riding a chicken. In the right panel, a naked woman tempts the saint, while above her a man and a woman ride a fish in the sky.

Spanish painter and sculptor Salvador Dalí's oil on canvas take on the subject in 1946 was produced for a competition for an artwork to appear in the 1947 film *The Private Affairs of Bel Ami*. Again, there are many surreal elements. A naked and kneeling St Anthony brandishes a cross against a procession of elephants with a powerful rearing horse at their head. The spindly-legged elephants bear various naked women and an obelisk. In the background, Spanish king Philip II's Escorial palace peeps through the clouds. The competition – co-judged by French-American painter Marcel Duchamp (*see* 2 September) – was won by German painter Max Ernst, who beat off rival artists who included British artists Leonora Carrington and Stanley Spencer as well as Dalí. All the artists were paid $500 for their entries.

ALSO ON THIS DAY 1904: Thai painter and illustrator Hem Vejakorn born · **1736:** Death of German architect Matthäus Pöppelmann · **1933:** Death of American stained-glass artist Louis Comfort Tiffany (*see* 18 February)

18 JANUARY

Blake sends a letter
about his *Last Judgment*, 1808

To Ozias Humphry Esqre

The Design of *The Last Judgment*, which I have completed by your recommendation for The Countess of Egremont, it is necessary to give some account of: & its various parts ought to be described, for the accomodation [*sic*] of those who give it the honour of attention.

Christ seated on the Throne of Judgment: The Heavens in Clouds rolling before him & around him, like a scroll ready to be consumed in the fires of the Angels; who descend before his feet with their four trumpets sounding to the four Winds.

Beneath; the Earth is convuls'd with the labours of the Resurrection; in the caverns of the Earth is the Dragon with seven heads & ten horns, Chained by two Angels & above his Cavern on the Earths Surface, is the Harlot also seized & bound by two Angels with Chains while her Palaces are falling into ruins & her Councellors & Warriors are descending into the Abyss in wailing and despair.

Hell opens beneath the Harlots seat on the left hand into which the Wicked are descending.

The right hand of the Design is appropriated to the Resurrection of the Just: the left hand of the Design is appropriated to the Resurrection & Fall of the Wicked.

Immediately before the Throne of Christ is Adam & Eve, kneeling in humiliation, as representatives of the whole Human Race; Abraham & Moses kneel on each side beneath them; from the Cloud on which Eve kneels & beneath Moses & from the Tables of Stone which utter lightnings; is seen Satan wound round by the Serpent & falling headlong; the Pharisees appear on the left hand pleading their own righteousness before the Throne of Christ: The Book of Death is opend on Clouds by two Angels: many groupes of Figures are falling from before the Throne & from the Sea of Fire which flows before the steps of the Throne; on which are seen the Seven Lamps of the Almighty, burning before the Throne. many Figures Chaind & bound together fall thro' the air, & some are scourged by Spirits with flames of fire into the Abyss of Hell which opens to receive them beneath, on the left hand of the Harlots seat; where others are howling & descending into the flames. & in the act of dragging each other into Hell & of contending in fighting with each other on the brink of Perdition....

The whole upper part of the Design is a view of Heaven opened; around the Throne of Christ, Four Living Creatures filled with Eyes, attended by seven Angels with the Seven Vials of the Wrath of God, & above them Seven Angels with the Seven Trumpets compose the Cloud, which by its rolling away displays the opening Seats of the Blessed, on the right & the left of which are seen the Four & Twenty Elders seated on Thrones to Judge the Dead....

Such is the Design which you my Dear Sir have been the cause of my producing & which but for you might have slept till the Last Judgment.

**William Blake, letter to Ozias Humphry,
18 January 1808**

English writer and artist William Blake (1757-1827; *see also* 28 November) wrote a detailed letter to the painter Ozias Humphry in which he described his new watercolour painting *The Last Judgment*. It had been commissioned via Humphry by the Countess of Egremont for Petworth House in Sussex. Blake was fixated on the theme and painted it more than half a dozen times, claiming that the concept and details of this painting had come from one of his many visions. It also built on an earlier depiction of the same subject that he had produced for the 1808 edition of *The Grave* by Scottish poet Robert Blair.

ALSO ON THIS DAY 1752: English architect John Nash born · **1934:** English illustrator Raymond Briggs born · **1980:** Death of English photographer Cecil Beaton (*see* 18 September)

19 JANUARY

Painter Paul Cézanne
is born, 1839

No one will ever paint like Cezanne for example, because no one will ever have his peculiar visual gifts; or to put it less dogmatically, will anyone ever appear again with so peculiar and almost unbelievable a faculty for dividing color sensations and making logical realizations of them? Has any-one ever placed his color more reasonably with more of a sense of time and measure than he? I think not, and he furnished for the enthusiast of today new reasons for research into the realm of color for itself.

American painter Marsden Hartley,
'Art and the Personal Life', 1928

French painter Paul Cézanne (1839-1906; *see also* 10 June) had strong ideas about what he was trying to achieve in his art and also about how his subjects should sit for the many portraits he painted throughout his life. Usually his subjects were friends, neighbours or family, including his wife Hortense, of whom he made about thirty portraits. He also painted at least ten of his uncle, Dominique Aubert, in the space of six months in 1866–67, dressing him up in a range of outfits, including as a Dominican monk and also in a tasselled blue cap.

Aubert got away lightly. 'Paul is a horrible painter as regards the poses he gives people in the midst of his riot of colour,' commented writer Antoine

Valabrègue who sat for him. 'Every time he paints one of his friends, it seems as though he were revenging himself on him for some hidden injury.'

Novelist Gustave Geffroy, who sat every day for three months, sensed Cézanne wasn't even interested in him. 'The library, the papers on the table, Auguste Rodin's little plaster model, the artificial rose which he brought at the beginning of our sittings, everything is first-rate,' said Geffroy. 'There is also a person in the scene.'

ALSO ON THIS DAY **1889:** Swiss painter and sculptor Sophie Taeuber-Arp born · **1954:** American photographer Cindy Sherman born · **1964:** Bahamian sculptor, performance artist and photographer Janine Antoni born

20 JANUARY

Sir John Soane's Museum is created on his death, 1837

Architecture from the earliest periods has engaged the attention of mankind, nor can this be wondered at when we see how necessary and how useful it is. It protects us from the shivering lightnings and furious tempests, from the heats of summer and the severities of winter; and by its powers the comforts, conveniences and refinements of life are increased. Architecture likewise defends us from ambitious neighbours; it instructs us also in the art of building ships, by whose assistance we are enabled, in defiance of winds and waves, to penetrate into the most distant parts of the globe, and to enrich our country with the various productions of other climes. Hence we may derive the origin of civil, military and naval architecture.

Sir John Soane, Royal Academy Lectures on Architecture: Lecture I, 1810

Sir John Soane (1753–1837) was the leading English architect of his age, with the Bank of England and Dulwich Picture Gallery among his finest works. Professor of Architecture at the Royal Academy in London, he was also a prolific collector of art in all its forms and kept it together at his home at Lincoln's Inn Fields.

His collection was vast and constantly expanding. Ancient works included the most expensive item bought by Soane (which was also his favourite):

the alabaster sarcophagus of the Egyptian pharaoh Seti I; William Hogarth's eight episodes of *The Rake's Progress*; paintings by Canaletto and Turner; and more than 30,000 architectural drawings, many by Soane and his pupils, but also including work by architects Sir Christopher Wren and Robert Adam.

Another highlight at his home, which was, in fact, three houses knocked together, was the Model Room where he gathered up a wide range of cork and plaster architectural models, such as a cork replica of Pompeii, as well as his own projects.

On his death, and disinheriting his troublesome eldest son along the way, his home became a museum on the strict instructions that it was preserved unchanged at the moment of his passing and that its collection be open to the public for free. About 100,000 people visit the museum annually.

ALSO ON THIS DAY 1872: American architect Julia Morgan born · **1900:** English painter, potter and muralist Dorothy Annan born · **1900:** Death of English painter and critic John Ruskin (*see* 16 April)

21 JANUARY

Edward Hopper finishes
Nighthawks, 1942

For an artist to be interesting to us he must have been interesting to himself. He must have been capable of intense feeling, and capable of profound contemplation. He who has contemplated has met with himself, is in a state to see into the realities beyond the surfaces of his subject. Nature reveals to him, and, seeing and feeling intensely, he paints, and whether he wills it or not each brush stroke is an exact record of such as he was at the exact moment the stroke was made.

**Robert Henri, Edward Hopper's teacher
at the New York School of Art and Design,
The Art Spirit, 1923**

Originally titled *Night Hawks*, this famous oil on canvas painting by American artist Edward Hopper (1882–1967) depicts people sitting in a glass-fronted New York diner. 'Unconsciously, probably,' he later said, 'I was painting the loneliness of a large city.' His wife Jo's comments for 21 January 1942 appear in the journal the couple kept in which Hopper made a sketch of each painting and she wrote explanatory comments.

She describes the scene as the night-time interior of a cheap restaurant, noting the main characteristics of each of the people inside including 'Man night hawk' wearing dark clothes and holding a cigarette (Jo was the model for the woman with red hair and Hopper used himself as a model for the two men), the diner's sign and the brick buildings opposite.

Hopper clearly stated the diner in the painting was based on one on Greenwich Avenue, Manhattan, which he then enlarged and simplified. Seekers of the exact location, though, have not managed to definitively track it down. Other suggestions for its inspiration include Vincent van Gogh's *Café Terrace at Night*, which was on show in New York while Hopper was working on *Nighthawks*, as well as the American writer Ernest Hemingway's short story, 'The Killers'.

Hopper's numerous preparatory sketches for *Nighthawks* are in a kind of storyboard format. Interestingly, English filmmaker Ridley Scott has described how he used a reproduction of the painting to show the production team on the 1982 film *Blade Runner* what kind of effect he was trying to achieve. *Nighthawks* also appears in the museum scene in the film *Ferris Bueller's Day Off* (*see* 5 June).

ALSO ON THIS DAY 1784: English painter Peter De Wint born · **1895:** Spanish fashion designer Cristóbal Balenciaga born · **1905:** French fashion designer Christian Dior born

22 JANUARY

Apple run '1984' ad for Macintosh computer, 1984

He thought of the telescreen with its never-sleeping ear. They could spy upon you night and day, but if you kept your head you could still outwit them. With all their cleverness they had never mastered the secret of finding out what another human being was thinking. Perhaps that was less true when you were actually in their hands.... They could not alter your feelings: for that matter you could not alter them yourself, even if you wanted to. They could lay bare in the utmost detail everything that you had done or said or thought; but the inner heart, whose workings were mysterious even to yourself, remained impregnable.

George Orwell, *Nineteen Eighty-Four,* **1949**

Soon to become the darling of creatives around the world, the only national airing of the advertisement for the Macintosh 128k came during a third quarter ad break in the Super Bowl XVIII coverage. It was seen by nearly 100 million people and then replayed endlessly in the following days on news and current affairs programmes.

English filmmaker Ridley Scott (b. 1937) directed the groundbreaking commercial, which was devised by Steve Hayden (who wrote the speech), Brent Thomas and Lee Clow at Chiat/Day Agency. Instead of actually showcasing the computer, this was the story of dour, grey-clothed, industrial workers with shaved heads on the receiving end of a speech from a Big Brother-ish face speaking to them via a huge screen ('Today, we celebrate the first glorious anniversary of the Information Purification Directives').

An athletic young woman (British discus thrower Anya Major, later to appear as Nikita in Elton John's music video) carrying a large hammer runs into shot, chased by armed police in riot gear. Wearing a T-shirt with a drawing of the computer on it, she then flings the hammer towards the screen and smashes it. 'On January 24th, Apple Computer will introduce Macintosh,' says the voiceover, accompanied by the text in Garamond. 'And you'll see why 1984 won't be like "1984".'

So much like the book of the same name by English writer George Orwell (1903-1950) in fact, that the author's estate argued it infringed copyright and sent Apple a cease and desist letter.

Despite initial reservations about its content from Apple's board of directors, since its premiere the dystopian advert has won many awards and regularly appears in 'Best ever ads' lists, even though it was never reshown.

ALSO ON THIS DAY **1802:** English-American architect Richard Upjohn born · **2010:** Student visitor accidentally falls onto Pablo Picasso's painting *The Actor* at the Metropolitan Museum of Art in New York causing a 15-cm (6-inch) tear (later fully repaired) · **2015:** Death of Canadian illustrator Margaret Bloy Graham

Zhu Yuanzhang establishes a golden age of Chinese art, 1368

But when the nation began to arouse itself, we...conceived the patriotic idea to save the people, and it pleased the creator to grant that our civil and military officers effected their passage across eastward to the left side of the river.... We were selected by our people to occupy the imperial throne of Zhongguo [China] under the dynastic title of 'the Great Ming'.... Although we are not equal in wisdom to our ancient rulers whose virtue was recognized all over the universe, we cannot but let the world know our intention to maintain peace within the four seas.

Ming History (Míng Shǐ), 1739

The three-hundred-year-long Ming dynasty (1368–1644) saw an incredible outpouring of work in all the creative arts. It was founded by the immensely successful military leader and former novice monk Zhu Yuanzhang, who aimed to rebuild the country after years of war and poor agricultural practices. The third emperor and son of Yuanzhang, Zhu Di (1360–1424), known as the Yongle emperor, oversaw the building of the Forbidden City in Beijing and the Porcelain Pagoda of Nanjing, which was nearly 80 metres (260 feet) high and built from porcelain bricks.

However, the major achievements in art were in painting, which increasingly incorporated calligraphy and pottery. Most famous today is the era's 'blue and white' ceramic work, much of which was produced in vast factories at Jingdezhen in Jiangxi province and designed very much for export and trade, as well as for the emperor to use as gifts. Innovations included the use of manganese to make the cobalt lines finer. Also very popular was Jingdezhen's jade-coloured greenware. Indeed, King Manuel I of Portugal told explorer Vasco da Gama as he set off for China at the end of the 15th century that in addition to bringing back precious spices he was also to return with plenty of porcelain. During the early Ming period, reign marks first began to be used.

Tombs from the period have also revealed spectacular works, such as the enormous gold belt decorated with gemstones found in the tomb of Prince Zhuang of Liang (1411–1441).

24 JANUARY

'The Family of Man' photography exhibition opens, 1955

But such is the irresistible nature of truth, that all it asks, and all it wants, is the liberty of appearing.

Thomas Paine, *The Rights of Man*, 1791

O wonderful, wonderful and most wonderful wonderful! and yet again wonderful...

William Shakespeare, *As You Like It*, Act 3, Scene 2, 1623

'The Family of Man' was a manifesto for peace, equality and solidarity put on in New York by the Museum of Modern Art's director of photography Edward Steichen (1879–1973). It was an enormous photo essay consisting of 503 photographs by 273 photographers (40 of whom were women) from 68 countries, including work by Robert Capa (*see* 6 June), Henri Cartier-Bresson, Dorothea Lange, Nina Leen, Robert Doisneau and Ansel Adams. When he approached photographers to submit their work, he said his goal was to show images 'made in all parts of the world, of the gamut of life from birth to death, with an emphasis on the everyday relationships of man to himself, to his family, to the community and to the world we live in'.

Grouped together under various heading – lovers, childbirth, household, careers, death – and finishing with an image of a hydrogen bomb, the prints had no captions but were exhibited alongside quotations chosen by photographer Dorothy Norman (1905–1997) from writers such as William Shakespeare and Thomas Paine.

Photos included a young Peruvian boy playing his flute, an Inuit mother kissing her child in an igloo, and the body of African American Robert McDaniels after he had been lynched in 1937, an image that was later withdrawn and did not make it into the exhibition's accompanying book. One of the most popular images was documentary photographer Dorothea Lange's 1936 *Migrant Mother*, which shows Florence Owens Thompson and her children in a camp for workers who had suffered major crop failure.

Overwhelmingly well-received and perceived as the exhibition that elevated photography to the status of an art form, American writer Susan Sontag and French critic Roland Barthes suggested it was merely sentimental and conventional humanism. After a long world tour, the exhibition was permanently installed at Clervaux Castle, Luxembourg, in 1994. Over the last sixty-five years, more than ten million people have visited it.

ALSO ON THIS DAY 1664: English architect John Vanbrugh baptized · **1923:** Aztec Ruins National Monument in New Mexico is established · **1926:** American sculptor Ruth Asawa born

25 JANUARY

Henry Fox Talbot's first photographic exhibition, 1839

No human hand has hitherto traced such lines as these drawings display; and what man may hereafter do, now that Dame Nature has become his drawing mistress, it is impossible to predict.

> **Michael Faraday, address to the Royal Institution, UK,**
> **25 January 1839**

Leaving aside the complex debate about who exactly invented photography, English photography pioneer William Henry Fox Talbot (1800–1877) was the first person to publicly exhibit the images he had created on 25 January 1839. Earlier at the Royal Institution, his friend the scientist Michael Faraday had given a lecture and then concluded by announcing Talbot's and Louis Daguerre's parallel invention (*see* 31 July).

Members were invited to examine Talbot's photographs, a slightly random collection that he had in fact made five years earlier, which he listed as:

flowers and leaves; a pattern of lace; figures taken from painted glass; a view of Venice copied from an engraving; some images formed by the Solar Microscope, viz. a slice of wood very highly magnified, exhibiting the pores of two kinds, one set much smaller than the other, and more numerous. Another Microscopic sketch, exhibiting the reticulations on the wing of an insect. Finally: various pictures, representing the architecture of my house in the country; all these made with the Camera Obscura in the summer of 1835.

'I do not profess to have perfected an Art, but to have *commenced* one,' wrote Talbot to William Jerdan, editor of the *Literary Gazette*, five days later, 'the limits of which it is not possible at present exactly to ascertain.'

ALSO ON THIS DAY 1628: Dutch painter Johannes van der Beeck (aka Torrentius) is found guilty of blasphemy, atheism and 'leading a frightful and pernicious lifestyle' · **1938:** Japanese manga artist Shotaro Ishinomori born · **2006:** A visitor to the Fitzwilliam Museum in Cambridge, England, accidentally trips and breaks three 17th-century Qing vases

26 JANUARY

Franklin has concerns about the US bald eagle symbol, 1784

For my own part I wish the bald eagle had not been chosen the representative of our country. He is a bird of bad moral character. He does not get his living honestly. You may have seen him perched on some dead tree near the river, where, too lazy to fish for himself, he watches the labour of the fishing hawk; and when that diligent bird has at length taken a fish, and is bearing it to his nest for the support of his mate and young ones, the bald eagle pursues him and takes it from him.

With all this injustice, he is never in good case but like those among men who live by sharping [cheating] & robbing he is generally poor and often very lousy. Besides he is a rank coward: the little king bird not bigger than a sparrow attacks him boldly and drives him out of the district. He is therefore by no means a proper emblem for the brave and honest Cincinnati of America who have driven all the king birds from our country.

Benjamin Franklin, letter to his daughter Sarah Bache, 26 January 1784

Choosing a symbol or a logo for an organization is a difficult process – it's hard to please everybody. The selection of a bald eagle as the emblem of the United States in 1782 certainly did not please Founding Father, politician and polymath Benjamin Franklin (1706–1790) as he outlined in a letter to his daughter on 26 January 1784, although this was never in fact sent.

Other birds suggested to the Great Seal committees included a rooster and a phoenix in flames, while Franklin also considered a rattlesnake and a turkey, as he went on to explain in his letter to Sarah:

> I am on this account not displeased that the figure is not known as a bald eagle, but looks more like a turkey. For in truth the turkey is in comparison a much more respectable bird, and withal a true original native of America.... He is besides, though a little vain & silly...a bird of courage, and would not hesitate to attack a grenadier of the British Guards who should presume to invade his farm yard with a red coat on.

According to the final committee in 1782, the olive branch and arrows held by the eagle in its talons represent the desire for peace but readiness for war. The eagle is facing the olive branch to indicate its ideal choice.

ALSO ON THIS DAY 1929: American cartoonist Jules Feiffer born · **1824:** Death of French painter Théodore Géricault (*see* 2 July) · **2000:** Death of English illustrator Kathleen Hale

27 JANUARY

Death of painter
John James Audubon, 1851

Mr Kidd, a promising young artist in landscape, only nineteen, breakfasted with me today, and we talked on painting a long time, and I was charmed with his talents, and thought what a difference it would have made in my life if I had begun painting in oil at his age and with his ability. It is a sad reflection that I have been compelled to hammer and stammer as if I were working in opposition to God's will, and so now am nothing but poor Audubon. I invited him to come to my rooms daily, and to eat and drink with me, and give me the pleasure of his company and the advantage of his taste in painting. I told him of my ardent desire to improve in the delightful art, and proposed to begin a new picture, in which he should assist with his advice; and proposing to begin it tomorrow, I took down my portfolio, to select a drawing to copy in oil. He had never seen my works before, and appeared astonished as his eyes ranged over the sheets. He expressed the warmest admiration, and said, 'How hopeless must be the task of my giving any instruction to one who can draw like this?' I pointed out to him that nature is the great study for the artist, and assured him that the reason why my works pleased him was because they are all exact copies of the works of God, who is the great Architect and perfect Artist; and impressed on his mind this fact, that nature indifferently copied is far superior to the best idealities.

John James Audubon, journal entry, 1 March 1827

American ornithologist and painter John James Audubon (born Jean Rabin, 1785–1851) was fascinated by birds from childhood and as a young man was an avid collector of birds' eggs and birds (which he stuffed himself) as well as other animals.

Audubon's best-known work is his *Birds of America* (*see* 17 July). Failing to find a publisher at home, he travelled with three hundred drawings to England where he was an instant success. Despite the huge printing expenses, he raised enough money to print and promote the gargantuan work, which features 435 hand-coloured prints made using engraved copper plates.

His goal was to produce images in as realistic style as possible, killing each bird then using wires to achieve a lifelike attitude. He painted mainly in watercolour but sometimes in gouache, adding coloured chalk or pastel for feathers. In 2010, a copy of *The Birds of America* was sold for £7.3 million at auction.

ALSO ON THIS DAY 1805: English painter and etcher Samuel Palmer born · **1850:** English painter John Collier born · **1885:** Japanese painter Seison Maeda born

28 JANUARY

Cellini on sculpture vs painting, 1546

I say that the art of sculpture, among all the arts connected with design, is at least seven times greater than any other, for the following reason: why, sir, a statue of true sculpture ought to have eight points of view, which ought all to boast equal excellence…. Painting, in fact, is nothing else much than a tree, a man, or any other object, reflected in the water. The distinction between sculpture and painting, is as great as between the shadow and the substance.

Benvenuto Cellini, letter to Benedetto Varchi, 28 January 1546

During the Italian Renaissance there was a lively debate about the relative merits of painting and sculpture, known as the 'paragone' or 'comparison'. One of those with especially strong views was goldsmith and sculptor Benvenuto Cellini (1500–1571). Unsurprisingly, sculptors were firm backers of sculpture, while painters felt painting was the higher art form.

In the 1540s, humanist Benedetto Varchi wrote to numerous well-known artists – including Cellini, who responded on 28 January 1546 – about their views and wrote up some of the results in his *Due Lezzioni di M. Benedetto Varchi* (Two Lessons of M. Benedict Varchi, 1549).

The arguments in favour of painting lay in its ability to render complex stories, the way it offered a full colour replica of life including light and shade, and that it required more mental than physical energy so was inherently nobler. Sculpture was claimed to have a stronger link to much-praised and much-copied ancient art, was more durable and provided three-dimensional multiple-viewing possibilities. Proponents also argued that it was just 'more real'. The debate invaded works of art themselves, as painters attempted to imitate sculptures and sculptors imitate paintings.

Cellini was very much 'Team Sculpture', but 'Team Painting' had numerous big hitters including Leonardo da Vinci (who expounded his views in *A Treatise on Painting*, or Codex Urbinas, contending that painting was a science), architect and author Leon Battista Alberti and painter and art historian Giorgio Vasari. Michelangelo, wisely, pointed out that it took artists longer to debate such topics than actually make art.

ALSO ON THIS DAY 1887: Work starts on the Eiffel Tower in Paris (*see* 31 March) · **1900:** American painter Alice Neel born · **1958:** The Lego company patents its brick design

Walt Disney starts
work as an animator, 1920

Lewis Carroll's *Alice in Wonderland* is a good example of the type of fanciful tale on the order of which animated cartoons could be made for children. The Mad Hatter would make an admirable figure to pace across the screen. An artist desiring to be the author of an animated story built on the model of Carroll's classics would need a gleeful imagination and a turn for the fantastic. And he would require, besides, if he hoped to draw characters of a par with Tenniel's depictions, more than the ordinary qualifications of a screen draftsman.

Edwin George Lutz,
***Animated Cartoons*, 1920**

On 29 January 1920, on his return to Kansas from France where he had been serving as an ambulance driver, Walt Disney (1901–1966) began his career in animation with a job at the Kansas City Slide Company (later Kansas City Film Ad Company) at $40 a week.

Until this point, Disney had only produced commercial art and still cartoons. Here he learned some basic stop-motion animation skills using puppets and cut-out figures with riveted joints, and started creating his own cartoon shorts called 'Laugh-o-grams' with friend and partner Ub Iwerks. One of their earliest productions was *Alice's Wonderland* (initially 'Alice in Slumberland', 1923), an innovative mixture of live action and animation lasting twelve minutes. Together they went on to make fifty-seven 'Alice' films.

Disney said that *Alice's Adventures in Wonderland* (see 16 December) was the story that most intrigued him from the moment he read it as a boy, partly because he felt English author Lewis Carroll had achieved the right mix of seriousness and fantasy. Disney's more recent inspiration for the 'Alice' films may well have been the book *Animated Cartoons* by American illustrator and author E. G. Lutz (1868–1951), which he is known to have enjoyed.

His interest in Alice continued for the next thirty years, buying the rights to English illustrator Sir John Tenniel's iconic illustrations, then lining up actor Mary Pickford for another film involving animation and live action in the 1930s. When that came to nothing, he worked on another version using

English writer Aldous Huxley's script in the 1940s, before finally producing his 1951 masterpiece.

ALSO ON THIS DAY 1888: Death of English painter and illustrator Edward Lear (*see* 3 February) · **1959:** Walt Disney's film *Sleeping Beauty* is released in the USA · **1959:** Death of South African painter and illustrator Winifred Brunton

30 JANUARY

Menai Suspension Bridge opens to the public, 1826

Mr Telford ascended to the point of fastening, and satisfied himself that a continuous and safe connection had been formed from the Caernarvon fastening on the rock to that on Anglesea [*sic*]. The announcement of the fact was followed by loud and prolonged cheering from the workmen, echoed by the spectators, and extending along the Straits on both sides, until it seemed to die away along the shores in the distance. Three foolhardy workmen, excited by the day's proceedings, had the temerity to scramble along the upper surface of the chain – which was only nine inches wide and formed a curvature of 590 feet – from one side of the Strait to the other!...

Mr Telford afterwards stated to a friend, only a few months before his death, that for some time previous to the opening of the bridge, his anxiety was so great that he could scarcely sleep; and that a continuance of that condition must have very soon completely undermined his health. We are not, therefore, surprised to learn that when his friends rushed to congratulate him on the result of the first day's experiment, which decisively proved the strength and solidity of the bridge, they should have found the engineer on his knees engaged in prayer.

Samuel Smiles, *The Life of Thomas Telford, Civil Engineer*, 1867

Until the bridge built by Scottish civil engineer Thomas Telford (1757–1834) spanned the gap between Anglesey/Ynys Môn and mainland Wales, the only way to cross the Menai Strait had been by foot at low tide. This was not a safe method and just as bad in a boat – the vessel could easily be swamped, stranded, wrecked or carried well away from landing points. Farmers on the island even swam their livestock across to get them to market.

The plans for a bridge were part of a larger project undertaken by Telford (*see* 26 November) who was improving the London–Holyhead road (eventually becoming the A5). He realized that a bridge would also improve transport connections with Ireland via the port town of Holyhead on Anglesey.

First, hollow towers of limestone were built on the two sides of the strait, linked by sixteen huge iron chain cables, each weighing about 120 tonnes (135 short tons), hung in loops. To prevent rusting, they were treated with linseed oil, then painted – Lewis Carroll's White Knight remarks on the issue to Alice in *Through the Looking-Glass* (*see* 16 December) when he sings the 'Haddocks' Eyes' song to her:

> I heard him then, for I had just
> Completed my design,
> To keep the Menai bridge from rust
> By boiling it in wine.

Remarkably, no scaffolding was used during construction as the strait was a busy thoroughfare for ships.

When it opened on 30 January 1826, the world's first major modern suspension bridge cut the journey from London to Holyhead from thirty-six to twenty-seven hours.

31 JANUARY

Rembrandt attends the dissection that inspires a painting, 1632

Few painters, indeed, have so full a claim to the merit of originality as Rembrandt. It would be hard to point out any of his predecessors to whom he is indebted for any part of his style, but he has opened a rich treasure of excellence for his successors to profit by. The full powers of the management of light and shade, which we denominate by the Italian phrase *chiar' oscuro*, were not known until Rembrandt developed them. It might have been supposed that the power and harmony, and splendour of Correggio left nothing to be desired in this department of the art, but Rembrandt gave to his masses a force and depth, and concentration, unequalled, and peculiar to himself. Nor is *chiar' oscuro* in his hands merely an instrument of picturesque effect; it is also a most powerful vehicle of sentiment, especially in subjects characterized by solemnity or terror.

Arthur Malkin, *The Gallery of Portraits*, 1834

The Anatomy Lesson of Dr Nicolaes Tulp, an oil painting on canvas by Dutch artist Rembrandt (1606–1669; *see* 25 July), captures the moment in January 1632 when Amsterdam's official city anatomist demonstrated the musculature of convicted robber Aris Kindt who had been hanged earlier in the day. Although anatomy lessons usually started with a chest opening, his anatomical detail has been praised for its general accuracy. It is also a fine example of Rembrandt's mastery of the chiaroscuro technique, strongly contrasting the light and dark sections of the painting to produce an intense effect. So closely was he associated with this style, that a similar approach in portrait photography is called 'Rembrandt lighting'.

The spectators who make up one of the artist's earliest group portraits include local doctors who paid to be included in the painting – their names are listed on the paper being held up by the man shown at the back. The work is also notable as it is signed 'Rembrandt', the first time the painter used his forename rather than the initials RHL.

In American author Donna Tartt's 2013 novel *The Goldfinch* (in which – spoiler alert – it is badly damaged in a bomb explosion; *see* 12 October), the protagonist's mother is critical of the painting, suggesting that rather than the general praise heaped upon it for its portrayal of the merits of the Enlightenment, she sees the image as a bit 'creepy', with the characters treating the occasion like a genial get-together. Elsewhere, French illustrator Albert Uderzo and writer René Goscinny (*see* 29 October) present a humorous homage to it in *Asterix and the Soothsayer* when a fish is dissected on a table to predict the future.

ALSO ON THIS DAY 1799: Swiss painter, cartoonist and caricaturist Rodolphe Töpffer born · **1960:** Death of French painter Auguste Herbin · **2000:** Death of Latvian-born American illustrator Gil Kane

February

William Morris
registers 'Trellis', 1864

For, and this is at the root of the whole matter, everything made by man's hands has a form, which must be either beautiful or ugly; beautiful if it is in accord with Nature, and helps her; ugly if it is discordant with Nature, and thwarts her; it cannot be indifferent: we, for our parts, are busy or sluggish, eager or unhappy, and our eyes are apt to get dulled to this eventfulness of form in those things which we are always looking at. Now it is one of the chief uses of decoration, the chief part of its alliance with nature, that it has to sharpen our dulled senses in this matter: for this end are those wonders of intricate patterns interwoven, those strange forms invented, that men have so long delighted in: forms and intricacies that do not necessarily imitate nature, but in which the hand of the craftsman is guided to work in the way that she does, till the web, the cup or the knife, look as natural, nay as lovely, as the green field, the river bank or the mountain flint. To give people pleasure in the things they must perforce use, that is one great office of decoration; to give people pleasure in the things they must perforce make, that is the other use of it.

William Morris, address to The Trades' Guild of Learning, London, 4 December 1877

Leading light in the 19th-century Arts and Crafts movement that strove to champion the pleasures of high-quality handmade products, English designer William Morris (1834–1896) was particularly attracted to the potentialities of wallpaper and produced a series of designs for his own company Morris, Marshall, Faulkner & Co. with repeating patterns that are still popular today.

His first design, registered on 1 February 1864, was 'Trellis', inspired by his own garden at Red House in Bexleyheath where he lived with his wife Jane in the early 1860s. Mirroring the wooden rose-covered trellises around his flowerbeds, 'Trellis' has a simple regular square pattern of bars adorned with red roses, and with birds drawn by Philip Webb (the architect who designed Red House), all on a pale blue background.

As well as an impressive output of writings and artistic works, Morris was also an able lecturer, speaking on art and society in general, including his socialist principles.

2 FEBRUARY

William Morris on the function of art schools, 1887

Common-sense would surely point out to people engaged in teaching drawing that the first thing to be done is to get the pupil into a habit of accuracy, to discourage anything like sloppiness or vagueness, while at the same time he has put before him the limits which the material he is working in puts to the representation of the object he is working from. It seems to me that the attempt to teach students 'style' which some of the writers whose correspondence you enclosed to me appear to advocate, is a great mistake, a putting of the cart before the horse; there is nothing gained in teaching a clever young man to pick up the more superficial part of the style of a *master*, though it is much easier to do so than to learn to draw clean and accurately what you have got before you.

The gist of the matter I think lies in this, art-education, like other education, can only give the pupil the instruments which he himself can use for his own self-education. You cannot by any system teach a man to be a characteristic painter or an original designer; but if he has the capacity in him you can shorten his labour of learning by using your experience and the experience of ages; and most people can be taught to draw fairly accurately; and even to colour well; i.e. their capacities can be developed to a certain extent by the teaching. This I repeat is the function of art schools.

William Morris, letter to Arthur Pearson, 2 February 1887

The February letter that English designer William Morris (1834–1896) sent to Manchester Art School student Arthur Pearson was in response to a request received from Pearson, who had written to twenty English artists asking for their opinions on a lecture given by painter J. H. E. Partington. In 'Belgian vs. South Kensington Art Teaching', the artist had compared the inflexibility of

Manchester's teaching to its more flexible Antwerp equivalent. The replies from Morris, John Ruskin, Sir John Everett Millais and Walter Crane were published in *The Architect* magazine and the *Manchester Guardian* later that month.

ALSO ON THIS DAY 1851: Mexican illustrator and engraver José Guadalupe Posada born · **1866:** Spanish painter Enrique Simonet born · **1977:** Pompidou Centre in Paris opens

3 FEBRUARY

A day in the artistic life of Edward Lear, 1859

XX1 Alas. – Yet somehow I rose better – whether from warmer weather, or from the stuff Mr Stansfeld gave me I cannot tell. The day has been pouringly wet all day – but warm. –

I painted at the Masada – (barring Greek lesson No. 2 –) & at 12 two Messrs Beauclerk, – & the Duchess of St Albans & her daughter came, (& a Mrs Bruce. Nobody more delightfully pleasant than that Duchess of St Albans ever saw I. – & after she went the young pleasant Beauclerk bought all the 3 remaining pictures. GOD BE THANKED. – S.W.C. came & drew afterwards – & at 5 I called on the Chetwodes, who are good but vastly silly folk. –

Came home, to write Greek & a letter to Ann, from whom I had a letter today.

**Edward Lear, diary entry,
3 February 1859**

Edward Lear (1812–1888) is best known today for his poetry, but he was also an accomplished artist who travelled widely throughout Europe and into Africa and Asia, as well as teaching painting to Queen Victoria and Elizabeth Gould (*see* 10 January). As a young man he quickly became a leading ornithological illustrator and pioneer of using live birds as models for his work. His first publication, at the age of nineteen, was *Illustrations of the Family of Psittacidae or Parrots* (1832). In his thirties he switched to landscapes and made many coloured wash drawings on his journeys that he then used as the basis for watercolours and oils on his return home.

Lear also kept a diary, always a Letts, and by 1885 he had filled sixty volumes. In the entry for 3 February 1859 – written when he was wintering in Rome where the Prince of Wales visited him later in the year – he indicates how many epileptic seizures he had that day using an X (so on this day he had two, the 1 indicating these were the first of that month) and then closes with a mention of his eldest sister Ann who brought him up.

ALSO ON THIS DAY 1468: Death of German printing-press pioneer Johannes Gutenberg · **1894:** American painter and illustrator Norman Rockwell born (*see 6 March*) · **1898:** Finnish architect Alvar Aalto born

4 FEBRUARY

Sir Walter Scott finds the Scottish crown jewels, 1818

My dear Croker,

I have the pleasure to assure you the Regalia of Scotland were this day found in perfect preservation. The Sword of State and Sceptre showed marks of hard usage at some former period; but in all respects agree with the description in Thomson's work. I will send you a complete account of the opening tomorrow, as the official account will take some time to draw up. In the meantime, I hope you will remain as obstinate in your belief as St Thomas, because then you will come down to satisfy yourself. I know nobody entitled to earlier information, save one, to whom you can perhaps find the means of communicating the result of our researches. The post is just going off.

Ever yours truly,

Walter Scott

**Sir Walter Scott, letter to John Wilson Croker,
4 February 1818**

The Scottish Crown Jewels, or Honours, have an odd history. They were used in 1543 to crown Mary, Queen of Scots, then James VI, Charles I and Charles II. During the Commonwealth they were hidden to evade Cromwell's destructive eyes, and then in 1707 after the Treaty of Union were placed in an oak trunk in the Crown Room at Edinburgh Castle and largely forgotten.

In 1818, the Prince Regent gave the very popular Scottish writer Sir Walter Scott (1771–1832) his consent to search the castle for the regalia, which he found on 4 February 1818. The gold crown, solid silver sceptre and Sword of State (a gift from Pope Julius II with a 1-metre/3-foot blade), as well as a silver-gilt wand whose purpose is uncertain, were discovered in exactly the same place they had been left.

In a follow-up letter to Irish politician John Wilson Croker, a confidant of the soon to be George IV, Scott wrote:

> The extreme solemnity of opening sealed doors of oak and iron, and finally breaking open a chest which had been shut since 7th March 1707, about a hundred and eleven years, gave a sort of interest to our researches, which I can hardly express to you, and it would be very difficult to describe the intense eagerness with which we watched the rising of the lid of the chest, and the progress of the workmen in breaking it open, which was neither an easy nor a speedy task. It sounded very hollow when they worked on it with their tools, and I began to lean to your faction of the Little Faiths. However, I never could assign any probable or feasible reason for withdrawing these memorials of ancient independence; and my doubts rather arose from the conviction that many absurd things are done in public as well as in private life, merely out of a hasty impression of passion or resentment. For it was evident the removal of the Regalia might have greatly irritated people's minds here, and offered a fair pretext of breaking the Union, which for thirty years was the predominant wish of the Scottish nation.

ALSO ON THIS DAY 1814: English painter and illustrator Luke Clennell produces a hand-coloured etching of the *Frost Fair* on the frozen River Thames · **1859:** The Codex Sinaiticus, containing the earliest complete copy of the Christian New Testament, is uncovered in Egypt · **1881:** French painter and sculptor Fernand Léger born

Manifesto of Futurism
is first published, 1909

1. We shall sing the love of danger, the habit of energy and boldness.
2. The essential elements of our poetry shall be courage, daring and rebellion.
3. Literature has hitherto glorified thoughtful immobility, ectasy and sleep; we shall extol aggressive movement, feverish insomnia, the double quick step, the somersault, the box on the ear, the fisticuff.
4. We declare that the world's splendour has been enriched by a new beauty; the beauty of speed. A racing motor-car, its frame adorned with great pipes, like snakes with explosive breath...a roaring motor-car, which looks as though running on shrapnel, is more beautiful than the VICTORY OF SAMOTHRACE.
5. We shall sing of the man at the steering wheel, whose ideal stem transfixes the Earth, rushing over the circuit of her orbit.
6. The poet must give himself with frenzy, with splendour and with lavishness, in order to increase the enthusiastic fervour of the primordial elements.
7. There is no more beauty except in strife. No masterpiece without aggressiveness. Poetry must be a violent onslaught upon the unknown forces, to command them to bow before man.
8. We stand upon the extreme promontory of the centuries!.... Why should we look behind us, when we have to break in the mysterious portals of the Impossible? Time and Space died yesterday. Already we live in the absolute, since we have already created speed, eternal and ever-present.
9. We wish to glorify War – the only health giver of the world – militarism, patriotism, the destructive arm of the Anarchist, the beautiful Ideas that kill, the contempt for woman.
10. We wish to destroy the museum, the libraries, to fight against moralism, feminism and all opportunistic and utilitarian meannesses.
11. We shall sing of the great crowds in the excitement of labour, pleasure or rebellion; of the multi-coloured and polyphonic surf of revolutions in modern capital cities; of the nocturnal vibration of arsenals and workshops beneath their violent electric moons; of the greedy stations

swallowing smoking snakes; of factories suspended from the clouds by their strings of smoke; of bridges leaping like gymnasts over the diabolical cutlery of sunbathed rivers; of adventurous liners scenting the horizon; of broad-chested locomotives prancing on the rails, like huge steel horses bridled with long tubes; and of the gliding flight of aeroplanes, the sound of whose screw is like the flapping of flags and the applause of an enthusiastic crowd.

Filippo Tommaso Marinetti,
'Initial Manifesto of Futurism', 1912

The Futurists of the early 20th century were keen to explore the energy and dynamism of the modern world in all its social and artistic aspects. Radical painters and sculptors, including Italian painters Giacomo Balla, Umberto Boccioni and Gino Severini, took technology rather than tradition as their inspiration, although it was not until the 1914 *Technical Manifesto of Futurist Painting* that any kind of artistic programme was developed.

Its first manifesto was written by the Italian poet, art theorist and the movement's co-founder Filippo Marinetti (1876–1944), who included it in a book of his poems in 1908. It was then published in February 1909 in the Italian newspaper *Gazzetta dell'Emilia* and later that month, in French, in *Le Figaro* in France.

Futurism inspired Vorticism in Britain, although its adherents were decidedly antagonistic to each other.

ALSO ON THIS DAY 1852: Hermitage Museum in St Petersburg opens · **1870:** English book illustrator and painter Charles Edmund Brock born · **1916:** German author Hugo Ball opens the Cabaret Voltaire nightclub in Zurich, paving the way for the founding of the Dada art movement

6 FEBRUARY

Death of landscape gardener Capability Brown, 1783

At Blenheim, Croome and Caversham we trace
Salvator's Wildness, Claud's enlivening grace,
Cascades and Lakes as fine as Risdale drew,
While Nature's vary'd in each charming view.

To paint his works wou'd Pousin's Powers require,
Milton's sublimity and Dryden's fire:
For both the Sister Arts in him combin'd,
Enrich the great ideas of his mind;
And these still brighten all his vast designs,
For here the Painter, there the Poet shines!
With just contempt he spurns all former rules,
And shows true Taste is not confin'd to schools.
He barren tracts with every charm illumes,
At his command a new Creation blooms;
Born to grace Nature, and her works complete,
With all that's beautiful, sublime and great!
For him each Muse enwreathes the Laurel Crown,
And consecrates to Fame immortal Brown.

Anon., *The Rise and Progress of the Present Taste in Planting Parks, Pleasure Grounds, Gardens*, 1767

English landscape architect Lancelot Brown (1716–1783), better known by his nickname 'Capability' for his tendency to tell his clients that their estates offered great 'capabilities' for improvement, designed more than 170 landscaped parks in England. Some of these are mentioned in the anonymous poem above, which also likens him to the landscape painters Salvator Rosa, Claude Lorrain, Jacob van Ruisdael and Nicolas Poussin.

Brown trained under the popular landscape architect and designer William Kent at Stowe in Buckinghamshire, becoming head gardener in 1742 and King George III's Master Gardener at Hampton Court Palace twenty years later. His natural approach with sweeping lawns and manmade lakes was a marked change from the previous formal style of garden design.

A commemorative fountain for him was unveiled in 2018 in the cloister garth in Westminster Abbey, London.

ALSO ON THIS DAY 1918: Death of Austrian painter Gustav Klimt · **1947:** Magnum Photos cooperative agency is founded · **2012:** Death of Spanish painter and sculptor Antoni Tàpies

'Bonfire of the vanities'
in Florence, 1497

I counsel you to return to God, to live after the manner of a good Christian, to repent the past and recur to piety. Otherwise, I make known to you that severe chastisement awaits you, and that you shall be scourged in your substance, your flesh and your kindred.

Likewise I announce to you that your life is near its end; that if you obey not my words, you will go to hell, and this letter will be brought up against you before the judgment-seat of God, and leave you no way of escape.

**Girolamo Savonarola, letter to the prince of Mirandola,
Count Galeotto Pico, March 1496**

In 1492, Italian Dominican friar Girolamo Savonarola (1452–1498) had a vision in which the motto 'Behold the sword of the Lord will descend suddenly and quickly upon the earth' appeared. Five years later on 7 February, this mission statement was manifested in one of the most famous acts of deliberate artistic destruction – the 'bonfire of the vanities' during the celebration of Florence's Carnival.

In the final years of the 15th century, Florence was a centre of artistic excellence. At the same time, Savonarola began a personal crusade against corruption in the Church and what he saw as increasingly cultural immorality/ secularism. Initially restricting himself to stirring prophesies, he moved on to inspiring followers, including the prince of Mirandola to whom he wrote the above letter, to scour the city for any kind of art – books, clothes, games and make-up, as well as paintings and sculpture, including work by Donatello – and add it to a gigantic, multi-layered, eight-sided wooden pyramid. It was said to be 18 metres (60 feet) high.

Savonarola was so charismatic that he numbered important artists among his followers. Fra Bartolomeo was inspired by him to give up painting for a while to become a Dominican friar, although he also produced the most famous painting of Savonarola. Sandro Botticelli was another follower as art historian Giorgio Vasari explained: 'He was so ardent a partisan that he was thereby induced to desert his painting, and, having no income to live on, fell into very great distress.'

Savonarola fell out of favour with the local and religious authorities and a year later he was burned to death on the same spot in Piazza della Signoria where the vanities had gone up in flames.

ALSO ON THIS DAY 1726: English painter Margaret Fownes-Luttrell born · **1845:** Drunk student William Mulcahy smashes the Portland Vase, Roman cameo glassware from *c.* AD 25 (and is sentenced to two months in prison) · **2013:** A 9/11 conspiracy theorist defaces *Liberty Leading the People* by French painter Eugène Delacroix with a black pen at the Louvre-Lens Museum, France

8 FEBRUARY

Caspar David Friedrich
defends Romanticism, 1809

If a picture seems soulful to the viewer, if it shifts his mind into a beautiful mood, then it has satisfied the first demand of a work of art, however poor it may be in terms of drawing, colour, manner and so on.

**Caspar David Friedrich, letter to Akademiedirektor Schulz,
8 February 1809**

German painter Caspar David Friedrich (1774–1840) is most widely known for his 1818 work *Wanderer above the Sea of Mist*, but he set out his credentials for landscape Romanticism in his oil painting *Cross in the Mountains* (1808), known as the *Tetschen Altar*, his first major work.

The painting shows Jesus crucified on a golden cross. He is shown silhouetted and in profile on a rock on top of a mountain crag, ringed with a mass of fir trees. Christ is illuminated by a religious light. Everything is portrayed in great detail – indeed, this was an aspect of the work strongly criticized by the art critic Basilius von Ramdohr, a contemporary of Friedrich's who argued that the viewer would simply be unable to see such fine detail. The quote above is Friedrich's response.

Ramdohr also objected to another aspect of the painting, the use of religious allegory in conventional landscape painting (moreover, Friedrich initially put it on show in his studio). 'It is true presumption when landscape painting wants to slink into the church and creep on to the altars,' complained Ramdohr. The spat between the two became an artistic debate about Romanticism in general known as the *Ramdohrstreit*.

Friedrich's original intention was to make a political statement with the painting by producing it for the pro-German Swedish king Gustav IV, but in the end it was commissioned by Countess Theresia von Thun-Hohenstein for her Catholic family's chapel in Tetschen, Bohemia, and presented in a special frame made by sculptor Christian Kühn featuring a wide range of Christian iconography (unfortunately, the Countess's mother refused to allow it to hang in the chapel and it remained in the Countess's bedroom instead).

ALSO ON THIS DAY 1807: English sculptor and zoologist Benjamin Waterhouse Hawkins born (*see* 31 December)· **1819:** English painter and critic John Ruskin born (*see* 13 May) · **1880:** German soldier and painter Franz Marc born

9 FEBRUARY

Van Gogh writes a thank-you letter to a critic, 1890

I was extremely surprised by the article on my paintings that you sent me.... I think that basically the writer writes it rather to guide not only me but also the other Impressionists.... He tells me simply that there's something good here and there, if you like, in my very imperfect work as well, and there's the consolatory side which I appreciate and which I hope I'm grateful for.... Then an article like that has its own merit as a critical work of art, as such I consider it worthy of respect, and the writer *must* use exalted tones, synthesize his conclusions, etc.

**Vincent van Gogh, letter to his brother Theo,
1 February 1890**

In January 1890, French poet, author and art critic Albert Aurier (1865–1892) wrote an article in the magazine *Mercure de France* highly praising the work of Dutch painter Vincent van Gogh (1853–1890; *see also* 17 June), which he had seen at the Salon des Indépendants in Paris in 1889 and then again at an exhibition in Brussels. He emphasized that it showed an excess of strength and nervousness as well as a violence of expression.

Van Gogh, who had been sent the article by his brother, art dealer Theo van Gogh, was, unsurprisingly, delighted and on 9 February wrote to Aurier from the asylum in Saint-Rémy, France, where he was currently residing, thanking him and explaining how the criticism had also given him insight into his own work. He also promised Aurier that he would send him more of his work, a study of cypresses in the corner of a wheat field on a summer's day, as a personal gift.

ALSO ON THIS DAY 1498: Leonardo da Vinci finishes *The Last Supper* mural in the Convent of Santa Maria delle Grazie, Milan · **1916:** Romanian-born French writer Tristan Tzara invents the term Dada (apparently at 6 p.m.; *see* 5 February 1916) · **1920:** Armenian-American painter Arshile Gorky (*see* 16 July) emigrates to the USA

10 FEBRUARY

Lichtenstein's *Look Mickey* is first exhibited, 1962

To all whom it may concern: Be it known that I, BENJAMIN DAY, of West Hoboken, in the county of Hudson and State of New Jersey, have invented a new and useful Improvement in Printing-Films; and I do hereby declare that the following is a full, clear, and exact description of the same.... It will also be understood that when several different films are used, each cast with a different face or different character of lines, grain, or stipple, then a still greater variety of finish may be given to the picture; and, in fact, any kind of stippling, graining, hatching, lining, or shading may be produced upon the picture with the utmost precision, rapidity, delicacy and excellence of finish, thus effecting a vast saving in time and labor in the production of difficult artistic work.

Benjamin Day, US patent application, 1878

The eponymous process for printing various shapes invented by American printer Benjamin Day (1810–1889), especially small coloured dots of equal sizes arranged closely together, was used in many comic books in the first half of the 20th century and most famously adopted by American artist Roy Lichtenstein (1923–1997; *see also* 28 July).

Indeed, Lichtenstein threw a Pop-art-shaped spanner into the world of art when his *Look Mickey* oil on canvas painting (1961) incorporating the Ben Day dots method went on show at the Leo Castelli Gallery in New York. Not only was it his first attempt at adapting/reorganizing a comic frame – here,

Mickey Mouse and Donald Duck fishing at a pier at the moment when Donald announces 'LOOK MICKEY, I'VE HOOKED A BIG ONE!!' – but also incorporating new techniques such as speech bubbles.

In an interview with Gene Swenson for *ARTnews* in November 1963, Lichtenstein emphasized that everything he did was distinct from the comic strips that inspired his work, and although perhaps only very slightly dissimilar, still distinctly different.

The show at the Leo Castelli Gallery featured other works produced along similar lines, including *Blam* (a pilot escapes a plane in flames) and *Engagement Ring* ('It's...it's not an engagement ring, is it?' a young woman asks her male companion), and sold out before opening day.

It was a revolutionary but not universally popular artistic style. In an article two years later, *Life* magazine asked whether Lichtenstein was the worst artist in America, suggesting that while some people would give the answer a 'resounding yes' many others found his work fascinating.

ALSO ON THIS DAY 1879: Death of French painter and sculptor Honoré Daumier (*see* 19 June) · **1940:** Tom and Jerry make their screen debut in the cartoon *Puss Gets the Boot* · **1969:** American sand painter and sculptor Joe Mangrum born

11 FEBRUARY

The birth of Brazilian modernism, 1922

There are two kinds of artists. One is composed of those who normally see things and consequently make pure art.... Those who trail this path are Praxiteles in Greece, Raphael in Italy, Rembrandt in Holland, Rubens in Flanders, Reynolds in England, Lenbach in Germany, Iorn in Sweden, Rodin in France, Zuloaga in Spain.... The other species is those who see nature abnormally, and interpret it in the light of ephemeral theories, under the cross-eyed suggestion of rebellious schools, appearing here and there as boils of decadence. They are the products of weariness and sadism of all periods of decadence: they are the fruits of the end of the season. Shooting stars, they shine for an instant, mostly with the light of scandal, and soon disappear in the darkness of oblivion.

Monteiro Lobato, exhibition review, *O Estado de S. Paulo* newspaper, 20 December 1917

It would be fair to say that Brazilian novelist and art critic Monteiro Lobato (1882–1948) was not won over by the work of Brazilian artist Anita Malfatti (1889–1964), which was shown in her one-woman 'Exposição de Pintura Moderna' (Modern Painting Exhibition) in São Paulo over the winter of 1917/18. Lobato was upset with many elements – her use of colour, her paintings of nudes, the very fact that she was a woman – but his review had quite the opposite effect. It in fact helped to trigger an entirely new movement as many artists working along similar aesthetic lines backed Malfatti's approach and gathered to plan a large-scale show.

The seven days of São Paolo's Modern Art Week that began on 11 February 1922 saw a unique outpouring of Brazilian artistry, with Brazilian modernist art created alongside many performances, lectures and writings. It met with a mixed reception, not everybody warming to the radical sculptures of Italian-Brazilian Victor Brecheret or the paintings of Malfatti, who had twenty on show, including *The Yellow Man* and *Woman with Green Hair*.

Among those pushing for change was the Grupo dos Cinco (Group of Five), five artists including writer Oswald de Andrade whose later manifesto (known as the *Manifesto Antropófago*) argued that one of Brazilian culture's greatest assets was its ability to borrow or 'cannibalize' from other civilizations and thus counter European supremacy. A rival group, The Nationalists, called for the total rejection of international influences.

De Andrade's wife Tarsila do Amaral was one of the key artists exhibiting during the week (*see also* 19 April). Among her most famous works were *A Negra* (1923), an image that recognized the African contribution to Brazil's multiracial culture, and her iconic *Abaporu* (1928), which inspired her husband's manifesto. By happy coincidence, a major retrospective of her work opened at the Museum of Modern Art in New York on 11 February in 2018.

ALSO ON THIS DAY **1800:** English photography pioneer William Henry Fox Talbot born · **1855:** American painter Ellen Day Hale born (and died 1940) · **1869:** German art collector Helene Kröller-Müller born

Edvard Munch's
The Scream is stolen, 1994

One evening I was walking along a path, the city was on one side and the fjord below. I felt tired and ill. I stopped and looked out over the fjord – the sun was setting, and the clouds turning blood red. I sensed a scream passing through nature; it seemed to me that I heard the scream. I painted this picture, painted the clouds as actual blood. The colour shrieked. This became *The Scream*.

**Edvard Munch, diary entry, Nice, France,
22 January 1892**

Just before 6.30 a.m. on 12 February 1994, two men placed a ladder against the wall of the National Gallery in Oslo. In just under a minute, they raced up it, smashed a window on the second storey, jumped in and cut Munch's 1893 painting *The Scream* from the wall using wire cutters. They then climbed out of the window (dropping it briefly in the process) and sped off, leaving behind a note saying 'Thanks for the poor security.'

An initial claim of responsibility by a Norwegian anti-abortion group was discounted and an undercover sting operation was set up in collaboration with British detectives including Charles Hill (*see* 11 January). Hill pretended to be a criminal art dealer representing the Getty Museum who was interested in paying £250,000 for the painting and, following a series of leads, he recovered the work undamaged on 7 May. Three of the men involved successfully appealed against their consequent conviction on a legal technicality. The fourth was Pål Enger who six years earlier had stolen another Munch work, *The Vampire*.

Norwegian painter Edvard Munch (1863–1944) produced four versions of *The Scream*, one of which was stolen from the Munch Museum in Oslo in 2004 at gunpoint and recovered two years later (*see* 22 August).

ALSO ON THIS DAY 1884: German painter and sculptor Max Beckmann born · **1947:** French fashion designer Christian Dior's 'New Look' propels Paris to the top of the fashion world · **2014:** Discovery of two new portraits (probably) of William Shakespeare announced: the Wörlitz portrait and the Boaden portrait

Academy accepts resignation of Thomas Eakins, 1886

My figures at least are not a bunch of clothes with a head and hands sticking out but more nearly resemble the strong living bodies that most pictures show. And in the latter end of a life so spent in study, you at least can imagine that painting is with me a very serious study. That I have but little patience with the false modesty which is the greatest enemy to all figure painting. I see no impropriety in looking at the most beautiful of Nature's works, the naked figure. If there is impropriety, then just where does such impropriety begin? Is it wrong to look at a picture of a naked figure or at a statue? English ladies of the last generation thought so and avoided the statue galleries, but do so no longer. Or is it a question of sex? Should men make only the statues of men to be looked at by men, while the statues of women should be made by women to be looked at by women only? Should the he-painters draw the horses and bulls, and the she-painters like Rosa Bonheur the mares and cows? Must the poor old male body in the dissecting room be mutilated before Miss Prudery can dabble in his guts?

Such indignities anger me. Can not anyone see into what contemptible inconsistencies such follies all lead? And how dangerous they are? My conscience is clear, and my suffering is past.

Thomas Eakins, letter of resignation to Edward Hornor Coates,
Chairman of the Committee on Instruction,
Pennsylvania Academy of the Fine Arts, 15 February 1886

American painter and photographer Thomas Eakins (1844–1916; *see also* 19 October) was also an important teacher, professor and director at the Pennsylvania Academy of the Fine Arts. A noted portraitist, he was especially interested in the nude human figure. However, his forthright behaviour and attitudes – when a female student asked him about the male pelvis, he undressed in his studio to give her a first-hand explanation – led to confrontation with the academy's board of directors. The final straw came when he took off a male model's loincloth during an anatomy lecture that included female students and, confronted with more accusations of inappropriate behaviour, Eakins was asked to resign.

Eakins, who always protested his innocence of all charges, was popular among both his male and female students and a large group of them formed the Art Students' League of Philadelphia to call for his reinstatement. Approximately thirty of them briefly set up a new art school, headed by Eakins, which explicitly studied the nude figure.

ALSO ON THIS DAY 1571: Death of Italian sculptor Benvenuto Cellini (*see* 28 January) · **1930:** Austrian painter and sculptor Ernst Fuchs born · **2000:** The day after Charles M. Schulz dies, the final *Peanuts* Sunday comic strip is published (*see* 2 October 1950)

14 FEBRUARY

Valentine's Day cards

Since on this ever Happy day,
All Nature's full of Love and Play
Yet harmless still if my design,
'Tis but to be your Valentine.

**Oldest printed Valentine's Day
card message, 1797**

Early messages of Valentine's love date back to the 15th century when, behind bars in the Tower of London, Charles, Duke of Orleans wrote a love poem to his wife. The oldest surviving example in English was written in 1477 by Margery Brews to her fiancé John Paston whom she calls her 'right well-beloved valentine'. But cards with artwork only began to be sent during the 18th century. The oldest-surviving handwritten card was sent in the 1790s with a message on the front:

Farewell you sweet and turtle dove.
On you alone, I fixed my love.
And if you never can be mine,
I never can no comfort find!

Above it, a dove with an envelope in its beak is encircled by clouds and flanked by two pairs of hearts.

The oldest-known printed Valentine card was published in 1797 with the message at the head of this entry and decorated with the now familiar combination of flowers, cupids and doves. It was sent by Catherine Mossday to a Mr Brown of Dover Place, Kent Road, London. Miss Mossday also added a handwritten message inside:

> Mr Brown,
> As I have repeatedly requested you to come I think you must have some reason for not complying with my request, but as I have something particular to say to you I could wish you make it all agreeable to come on Sunday next without fail and in doing you will oblige your well wisher.
> Catherine Mossday.

Valentine cards were popularized in the United States by Esther Howland (1828–1904) from Massachusetts, who set up a card business in 1849 and grew it over the following decades into an extremely profitable business. Among her inventions were 'lift-up' cards made up of layers of ornately worked lace, three-dimensional scenes and a bouquet of flowers that moved when an attached piece of string was pulled. Her private life is somewhat obscure but she never married.

ALSO ON THIS DAY **1404:** Italian architect and polymath Leon Battista Alberti born · **1849:** James Knox Polk becomes the first serving US president to have his photograph taken (by Matthew Brady) · **1990:** NASA's *Voyager 1* spacecraft takes the Pale Blue Dot photograph of Earth

15 FEBRUARY

Ronald Searle is captured as Singapore surrenders to Japan, 1942

Sapper Ronald Searle R.E., Cambridge artist and cartoonist, using paints smuggled to him by Korean guards and brushes made from hairs from a cat's tail while a prisoner of the Japanese, painted a complete record of the scenes of horror and brutality on the Thailand 'Death Railway' and the Changhi prison camp.

When he was drafted from Britain to Mombasa in 1941, he decided to keep a day-to-day picture diary of life in the forces. He was captured at Singapore and was a prisoner for four years. 'We were so hungry in the Japanese camps that we ate cats,' he told me in London yesterday. 'The tails were always saved to make my brushes.'

Searle showed me hundreds of drawings he brought out of captivity. They are an astonishing record of cruelty, suffered by British prisoners. Men being whipped for trivial offences, men dying of hunger and thirst.... Joyous scenes when the camp was liberated.

'I had to do something to preserve my sanity, and so I painted,' said Searle....

An exhibition of Searle's line drawings and paintings is being held at the Cambridge School of Art this week.

**Reynolds News and Sunday Citizen newspaper,
2 December 1945**

After two years as a student at the Cambridge College of Arts and Technology in the UK, English illustrator Ronald Searle (1920–2011) enlisted in the British army in 1939. He was taken prisoner by Japanese forces on 15 February 1942 and spent the rest of the war in Changi Prison in Singapore or in the Kwai jungle, forced to work on the Death Railway, which ran from Thailand to Burma (now Myanmar).

Although severely ill and close to death during his time in the camps, Searle sketched his surroundings on a daily basis and even managed to set up an underground magazine, 'Survivor', written, illustrated (by Searle) and produced by prisoners of war. He also swapped drawings with other inmates for cigarettes and paper to continue his work. All his art was hidden from the Japanese soldiers, sometimes even under the beds of fellow prisoners dying of cholera. Many of these drawings were published in his book, *Ronald Searle: To the Kwai and Back, War Drawings 1939–1945* (1996).

After the war, Searle worked as a courtroom artist at the Nuremberg trials and the 1961 trial of Nazi war criminal Adolf Eichmann.

ALSO ON THIS DAY 1904: English muralist and painter Mary Adshead born · **1954:** American animator Matt Groening born · **1998:** English sculptor Antony Gormley instals the *Angel of the North* near the A1 and A167 roads at Gateshead, England

Howard Carter unseals
Tutankhamun's burial chamber, 1923

When the hole was wide enough Carter had a good look in and found we could just get round the right side of the tabernacle and walk along. He reported the outer door of the tabernacle was open, but that there was a second smaller one inside with the door still sealed and that there was another chamber opening off to the right. We then passed in our big travelling electric light, and Carnarvon and Lacau went in to see. Then Lady Evelyn – the only woman present, with Sir William Garstin, and then the others two by two. It was curious to watch them come out. With hardly an exception each person threw up his hands and gasped. Lucas and I went in together when it came to our turn. There was just room to squeeze round the corner of the tabernacle and walk along the side of it. In the middle were the great swing doors with open bars. Within you could see the second structure with sealed door and above it, on a frame, a pall dropping over it, of linen, spangled with gold stars.

Between the first and second tabernacles there were two wonderful alabasters, one in the form of a cat or lioncub. Passing along, you came on the right to a low open doorway, and looking into this you saw facing you against the far wall, the most impressive monument I've ever seen – a huge wooden shrine covered with gold to contain the canopic jars, and full standing guarding it one on each side there were four goddesses, the most lovely female figures, absolutely natural and lifelike in their poise, one with back turned and two looking sideways over their shoulders. For modelling I really think they beat anything I have ever seen from any country. For the rest, the chamber was full, boxes mostly. One we looked into and it contained a most lovely gold and ostrich feather fan, apparently in perfect condition. There were also a number of boats, two more chariots and a number of other things. My mind was too confused and excited to take them in. The whole thing was really almost painfully impressive. With one exception of the hurried visit of the thieves some ten years after the King's death, none had set foot in the chamber since the King was laid to rest more than three thousand years before. One didn't dare let one's imagination get too vividly to work. The figures of the goddesses alone were so beautiful that they made a lump come in one's throat. It was a quarter past two when we went down into the tomb, and it was after five when we came out, and I think we were all fairly dazed, too dazed even to realize what we had found. Now it is all buried deep underground again waiting for next season's work.

Carter came back to dinner with us that night, and we were all more or less like crazy people. The excitement had been too much for us, and I'm sure anyone coming in would have said we all had been taking too much to drink.

An unforgettable experience and impossible to get onto paper.

Arthur Mace, diary entry, 3 March 1923

English archaeologist Arthur Mace (1874–1928) was a key member of the team led by archaeologist Howard Carter (1874–1939) that discovered Tutankhamun's tomb in the Valley of the Kings in Egypt in November 1922 (*see also* 12 August).

ALSO ON THIS DAY 1543: Japanese painter Kanō Eitoku born · **1740:** Italian typographer and engraver Giambattista Bodoni born · **1878:** English tarot card illustrator Pamela Colman Smith born

17 FEBRUARY

Armory Show opens in New York, 1913

The recent 'International Exhibition of Modern Art' in New York was really noteworthy. Messrs Davies, Kuhn, Gregg and their fellow members of the Association of American Painters and Sculptors have done a work of very real value in securing such an exhibition of the works of both foreign and native painters and sculptors. Primarily their purpose was to give the public a chance to see what has recently been going on abroad. No similar collection of the works of European 'moderns' has ever been exhibited in this country. The exhibitors are quite right as to the need of showing to our people in this manner the art forces which of late have been at work in Europe, forces which cannot be ignored.

This does not mean that I in the least accept the view that these men take of the European extremists whose pictures are here exhibited. It is true, as the champions of these extremists say, that there can be no life without change, no development without change, and that to be afraid of what is different or unfamiliar is to be afraid of life. It is no less true, however, that change may mean death and not life, and retrogression instead of development. Probably we err in treating most of these pictures seriously. It is likely that many of them represent in the painters the astute appreciation of the powers to make folly lucrative which the late P. T. Barnum showed with his faked mermaid. There are thousands of people who will pay small sums to look at a faked mermaid; and now and then one of this kind with enough money will buy a Cubist picture, or a picture of a misshapen nude woman, repellent from every standpoint.

Theodore Roosevelt, 'A Layman's Views of an Art Exhibition',
***Outlook*, 29 March 1913**

America's first major modern art exhibition, which ran for three days at the 69th Regiment Armory in New York and introduced a new European approach to art, caused a scandal. Among the most controversial works were French painter Henri Matisse's *Blue Nude* (burned in effigy by art students when the show moved to Chicago) and French-American artist Marcel Duchamp's *Cubist Nude Descending a Staircase*, about which former US president Theodore Roosevelt commented: 'He is nuts and his imagination has gone wild.'

Roosevelt (1858–1919; *see also* 3 October) was among those who had mixed feelings about the show. While he admired the originality and enterprise of the project, he was not personally keen on many of the works on display.

ALSO ON THIS DAY 1854: Death of English painter, illustrator and engraver John Martin · **1923:** English archaeologist and Dead Sea Scrolls scholar John Allegro born (and died 1988) · **1966:** Death of German-American painter Hans Hofmann

18 FEBRUARY

Louis Comfort Tiffany is born, 1848

One of the earliest designs for personal jewelry which occurred to Mr Tiffany is the flower of the wild carrot, called Queen Anne's Lace. This charming weed is found everywhere. Its unpretending wheel formed of a great number of small white flowers, sometimes of a delicate mauve, will often carry a small dark floweret in the centre of the disk. This wheel is reproduced in white enamel on silver, with a garnet at the centre. A dragonfly for a hat-pin is enameled and set with opals on a platinum base. A marine motif, half crab, half octopus, with the writhing feet split into two or more special ends, is arranged for a brooch and set with opals, sapphires and rubies. This piece is now in the Walters Gallery. A girdle of silver ornamented with enamels, has berries formed of opals. A decoration for the head is a branch of blackberries, the leaves made of filigree of gold and silver, enameled, the berries composed of clusters of dark garnets. Another design is the dandelion full blown with seed, the 'four o'clock'. A third is a spray of the little spirea flower.

Charles de Kay,
***The Art Work of Louis C. Tiffany*, 1914**

American jeweller and stained-glass artist Louis Comfort Tiffany (1848–1933) mastered numerous artistic disciplines. He initially trained as a painter before turning to glassmaking, and in particular elaborate and highly coloured stained glass, developing a unique kind of iridescent glass, Favrile. Inspired chiefly by the natural world, he was the first design director at Tiffany & Co., founded by his father Charles, as well as a highly successful interior designer, with commissions ranging from Mark Twain's house to the White House under President Chester Arthur. Tiffany worked in almost every medium, including pottery, mosaics, enamel and metalwork, as well as the leaded stained-glass window work with which he is particularly associated today, and built his own remarkable eighty-four-room mansion, Laurelton Hall on Long Island, New York. Even his biography, dictated to art historian Charles de Kay, is a work of art, limited to 502 copies (10 for family members on parchment, the rest on Japan paper) with a highly decorative cover of gold over a papier-mâché binding, which he designed himself.

ALSO ON THIS DAY 1455: Death of Italian painter Fra Angelico · **1564:** Death of Italian painter, sculptor and architect Michelangelo (*see* 1 November) · **1934:** Spanish fashion designer Paco Rabanne born

The era of Byzantine
Iconoclasm ends, 843

Supported by the Holy Scriptures and the Fathers, we declare unanimously, in the name of the Holy Trinity, that there shall be rejected and removed and cursed out of the Christian Church every likeness which is made out of any material and colour whatever by the evil art of painters.

Whoever in future dares to make such a thing, or to venerate it, or set it up in a church, or in a private house, or possesses it in secret, shall, if bishop, presbyter, or deacon, be deposed; if monk or layman, be anathematised, and become liable to be tried by the secular laws as an adversary of God and an enemy of the doctrines handed down by the Fathers....

If anyone ventures to represent the divine image (karakthr) of the Word after the Incarnation with material colours, let him be anathema!

If anyone ventures to represent in human figures, by means of material colours, by reason of the Incarnation, the substance or person (ousia or hypostasis) of the Word, which cannot be depicted, and does not rather confess that even after the Incarnation He [i.e., the Word] cannot be depicted, let him be anathema!

Edict, Iconoclastic Council of Hieria, 754

The war against religious images and icons in the Byzantine Empire raged between 726 and 842. The initial ban was made by Emperor Leo III with the backing of the Orthodox Church leaders – though at no time by the Papacy – and was followed by mass destruction and persecution of those who refused to submit. The edict of 754 was the Church's first full official endorsement of the iconoclastic position.

The reasons for the ban are not entirely clear and may be linked to a volcanic eruption in 726 in the Aegean Sea near the island of Santorini, which caused a tsunami and multiple deaths and some thought indicated God's wrath. Others suggest it was more a political move against the increasing power of the monasteries or was the result of the influence of the Islamic prohibition of imagery. There was also an argument that held it was impossible to adequately portray both the human and divine elements of Jesus, either separately or at the same time.

The iconoclasm was officially ended on 19 February 843 by proclamation of Empress Theodora, but the controversy still rumbled on and was among the causes of the Great Schism of 1054 between the Roman Catholic Church and the Eastern Orthodox Church.

Painter George Frederic Watts marries actress Ellen Terry, 1864

In the middle of the run of 'The American Cousin' I left the stage and married. Mary Meredith was the part, and I played it vilely. I was not quite sixteen years old, too young to be married even in those days, when everyone married early. But I was delighted, and my parents were delighted, although the disparity of age between my husband and me was very great. It all seems now like a dream – not a clear dream, but a fitful one which in the morning one tries in vain to tell. And even if I could tell it, I would not. I was happy, because my face was the type which the great artist who had married me loved to paint. I remember sitting to him in armour for hours and never realizing that it was heavy until I fainted!

The day of my wedding it was very cold. Like most women, I always remember what I was wearing on the important occasions of my life. On that day I wore a brown silk gown which had been designed by Holman Hunt, and a quilted white bonnet with a sprig of orange-blossom, and I was wrapped in a beautiful Indian shawl. I 'went away' in a sealskin jacket with coral buttons, and a little sealskin cap. I cried a great deal, and Mr Watts said, 'Don't cry. It makes your nose swell.'

Ellen Terry, *The Story of My Life*, 1908

English painter and sculptor George Frederic Watts (1817–1904) was regarded as one of the finest Victorian painters and was one of the first to be awarded the Order of Merit; he has been described as 'England's Michelangelo'.

He was first introduced to the teenage actress Ellen Terry (1847–1928) by a mutual friend, dramatist and editor of *Punch* magazine, Tom Taylor. Watts initially felt Terry could be his great muse and model and considered adopting her before deciding on marriage despite the age difference (he was forty-six and Terry was sixteen) and little encouragement from his circle of friends.

There are five surviving portraits of Ellen Terry by Watts, of which the most famous is his Pre-Raphaelite painting, *Choosing*, which shows her deliberating between camellias (gorgeous but with little scent) and violets (less glamorous but a finer scent), a symbolic choice between worldly goods and loftier virtues – 'I paint ideas,' said Watts, 'not things.' Sadly, the marriage did not last. Terry returned to her family ten months later and the couple were amicably divorced in 1877.

ALSO ON THIS DAY **1872:** The Metropolitan Museum of Art opens in New York · **1902:** American photographer Ansel Adams born · **1943:** First of American artist Norman Rockwell's 'Four Freedom' paintings (*see* 6 March) is published in the *Saturday Evening Post*

21 FEBRUARY

Nicholas Brend leases land for the Globe Theatre, 1599

On 21st September after lunch, about two o'clock, I and my party crossed the water, and there in the house with the thatched roof witnessed an excellent performance of the tragedy of the first Emperor Julius Caesar.... The playhouses are so constructed that they play on a raised platform, so that everyone has a good view. There are different galleries and places, however, where the seating is better and more comfortable and therefore more expensive. For whoever cares to stand below only pays one English penny, but if he wishes to sit he enters by another door, and pays another penny, while if he desires to sit in the most comfortable seats which are cushioned, where he not only sees everything well, but can also be seen, then he pays yet another English penny at another door. And during the performance food and drink are carried round the audience, so that for what one cares to pay one may also have refreshment.

Thomas Platter, diary entry,
21 September 1599

Doctor and traveller Thomas Platter (1574–1682) from Basel visited England in 1599 as part of a wider tour of Europe. In September, he went to see a performance of *Julius Caesar* (probably by William Shakespeare) at the newly built Globe Theatre in London and provided the earliest account of its architecture. The Globe was the outdoor playhouse home of the Lord Chamberlain's Men, later known as the King's Men, after they were initially based in Shoreditch.

One night in late December 1598, actor Richard Burbage and a group of friends and workmen dismantled the company's previous home, The Theatre in Shoreditch, built by Burbage's father, carried it section by section to Southwark and stored it in a warehouse belonging to one of the leading theatre carpenters of the day, Peter Street. Incorporating additional timber to increase its size, it was then reassembled as the Globe later in the spring of 1599 to designs by Burbage's brother Cuthbert on a rather marshy site not far from the riverbank. This plot belonged to local landowner Nicholas Brend (*c.* 1560–1601), who leased it to the players on 21 February 1599. One story has it that as it was a cold winter and the Thames had frozen over, the actors carried the beams across the ice (a nice story, but it was almost certainly too thin for them to have done so and it was done rather by ferry). The theatre reopened in the summer, just in time for Platter to enjoy Shakespeare's retelling of Caesar's demise.

Estimates suggest the three-storey Globe was more of polygon than simply round, had a diameter of about 30 metres (100 feet) and was large enough for an audience of approximately three thousand people in the pit at the front or seated in the main amphitheatre. The raised stage extended into the centre of the auditiorium with a balcony for the musicians, which was sometimes also used for staging.

The Globe burned down on 29 June 1613 after the thatched roof caught fire during a performance of *Henry VIII*, but was rebuilt the following year; it closed its doors in 1642. In 1997, the Shakespeare's Globe reconstruction of the theatre opened close to the original site.

Bernini's St Peter's Baldachin is inaugurated, 1633

Beneath the chapel is a vault lined with sarcophagi of the Corsini. Its altar is surmounted by a magnificent Pietà – in whose beautiful and impressive figures it is difficult to recognise a work of the usually coarse and theatrical artist Bernini.

**Augustus Hare, on Bernini's *Pietà* in the Basilica of St John Lateran, Rome,
Walks in Rome, 1875**

The reputation of the 17th-century Italian Renaissance polymath Gian Lorenzo Bernini (1598–1680) yo-yoed both during his lifetime and after his death, waning in the 18th and 19th centuries (as the above quotation from English travel writer Augustus Hare indicates), but it has fully recovered over the last century. In fact, the painter, theatre designer, actor and scriptwriter was also a notable architect whose work on the bronze canopy known as St Peter's Baldachin is a fine example of the integration of sculpture and architecture.

Commissioned by Pope Urban VIII, Bernini's Baroque-style baldachin covers the high altar in the crossing of St Peter's Basilica in the Vatican City, and was built between 1623 and 1634 to indicate the tomb of St Peter underground. The canopy is held up by four 20-metre (65-foot) helical columns standing on a marble plinth. Above, four double-life-size angels stand at each corner, with a gilded cross on a sphere at the very top. Much of the bronze is likely to have come from the ceiling of the ancient Roman Pantheon.

Details on the baldachin reflect that the work was commissioned by Pope Urban, whose name was Maffeo Barberini. Thus, the heraldic bee emblem of the Barberini family is a prominent feature. One of the most notable sections is the series of coats of arms that appear to portray the stages of childbirth.

ALSO ON THIS DAY **1882:** English sculptor, typographer and printmaker Eric Gill born · **1925:** American illustrator Edward Gorey born · **1987:** Death of American mixed-media artist Andy Warhol (*see* 9 July)

Civilisation: A Personal View is first broadcast, 1969

Civilisation: 1: The Skin of Our Teeth
A personal view by Kenneth Clark

In this the first of a new documentary series of thirteen programmes, one of our most distinguished art historians and critics Sir Kenneth Clark examines the ideas and values which to him give meaning to the term Western Civilisation. Tonight he looks at the Dark Ages, the six centuries following the collapse of the Roman Empire. Travelling from Byzantine Ravenna to the Celtic Hebrides, from the Norway of the Vikings to Charlemagne's chapel at Aachen, he unravels the extraordinary story of how European thought and art were saved by 'the skin of our teeth'.

Radio Times, 20 February 1969

Sandwiched between a variety show featuring the Kuban Cossacks and a documentary about the life and music of Austrian composer Anton Bruckner, *Civilisation: A Personal View* made its debut on Sunday, 23 February 1969 at 8.25 p.m. and was an immediate hit, racking up viewing figures of one million.

Its writer and presenter English art historian Sir Kenneth Clark (1903–1983) had already worked on several television programmes about art history as well as running the Ashmolean Museum in Oxford and Britain's National Gallery in London (*see* 23 August). In the eyes of Sir David Attenborough, controller of the newly launched BBC Two channel, this made him the ideal choice to showcase the marvels of colour television and filming started in 1966.

Over the following months, Clark offered his personal take on Western art and architecture as well as philosophy, drama, literature and music, as he toured thirteen countries and more than one hundred locations. Each episode was repeated later in the week. The book of the series became a bestseller.

At the end of the thirteen episodes, journalist and critic Stanley Reynolds reviewed the series in the *Guardian* newspaper on 19 May. 'Sir Kenneth's series', he wrote, 'with its constant praise of the unfashionable heroic man, has shone out brightly among the grey and gutless expediency of contemporary criticism.'

24 FEBRUARY

John Evelyn enjoys an architectural walk in Rome, 1645

We walked to St Roche's and Martine's, near the brink of the Tiber, a large hospital for both sexes. Hence, to the Mausoleum Augusti, between the Tiber and the Via Flaminia, now much ruined, which had formerly contended for its sumptuous architecture. It was intended as a cemetery for the Roman emperors, had twelve ports and was covered with a cupola of white marble, environed with stately trees and innumerable statues, all of it now converted into a garden. We passed the afternoon at the Sapienza, a very stately building full of good marbles, especially the portico, of admirable architecture. These are properly the University Schools, where lectures are read on Law, Medicine and Anatomy, and students perform their exercises.

Hence, we walked to the church of St Andrea della Valle, near the former Theater of Pompey, and the famous Piccolomini, but given to this church and the Order, who are Theatins. The Barberini have in this place a chapel, of curious incrusted marbles of several sorts, and rare paintings. Under it is a place where St Sebastian is said to have been beaten with rods before he was shot with darts. The cupola is painted by Lanfranc, an inestimable work, and the whole fabric and monastery adjoining are admirable.

John Evelyn, diary entry, 24 February 1645

English writer John Evelyn (1620–1706; *see also* 21 June) is best remembered now for his diary. Unlike his contemporary Samuel Pepys (*see* 17 March), Evelyn did not make daily entries and sometimes caught up using notes. Nor is it as salacious as Pepys's (though he was a friend of Charles II and the diary includes references to his mistresses, including actress Nell Gwynn), but it does cover a much wider range of dates, from about 1640 to the very end of his long life.

But Evelyn (motto: 'explore everything, keep the best') was far more than a diarist. He was a founding member of the Royal Society, an architect, a bibliophile, a notable horticulturalist and among his literary correspondents were polymath Sir Thomas Browne, wood carver Grinling Gibbons, Anglo-Irish scientist Robert Boyle and architect Sir Christopher Wren, as well as Pepys.

When Evelyn wrote about his walk in Rome on 24 February 1645, as well as on a kind of Grand Tour of Italy and France, he was also escaping the horrors of the English Civil War.

ALSO ON THIS DAY 1910: Death of Turkish painter, museum curator and archaeologist Osman Hamdi Bey · **1836:** American painter Winslow Homer born · National Artist Day in Thailand

25 FEBRUARY

The first Anderson shelter is erected in London, 1939

Air Raid Warnings

When air raids are threatened, warning will be given in towns by sirens or hooters, which will be sounded, in some places by short blasts, and in other places by a warbling note, changing every few seconds. In war, sirens and hooters will not be used for any other purpose than this.

The warning may also be given by the Police or Air Raid Wardens blowing short blasts on whistles.

When you hear the warning, take cover at once. Remember that most of the injuries in an air raid are caused not by direct hits by bombs, but by flying fragments of debris or bits of shells. Stay under cover until you hear the sirens or hooters sounding continuously for two minutes on the same note, which is the signal 'Raiders Passed'.

If poison gas has been used, you will be warned by means of hand rattles. Keep off the streets until the poison gas has been cleared away. Hand bells will be rung when there is no longer any danger. If you hear the rattle when you are out, put on your gas mask at once and get indoors as soon as you can.

Make sure that all members of your household understand the meanings of these signals.

UK government, *Some Things You Should Know If War Should Come, Public Information Leaflet No. 1*, July 1939

Plans for civilian protection from air raids in the UK had been underway well before the beginning of the Second World War in 1939. One of the earliest provisions was the Anderson shelter, designed in 1938 by Dr David Anderson, William Paterson and Oscar Carl Kerrison and first built in Islington, London, on 25 February 1939. A shed-like galvanized corrugated steel structure of 2 × 1.4 metres (6½ × 4½ feet), the shelter was erected in domestic back gardens sunk 1.2 metres (4 feet) into the ground and then covered with earth. Able to accommodate up to six people, they were provided to more than three million people living in the most exposed locations and were free to those earning under £5 a week (£7 to everyone else).

Although they undoubtedly saved lives, they were of no use to those without gardens and were uncomfortable and prone to damp. They gradually fell out of use, to be replaced by the cage-like indoor Morrison shelters. After the war, many Anderson shelters continued life as chicken coops or tool sheds.

ALSO ON THIS DAY 1723: Death of English architect Christopher Wren · **1841:** French painter and sculptor Pierre-Auguste Renoir born (*see* 26 August) · **1988:** English photograph colourizer Tom Marshall born

26 FEBRUARY

Rubens is commissioned to paint the Marie de' Medici Cycle, 1622

He made spirited sketches of each subject, which he gave to his pupils to work from under his constant superintendence, by which means this prodigious work was completed in less than two years, although from the previous correspondence it is evident that Rubens was also engaged upon other pictures. Nineteen were painted at Antwerp in his own studio, the two largest on his return to Paris, where he finished the portraits of several of the principal characters, and superintended placing them in the Palace of the Luxembourg. While thus engaged, the Queen, who took a particular pleasure in his conversation, frequently honoured him with visits. She was so delighted with these extraordinary works of art that she requested Rubens to paint four portraits.... When the whole series was finished, Rubens had the honour to conduct the Queen, attended by many distinguished persons, through the gallery, and to explain the meaning of the numerous allegories. A few days after he had an audience of Her Majesty, who gave him many splendid presents, and he quitted Paris.

William Sainsbury, on the Marie de' Medici Cycle,
in *Original Unpublished Papers Illustrative of the Life of Sir Peter Paul Rubens*, 1859

The twenty-four paintings by Flemish artist Peter Paul Rubens (1577–1640) that make up the Marie de' Medici Cycle (1622–25) were commisioned by the widow of Henry IV of France, Marie de' Medici, who hung them in the Luxembourg Palace in Paris.

The first twenty-one paintings are essentially a pictorial biography of the life of Marie (1575–1642) – from birth, through marriage, to her position as regent – in mostly allegorical terms to avoid causing any political upset. These were:

The Destiny of Marie de' Medici
The Birth of the Princess
Education of the Princess
The Presentation of Her Portrait to Henry IV
The Wedding by Proxy of Marie de' Medici to King Henry IV
The Disembarkation at Marseilles
The Meeting of Marie de' Medici and Henry IV at Lyons
The Birth of the Dauphin at Fontainebleau
The Consignment of the Regency
The Coronation in Saint-Denis
The Death of Henry IV and the Proclamation of the Regency
The Council of the Gods
The Regent Militant: The Victory at Jülich
The Exchange of the Princesses at the Spanish Border
The Felicity of the Regency of Marie de' Medici
Louis XIII Comes of Age
The Flight from Blois
The Negotiations at Angoulême

The Queen Opts for Security
Reconciliation of the Queen and her Son
The Triumph of Truth

These were followed by three portraits of her, her father Francesco I and her mother Johanna of Austria.

In a letter to his friend French astronomer Nicolas-Claude Fabri de Peiresc in May 1625, Rubens said that Marie and her son Louis XIII were highly satisfied with the paintings. A similar cycle by Rubens with Henry IV as the focus was planned but never went further than some sketches, not least because Louis, with whom Marie de' Medici had a prickly relationship once he became king, exiled her from France in 1631.

ALSO ON THIS DAY 1808: French painter and sculptor Honoré Daumier born (*see* 19 June) · **1829:** German-American fashion designer Levi Strauss born · **2001:** The Taliban destroy two enormous statues of the Buddha in Bamiyan, Afghanistan

27 FEBRUARY

First sight of Picasso's
Les Demoiselles d'Avignon, 1907

Dined at Picasso's in the evening, saw his new painting: even colours, rose-coloured flesh and flowers, etc, simple heads of women and men too. Admirable language that no literature can express.

Guillaume Apollinaire, diary entry,
27 February 1907

Spanish painter and sculptor Pablo Picasso (1881–1973; *see* 26 April) and his friend French poet and critic Guillaume Apollinaire (1880–1918; *see* 7 September) shared an interest in African sculptures. However, Apollinaire's first reaction to Picasso's *Les Demoiselles d'Avignon* (1907), which was inspired by them, was decidedly lukewarm when he was shown the painting on 27 February.

Reactions to Picasso's famous work of art, a groundbreaking painting of a group of five female prostitutes, varied immensely. The artist himself said that, inspired by primitive masks, he had been able to 'liberate an utterly original artistic style of compelling, even savage force', while his friend French painter Georges Braque compared the painting to drinking petrol and spitting fire.

American writer Gertrude Stein, a major collector of Picasso's work, described it in her autobiography as 'a strange picture of light and dark...all of it rather frightening'. Russian art collector Sergei Shchukin was even more upset, exclaiming: 'What a loss to French art!' Picasso's artistic rival Henri Matisse (*see* 17 October) found it especially objectionable, but at least partly because its notoriety threatened to eclipse his own fame.

'He has painted, or rather daubed, five women who are, if the truth be told, all hacked up, and yet their limbs somehow manage to hold together,' wrote *Le Cri de Paris* magazine in July 1916 when it was finally first exhibited. 'They have, moreover, piggish faces with eyes wandering negligently above their ears.'

Others were more far-sighted, such as Picasso's art dealer Daniel-Henry Kahnweiler, who described the work as the beginning of Cubism.

ALSO ON THIS DAY 1622: Dutch painter Carel Fabritius born (*see* 12 October) · **1799:** English artist and architect Frederick Catherwood born · **1964:** Death of Australian-American costume designer Orry-Kelly

28 FEBRUARY

The Artists Rifles volunteer corps is established, 1860

I am now an artist in a wider sense.... Every man must do his bit in this horrible business so I have given up painting and bid it adieu for who knows how long to take up this queer business of soldiering.

Paul Nash, letter to English poet Gordon Bottomley, September 1914

The British army's Artists Rifles volunteer regiment was set up on 28 February 1860 by art student Edward Sterling as a proactive measure against a perceived threat of French invasion. At its heart were painters and architects, as well as musicians, writers, actors and others involved in creative industries. Initially headquartered at Burlington House in London, its founding members included Frederic, Lord Leighton, George Frederic Watts, Sir John Everett Millais, William Morris, Dante Gabriel Rossetti and Edward Burne-Jones.

Although generally dedicated to the task in hand, there were some issues. Painter William Holman Hunt (*see* 30 August) kept losing parts of his disassembled rifle and writer Ford Madox Ford accidentally shot his own dog during target practice. In his memoirs, portrait painter, sculptor, stained-glass designer and mosaicist Sir William Blake Richmond recounts that textile designer William Morris (*see* 1 February) often mixed up right and left when turning, while Rossetti (*see* 30 August) was particularly argumentative: 'He wished to know the exact reason for every movement which he and his comrades were told to execute.'

Richmond recounts that it was a time-consuming passion – they drilled twice a day (7–9 a.m., then 4–7 p.m.), and at least all afternoon on Saturdays. They carried out route marches and sham skirmishing on Wimbledon Common and Hampstead Heath.

The Artists Rifles fought in the Boer Wars and while membership broadened significantly, among those who signed up during the First World War were artist brothers Paul Nash and John Nash. During the war, more than 15,000 men passed through the battalion, which saw action in France and sustained very high casualties.

Since 1860, the 'Rifles' has had various name changes and is now the 21st Special Air Service Regiment (Artists) (Reserve).

ALSO ON THIS DAY 1820: English illustrator Sir John Tenniel born (*see* 16 December) · **1929:** Canadian-American architect Frank Gehry born · **1935:** Viking Ladby Ship is discovered on Funen, Denmark

29 FEBRUARY

<h1 style="text-align:center">Sculptor Augusta Savage
is born, 1892</h1>

Lift ev'ry voice and sing
Till earth and heaven ring,
Ring with the harmonies of Liberty;
Let our rejoicing rise
High as the listening skies,
Let it resound loud as the rolling sea.
Sing a song full of the faith that the dark past has taught us,

Sing a song full of the hope that the present has brought us.
Facing the rising sun of our new day begun,
Let us march on till victory is won.

James Weldon Johnson,
'Lift Ev'ry Voice and Sing' lyrics, 1900

Despite her father's strong disapproval, American artist Augusta Savage (1892–1962) studied sculpture at Cooper Union in New York during which time she was turned down for a summer course at the Fontainebleau School of Fine Arts in France solely on the basis of being black. Her appeal against the decision made headlines in the media and marked the start of her efforts to fight for equal rights for other African Americans in the world of art.

After studying and working in Europe, she returned to the United States where she became the first African American artist to be elected to the National Association of Women Painters and Sculptors and the first to open her own gallery, Salon of Contemporary Negro Art. She was also an integral part of the 306 Group of African American artists based in Harlem.

Although she made a name for herself as a portrait sculptor, producing busts of prominent civil rights activists including W. E. B. Du Bois and Marcus Garvey, the work that made her name was her nearly 5-metre (16-foot) plaster sculpture *Lift Every Voice and Sing* (1939), a commission for the 1939 New York World's Fair inspired by the song of the same name written by James Weldon Johnson in 1900.

Also known as *The Harp*, Savage's sculpture showed a dozen young African Americans as the strings on a harp, the sounding board morphed into the arm and hand of God, and a small figure kneeling in front of it. It was destroyed at the end of the fair along with much of the art. In fact little of her art remains, partly because she lacked the funds to work in more lasting media such as bronze, although her plaster bust of a young boy, *Gamin* (c. 1929), is on permanent display at the Smithsonian American Art Museum in Washington DC.

Her output dropped in later years when she moved to the Catskill Mountains, New York, but she remained a keen teacher and educator until her death in relative obscurity in 1962.

March

Damien Hirst's shark
goes on display, 1992

But you didn't, did you?

**Damien Hirst, quoted in Lynn Barber, 'Saatchi Gallery:
Bleeding Art', _Observer_, 20 April 2003**

On 1 March 1992, _The Physical Impossibility of Death in the Mind of Someone
Living_ (1991) by English artist Damien Hirst (b. 1965; _see also_ 25 December)
first appeared at Charles Saatchi's new exhibition series 'Young British Artists'
at the Saatchi Gallery, London. The 4-metre (13-foot) tiger shark conserved
behind glass in formaldehyde – a representation of the tension between life
and death, a kind of Schrödinger's shark – immediately become the iconic
symbol of the Britart movement.

The shark was caught at Hervey Bay in Australia by a fisherman whom
Hirst had instructed to find something 'big enough to eat you'. Commissioned
by Saatchi himself for £50,000 (or as the _Sun_ newspaper's headline put it
'£50,000 for fish without chips'), it was later sold by him in 2004 for an
estimated $8 million.

After years of deteriorating in the giant glass vitrine, a fin dropped off
and the skin wrinkled and went green. Consequently, the original shark was
replaced in 2006 by another shark from Australia, leading to philosophical
questions about whether it was still the same artwork and adding to the
debate about its portrayal of death and decay.

Over the years, Hirst developed a comeback to people who criticized the
work by saying that they or anybody else could have produced it: 'But you
didn't, did you?'

ALSO ON THIS DAY 1812: English architect Augustus Pugin born · **1869:** US postage stamps show
pictorial scenes for the first time: a post horse and rider, a locomotive, a shield and eagle, and a
ship, the _Adriatic_ · **1973:** Pink Floyd release _Dark Side of the Moon_ with a record sleeve depicting a
glass prism dispersing light into colour designed by English graphic designer Storm Thorgerson

London premiere of *The Rebel* stars Tony Hancock, 1961

Children delight in scribbling; we scold where we should carefully govern. The very first drawings of little children are for some time only incoherent scribbles, yet they like it; the muscular action itself is pleasant. It is this same natural activity pressed into service and disciplined which enabled the Greeks with pleasure to draw as Mr Ablett has done the so-called honeysuckle ornament. It is a force of great value when so controlled. There is another delight of children, especially valuable in decoration. They enjoy repetition; and that too for many purposes the teacher needs. If a child follows its bent and draws animals its own way, in action, and repeats them, outlines them, and colours them too, he will produce a drawing which may be comparable to the archaic period of more than one historic school.

English art educator Ebenezer Cooke,
International Health Exhibition,
Conference on Education, London, 1884

In 1961, after considerable success on radio and television, English comedian Tony Hancock (1924–1968) starred in his first leading film role in *The Rebel*. Playing a discontented London office worker, Hancock decides to leave London and head for Paris to turn his hobby as an artist – he is working on an enormous stone sculpture *Aphrodite at the Waterhole* in his lodgings – into a full-time career. The script by Ray Galton and Alan Simpson was a satire on modern art and existentialist philosophy – while Hancock's childish and inept works are admired by the young 'Beat' set who christen it the 'Infantile' and 'Shapeist' school of art, a mix-up with his (talented) room-mate's paintings sees him become briefly famous before the deception is uncovered.

The film features actor Dennis Price as Jim Smith, a parody of the Spanish artist Salvador Dalí who, complete with curly moustache, has a cow in his bedroom and sleeps at the bottom of a fish tank. In another scene Hancock hurls paint onto a vast canvas then walks and cycles around on it, a nod to American painter Jackson Pollock (*see* 30 October) and the work of English Action painter William Green.

All Hancock's paintings in the film, including the memorable *Ducks in Flight Around the Eiffel Tower*, and those created by his flatmate played by Paul Massie, were by English artist Alistair Grant (1925–1997), who was commissioned to produce work along the lines of Pablo Picasso and sculptor Sir Jacob Epstein.

After the film was finished, Elstree Studios threw away all the artwork, but in 2002 the London Institute of Pataphysics recreated the Hancock works for a show at The Foundry in London ('Anthony Hancock Paintings & Sculpture: A Retrospective Exhibition'), including a live reconstruction of the Action painting. The catalogue described *The Rebel* as a 'bio-documentary account of his Paris years…a film whose treatment of his work is far from reverential'.

In an article for the *Guardian* newspaper in 2012, Galton and Simpson revealed that German-born British painter Lucian Freud had once said *The Rebel* was the greatest film about modern art every made.

ALSO ON THIS DAY 1545: English scholar Thomas Bodley, founder of the Bodleian Library, Oxford, England, born · **1904:** American illustrator Dr Seuss (Theodor Geisel) born · **1959:** Hungarian-French artist Victor Vasarely patents his geometric cut-outs method, *unités plastiques*

3 MARCH

The Teatro Olimpico
opens with *Oedipus Rex*, 1585

The Theater of Palladios ordering the front of the Sceane of Bricke covered with stcco full of ornament and stattues as in the designe I have. The Prospectives ar 5: the wiedest is a streete of houses Temples and suchlicke in front; at yᵉ end of yᵉ scene an arck triumfall Painted; all thec houses on yᵉ sides ar of Releave; the windoues look out and maad with bourdes inwardes to maak a thicknes; the Collombs wear flatt but roud tourd the edges; yᵉ Stattues of marbel and bronzo finto, I mean thos in shortining ar flatt but of hole Releafe, wch shew strangly a neear but a farr of well. On the Passages of the sides all the lightes wear Placet wch, as the said, sheawed exelently the flouer was Playne Boardes but Painted lyke Pauement; yᵉ Cornishes wear Splaie Peeces of Deael bourdes and Painted slightly. The rufe was yᵉ rafters and tiles covered with canvase; the cheaf artifice was that whear so ever you satt you sawe on of thes Prospectes. In this Sceane thear is no apparitions of nugolo and such licke but only the artifice of the seeane in Prospective Carrieth ytt...an otangell tempell an other in collomes againste yt and Pallases on each side of them.

Inigo Jones, notes (1613–14) on the flyleaf of his copy
of Andrea Palladio's *I Quattro libri dell'architettura*, 1601

The Teatro Olimpico in Vicenza, Italy, was the final work of Italian architect Andrea Palladio (1508–1580) and one of his finest, started just before his death and finished in 1585 by his son Silla and local architect Vincenzo Scamozzi. Famous visitors included English architect Inigo Jones (1573–1652; *see* 27 April), who visited the Teatro Olimpico in 1613 and 1614, and German writer Johann Wolfgang von Goethe, who called it 'indescribably beautiful'.

Palladio's design was inspired by ancient Roman theatres, with an elliptical seating area. Its most remarkable feature is in fact Scamozzi's wood and stucco *trompe l'oeil* marble stage set, in place for opening night and still operational today, depicting several long streets disappearing into the distance.

ALSO ON THIS DAY 1792: Death of Scottish architect Robert Adam · **1914:** Danish painter and sculptor Asger Jorn born · **1983:** Death of Belgian illustrator Hergé (Georges Remi)

4 MARCH

Beatrix Potter writes a picture letter, 1897

My dear Noel

Here is another picture of the owl and the pussy cat, after they were married. It is funny to see a bird with hands, but how could he play the guitar without them?

I must tell you about the wind in our garden on Wednesday night. It was so rough I went out after dark, all wrapped up with galoshes on, and brought in my rabbit in a basket. Next morning the hutch was blown right over.

I remain yours aff.

Beatrix Potter

Beatrix Potter, letter to Noel Moore, 4 March 1897

English book illustrator Beatrix Potter (1866–1943) wrote many letters with illustrations – she called them 'picture letters' – to her friends' children as well as her own family. Indeed, the first inklings of *Peter Rabbit* came in an eight-page letter written in September 1893 to Noel Moore, the young son of her former governess, Annie Moore (*see also* 2 October).

On 4 March 1897, her correspondence with Noel continued as she explored Edward Lear's 'The Owl and the Pussy Cat', one of her favourite poems (she later used it as inspiration for her *Tale of Little Pig Robinson*, 1930). She had written to Noel in a letter the month before about the poem and the illustrations in the March letter include one of the owl tasting the famous honey from a saucer while holding a spoon, and the cat fishing, having already attached four successfully caught fish to the mast.

ALSO ON THIS DAY **1602:** Japanese painter Kanō Tan'yū born · **1890:** Britain's longest bridge, the Forth Bridge, is opened · **1989:** Louvre Pyramid, Paris, designed by Chinese-American architect Ieoh Ming Pei, is inaugurated

5 MARCH

Alberto Korda photographs Che Guevara, 1960

As we say farewell to the dead today, I have no other thought than the idea which symbolizes this struggle: let them rest together, in peace; together, workers and soldiers; together in their graves, as together they fought and died, and as together we are prepared to die. As we say goodbye we make this promise: Cuba will not be intimidated; Cuba will not turn back; the revolution will not halt; the revolution will not turn back; the revolution will continue forward, victoriously; the revolution will continue going ahead without breaking step. That is our promise, not to those who have died, because dying for the country is to live, but to the comrades whom we will always remember as something of ourselves. They will live on in the heart of the nation.

Fidel Castro, speech at the funeral of victims of the *La Coubre* ship explosion in Havana, 5 March 1960

On 5 March 1960, while Cuba's leader Fidel Castro was making his speech following the probable sabotage of a Cuban vessel the day before in Havana harbour, Cuban photographer Alberto Korda (1928–2011) noticed the thirty-one-year-old Argentine revolutionary Che Guevara (1928–1967), the country's new Minister of Industry. He picked up his Leica M2 with its 90mm lens and quickly took a look.

Korda was only about 9 metres (30 feet) away from his subject and says he was drawn by Guevara's 'absolute implacability'. He took two shots, one vertical and one horizontal, with no time for more before Guevara moved away. Korda was delighted with the result, which he slightly edited to remove some palm branches and the face of fellow guerrilla leader Jorge Masetti, who was stood next to Guevara. However, Korda's editor at the *Revolución* newspaper where he worked was less keen and decided against using it. Instead, Korda hung it in his flat.

It was not widely known until 1967 when Korda gave two prints of it to Italian publisher Giangiacomo Feltrinelli who used it to publicize Che Guevara's struggle and execution.

The shot – known as *Guerrillero Heroico* – has since become one of the most iconic images of the modern world, a universal symbol of rebellion and the fight against oppression. It has also been reproduced in countless media and merchandised in every way possible, although Korda was insistent it should not be trivialized and only used to further goals that Che Guevara would have supported.

ALSO ON THIS DAY **1512:** Flemish cartographer Gerardus Mercator born · **1637:** Dutch painter Jan van der Heyden born · **1696:** Italian painter Giovanni Tiepolo born

6 MARCH

Rockwell's *Freedom from Want* is published, 1943

In the future days, which we seek to make secure, we look forward to a world founded upon four essential human freedoms. The first is freedom of speech and expression – everywhere in the world. The second is freedom of every person to worship God in his own way – everywhere in the world. The third is freedom from want – which, translated into world terms, means economic understandings which will secure to every nation a healthy peacetime life for its inhabitants – everywhere in the world. The fourth is freedom from fear – which, translated into world terms, means a world-wide reduction of armaments to such a point and in such a thorough fashion that no nation will be in a position to commit an act of physical aggression against any neighbor – anywhere in the world.

US President Franklin D. Roosevelt, State of the Union Address
(Four Freedoms speech), 6 January 1941

The rousing human rights speech made in 1941 by President Franklin D. Roosevelt (1882–1945; *see also* 12 April) as war raged in Europe inspired American painter and illustrator Norman Rockwell (1894–1978) to produce his 'Four Freedoms' series of oil paintings. Published over four weeks in 1943 in the *Saturday Evening Post*, the third of them, *Freedom from Want*, became a hugely popular depiction of Thanksgiving.

Coming after *Freedom of Speech* (a working-class man speaks his mind at a town meeting) and *Freedom of Worship* (eight people of various faiths in prayer), and before *Freedom from Fear* (parents look on while their children sleep in their beds), *Freedom from Want* shows a group of the artist's friends and family at table as his cook Mrs Thaddeus Wheaton brings in a large turkey. Rockwell started painting it on Thanksgiving Day 1942, having taken a photograph of the event and individually of the eleven people present as a starting point.

Although Rockwell (*see also* 1 April) was pleased with the result, he did have later misgivings about the size of the turkey he painted at a time when Europe was enduring major shortages.

ALSO ON THIS DAY 1475: Italian painter, sculptor and architect Michelangelo born (*see* 1 November) · **1940:** Canadian painter Ken Danby born · **1986:** Death of American painter Georgia O'Keeffe (*see* 1 June)

Kristen Visbal's *Fearless Girl*
is installed in New York, 2017

Women's rights are human rights. But in these troubled times, as our world becomes more unpredictable and chaotic, the rights of women and girls are being reduced, restricted and reversed. Empowering women and girls is the only way to protect their rights and make sure they can realize their full potential.

Historic imbalances in power relations between men and women, exacerbated by growing inequalities within and between societies and countries, are leading to greater discrimination against women and girls. Around the world, tradition, cultural values and religion are being misused to curtail women's rights, to entrench sexism and defend misogynistic practices.

Women's legal rights, which have never been equal to men's on any continent, are being eroded further. Women's rights over their own bodies are questioned and undermined. Women are routinely targeted for intimidation and harassment in cyberspace and in real life. In the worst cases, extremists and terrorists build their ideologies around the subjugation of women and girls and single them out for sexual and gender-based violence, forced marriage and virtual enslavement.

Despite some improvements, leadership positions across the board are still held by men, and the economic gender gap is widening, thanks to outdated attitudes and entrenched male chauvinism. We must change this, by empowering women at all levels, enabling their voices to be heard and giving them control over their own lives and over the future of our world.

UN Secretary-General António Guterres,
Message for International Women's Day, 2017

On 7 March 2017, the day before International Women's Day in 2017, the *Fearless Girl* bronze statue of a steadfast young girl with her hands on her hips was installed at Bowling Green, New York, opposite Italian-American artist Arturo Di Modica's *Charging Bull* sculpture.

The 127-cm (50-inch)-high statue was commissioned by State Street Global Advisors to encourage companies to appoint more women to their boards, or as it's maker American sculptor Kristen Visbal (b. 1962) put it: 'a humorous yet meaningful message of collaboration, of significance. A shout out for women in business and what they meant to our collective future.' Visbal used two children from Delaware as models for the work.

It has since been relocated and now stands in front of the New York Stock Exchange. Reproductions of it have been set up in Oslo, Melbourne in Australia, and in London's Paternoster Square near the Stock Exchange.

ALSO ON THIS DAY 1765: French photography pioneer Nicéphore Niépce born (*see* 31 July) · **1872:** Dutch painter Piet Mondrian born (*see* 24 September) · **1996:** Hubble Space Telescope takes the first photographs of the surface of Pluto

8 MARCH

Nelson's Pillar in Dublin is destroyed by a bomb, 1966

By the blessing of Almighty God to commemorate the transcendent heroic achievements of the right honourable Horatio Lord Viscount Nelson, Duke of Bronti in Sicily, Vice-Admiral of the White Squadron of His Majesty's Fleet who fell gloriously in the battle of Cape Trafalgar on the 21st day of October 1805 when he obtained for his country a victory over the combined fleets of France and Spain unparalleled in navy history. This first stone of a triumphal pillar was laid by his Grace Charles Duke of Richmond and Lennox, Lord Lieutenant General and General Governor of Ireland, on the 15th Day of February in the year of our Lord, 1808, and in the 48th Year of our most gracious sovereign George the Third, in the presence of the Committee appointed by the Subscribers for erecting this monument.

Inscription on Nelson's Pillar plaque, Dublin, laid with the foundation stone, 15 February 1808

To mark British naval commander Horatio Nelson's victory at the 1805 Battle of Trafalgar, the Dublin authorities decided to build a celebratory pillar. On top of the granite column designed by English architect William Wilkins (1778–1839) and Irish architect Francis Johnston (1760–1829) stood a statue of the vice-admiral by the Irish sculptor Thomas Kirk (1781–1845), looking across the city from its location on Sackville Street (later O'Connell Street).

The pillar was finished in 1809 and open to the public from October that year on the anniversary of the battle. It reached 40 metres (134 feet) high and Nelson's victories were marked on the pedestal. Inside, a 168-step spiral stairway led to a small viewing platform just below the statue. Although it became a popular tourist attraction, it met with mixed reactions politically and over the next 150 years there were various demands to have it removed.

On the night of 7/8 March 1966, dissident IRA volunteers left a bomb inside, which when it exploded took off Nelson's statue and the top half of the pillar. What remained was destroyed in a controlled explosion by the Irish Army on 14 March. Debris was collected by members of the crowd watching its end, although Nelson's head can still be seen in the Reading Room of the Dublin City Library and Archive on Pearse Street.

The pillar was replaced by the Spire of Dublin (*An Túr Solais*), a pin-like monument 120 metres (394 feet) high.

ALSO ON THIS DAY 1826: Estonian painter Johann Köler born · **1924:** English sculptor Anthony Caro born · **2006:** *Little Mermaid* statue in Copenhagen is vandalized (again, *see* 6 January 1998)

9 MARCH

Anna Hyatt Huntington reveals her Lincoln statue, 1962

In all this, book-learning is available. A capacity, and taste, for reading, gives access to whatever has already been discovered by others. It is the key, or one of the keys, to the already solved problems. And not only so. It gives a relish, and facility, for successfully pursuing the [yet] unsolved ones.

Abraham Lincoln, 'Address to the Wisconsin State Agricultural Society', 1859

In an interview with the *New York Times* published the day before her birthday in 1962, headed 'Sculptor Regards 86th Birthday as Just Another Day to Work', American specialist equestrian sculptor Anna Hyatt Huntington (1876–1973) explained how the celebrations would not alter her regular schedule of two or three hours' work a day. In the article, she talked about her latest and just-finished work that had taken three years and was still in scaffolding in her studio, a gigantic 4-metre (14-foot) bronze entitled *On the Circuit*.

It shows US president Abraham Lincoln (1809–1865) as a young lawyer in his thirties, reading a book held in his right hand while sat on his grazing horse whose reins he holds in his left, a testament to his belief in the power of education. The first casting was installed at the entrance courtyard of the Illinois State Pavilion at the 1964 World's Fair and is now located at New Salem Historic Park, New Salem, Illinois.

ALSO ON THIS DAY 1454: Italian cartographer Amerigo Vespucci born · **1850:** English sculptor Hamo Thornycroft born · **2017:** Death of English painter Howard Hodgkin

10 MARCH

A suffragette takes a meat cleaver to the *Rokeby Venus*, 1914

I have tried to destroy the picture of the most beautiful woman in mythological history as a protest against the Government for destroying Mrs Pankhurst, who is the most beautiful character in modern history. Justice is an element of beauty as much as colour and outline on canvas. Mrs Pankhurst seeks to procure justice for womanhood, and for this she is being slowly murdered by a Government of Iscariot politicians. If there is an outcry against my deed, let every one remember that such an outcry is an hypocrisy so long as they allow the destruction of Mrs Pankhurst and other beautiful living women, and that until the public cease to countenance human destruction the stones cast against me for the destruction of this picture are each an evidence against them of artistic as well as moral and political humbug and hypocrisy.

Mary Richardson, statement to the Women's Social and Political Union (WSPU), 10 March 1914

On 9 March 1914, Emmeline Pankhurst's talk in Glasgow was broken up unceremoniously by police who used excessive violence in arresting her and other attendees. Angered by the assault on the British suffragist, Canadian suffragette Mary Richardson (1823–1961) put her pre-planned scheme into action.

She walked into the National Gallery in London and wandered around, carrying a notebook in her hand and a meat cleaver up her sleeve, held in by safety pins. After quietly sketching various paintings and with the attendant distracted by his newspaper, Richardson approached Spanish painter Diego Velázquez's *Rokeby Venus* (1647–51) and smashed the glass protecting it. Before she was overpowered, she managed to slash the painting five times. The following day, Richardson was sentenced to six months in prison for malicious damage. Despite the damage, the painting was successfully restored.

This was not Mary Richardson's first brush with the law, having spent time in prison for various other counts of arson and damage. Nor was it the first suffragette attack on art – an earlier strike had been made in April 1913 at Manchester Art Gallery (*see* 3 April).

Although her chief motive was to draw attention to the suffragette cause, Richardson also added in an interview in 1952 that: 'I didn't like the way men visitors to the gallery gaped at it all day.'

ALSO ON THIS DAY 1787: English painter William Etty born · **1876:** American sculptor Anna Hyatt Huntington born (*see* 9 March) · **1913:** French sculptor Camille Claudel (*see* 8 November) is committed to psychiatric hospital for the rest of her life

11 MARCH

Charlotte Brontë praises Thackeray's artistic skills, 1848

I have not the skill you attribute to me. It is not enough to have the artist's eye, one must also have the artist's hand to turn the first gift to practical account. I have, in my day, wasted a certain quantity of Bristol board and drawing-paper, crayons and cakes of colour, but when I examine the contents of my portfolio now, it seems as if during the years it has been lying closed some fairy had changed what I once thought sterling coin into dry leaves, and I feel much inclined to consign the whole collection of drawings to the fire; I see they have no value. If, then, *Jane Eyre* is ever to be illustrated, it must be by some other hand than that of its author. But I hope no one will be at the trouble to make portraits of my characters. Bulwer and Byron heroes and heroines are very well, they are all of them handsome; but my personages are mostly unattractive in look, and therefore ill-adapted to figure in ideal portraits. At the best, I have always thought such representations futile. You will not easily find a second Thackeray. How he can render, with a few black lines and dots, shades of expression so fine, so real; traits of character so minute, so subtle, so difficult to seize and fix, I cannot tell, I can only wonder and admire. Thackeray may not be a painter, but he is a wizard of a draughtsman; touched with his pencil, paper lives. And then his drawing is so refreshing; after the wooden limbs one is accustomed to see portrayed by commonplace illustrators, his shapes of bone and muscle clothed with flesh, correct in proportion and anatomy, are a real relief. All is true in Thackeray. If Truth were again a goddess, Thackeray should be her high priest.

Literary reader and publisher William Smith Williams, who encouraged English writer Charlotte Brontë (1816–1855) and published her novel *Jane Eyre*, had suggested that she might like to illustrate the third edition. The second edition was dedicated to the novelist William Makepeace Thackeray (1811–1863; *see also* 6 September) who illustrated his own books, including *Vanity Fair*.

The letter above is her reply to Williams.

ALSO ON THIS DAY 1819: Henry Tate, English businessman and founder of the Tate Gallery, London, born · **1930:** English artist David Gentleman born · **1932:** Death of English painter Dora Carrington

12 MARCH

Dennis the Menace
debuts in *The Beano*, 1951

These cigarettes are made from the FINEST TOBACCO and will be found rich and cool in smoking.

Each cigarette is stamped PLAYER'S 'MEDIUM' NAVY CUT

'It's the tobacco that counts'

Dennis the Menace made his first appearance in *The Beano* comic No. 452, which went on sale on 12 March 1951. In the nine-frame strip he goes for a walk with his dad and his dog in the park, fails to observe signs requesting him to keep off the grass and is finally put on the leash by his father. He was drawn by Scottish cartoonist David Law (1908–1971; he also produced Corporal Clott for *The Dandy* and Beryl the Peril for *The Topper*) until 1970. Although his iconic red and black striped jumper was not in place until May that year, in his first outing he does have messy black hair and is wearing shorts.

Over the years Dennis's father grew taller and the strips in the comic grew larger, from half a page to a full page. Dennis himself undergoes various changes in size and in 2015 it was revealed that the current Dennis is in fact the original Dennis's son.

The inspiration for Dennis – not to be confused with his namesake in America who entirely coincidentally appeared on exactly the same day – was the 1935 music hall song 'Dennis the Menace from Venice' by American actor and songwriter Eddie Pola. It's focus was a gondolier lothario that *Beano* editor George Moonie, having heard the song, felt could be reused as a cartoon character.

ALSO ON THIS DAY 1586: Greek artist El Greco (*see* 7 April) wins commission for his painting *The Burial of the Count of Orgaz* · **1901:** Whitechapel Gallery opens in London · **1913:** Foundation stone of Canberra, Australia, is laid

13 MARCH

The unveiling of *Christ the Redeemer of the Andes*, 1904

These mountains will fall before the peace sworn between Chileans and Argentinians at the foot of Christ, the Redeemer is broken.

Christ the Redeemer of the Andes
monument inscription

The *Christ the Redeemer of the Andes* monument is a symbol of peace that stands 3,832 metres (12,570 feet) high in the Andes mountains on the border between Chile and Argentina. The 7-metre (23-foot)-tall statue, which stands on a whitewashed granite pedestal, was created by Argentinian sculptor

Mateo Alonso (1878–1955) to mark the peaceful end of a frontier conflict between the two countries.

Initially, it was erected in the Dominican-run Collège Lacordaire in Buenos Aires on 13 March 1904, some 1,200 km (745 miles) away, but was moved in early 2004 in a number of sections by train and mule. The figure stands on a globe and faces the border line, holding a large cross in his left hand (the current is a replica of the original, which suffered weather damage) and raising his right in a blessing.

Reaching the statue is not easy, with access via a narrow dirt road that has multiple hairpin turns and is not open during winter.

ALSO ON THIS DAY 1825: Norwegian painter Hans Gude born · **1870:** American painter William Glackens born · **1962:** Death of Irish sculptor Anne Acheson

14 MARCH

The Dinner Party
by Judy Chicago opens, 1979

To be a king and wear a crown is a thing more glorious to them that see it than it is pleasant to them that bear it. For myself I was never so much enticed with the glorious name of a King or royal authority of a Queen as delighted that God hath made me his instrument to maintain his truth and glory and to defend his kingdom as I said from peril, dishonour, tyranny and oppression. There will never Queen sit in my seat with more zeal to my country, care to my subjects and that will sooner with willingness venture her life for your good and safety than myself. For it is my desire to live nor reign no longer than my life and reign shall be for your good. And though you have had, and may have, many princes more mighty and wise sitting in this seat, yet you never had nor shall have, any that will be more careful and loving.

**Queen Elizabeth I of England, speech to the House of Commons, London,
30 November 1601**

American artist Judy Chicago (b. 1939) attended a dinner party in the early 1970s where, despite all the women at the table having doctorates, it was the men who held forth. This was the spur to produce her feminist installation *The Dinner Party* (1974–79) with the aim of correcting the omission of women from history.

The work is based around a triangular table with thirteen place settings along each 15-metre (48-foot) side. At each setting is a runner embroidered with the name of an important woman from history, with a hand-painted plate, cutlery and gold chalice. The plates are decorated with vulva or butterfly emblems appropriate for the named woman. These are:

Wing I – Prehistory to the Roman Empire: Primordial Goddess, Fertile Goddess, Ishtar, Kali, Snake Goddess, Sophia, Amazon, Hatshepsut, Judith, Sappho, Aspasia, Boudicca and Hypatia

Wing II – Christianity to the Reformation: Marcella, Saint Bridget, Theodora, Hrosvitha, Trota of Salerno, Eleanor of Aquitaine, Hildegarde of Bingen, Petronilla de Meath, Christine de Pisan, Isabella d'Este, Elizabeth I, Artemisia Gentileschi and Anna van Schurman

Wing III – American Revolution to present day: Anne Hutchinson, Sacajawea, Caroline Herschel, Mary Wollstonecraft, Sojourner Truth, Susan B. Anthony, Elizabeth Blackwell, Emily Dickinson, Ethel Smyth, Margaret Sanger, Natalie Barney, Virginia Woolf and Georgia O'Keeffe.

The table stands on a floor of white lustre-glazed triangular-shaped tiles, each bearing the name of 998 women who have had some impact on women's lives. It also accidentally features one man, the ancient Greek sculptor Kresilas, who was thought for many years to be a woman.

After its opening in March 1979 at the San Francisco Museum of Modern Art, *The Dinner Party* toured three countries and sixteen venues and is now a permanent exhibit at the Brooklyn Museum in New York.

ALSO ON THIS DAY **1617:** Diego Velázquez is licensed in Seville, Spain, as a Master Painter · **1853:** Swiss painter Ferdinand Hodler born · **1911:** Japanese origamist Akira Yoshizawa born

The Helga paintings are 'revealed', 1986

'Such close attention by a painter to one model over so long a period of time is a remarkable, if not singular, circumstance in the history of American art,' writes John Wilmerding, deputy director of the National Gallery of Art and curator of the exhibition. 'This show marks the first time the artist has permitted into public view a large suite of sequential drawings related to a single work.'

**National Gallery of Art, Washington DC, press release
for its exhibition of Andrew Wyeth's 'Helga Pictures', 3 February 1987**

Between 1971 and 1985, American artist Andrew Wyeth (1917–2009) produced about 240 paintings and drawings of his neighbour in Chadds Ford, Pennsylvania, Helga Testorf. The works show Testorf in a variety of scenes, nude and clothed, indoors and outdoors, and the finished pictures were kept at the home of another neighbour.

There was an immediate worldwide media frenzy when the pictures were 'discovered' by American art collector Leonard Andrews on 15 March 1986, although it soon became clear that they were not quite as 'unknown' as Wyeth and his wife Betsy had suggested. Andrews reported that the mixture of watercolour, drybrush and pencil works were unframed and many leaning casually against walls.

Although Andrews described the size of the collection as overwhelming and a 'national treasure', the quality of the work divided critics, among them Australian art critic Robert Hughes (*see* 21 September), who wrote in his 2016 book *The Spectacle of Skill*: 'This was the greatest and perhaps the defining art-world hype of the 1980s.'

ALSO ON THIS DAY 1611: Flemish painter Jan Fyt born · **1673:** Death of Italian painter Salvator Rosa · **1967:** Japanese manga artist Naoko Takeuchi born

The *Ecce Homo* restoration interpretation centre opens, 2016

This is the result of two hours of devotion to the Virgin of Mercy

Elías García Martínez, dedication, *Ecce Homo* fresco, 1930

Cecilia Giménez hit the world's headlines in 2012 when her restoration of Spanish painter Elías García Martínez's 1930 fresco *Ecce Homo* in the Sanctuary of Mercy church, Borja, Spain, went...a bit wrong.

Martínez (1858–1934) was a professor at Zaragoza's School of Art and his *Ecce Homo* shows a traditional head and shoulders portrait of Jesus, crowned with thorns. It was competently done, but entirely unremarkable. By 2012, parts of the work were flaking off and it was decided to restore it, partly using funds donated by the painter's grand-daughter.

Despite her best intentions, the eighty-one-year-old Doña Cecilia Giménez's work on the fresco was not up to professional standards – although she protested that she had not been allowed to finish before the restoration was made public – and the result was described as more like *Ecce Mono* ('Behold the Monkey') than *Ecce Homo* ('Behold the Man'). Initially it was thought that it had been the victim of vandalism before the full story became clear. The transformed *Ecce Homo* became an internet meme and was widely ridiculed in the media.

Yet interest was so enormous that 40,000 people came to see the fresco in 2013 and the church made a small charge to see it, the proceeds going to charity. Four years later, tourist numbers had risen from 6,000 to more than 60,000. While numbers have dropped a little since those heady days, the consequent increase in donations to the church has helped to fund a care home for older residents in the community. The local wine producer Bodegas Ruperte even launched a special 'El Ecce Homo' brand.

An interpretation centre dedicated to the fresco's recent history opened on 16 March 2016. It includes photos, videos and a wide range of merchandise, as well as the opportunity for visitors to try their hands at producing their own version.

ALSO ON THIS DAY **1774:** English cartographer Matthew Flinders born · **1822:** French painter and sculptor Rosa Bonheur born (*see* 30 July) · **1991:** Death of Australian painter Jean Bellette

Samuel Pepys sits for his portrait, 1666

Up, and to finish my Journall, which I had not sense enough the last night to make an end of, and thence to the office, where very busy all the morning. At noon home to dinner and presently with my wife out to Hales's, where I am still infinitely pleased with my wife's picture. I paid him 14*l.* for it, and 25*s.* for the frame, and I think it is not a whit too deare for so good a picture. It is not yet quite finished and dry, so as to be fit to bring home yet. This day I begun to sit, and he will make me, I think, a very fine picture. He promises it shall be as good as my wife's, and I sit to have it full of shadows, and do almost break my neck looking over my shoulder to make the posture for him to work by. Thence home and to the office, and so home having a great cold, and so my wife and Mrs Barbary have very great ones, we are at a loss how we all come by it together, so to bed, drinking butter-ale.

Samuel Pepys, diary entry, 17 March 1666

Initially identified simply as *Portrait of a Musician* until the middle of the 19th century, the portrait by John Hayls (or Hales) that Samuel Pepys (1633–1703; *see also* 9 May) describes in his journal on 17 March 1666 is the one of the famous diarist that is most familiar to us in the 21st.

Pepys is shown holding sheet music for 'Beauty, Retire', his own setting of English poet and playwright Sir William Davenant's verse lines from *Siege of Rhodes*, in a bunched leaf frame, a style of which Pepys was particularly fond. Pepys was very keen on his frames and mentions his unhappiness at the damage done to them by the Great Fire of London later that year.

Pepys reports more sittings on 20 March ('I do not fancy that it has the ayre of my face'), the 23rd ('it comes on a very fine picture'), 28th ('it is become mighty like') and 30th ('sat till almost quite darke upon working my gowne, which I hired to be drawn in; an Indian gowne, and I do see all the reason to expect a most excellent picture of it'). Throughout, Pepys describes these sittings as far from sombre with other friends present and music and singing an accompanying part of the process, and he concludes that as a result 'the picture goes on the better for it'. On 16 May, he paid Hayls and notes that he is 'very well satisfied'.

Hayls (1600?–1679) was a popular English portraitist in the mid-17th century and also painted Mrs Pepys as St Catherine in 1666. However, Pepys was not a wholly uncritical fan – on 25 March the following year he visits the leading court portrait painter of the day, Sir Peter Lely: 'Called at Mr Lilly's, who was working; and indeed his pictures are without doubt much beyond Mr Hales's.'

ALSO ON THIS DAY 1686: French painter Jean-Baptiste Oudry born · **1846:** English illustrator Kate Greenaway born · **1889:** Irish illustrator and stained-glass designer Harry Clarke born

18 MARCH

The first work of art is produced in space, 1965

Imagine you are fully dressed in your warmest clothes, then you have skiing gear on top of that, a motorbike helmet and you are strapped to a chair in a tiny, tiny circular spacecraft, which is orbiting the Earth at a very high speed.

Curator Natalia Sidlina, interview with Mark Brown,
Guardian, **31 August 2015**

Aboard the cramped Voskhod 2 spacecraft, 18 March 1965 became a very stressful day for Russian cosmonaut Alexei Leonov (1934–2019) when, after making history on the first ever spacewalk, he realized that his spacesuit had expanded so much that he was unable to get back into the capsule. After some swift thinking – he opened a valve to deflate the suit and reduce the pressure, a very risky procedure – he managed to squeeze back in.

Rather than simply taking it easy as they prepared for re-entry, however, he pulled out his sketchpad...

The work he produced is called *Sunrise*, a series of black, red, yellow and blue colour arcs in the shape of a rainbow with a small red ball in the centre. It is not perhaps the most spectacular piece of art ever produced, but as curator Natalia Sidlina pointed out, this image of an orbital sunrise was created under the most difficult conditions, not to mention his brush with death in space a few minutes earlier. He solved the problem of how to use pencils and paper

in zero gravity by weighing down the packet of pencils with an ingeniously
low-tech rubber band around his wrist, with string attached to each pencil
to stop them drifting off. The drawing and pencils went on display in London
at the Science Museum's 'Cosmonauts: Birth of the Space Age' exhibition in
2015, curated by Sidlina.

Leonov, awarded the highest distinction of Hero of the Soviet Union for his
inaugural spacewalk, had in fact studied as an artist at the Academy of Arts
in Riga, Latvia, but dropped out because he was unable to fund his studies.
In later life, he produced a considerable body of space art, including portraits
of his colleagues while in space and in particular a self-portrait of his 1965
spacewalk, the oil painting *Over the Black Sea* (1973).

ALSO ON THIS DAY 1578: German painter Adam Elsheimer born · **1862:** Swedish painter Eugène
Jansson born · **1990:** Art worth $500 million is stolen from the Isabella Stewart Gardner
Museum, Boston (none has been recovered)

19 MARCH

The first stone is laid
for the Sagrada Família, 1882

The greatest piece of creative architecture in the last twenty-five years. It
is spirit symbolised in stone!
American architect Louis Sullivan, 1922

For the first time since I had been in Barcelona I went to have a look at the
cathedral – a modern cathedral, and one of the most hideous buildings in
the world. It has four crenellated spires exactly the shape of hock bottles.
Unlike most of the churches in Barcelona it was not damaged during the
revolution – it was spared because of its 'artistic value', people said. I think
the Anarchists showed bad taste in not blowing it up when they had the
chance, though they did hang a red and black banner between its spires.
George Orwell, *Homage to Catalonia*, 1938·

Fundraising for what was to become the Roman Catholic Basílica de la Sagrada
Família in Barcelona began in 1874, the land to build it on was bought seven
years later and the cornerstone was laid on 19 March 1882. It has caused

106

mixed feelings ever since, one of its fiercest critics being the English writer George Orwell (1903–1950; *see also* 22 January) who visited it while he was in the city fighting during the Spanish Civil War.

The first architect in charge was Francisco de Paula del Villar y Lozano (1828–1901), but he was soon replaced by the man who is now most closely associated with the still unfinished building, Catalan architect Antoni Gaudí (1852–1926). Gaudí masterminded the critical first stages, altering Villar's early work and bringing a mixture of Art Nouveau and Gothic elements to the build.

His initial work on the Nativity Facade, with all the arches and figures to be painted in a range of bright colours, indicated the direction he wanted to take. His columns inside the building are based around a series of unique geometric variations, evolving as they rise higher. Everywhere there are abstract and curving forms.

Gaudí died in 1926, a few days after being hit by a tram and with more than three-quarters of the cathedral still to be built. He was buried in the crypt. In 2010, Pope Benedict XVI consecrated the Sagrada Família as a minor basilica.

ALSO ON THIS DAY 1601: Spanish architect, painter and sculptor Alonso Cano born · **1864:** American painter Charles Marion Russell born (*see* 27 March) · **1895:** French motion picture pioneers Auguste and Louis Lumière record their first shots using their new cinematograph camera

20 MARCH

The Nazis burn 5,000 works of art, 1939

No picture receives clemency. The Führer is also for expropriation without compensation. We will swap a few of the works abroad for real masterworks. For this reason, the Führer is setting up a commission under my chairmanship.

Joseph Goebbels, diary entry, 13 January 1938

After the Nazi-organized Degenerate Art exhibition closed (*see* 4 June), the authorities developed three options to deal with the 16,000 works of art they had confiscated over the previous few years and stored in a warehouse on Köpenicker Strasse in Berlin. Only one official list of this art exists and this is partial and not entirely accurate. A more exhaustive inventory created in 1941/2 emerged in 1997 in the collection of Austrian art dealer Harry Fischer, whose widow had donated it along with other books, journals and exhibition catalogues to the Victoria and Albert Museum in London.

Initially, the Nazis offered all the confiscated artwork for sale to foreign collectors and museums via trusted art dealers or exchanged it for art they regarded as 'decent'. This process left about five thousand works that nobody appeared to want – those with an X by them on the Harry Fischer list – so on 20 March 1939, these paintings, drawings, prints and sculptures were simply burned in the courtyard of the main fire station in Berlin. This was a fairly low-key event and there is no official record or photograph of the burning, or even a mention in the voluminous diaries of Nazi Minister for Propaganda Joseph Goebbels (1897–1945; *see also* 4 June).

It is hard to know exactly what was lost as works are still emerging, despite being marked with an X. For many years, for example, it was thought German painter Otto Dix's powerful *The Trench* had disappeared into the flames but in fact it had been sold.

ALSO ON THIS DAY 1836: English painter and illustrator Edward Poynter born · **1840:** Russian painter Illarion Pryanishnikov born · **1999:** Death of English painter Patrick Heron

21 MARCH

Tsar Alexander III opens the first Fabergé egg, 1885

Vous êtes un génie incomparable.

Russian Dowager Empress Maria Feodorovna to Peter Carl Fabergé, on receiving her annual egg, 1914

There is a long history of decorated eggs in Russia and pre-Fabergé porcelain eggs had been popular for many years. The first Fabergé egg was made for Tsar Alexander III (1845–1894) as an Easter present for his wife, the Empress Maria Feodorovna (1847–1928), and perhaps also to mark the twentieth anniversary of their engagement. Created in the workshops of Russian jeweller Peter Carl Fabergé (1846–1920) in St Petersburg, probably by Finnish goldsmith and jeweller Erik Kollin (1836–1901), it is known as the Hen Egg – within the gold shell covered in white enamel is a gold 'yolk' that itself contains a gold hen. Originally, the hen opened to reveal a tiny diamond replica of the imperial crown on which a ruby pendant hung, though these have been lost.

On 21 March 1885, the Tsar wrote to the Grand Duke Vladimir Alexandrovich thanking him for arranging the order, which he said was fine and exquisite. Apparently, the Tsarina, too, was very pleased with the egg, which stayed in the imperial Anichkov Palace in St Petersburg until the Russian Revolution of 1917.

After the revolution, along with many other Romanov treasures, the now large egg collection was removed on Lenin's orders to the Kremlin Armoury Museum in Moscow. A number of the eggs were then bought by a London dealer, sold various times at auction in the 20th century, and finally bought by Russian businessman Viktor Vekselberg. He donated his collection, including the first Fabergé egg, to the Fabergé Museum in St Petersburg in 2013.

Fabergé made a total of sixty-nine eggs, mostly for Alexander III and his son Nicholas II to be given as presents, of which fifty-seven have survived.

ALSO ON THIS DAY 1859: Scottish National Gallery opens in Edinburgh · **1887:** Australian painter Clarice Beckett born · **1938:** English book illustrator Michael Foreman born

22 MARCH

The Emerald Buddha reaches its final resting place, 1784

The temples erected in modern times by royal and noble families and by the people are built with a view that they should form a memorial of their family, a place where their ashes may be buried, where their memory will be kept, and where, in providing for the priests, they also provide for the spiritual welfare of the people. Famous, of course, is the Wat Phra Keo, which contains the Emerald Buddha, and which may be considered the temple of the present dynasty, for, commenced in the first reign, all succeeding kings have contributed to its embellishment.

Oskar Frankfurter, 'Buddhism',
in *Twentieth Century Impressions of Siam*, 1908

Wat Prakeo, the temple within the palace walls, is the shrine of the so-called 'Emerald Buddha', a little figure made of green jade and standing about eighteen inches high.

Arnold Wright, 'Bangkok',
in *Twentieth Century Impressions of Siam*, 1908

The story of the creation of the Emerald Buddha, Thailand's most sacred religious icon, is included in various sources, including the 15th-century *Chronicle of the Emerald Buddha* by Brahmarājapañña. It tells how a holy man Nagasen was helped by Vishnu and Indra to create a special likeness of the Buddha out of a highly precious stone to help spread his teachings.

The Buddha is probably made of jasper rather than jade (the emerald is a reference to its green colour), is seated in the virasana pose and is 66 cm (26 inches) high rather than the height estimated by Wright in the ground-breaking English language history of the country quoted above. The Buddha's hands are resting on the lap in the dhyana mudra position (right palm resting in the palm of the left hand, both facing up, the thumbs touching), which indicates meditation, and there is a gold third eye above its eyebrows. It has three sets of gold costumes, one each for the summer, rainy and winter seasons, changed by the King of Thailand.

Over its lifetime, the Emerald Buddha has travelled widely. Legend places it variously in Sri Lanka, Cambodia and Thailand, where it was supposedly discovered in 1434 after lightning hit a Buddhist stupa in Chiang Rai. It was then moved to Lampang, to Chiang Mai in 1468, then to Luang Prabang and Vientiane (both now in Laos), and finally on 22 March 1784 to its present permanent home in the Wat Phra Kaew temple in the grounds of Bangkok's Grand Palace.

ALSO ON THIS DAY 1599: Flemish painter Sir Anthony van Dyck born (*see* 12 July) · **1846:** English illustrator Randolph Caldecott born · **1912:** American-Canadian painter Agnes Martin born

Michelangelo's kidney stones are on the mend, 1549

The last time I wrote to you I mentioned the evil of my stone, which is a most cruel thing, as anyone who has suffered it knows. Then I was given to drink a particular kind of water that has made me produce so much thick white substance in my urine with a few pieces of the stone that I am a lot better and hope that shortly I will be free, thanks to God.

Michelangelo, letter to his nephew Lionardo,
23 March 1549

From 1548 onwards, Italian painter and sculptor Michelangelo (1475–1564; *see also* 1 November) suffered a number of health problems including arthritis and kidney stones (one theory has it that he included the shape of a kidney in *Separation of Land and Water* in his Sistine Chapel ceiling). This illness partly accounts for his rather testy letters to his nephew Lionardo, despite the latter's regular gifts of food and drink.

He was treated by the noted anatomist Realdo Colombo, a surgeon at the University of Padua, and the two even discussed working on an illustrated book of anatomy together. His friend, the art historian Giorgio Vasari, notes this in his description of the artist's general health in his *Lives of the Artists*:

> I must record that the master's constitution was very sound, for he was lean and well knit together with nerves, and although as a boy he was delicate, and as a man he had two serious illnesses, he could always endure any fatigue and had no infirmity, save that in his old age he suffered from dysuria and from gravel, which in the end developed into the stone; wherefore for many years he was syringed by the hand of Maestro Realdo Colombo, his very dear friend, who treated him with great diligence.

ALSO ON THIS DAY 1769: English cartographer William Smith born · **1874:** German-American painter and illustrator J. C. Leyendecker born · **1887:** Spanish painter and sculptor Juan Gris born

David Hockney finds inspiration from a cha-cha, 1961

Dancing as an art, we may be sure, cannot die out, but will always be undergoing a rebirth. Not merely as an art, but also as a social custom, it perpetually emerges afresh from the soul of the people...an art which has been so intimately mixed with all the finest and deepest springs of life has always asserted itself afresh. For dancing is the loftiest, the most moving, the most beautiful of the arts, because it is no mere translation or abstraction from life; it is life itself.

Havelock Ellis, *The Dance of Life*, 1923

At the Royal College of Art in 1961, English painter David Hockney (b. 1937) was attracted to fellow student Peter Crutch. Realizing this, Crutch did a special cha-cha dance for Hockney who was subsequently inspired to make a painting of it. In *The Cha-Cha That Was Danced in the Early Hours of 24th March, 1961* against three large blocks of colour, 'Peter' is shown in the middle of his dance. In the centre two hearts overlap as the words 'cha-cha' dance around his body. The cha-cha had been invented in the early 1950s and the first cha-cha song 'La Engañadora' in 1953 set off a craze for the rest of the decade.

There are other textual elements in the painting. Along the bottom run the words 'I love every moment', a quote from the 1961 UK number one hit single 'Poetry in Motion' sung by Johnny Tillotson, while behind the dancer's shoulder is part of the wording from an ointment medication packaging that reads 'penetrates deep down / gives instant relief from'. The figure is reflected in a mirror behind, an element that appears elsewhere in Hockney's early work, including *Mirror, Mirror on the Wall* (1961), which also includes part of the text from a poem by the Greek poet C. P. Cavafy about mirrors.

The oil on canvas painting was first shown at the Kasmin Gallery in London two years later, in Hockney's first exhibition 'Paintings with People In', the title indicating a reaction to the then vogue for abstractionist works. Hockney moved to Los Angeles in 1964; Crutch went on to become a successful furniture designer.

ALSO ON THIS DAY 1834: English textile designer William Morris born (*see* 1 February) · **1886:** American photographer Edward Weston born · **1948:** Death of Swedish painter Sigrid Hjertén

The Kramer painting
is first exhibited, 1992

The breed of dogs kept by the monks to assist them in their labours of love has been long celebrated for its sagacity and fidelity. All the oldest and most tried of them were lately buried, along with some unfortunate travellers, under a valanche [*sic*]; but three or four hopeful puppies were left at home in the convent, and still survive. The most celebrated of those who are no more was a dog called Barry. This animal served the hospital for the space of twelve years, during which time he saved the lives of forty individuals. His zeal was indefatigable. Whenever the mountain was enveloped in fogs and snow, he set out in search of lost travellers. He was accustomed to run barking until he lost breath, and would frequently venture on the most perilous places. When he found his strength was insufficient to draw from the snow a traveller benumbed with cold, he would run back to the hospital in search of the monks.

English author Thomas Byerley on St Bernard dogs,
in *The Percy Anecdotes*, 1826

'The Letter', an episode in the third season of the US comedy series *Seinfeld* that aired on 25 March 1992, features a three-quarter-length oil painting of Kramer (Michael Richards), which has been created by Jerry Seinfeld's girlfriend Nina (Catherine Keener). Art collectors Mr and Mrs Armstrong (Elliott Reid and Justine Johnston) take turns in elaborating on the work, Mrs Armstrong generally positive ('I detect a nobility of attitude and unwavering loyalty. Much like the St Bernard.'), Mr Armstrong rather less so ('Like a cockroach, clinging to a sewer crate.'), until finally agreeing that they both love it.

Their conversation has helped to make this one of the most popular episodes of the series. Mr Armstrong's phrase 'He is a loathsome, offensive brute' has also become a regularly used description of something terrible yet scintillating. *The Kramer*, as it is known, was painted by American illustrator Larry Salk (1936–2004) who produced many movie posters, including for *Superman III*.

Other artworks that play a key part in *Seinfeld* include the *Fusilli Jerry* pasta statue; *The Timeless Art of Seduction* photo of George Costanza (Jason

Alexander) wearing only his boxer shorts and socks while posing on a couch (*The Package*); and the porcelain statue of a young 1920s girl in evening dress (*The Statue*).

ALSO ON THIS DAY **1736:** Death of English architect Nicholas Hawksmoor · **1867:** American sculptor Gutzon Borglum born (*see* 4 October) · **1916:** Indian artist S. M. Pandit born

26 MARCH

Modigliani works on
The Amazon, 1909

My dearest Paul, It looks like it's too late to submit something to the Salon d'Automne. But please send me registration forms. You can find them in all artists' shops. This means that I have worked a little. To exhibit or not to exhibit, in the end it's all the same to me, but... You will see me arrive physically and sartorially renewed. Ah! My friend, I jump for joy – in my heart – at the idea of returning to Paris...but you are busy, you are at work, poor chap! Send my very affectionate greetings to Jean. In about twenty days I'll see you all again. Regards to your parents. In any case, send me news about the Salon d'Automne.

Amedeo Modigliani, letter to Paul Alexandre, 5 September 1909

Italian painter Amedeo Modigliani (1884–1920) grew up in Italy but spent most of his working life in Paris. While his patron and friend Dr Paul Alexandre was away from the city, he asked his younger brother Jean to keep an eye on the artist while he worked because, as the above letter indicates, Modigliani was rather haphazard in his methods and general approach to his art. To keep him out of mischief, Jean commissioned a portrait of his lover, the socialite Baroness Marguerite de Hasse de Villers. On 26 March 1909, Jean wrote to Paul saying that he was usually seeing Modigliani quite regularly, although he had not seen him for several days and when he called in, the artist was penniless and starving. Jean reports that he had been working on the portrait, though had to persuade him from throwing it in the fire.

The sittings did not go well and in the end, the Baroness did not buy the finished painting *The Amazon*, Paul Alexandre doing so on his return to capital. Modigliani, often fuelled by excessive alcohol consumption, behaved erratically with many of his models, and the Baroness became so irritated by endless sittings in his studio that she finally gave him a week to finish the work before she gave up on the project. One source of the problem was that Modigliani dithered over the colour of the riding jacket. Although she wore her favourite red one, he was keen to paint it yellow (indeed, the alternative name for the painting is *Woman in Yellow Jacket*). He also threatened to destroy the work several times because he was unsatisfied with it.

In the final portrait, the Baroness stands boldly regarding the viewer dressed elegantly to go riding, her fine cheekbones accentuated in almost masklike fashion.

ALSO ON THIS DAY **1881:** Italian fashion designer Guccio Gucci born · **1928:** The China Academy of Art is founded · **2019:** Detectives recover Pablo Picasso's painting *Buste de Femme* two decades after its theft

27 MARCH

Charles Marion Russell
writes to a friend, 1920

Friend Perc. You are right. I've reached another station. The road has been long but my friends have made it a pleasant one. And it is good to know when I'm past the half way road ranch that my friends still greet me at the stations.

Best wishes to you and yours, Your friend

C. M. Russell

> **Charles Marion Russell, letter to Percy Raban,**
> **27 March 1920**

American painter Charles Marion Russell (1864–1926) left school at sixteen to work on a sheep ranch, travelling on to Montana where he worked as a cowboy. Here he began sketching the work of his fellow camp workers before making the jump to working as an artist full-time, producing oils, watercolours, pen and inks, and even bronze statues of the Old American West's peoples – he was an early believer in the rights of Native Americans – and landscapes. As a result, he became known as the 'cowboy artist'.

Russell was also a keen letter writer, keeping in regular contact with his family and friends. His letters usually started with an ink sketch or watercolour, followed by the text, which wrapped around it, and he was often relaxed about grammar and punctuation. The letter written on 27 March 1920 to Percy Raban, a reporter for the *Great Falls Tribune* who had sent him birthday wishes a week earlier, was marked as from Pasadena (which he spells 'Pasadina'), California, as Russell headed towards his home in Great Falls, Montana. It shows a stagecoach pulled by six horses resting at a rural saloon bar, passengers and drinkers shaking hands. Among his many other letters is one sent to his family informing them of his imminent return home that has no text but is simply a cowboy going into his childhood home. Russell often did a first draft of a letter before working on a final version.

28 MARCH

Mary Berry visits sculptor Antonio Canova, 1784

With Mr Botoni to a sculptor who is making a monument for Pope Gaganelli. He is the young man who was the son of a peasant near Venice. Untaught, he did wonders in the way of sculpture; he has been but two years in Rome and has already made such progress as to surprise everybody of his professon. A Theseus sitting triumphantly over the Minotaur might almost rival some of the chefs d'oeuvre of antiquity.

Mary Berry, journal entry,
28 March 1784

When English author Mary Berry (1763–1852) travelled through Europe with her father and sister in 1783 she began writing her voluminous journals, published after her death as *Journals and Correspondence* (1865). During their visit to Rome, Berry recounts how she was introduced to the rising star of the Neoclassical Italian art world, sculptor Antonio Canova (1757–1822).

The monument Berry mentions in her journal on 28 March is Canova's well-regarded monumental tomb of Pope Clement XIV, which he worked on between 1783 and 1787 for the Church of Santi Apostoli in Rome.

The second work she refers to is his 1782 *Theseus and the Minotaur*, commissioned by Girolamo Zulian, the ambassador to Rome from Venice where Canova was born. Inspired by Ovid's *Metamorphoses*, rather than depicting the battle between them, the marble statue shows Theseus sitting on top of the creature he has just dispatched. This portrayal was suggested by Canova's friend the Scottish art dealer and painter Gavin Hamilton who advised such a grouping would be better received than something more warlike. It was the work that really made Canova's name, astounding people that it was his own work rather than a copy of an original Greek statue. It is now owned by the Victoria and Albert Museum in London.

ALSO ON THIS DAY **1472:** Italian painter Fra Bartolomeo born · **1483:** Italian painter Raphael (Raffaello Sanzio da Urbino) probably born (*see* 7 October) · **1566:** Grand Master Jean de Valette lays the foundation stone of Malta's capital city, Valletta

29 MARCH

The Terracotta Army is unearthed in China, 1974

When the First Emperor ascended the throne, the digging and preparation at Mount Li began. After he unified his empire, 700,000 men were sent there from all over his empire. They dug down deep to underground springs, pouring copper to place the outer casing of the coffin. Palaces and viewing towers housing a hundred officials were built and filled with treasures and rare artifacts. Workmen were instructed to make automatic crossbows primed to shoot at intruders. Mercury was used to simulate the hundred rivers, the Yangtze and Yellow River, and the great sea, and set to flow mechanically. Above, the heaven is depicted, below, the geographical features of the land. Candles were made of 'mermaid''s fat which is calculated to burn and not extinguish for a long time. The Second Emperor said: 'It is inappropriate for the wives of the late emperor who have no sons to be free', ordered that they should accompany the dead, and a great many died. After the burial, it was suggested that it would be a serious breach if the craftsmen who constructed the tomb and knew of its treasure were to divulge those secrets. Therefore, after the funeral ceremonies had completed, the inner passages and doorways were blocked, and the exit sealed, immediately trapping the workers and craftsmen inside. None could escape. Trees and vegetation were then planted on the tomb mound such that it resembled a hill.

Sima Qian, *Shiji, or The Records of the Grand Historian*, c. 94 BC

Pieces of terracotta and masonry had frequently been reported around Mount Li, just outside the city of Xi'an. But it wasn't until farmers digging a well to cope with a bad drought in 1974 came across something rather more substantial about a metre down that archaeologists realized they had stumbled across a buried army.

Ten years earlier, some figures had already been found nearby, including three kneeling crossbowmen, but this find was an entire defence force of more than eight thousand terracotta figures buried with the first emperor of unified China, Qin Shi Huang, about AD 209 to guard him as he entered the afterlife. No contemporary accounts mention their existence, although – like the entry above by Chinese historian Sima Qian from his monumental and groundbreaking chronicle *Shiji* – they do list the burial ceremonies of the emperor, including the burial of luxurious objects and servants, and the construction of one hundred rivers of mercury to simulate water (though once regarded as a fanciful story, the soil around the area has been tested and has an unnaturally high mercury content).

The individual work on the figures is remarkable. They are life-size, although of different heights according to their importance, the generals being the tallest. Although moulding techniques produced ten basic fact types, each face is unique – the craftsmen created individual characteristics such as smiles or features representing emotions like bravery or honesty. Nearly all have moustaches, the aesthetic custom of the time, of which there are seven varieties from bushy to handlebar. The figures' clothing is also very diverse, including many combinations of armour; most would have been holding real weapons. While many of the figures have been looted or disintegrated, thousands of bronze swords, axes and shields have survived.

As well as soldiers (infantry, cavalry, archers), there are servants, acrobats, hundreds of horses and more than 130 chariots, serving as a microcosm of the emperor's palace. All the figures seen today in the museum complex would also have been brightly coloured with a lacquer finish for extra realism.

One theory is that they are so lifelike partly because ancient Greek sculptors travelled to the country and helped with their designs.

Intriguingly, the tomb of Emperor Qin Shi Huang remains unopened due to fears that the contents would instantly flake or crumble when revealed to the open air.

ALSO ON THIS DAY **1802:** German painter Johann Moritz Rugendas born · **1891:** Death of French painter Georges Seurat · **1959:** Austrian-born American film director and producer Billy Wilder's film *Some Like It Hot* released in New York

30 MARCH

Picasso produces a Vollard Suite etching, 1933

As for Vollard, did you realize the huge size of his legacy? There are discoveries everywhere, valuable pieces scattered, nothing on show nor documented, precious finds under stacks of canvases, all priceless.

Jacques-Émile Blanche, letter to Maurice Denis, December 1939

When French art dealer Ambroise Vollard (1867–1939) was killed in a car crash on his way to his home in Paris, nobody knew the extent of his private collection, as the letter from portrait painter Jacques-Émile Blanche to art theorist and painter Maurice Denis indicates.

Vollard was an early vocal champion of an impressive roll of artists including Henri Matisse, Paul Cézanne, Vincent van Gogh, Pierre-Auguste Renoir, Paul Gauguin and especially Spanish painter and sculptor Pablo Picasso (1881–1973; *see also* 27 February). He organized Picasso's first one-man show in Paris in 1901 and, after their relationship cooled, commissioned a series of etchings from him.

These one hundred works by Picasso – started in 1930, produced largely in 1933 and finished in 1937 – became known as the Vollard Suite. Printing the 230 full sets of etchings took printmaker Roger Lacourière another two years. *Le Repos du Sculpteur devant le Jeune Cavalier* (Sculptor, reclining model, and sculpture of a horse and youth), created on 30 March 1933, is among many of the works inspired by classical civilization. The etchings also show the influence of Picasso's mistress and model Marie-Thérèse Walter.

As a result of Vollard's sudden death and the coming of the Second World War, the etchings did not emerge into the wider public view until 1950.

ALSO ON THIS DAY **1746:** Spanish painter Francisco Goya born (*see* 4 April) · **1853:** Dutch painter Vincent van Gogh born (*see* 17 June) · **1892:** Italian painter and sculptor Fortunato Depero born

31 MARCH

The Eiffel Tower officially opens, 1889

Because we are engineers, do we then believe that beauty does not concern us in our constructions and that at the same time that what we make solid and durable we do not strive to make elegant? Do not the real conditions of force always conform to the hidden rules of harmony? The first principle of architectural aesthetics is that the essential lines of a monument are determined by perfect appropriation for its destination. What condition did I have, above all, to take into account in my turn? Wind resistance. Well, I claim that the curves of the four edges of the monument as the calculation provided them, will give an impression of beauty, because they will translate to the eyes the boldness of my design.

There is, moreover, in the colossal an attraction, a peculiar charm to which ordinary theories of art are hardly applicable. Would it be argued that it is by their artistic value that the pyramids have so strongly struck the imagination of mankind? What is it, after all, other than artificial mounds? And yet who is the visitor who stays cold in their presence? Who hasn't returned full of irresistible admiration? And where is the source of this admiration, if not in the immensity of the effort and the grandeur of the result?

Gustave Eiffel, response to protest against the Eiffel Tower,
***Le Temps* newspaper, 14 February 1887**

French civil engineer Gustave Eiffel (1832–1923) was very proud of his tower and was delighted to lead a party of construction workers, civic dignitaries and members of the press up the new construction at the official opening on 31 March 1889 (not everybody made it to the top).

120

But not everyone loved the tower. Eiffel's earlier heartfelt comments in *Le Temps* in 1887 followed a campaign calling for building work on the tower to stop, not only because some felt it simply would not be safe, but also on aesthetic grounds. Among the loudest of the naysayers was the 'Committee of Three Hundred', which included many notable figures in the art world, led by architect Charles Garnier who had designed the Paris Opera House. In an open letter, they compared the tower unfavourably to other popular works of architecture in the city – Notre Dame, the Louvre, the Arc de Triomphe – suggesting Eiffel's effort was in fact a 'metal asparagus' and akin to a hateful and gigantic black chimney that would blot out everything else.

The story goes that writer Guy de Maupassant disliked it so much that he had lunch in the café at the bottom of the tower every day because this was the only spot in the city where he could not see it.

ALSO ON THIS DAY 1835: American stained-glass designer and muralist John La Farge born · **1837:** Death of English painter John Constable (*see* 11 June) · **1885:** Bulgarian artist Jules Pascin born

April

Rockwell's first
April Fool cover, 1943

If you can find twenty-five of them you are shooting par. If you can find thirty-five you're bogey plus, and if you find more than that, you ought to start discovering new stars with the naked eye.

Saturday Evening Post, 3 April 1943

In 1943, the first of three April Fool issue covers by American painter and illustrator Norman Rockwell (1894–1978; *see also* 6 March) appeared in the *Saturday Evening Post*, the newspaper with which he was most closely associated. It featured dozens of impossible, incredible or simply daft elements spread over the entire cover, which shows two elderly people playing checkers. Among them were the wrong numbers of squares on the chequers board, rubbers on both ends of a pencil, upside down wallpaper, a car tyre in the frame of the fireplace, a bottle and a glass floating in the air, Rockwell's signature in reverse on the bottom right of the painting, and a clock with the letters A P R I L F O O L replacing the numbers.

Rockwell produced two more covers along similar lines, in 1945 (featuring a young girl and an old man looking at dolls) and 1948 (a man wearing skis leaning against a tree and 'fishing' out of a can of tomatoes).

ALSO ON THIS DAY (other hoaxes...) **1928:** German magazine *Uhu* 'reveals' that X-rays show English painter Thomas Gainsborough's *The Blue Boy* is in fact a girl · **1935:** *Berliner Illustrirte Zeitung* newspaper claims that restoration work 'shows' the *Mona Lisa* was initially frowning but Leonardo da Vinci painted over it · **1950:** Dutch radio station VARA announces that Rembrandt's *The Night Watch* is 'dissolving' after the wrong liquid was used to clean it (*see also* 14 September)

Erik Satie composes
a song for Suzanne Valadon, 1893

'Bonjour Biqui, Bonjour!'
Erik Satie, song written for Suzanne Valadon, 2 April 1893

As well as a successful painter and artists' model, French painter Suzanne Valadon (1865–1938) captivated many men's hearts. Among them was the French composer Erik Satie (1866–1925), perhaps best known for his *Gymnopédies*, who became quite besotted by her.

The two had a six-month affair and Valadon painted his portrait, probably her first work in oils and one that was to become one of her most famous pieces. On 2 April 1893, Satie wrote a four-bar song for her, 'Bonjour Biqui, Bonjour!' (Biqui was his pet name for her). The score also includes a large drawing of Valadon by Satie, which he captioned 'Authentic Portrait of Biqui'.

Satie wrote many love letters to Valadon that he never sent and it is also unlikely she ever knew about this song.

ALSO ON THIS DAY 1647: German-born scientific illustrator Maria Merian born · **1891:** German painter and sculptor Max Ernst born · **1920:** English animator Jack Stokes born

Three suffragettes attack paintings
in Manchester, 1913

Suffragist Madness – Pictures Smashed in Manchester, Outrage at City Art Gallery
The latest outrage by the militant suffragettes in Manchester was a wanton attack last night upon some of the most valuable pictures in the permanent collection of the City Art Gallery.

Several of the works of art were mutilated, hammers being thrust through the canvasses. Among the pictures to suffer was *The Prayer*, one of the most valuable in the collection.

The officials were preparing to close the Gallery just before nine o'clock when two of the attendants heard the repeated cracking of glass in the large room, they at once rushed into the room and there found three women running around it breaking the glass of the largest and most important pictures in the collection. They had just completed their work on the right side of the room, and were at the moment within reach of two more large pictures – one by Millais and the other by Watts.

The women were at once arrested and gave their names as Annie Briggs (48), Lillian Forrester (33) and Evelyn Manesta (25). Each of them furnished a Manchester address and were afterwards liberated on bail pending their appearance at the City Police Court today.

Among the damaged pictures: *The Last Watch of Hero* by Leighton; *The Prayer* and *Paola and Francesca* by Watts; *Astarte Syriaca* by Rossetti; *Sibylla Delphica* by Burne Jones; *The Flood* and also *Birnam Woods* by Millais; *The Last of the Garrison* by Briton Rivière; and *The Shadow of the Cross* by Holman Hunt.

The damage to the glass alone was estimated at £170, and in some cases the canvas of the pictures themselves had been damaged and further examination would be necessary.

Manchester Evening News, 4 April 1913

For several years preceding the incident at Manchester Art Gallery on 3 April 1913, the Women's Social and Political Union (WSPU) had become more militant in its escalating drive for women's rights. At the Old Bailey in London the day before Annie Briggs, Lillian Forrester and Evelyn Manesta attacked fourteen paintings by Frederic, Lord Leighton, George Frederic Watts, Sir John Everett Millais, Edward Burne-Jones and William Holman Hunt, suffragist leader Emmeline Pankhurst had been sentenced to three years in prison for inciting violence (*see also* 10 March).

At their trial on 22 April, none of the women denied the charges but did make speeches to the jury, arguing that women were in an intolerable position and that their actions were not malicious but political; Briggs was acquitted, Forrester received a three-month custodial sentence and Manesta one month.

ALSO ON THIS DAY 1897: Vienna Secession movement is founded by Austrian artists, including its first president, Gustav Klimt · **1904:** Amercian dinnerware and furniture designer Russel Wright born · **2011:** Chinese artist Ai Weiwei is arrested in China on charges of tax evasion

The CND peace symbol
is unveiled in public, 1958

Symbols grow. They come into being by development out of other signs, particularly from likenesses or from mixed signs partaking of the nature of likenesses and symbols. We think only in signs. These mental signs are of mixed nature; the symbol-parts of them are called concepts. If a man makes a new symbol, it is by thoughts involving concepts. So it is only out of symbols that a new symbol can grow.... A symbol, once in being, spreads among the peoples. In use and in experience, its meaning grows.

American philosopher Charles Sanders Peirce, 'What is a Sign?', 1894

English textile designer, appliqué specialist and committed pacifist Gerald Holtom (1914–1985) designed the UK's Campaign for Nuclear Disarmament (CND) logo, which was aired for the first time at the start of the anti-nuclear-weapon Aldermaston March demonstrations held over the Easter weekend of 1958.

Holtom's first thought was to use the Christian cross as the main image or Pablo Picasso's dove, but rejected them partly because various church ministers he spoke to were hesitant about using the former, while the latter had unfortunate associations with Stalinist propaganda.

The design combined the semaphore signals for N and D (Nuclear Disarmament), while the damaged cross stood for the threat of the death of mankind, all encased in a circle symbolizing the unborn child. It is likely that Holtom's reasoning came via his reading of German designer Rudolph Koch's 1930 popular history of ancient and medieval symbols, *The Book of Signs*, which had recently been republished. Later, he also pointed out that by inverting the symbol it not only suggested the Christian tree of life symbol, but also represented U in semaphore signalling, which stands for Unilateral.

His explanation of the symbol's creation given in a letter – that inspiration came partly from Spanish painter Francisco Goya's *The Third of May 1808* (1814) – is slightly inaccurate because, in the painting, the man about to be shot has his hands in a raised V position rather than a downward one. The inspiration is more likely to have been from one of Goya's *Disasters of War* etchings, which does show a peasant in exactly this pose.

For the CND march that started on 4 April 1958, Holtom's studio produced five hundred cardboard lollipop sticks, half in the most recognizable black on white format (for Good Friday and Saturday), but half in white on green (Easter Sunday and Monday) to correspond with the Church's liturgical colour change over Easter.

Simple to reproduce and never copyrighted, it quickly became a popular and widespread symbol of peace in general.

ALSO ON THIS DAY 1648: Anglo-Dutch wood carver Grinling Gibbons born · **1843:** American painter William Henry Jackson born · **2013:** Death of American comics artist Carmine Infantino

5 APRIL

Linear B clay tablets
are uncovered at Knossos, 1900

On 5 April, however, an entire hoard of these clay documents, many of them perfect, was discovered amidst a deposit of charred wood in a bath-shaped receptacle of terracotta set close against the southern wall of the small chamber, already mentioned, to the West of the Clay Area.... The use indeed of bath-like vessels for other objects in Mycenaean Crete is shown by the occurrence of similarly shaped receptacles in the numerous tombs of the island, there used as ossuaries, and perhaps sarcophagi, indifferently with clay imitations of the wooden chests of contemporary Egypt. Like the chests however they are in this case specially fitted with a gabled cover, and that these recipients were specially made for a mortuary.... From this time on discoveries of hoards of inscribed tablets, often associated with remains of coffers of clay, wood or gypsum, were frequent throughout the excavation.

Sir Arthur Evans, report in *The Annual of the British School at Athens*, 1900

In 1900, English archaeologist Sir Arthur Evans (1851–1941) had been excavating the Knossos site on the island of Crete for only a fortnight before he stumbled across the clay tablets that carried what came to be known as the Linear B script. Using a mix of syllabic and ideographic signs, the script is a kind of shorthand for writing Bronze Age Mycenaean Greek, which was only deciphered much later by architect Michael Ventris.

On 30 March, Evans found 'part of an elongated clay tablet with a chisel-like end, engraved with what appeared to be signs and numbers' that reminded him of a similar fragment he had seen four years earlier. Four days later, more pieces of tablet were found, and then on 5 April came the major discovery ('A great day!' he entered in his diary).

Writing to his father on 15 April, Evans noted:

The great discovery is whole deposits, entire or fragmentary, of clay tablets analogous to the Babylonian but with inscriptions in the prehistoric script of Crete. I must have about seven hundred pieces by now. It is extremely satisfactory, as it is what I came to Crete seven years ago to find, and it is the coping stone to what I have already put together. These inscriptions engraved on the wet clay are evidently the work of practised scribes, and there are also many figures no doubt representing numerals. A certain number of characters are pictographic, showing what the subject of the documents was. Thus in one chamber occurred a series with chariots and horses' heads on them, others show vases etc.

ALSO ON THIS DAY **1709:** Death of French painter and art theorist Roger de Piles · **1723:** Death of Austrian architect Johann von Erlach · **1938:** American land artist and sculptor Nancy Holt born (*see* 20 July)

6 APRIL

James Russel considers making a Grand Tour guidebook, 1748

It was much to my satisfaction to be inform'd that my Letters were arriv'd safe, and that the subjects were to your liking. Curious and diverting subjects are not wanting in this place, but have occasion for more skill and time than I am master of: however, since it is your pleasure, I shall do my best to transmit something now and then. I here send you some addition to the Account of the Churches at Florence: to go through the whole will require some time, there being above 60 churches &c. besides palaces &c. and at present on holy days, and leisure time I am taken up with going through those of Rome.

James Russel, letter to his father Reverend Richard Russel, 6 April 1748

In yours to me, of 6 April you sent a Continuation of the Account of the Churches at Florence, and desired to know where you left off in the preceding Account: the Church mentioned last was S.S Nunziata or Annunciata. As you say there are above 60 Churches, I apprehend, that to go through them all, in so particular a manner, tho' the subject be of use, as well as entertainment, to Painters and Connoisseurs, will seem tedious to the generality of readers. But every particular would be very proper for the Pocket Volume, which you design. You will judge the better what to do, when you shall have gone through what has been made public.

Reverend Richard Russel, letter to James Russel, August 1748

Rather forgotten today, English artist James Russel (1720–1763) spent more than two decades living in Rome and Italy in the mid-18th century when the Grand Tour was beginning to become hugely popular. He was very well regarded in his day and his paintings such as *British Connoisseurs in Rome* – a painting of half a dozen of such tourists in front of the Colosseum that prefigures the 21st-century holiday snap – are a useful historical resource to the life of rich young men on their European jaunts. Russel was particularly interested in the excavations at Herculaneum and guided other tourists around them and those at nearby Pompeii. He also acted as a kind of agent for Italian artists in their dealings with English buyers.

James Russel sent a series of letters back home about life in the country's British community and his artistic work there, the importance of patronage and the social connections that were a central part of his business network. His family decided to turn the letters into book form in 1748 and 1750 and, when these became popular, Russel also considered publishing a kind of small *vade mecum* guidebook, as this correspondence with his father suggests, although it sadly came to nothing.

ALSO ON THIS DAY 1766: German painter Wilhelm von Kobell born · **1860:** French jewelry designer René Lalique born · **1888:** German artist and filmmaker Hans Richter born

El Greco's death reveals the extent of his library, 1614

On 7 April 1614, Domenico Greco died. He made no will. He received the sacraments, was buried in Santo Domingo el Antiguo, and gave candles.

Book of Funerals for the Parish of Santo Tomé, 1601–1614

When Greek artist El Greco (Doménikos Theotokópoulos, 1541–1614) died on 7 April in Toledo, Spain, his son Jorge Manuel Theotokópouli immediately drew up an inventory of his possessions (another was made seven years later). These show that his father had 143 (mostly finished) paintings, 45 models in clay, wax and plaster, 120 drawings, 200 engravings and an impressive collection of about 130 books.

Although there was no Plato in the book collection, there were general classics, such as Homer, Appian (*Civil Wars*), Xenophon, Petrarch, Ariosto and Lucian. Also included were the *Decrees of the Council of Trent* (*see* 4 December) and the writings of the Early Church Fathers, including John Chrysostom, to help the artist ensure his works were canonically accurate. There is no particularly unusual or remotely heretical title.

Since a knowledge of architecture was required as part of a proper artistic education, it is unsurprising that the inventory also includes important architectural treaties of the day, such as those by Italians Andrea Palladio (*see* 3 March) and Sebastiano Serlio. Here too is *De Architectura* by Roman architect Vitruvius and Italian art historian Giorgio Vasari's *Lives of the Artists*. These are full of thousands of words of El Greco's annotations, written clearly but not in remarkably fluent Spanish. He mentions his indifference to Michelangelo's work as a painter, is rather scathing in his assessment of Vasari's own paintings in the *Lives* (especially in comparison to Italian painter Giovanni Bellini), and in his Vitruvius, he writes of his belief in the supremacy of painting over architecture.

ALSO ON THIS DAY **1941:** English puppet maker Peter Fluck born · **1960:** English costume designer Sandy Powell born · **1965:** English painter and photographer Alison Lapper born

The *Venus de Milo* is discovered, 1820

We have before us in the statue of the Venus of Milo one of the greatest masterpieces of ancient Hellas, and it is of secondary importance whether or not it was the artist's intention to represent the goddess of love and beauty. Surely this work of art represents womanhood at its best – a noble feminine figure in full maturity, not a maiden but fully developed, a wife or mother; and yet not as a mother with a child, nor as a wife with her husband, but simply as a woman. There is nothing frivolous about her, no coquetry, nothing amorous. Her eyes betray not the slightest touch of a sensual emotion, not that sentimental moistness, τὸ ὑγρόν as the Greeks called it, and thereby the artist succeeded in transfiguring naked beauty by a self-possessed chastity unrivalled in the art of statuary. The consensus of art admirers, which is almost, though not quite, universal, sees in this marble the great mother-goddess, *das ewig Weibliche*, idealized femininity, the goddess of beauty and love, whom the Greeks called Aphrodite and the Romans Venus.

Paul Carus, *The Venus of Milo*, 1916

The *Venus de Milo*'s history is decidedly murky. She was probably found on 8 April 1820 (a February date is also possible) on the Aegean island of Melos (also called Milos) by local farmers (choose from half a dozen potential claimants) and is likely to represent the Greek goddess of love Aphrodite whose Roman name is Venus (although she could also be the sea goddess Amphitrite). It was made around AD 100, perhaps by Alexandros of Antioch (not, as once thought, Praxiteles).

What is pretty certain is that the marble statue was found without arms and in two main pieces – the torso and the lower legs and drapes – with a few other fragments including part of a hand holding an apple. Also lost were items of jewelry and possibly paint. Slightly larger than life-size, the statue is just over 2 metres (6 feet 8 inches) high and definitely on permanent display in the Louvre in Paris.

ALSO ON THIS DAY 1093: Winchester Cathedral is consecrated by Walkelin, Bishop of Winchester · **1941:** English fashion designer Vivienne Westwood born · **1973:** Death of Spanish painter and sculptor Pablo Picasso (*see* 30 March)

Saddam Hussein's statue is toppled, 2003

LT GEN SIR ANTHONY PIGOTT: Nobody had won anything, when the statue was pulled down. Nobody had won anything. That was the start of the...
SIR RODERIC LYNE: President Bush thought he had won something, he declared 'Mission accomplished', but you disagree with that?
LT GEN SIR ANTHONY PIGOTT: Well I'm just saying.... The President can do what he likes, he earns more money than I do, but how could it be? It was not the end of the campaign, it was the end of a particular and not overtaxing military task to the United States armed forces.

**Lieutenant-General Sir Anthony Pigott, witness,
to Sir Roderic Lyne, The Iraq Inquiry, 4 December 2009**

The bringing down of the statue of Saddam Hussein in Baghdad's Firdos Square in 2003 was a symbolic moment in the invasion of Iraq by US-led coalition forces. The 12-metre (40-foot) bronze statue that depicted the country's president standing upright with his raised arm stretched out had only been in place for a year.

Attacks on the figure began on the afternoon of 9 April, including a failed attempt using a sledgehammer by weightlifter and wrestler Kadhem Sharif. A more professional effort was later led by a US Marines unit who took it down with an M88 armoured recovery vehicle. The small group of local Baghdad citizens watching the demolition then chopped off the head, jumped on the remains and pulled the torso through the city's streets while passers-by whacked it with their shoes.

Fortuitously, in terms of publicity, the world's press were staying in the Palestine Hotel located in Firdos Square. Indeed, journalist Robert Fisk writing in the *Independent* two days later suggested it was the most staged photo opportunity since Iwo Jima (*see* 23 February 1945), adding that instead of liberating Baghdad, it had merely opened the doors to mass looting opportunities.

Parts of the statue, especially the left leg, have since appeared on online auction sites, although provenance has been a problematic issue.

ALSO ON THIS DAY 1806: English engineer Isambard Kingdom Brunel born · **1830:** English cinematography pioneer Eadweard Muybridge born (*see* 15 June) · **1978:** Death of Welsh architect Clough Williams-Ellis

Easter Island's statues
are first documented, 1722

What the form of worship of these people comprises we were not able to gather any full knowledge of, owing to the shortness of our stay among them; we noticed only that they kindle fire in front of certain remarkably tall stone figures they set up; and, thereafter squatting on their heels with heads bowed down, they bring the palms of their hands together and alternately raise and lower them. At first, these stone figures caused us to be filled with wonder, for we could not understand how it was possible that people who are destitute of heavy or thick timber, and also of stout cordage, out of which to construct gear, had been able to erect them; nevertheless some of these statues were a good 30 feet in height and broad in proportion. This perplexity ceased, however, with the discovery, on removing a piece of the stone, that they were formed out of clay or some kind of rich earth, and that small smooth flints had been stuck over afterwards, which are fitted very closely and neatly to each other, so as to make up the semblance of a human figure. Moreover, one saw reaching downwards from the shoulders a slight elevation or prominence which represented the arms, for all the statues seem to convey the idea that they were hung about with a long robe from the neck right down to the soles of the feet. They have on the head a basket heaped up with flints painted white deposited in it.

Jacob Roggeveen, ship's log, 10 April 1722

Dutch explorer Jacob Roggeveen (1659–1729) first sighted and named Rapa Nui as Easter Island on Easter Sunday, 5 April 1722, as he searched for Terra Australis (a non-existent southern continent shown on maps from the 15th century). Five days later, men from his ship went ashore and came across the huge stone statues called *moai*.

Carved between AD 1100 and 1680, there are nearly nine hundred statues made out of solidified volcanic ash or 'tuff'. They are most famous for their heads, but many have torsos, some are entire figures and others are kneeling. The transportation of these heavy works is still the matter of some debate; British explorer Captain James Cook, visiting in 1774, notes in his journal that 'they must have been a work of immense time, and sufficiently shew the ingenuity and perseverance of these islanders in the age in which they were built' (*see also* 13 July).

For Roggeveen, 10 April was a memorable day. As well as sighting the statues – it seems likely he did not get close to them – his men shot ten local islanders in a skirmish, an incident that surprisingly does not seem to have affected their cordial relationship.

ALSO ON THIS DAY 1858: Big Ben bell at Palace of Westminster, London, is recast · **1934:** *The Just Judges* panel of the *Ghent Altarpiece* by Dutch painter Jan van Eyck is stolen from St Bavo's Cathedral, Ghent, Belgium, and never recovered · **2019:** Event Horizon Telescope takes the first photograph of a black hole

11 APRIL

Frederic Remington goes sketching in New Mexico, 1907

We can no longer stand the altitudes. My heart nearly stopped when I took a bath this morning. We are overcome by altitude. Went down to Alamagordo [*sic*] – engineer pulled the air on us and nearly killed half dozen people in caboose by shock. I sketched bluffs at sunset and had terrible ride home across irrigating ditches.

**Frederic Remington, diary entry,
11 April 1907**

American painter, writer and sculptor Frederic Remington (1861–1909) focused his work on the Native Americans of the Old West and the cowboys and soldiers who lived and worked in frontier country. He worked regularly for *Harper's Weekly*, *Cosmopolitan* and many other magazines, and made regular trips to the west from his New York home for inspiration.

His diary entries are regular, often brief and include plenty of general day-to-day details, as well as documenting his life in art. Here are his thoughts on the two days before he made his trip to Alamogordo:

Tuesday, 9 April 1907
Came up 900 ft. to Cloudcroft all pines and not very paintable. Horrible dinner. Something must be done...

Wednesday, 10 April 1907

Sketched all day – Mountain and horses beautiful weather fine sunsets on pine tress [*sic*]. Picture 'The dead cow boy and outlaw horse'.... Henry wants to go Grand Canyon.

And here he is on 26 June the following year:

A lollipaloozies Day – made sketch Pete's cabin – a true impressional use of the vivid greens of summer which it is hard to make interesting but I got the violet light all right.

ALSO ON THIS DAY 1749: French painter Adélaïde Labille-Guiard born · **1869:** Norwegian sculptor Gustav Vigeland born · **1958:** Death of Russian painter Konstantin Yuon

12 APRIL

President Roosevelt dies while sitting for a portrait, 1945

You should really paint the President. He has such a remarkable face. There is no painting of him that gives his true expression. I think you could do a wonderful portrait, and he would be such an interesting person to paint! Would you do a portrait of him if it was arranged?

Lucy Mercer Rutherfurd to Elizabeth Shoumatoff (attributed)

Moscow-born, Long Island-based portrait artist Elizabeth Shoumatoff (1888–1980) had spent two days painting a watercolour portrait of US president Franklin D. Roosevelt (1882–1945; *see also* 6 March). At first slightly reluctant to take on the commission, not least because she was a Republican rather than a Democrat, the two got along very well and she spent a couple of hours each morning working with him. Lucy Mercer Rutherfurd (1891–1948), who had an affair with Roosevelt, was also present at the sittings. On the second day, Shoumatoff heard that her brother Andrey had suffered a heart attack.

At about noon on the third day, 12 April 1945, Roosevelt is reported to have said: 'I have a terrific pain in the back of my head', although Shoumatoff did not remember him uttering any words. He then fell forward. Shoumatoff shouted for help and knocked over the easel as she rushed to tell the security agents nearby. The President never regained consciousness and died three hours later from a massive cerebral haemorrhage.

Elizabeth Shoumatoff did not finish the head and shoulders painting of the sitting president, which now hangs at Roosevelt's former getaway (now his museum), the Little White House in Warm Springs, Georgia, but she did complete a second, almost identical, version.

ALSO ON THIS DAY **1484:** Italian architect Antonio da Sangallo the Younger born · **1845:** Swedish painter Gustaf Cederström born · **1885:** French painter Robert Delaunay born

13 APRIL

Thomas Coke buys
a statue of Diana, 1717

I told you in my last [letter] of an imbroylio I have had about a fine antique statue Mr Coke bought [he] got it safe away to Leghorn [the port of Livorno] when it was descover'd here they sent a corrier & had it sequesterd & would have confin'd Mr Coke and I was to have been sent away from Rome, but at last all was ajusted & he has got ye statue – I am hard at work now & will study hard to despacth that I may do something yet will be agreeable to my genorus friends when I come home. I can assure you am quite wery with living this power malancoly life, but I hope shall be reviv'd when I see all my friends in England.

William Kent, letter to Burrell Massingberg, 15 June 1717

While Thomas Coke (1697–1759), the 1st Earl of Leicester (fifth creation), was on his Grand Tour of Europe with English architect William Kent (c. 1685–1748) between 1712 and 1718, he spent a considerable sum on buying paintings and sculpture. Among them was a marble statue of Artemis/Diana – from c. AD 200, a copy of a 4th-century-BC figure – which he bought on 13 April 1717 for 900 crowns.

This caused some major issues for him and Kent, as Kent mentions in the letter to his friend Massingberg on 15 June, because the earl had neglected to obtain the correct papal export licence. Happily for them, however, the Duke of Tuscany stepped in and smoothed the way so that Coke and Kent could

136

continue to tour and shop. Among Coke's purchases were sixty ancient Roman marble sculptures, including a bust of Thucydides, a naked Poseidon and a statue of the Empress Livia 2.2 metres (7 feet 4 inches) in height.

Diana was the most expensive item he acquired for his collection of art at Holkham Hall, the country house in Norfolk, England, that he later built with Kent around the enormous amount of art he brought back from Europe at almost ruinous expense. The sculpture of Diana is 1.9 metres (6 feet 3 inches) high and is shown wearing a 'peplos' robe and carrying a bow in her left hand, while her right reaches for an arrow from the quiver on her back. She is on permanent display today in Holkham Hall's Statue Gallery.

ALSO ON THIS DAY 1780: Irish engineer Alexander Mitchell born · **1860:** Belgian painter James Ensor born · **1910:** Death of Scottish painter Sir William Quiller Orchardson

14 APRIL

A weeping statue attracts international attention, 1949

For that statues have appeared to sweat, and shed tears, and exude something like drops of blood, is not impossible; since wood and stone often contract a mould which is productive of moisture, and cover themselves with many colours, and receive tints from the atmosphere; and there is nothing in the way of believing that the Deity uses these phenomena sometimes as signs and portents. It is possible also that statues may emit a noise like a moan or a groan, by reason of a fracture or a rupture, which is more violent if it takes place in the interior.

Plutarch's *Lives*, c. early 2nd century AD

Statues of religious figures (usually the Virgin Mary) that weep tears of blood or other liquids have a long history and are still being reported today. One case that particularly grabbed the headlines was a plaster statue of St Anne owned by eleven-year-old Shirley Anne Martin from Syracuse, New York State, which began weeping tears after it was partly damaged in an accident. The local press ran a story about it on 13 April 1949 after police were called in to deal with the crowds of people who had gathered.

On the 14th, it was reported by media around the world and Shirley Anne travelled to New York where she appeared on the CBS radio and television talk show *We, the People*. She explained that she had no powers but she felt the tears of the statue were happy ones, not sad ones.

The news cycle then moved on and the statue was forgotten until Shirley was interviewed on the 50th anniversary of the phenomenon; she reported that the statue continued crying until she got married in 1954 and then stopped.

ALSO ON THIS DAY 1434: Foundation stone of Nantes Cathedral, France, is laid · **1527:** Flemish cartographer Abraham Ortelius born · **1827:** English ethnologist and museum founder Augustus Pitt Rivers born

15 APRIL

The first Impressionist exhibition opens in Paris, 1874

Very gently then, in my most innocent manner, I brought him to M. Pissarro's Ploughed Field. On seeing this spectacular landscape, the fine man thought that something was wrong with the lenses of his spectacles. He carefully cleaned them, then put them back on his nose.

'By Michalon!' he exclaimed, 'what is this?'
'You can see...hoar frost on deeply ploughed furrows.'
'Furrows? Frost? But these are scrapings of a palette placed evenly on a dirty canvas. There is no tail nor head, no top, or bottom, no front nor back.'
'Maybe...but the impression is there.'
'Well, it's a funny impression.... And what's that?'
'An Orchard, by Mr Sisley. Look at the small tree on the right; it's cheerful, but the impression...'
'Let me alone with your impression!... It's a dog's dinner.'

Louis Leroy, 'The Exhibition of the Impressionists',
Le Charivari **magazine, 25 April 1874**

The French Société Anonyme des Peintres, Sculpteurs et Graveurs (Anonymous Society of Painters, Sculptors and Engravers) was established in 1873 and its first exhibition opened in Paris the following year on 15 April at the studio of photographer Gaspard-Félix Tournachon, known as Nadar.

The review of the exhibition by French art critic Louis Leroy (1812–1885) shows he was unimpressed with the work of, among others, Claude Monet, Camille Pissarro, Alfred Sisley, Edgar Degas and Paul Cézanne. However, his derisive description of their work stuck and the artists themselves began to use the term 'Impressionists' three years later (*see also* 13 November).

ALSO ON THIS DAY 1452: Italian painter, sculptor and inventor Leonardo da Vinci born (*see* 28 September) · **1832:** German illustrator and painter Wilhelm Busch born · **2019:** The cathedral of Notre-Dame, Paris, sustains major fire damage

16 APRIL

John Ruskin records a nasty dream about his Turner, 1873

Wednesday. Y[esterday] a hot, thunderous day. I very languid and ill, hearing from Joanna of her mother's death. My work all hanging fire sadly.

John Ruskin, diary entry,
16 April 1873

English painter J. M. W. Turner (1775–1851; *see also* 6 September) made several painting trips to Switzerland in the 1840s and one of his most inspiring visits was to Flüelen on Lake Lucerne, views of which he depicted in a number of watercolours when he returned home. These were his final masterpieces as his health started to fail.

English polymath John Ruskin (1819–1900; *see also* 13 May) loved the work and was one of its earliest buyers, describing the Flüelen painting of his dream as:

the last Alpine drawing Turner ever made with loving power; – not unabated power, – for it was painted in 1845, the year of his failure; and it shows, in the foreground work, incipient conditions of fatal decline. But his love for the scene remains unabated – for it is the old place, Fluelen, the scene of that great Famley drawing, now fading away into a mere dream of departing light.

Ruskin even travelled to Flüelen in 1852 to try and establish where Turner had stood to capture the scene, writing to his father regretfully that 'there is no point from which he could have got his view. He supposes himself in the air.'

Despite Ruskin's enthusiasm for the painting, he sold the original but had a copy made by William Ward.

ALSO ON THIS DAY 1635: Dutch painter Frans van Mieris the Elder born · **1660:** Anglo-Irish collector Sir Hans Sloane born (*see* 15 January) · **1821:** English painter Ford Madox Brown born

17 APRIL

Charles Gough sets out on a fateful walk, 1805

A BARKING sound the Shepherd hears,
A cry as of a Dog or Fox;
He halts, and searches with his eyes
Among the scattered rocks:
And now at distance can discern
A stirring in a brake of fern;
And instantly a Dog is seen,
Glancing from that covert green.
The Dog is not of mountain breed;
Its motions, too, are wild and shy;
With something, as the Shepherd thinks,
Unusual in its cry:
Nor is there any one in sight
All round, in Hollow or on Height;
Nor shout, nor whistle strikes his ear;
What is the Creature doing here?

It was a Cove, a huge Recess,
That keeps till June December's snow
A lofty Precipice in front,
A silent Tarn below!
Far in the bosom of Helvellyn,

Remote from public Road or Dwelling,
Pathway, or cultivated land;
From trace of human foot or hand.

There, sometimes does a leaping Fish
Send through the Tarn a lonely cheer;
The Crags repeat the Raven's croak,
In symphony austere;
Thither the Rainbow comes – the Cloud –
And Mists that spread the flying shroud;
And Sun-beams; and the sounding blast,
That, if it could, would hurry past,
But that enormous Barrier binds it fast.
  William Wordsworth, 'Fidelity', 1807

English watercolourist Charles Gough (1784–1805) achieved a level of fame in death that he never managed in life. On 17 April 1805, he and his spaniel Foxie set out for a walk over Helvellyn towards Grasmere in the Lake District and was never seen alive again. His remains were found on 27 July, Foxie barking beside the corpse (at which some newspaper reports suggested mischievously she had nibbled); it seems likely that he had fallen from the Striding Edge route – which continues to claim lives because of its tricky conditions – and died either of his injuries or exposure.

His death in these sublime surroundings quickly became an inspiration to the English Romantic movement. Sir Edwin Landseer painted the rocky scene of heroic loyal Foxie anxiously attending to her master after the fall in his *Attachment*, as did Francis Danby in *The Precipice*, and both William Wordsworth in 'Fidelity' (see above for the first few stanzas) and Sir Walter Scott (*see* 4 February) in 'Helvellyn' wrote poems about the incident.

ALSO ON THIS DAY **1816**: English chapel-building benefactor Thomas Hazlehurst born · **1930**: Death of Russian stage designer Alexander Golovin · **2012**: The British Library buys the 7th-century St Cuthbert Gospel, Europe's oldest fully intact book, for £9 million

Angelica Kauffman complains
to the Royal Academy, 1775

Gentlemen!

I have had the honour of a visit from Sir Will. Chambers, the purpose of which was to reconcile me to submit to the exhibition of a picture which gave me offence. However I may admire the dignity of the gentlemen who are superior to the malignity of the author, I should have held their conduct much more in admiration, if they had taken into consideration a Respect to the sex which it is their glory to support.

If they fear the loss of an Academician who pays no respect to that sex, I hope I may enjoy the liberty of leaving to them the pleasure of that Academician and withdrawing one object who never willingly deserved his or their ridicule.

I beg leave to present my respects to the society and hope they will always regard their own honour. I have but one request to make, to send home my pictures if that is to be exhibited.

**Angelica Kauffman, letter to the Royal Academy of Arts, London,
18 April 1775**

Swiss painter Angelica Kauffman (1741–1807) was one of the two female founder members of London's Royal Academy in 1768, but although recognized as a superb artist, she still suffered considerable discrimination (*see* 25 April). When Irish painter and fellow Academy co-founder Nathaniel Hone (1718–1784) submitted and had accepted his painting *The Conjuror* to the 1775 Summer Exhibition, Kauffman complained forcefully, asking for her own works to be returned if they allowed Hone's work to remain on show.

The Conjuror less than subtly alluded to whispers of Kauffman's alleged affair with Sir Joshua Reynolds, the Academy's first president (*see* 8 May) – Kauffman is shown as a child resting on Reynolds's knee, while in the background are prints of various naked figures, including a small nude caricature of Kauffman that Hone later painted out. Kauffman's argument that the painting was offensive was taken seriously and the Royal Academy's

Hanging Committee took it down (although Hone exhibited it himself at a one-man exhibition).

When Kauffman's female Academician co-founder English painter Mary Moser died in 1819 (*see* 25 April), no women were elected to the Academy until artist Dame Laura Knight in 1936.

ALSO ON THIS DAY 1506: The cornerstone of St Peter's Basilica in the Vatican City is laid · **1898:** Death of French painter Gustave Moreau · **1944:** Scottish sculptor and photographer Philip Jackson born

19 APRIL

Tarsila do Amaral spells out her artistic intent, 1923

I feel myself ever more Brazilian. I want to be the painter of my country. How thankful I am for having spent all my childhood on the fazenda [farm]. The memories of that time have grown precious to me. In art, I want to be the little bumpkin girl from São Bernardo, playing with straw dollies, like in the painting on which I am now working.... Don't think that this tendency is viewed negatively here. On the contrary. What they want here is that each one brings the contribution of their own country. This explains the success of the Russian ballet, Japanese graphics and black music. Paris has had enough of Parisian art.

**Tarsila do Amaral, letter to her parents,
19 April 1923**

While Brazilian artist Tarsila do Amaral (1886–1973) was strongly associated with Brazilian modernism and indigenous culture – and indeed a member of the Grupo dos Cinco (Group of Five) movement (*see* 11 February) – her style was also influenced by her travels in Europe and particularly France.

After a rural childhood in Brazil, she studied in Paris in the early 1920s with French painter and sculptor Fernand Léger and painter André Lhote at the Académie Julian, where Cubism and Futurism became all the rage and there was a growing interest in non-European art and 'primitivism'. During this period, she produced one of her most famous works, the Cubist *A Negra*, a painting of a large black woman with one breast prominently exposed.

After travelling through Europe, she held her first solo exhibition in Paris in 1926, receiving positive reviews from both European modernists and Brazilian nationalists. She was careful in the development of this crossover image, smoking Brazilian cigarettes while wearing the latest fashion designed by French couturier Paul Poiret. She and her husband, the Brazilian writer Oswald de Andrade, lived in Montmartre and served traditional Brazilian meals at dinner parties there.

ALSO ON THIS DAY **1588:** Death of Italian painter Paolo Veronese · **1768:** Death of Italian painter Giovanni Canal (aka 'Canaletto') · **1957:** Pablo Picasso meets Lump the dog for the first time (*see* 30 March)

20 APRIL

The Frida Kahlo Barbie® doll is banned in Mexico, 2018

Critics say that the doll is more Barbie-like than Frida-like: that it doesn't reflect Kahlo's heavy, nearly conjoined eyebrows, and they say its costume doesn't accurately portray the elaborate Tehuana-style dresses the artist wore.

Guardian, 9 March 2018

Mattel's launch of a Frida Kahlo Barbie® doll hit a bump in the road when the Mexican artist's great-niece Mara de Anda Romeo's campaign to halt its sales were temporarily upheld in Mexico, on the basis that the company did not own the rights to Kahlo's image.

The official description of the doll said it was part of the toy company's ongoing series paying tribute to courageous female role models, and that Frida Kahlo (1907–1954; *see* 20 October) had been chosen for her originality and 'unwavering passion'.

Those opposed to the doll cited various physical aspects of its depiction of the artist – its unrealistic eyebrow treatment, failure to deal with Kahlo's physical disabilities and its inauthentic dress – as well as the entire commercialization of her name as part of the 'Inspiring Women' series. Among the critics was Mexican-American actress Salma Hayek (who portrayed Kahlo in a 2002 biopic), who pointed out that it was unfathomable that Frida Kahlo, who never attempted to look like anyone else, had been turned into a Barbie doll.

144

Mattel went on to win the battle to continue selling the doll, which featured a 'Fashionista standard torso' wearing 'Long Dress, Fringe Shawl, Floral Head piece, Flats' and earrings and necklace accessories, retailing at $29.99.

ALSO ON THIS DAY 1840: French painter Odilon Redon born · **1850:** American sculptor Daniel Chester French born · **1893:** Catalan painter and sculptor Joan Miró born

21 APRIL

A photo of the Loch Ness Monster appears, 1934

On another occasion also, when the blessed man was living for some days in the province of the Picts, he was obliged to cross the river Nesa (the Ness); and when he reached the bank of the river, he saw some of the inhabitants burying an unfortunate man, who, according to the account of those who were burying him, was a short time before seized, as he was swimming, and bitten most severely by a monster that lived in the water; his wretched body was, though too late, taken out with a hook, by those who came to his assistance in a boat. The blessed man, on hearing this, was so far from being dismayed, that he directed one of his companions to swim over and row across the coble that was moored at the farther bank. And Lugne Mocumin hearing the command of the excellent man, obeyed without the least delay, taking off all his clothes, except his tunic, and leaping into the water. But the monster, which, so far from being satiated, was only roused for more prey, was lying at the bottom of the stream, and when it felt the water disturbed above by the man swimming, suddenly rushed out, and, giving an awful roar, darted after him, with its mouth wide open, as the man swam in the middle of the stream. Then the blessed man observing this, raised his holy hand, while all the rest, brethren as well as strangers, were stupefied with terror, and, invoking the name of God, formed the saving sign of the cross in the air, and commanded the ferocious monster, saying, 'Thou shalt go no further, nor touch the man; go back with all speed.' Then at the voice of the saint, the monster was terrified, and fled more quickly than if it had been pulled back with ropes, though it had just got so near to Lugne, as he swam, that there was not more than the length of a spear-staff

between the man and the beast. Then the brethren seeing that the monster
had gone back, and that their comrade Lugne returned to them in the boat
safe and sound, were struck with admiration, and gave glory to God in the
blessed man.

The most famous photograph of the legendary Scottish Loch Ness monster's
neck and head was 'taken' by London doctor Robert Wilson and published
in the *Daily Mail* on 21 April 1934. Known as 'The Surgeon's Photograph', the
image was taken seriously by many until the 1990s, when it was revealed,
unsurprisingly, that it was a hoax, created using a toy submarine.

ALSO ON THIS DAY 1868: American painter Alfred Maurer born · **1913:** English photographer
Norman Parkinson born · **1969:** Mick Jagger briefs Andy Warhol on the design of the Rolling
Stones album *Sticky Fingers*

22 APRIL

Arthur Nantel paints
the Second Battle of Ypres, 1915

We knew there was something wrong. We started to march towards Ypres
but we couldn't get past on the road with refugees coming down the road.
We went along the railway line to Ypres and there were people, civilians and
soldiers, lying along the roadside in a terrible state. We heard them say it was
gas. We didn't know what the Hell gas was. When we got to Ypres we found
a lot of Canadians lying there dead from gas the day before, poor devils, and
it was quite a horrible sight for us young men. I was only twenty so it was
quite traumatic and I've never forgotten nor ever will forget it.

Canadian artist Arthur Nantel (1874–1948) enlisted with the 14th Royal
Montreal Battalion in August 1914, aged forty-one, and was captured at
the Second Battle of Ypres in Belgium. As a prisoner of war, he was sent
to the Giessen Camp, which initially had a reputation of being one of the

more humanely run camps. It also housed other artists and until 1917 they were given a special small shed, nicknamed the Giessen Studio, in which to work on canvases and also anything else they could find, including ration tin lids. The camp authorities encouraged Nantel to continue painting and when released at the end of the war, he returned home with thirty works. These were exhibited in London in 1919 and were later acquired by the Canadian War Memorials Fund art programme; they are now held by the Canadian War Museum in Ottawa.

As well as chronicling life as a prisoner of war, including Christmas Eve 1916, among Nantel's work was his *7 a.m., April 22nd, 1915*, a panoramic view from an elevated vantage point on the first day of the Second Battle of Ypres. Later in the day, the German army employed poison gas for the first time in the war, launching 160 tons of chlorine gas into the northeasterly wind towards the Allied troops, many of whom were Canadian and French.

ALSO ON THIS DAY 1917: Australian painter Sidney Nolan born · **1926:** Scottish architect James Stirling born · **1938:** Japanese fashion designer Issey Miyake born

23 APRIL

The first YouTube video is uploaded, 2005

Members of the Royal Institution and other visitors to a laboratory in an upper room in Frith-Street, Soho, on Tuesday saw a demonstration of apparatus invented by Mr J. L. Baird, who claims to have solved the problem of television.... For the purposes of the demonstration the head of a ventriloquist's doll was manipulated as the image to be transmitted, though the human face was also reproduced.... The image as transmitted was faint and often blurred, but substantiated a claim that through the 'Televisor' as Mr Baird has named his apparatus, it is possible to transmit and reproduce instantly the details of movement, and such things as the play of expression on the face. It has yet to be seen to what extent further developments will carry Mr Baird's system towards practical use.

The Times, **28 January 1926**

Scottish inventor John Logie Baird's choice of subject for the first transmission of television seems as random as that chosen by the founders of YouTube. The first item on the video-sharing site was uploaded on 23 April 2005 by the company's co-founder Jawed Karim. 'Me at the zoo' is a simple eighteen-second recording made by his friend Yakov Lapitsky at the San Diego Zoo. Karim talks about the elephants' long trunks and how cool they are. It has since been viewed more than 100 million times and ushered in an era of amateur self-broadcasting.

24 APRIL

Thomas Rowlandson
publishes *Cat in a Bowl*, 1811

There are certain subjects of his composition, carried through with a compatibility of style so truly original, and so replete with painter-like feeling that Sir Joshua Reynolds and Mr West pronounced them wonders of art.

Henry Angelo, on Thomas Rowlandson's art,
in *Reminiscences of Henry Angelo, with Memoirs of His Late Father and Friends*, 1828

English caricaturist Thomas Rowlandson (1757–1827) produced a number of scathing prints of the great and the good of his day, biting social commentary and London street life, as well as straightforward images, such as the illustrations of the noted fencing academy owned by his friend Henry Angelo (1756–1835). Many of his illustrations feature plenty of female nudity.

Among his works was a series of colourful prints under the general heading of *Rural Sports*. Published on 24 April 1811, *Cat in a Bowl* shows villagers laughing as they watch a cat in a bowl drifting on a pond. It is one of the tamest of the series, as is *A Cricket Match Extraordinary*, which simply shows women playing cricket. Slightly more saucy is *A Pleasant Way of Making Hay* in which two men and two women romp in the fields in front of several hay carts.

Clothing is less in evidence in other examples of *Rural Sports*. In *A Game at Quoits*, a woman bares her breasts as she talks to a man in front of the village inn, while in the chaos of a large hot air balloon drifting away in *Balloon Hunting*, various women fall out of a cart, one of whom in doing so exposes her breasts, as in the distance a woman floats in the air with her parasol and her bottom exposed. The double-entendre of *Coney Hunting* is particularly graphic, showing two men at a stile, ogling three women in a field, naked and legs akimbo.

ALSO ON THIS DAY 1904: Dutch-American painter Willem de Kooning born · **1931:** English painter Bridget Riley born · **1972:** Death of Filipino painter Fernando Amorsolo

25 APRIL

The first Royal Academy exhibition opens, 1769

As the present exhibition is part of the institution of an Academy supported by royal munificence, the public may naturally expect the liberty of being admitted without any Expence.

The Academicians therefore think it necessary to declare that this was very much their desire, but that they have not been able to suggest any other means than that of receiving money for admittance to prevent the room from being filled by improper persons to the entire exclusion of those for whom the exhibition is apparently intended.

Notice in *The Exhibition of the Royal Academy* catalogue, 1769

The Summer Exhibition has been held by the Royal Academy in London every year since 1769 when 136 works went on show from 25 April until 27 May. From the outset, the guiding principle was to make it an open submission exhibition for all artists and available to the public.

The founders of the Royal Academy were celebrated in German-born painter Johann Zoffany's group portrait *The Academicians of the Royal Academy* (1771–72) at a life class... well, most of them. Zoffany missed out the two women founders, English painter Mary Moser and Swiss painter Angelica Kauffman (*see* 18 April), including only vague portraits of them on the back wall. Indeed, the next female Royal Academician after Moser's death was English artist Dame Laura Knight, who was elected in 1936, and women were not invited to the Academy's annual dinner for another thirty years after that.

26 APRIL

The bombing of Guernica inspires Picasso, 1937

When the Civil War broke out in Spain, Franco sent a call for help to Germany and asked for support, particularly in the air. One should not forget that Franco with his troops was stationed in Africa and that he could not get the troops across, as the fleet was in the hands of the Communists, or, as they called themselves at the time, the competent Revolutionary Government in Spain. The decisive factor was, first of all, to get his troops over to Spain.

The Fuehrer thought the matter over. I urged him to give support under all circumstances, firstly, in order to prevent the further spread of communism in that theatre and, secondly, to test my young Luftwaffe at this opportunity in this or that technical respect.

Hermann Göring, Nuremberg Trial Proceedings, 14 March 1946

The oil painting *Guernica*, by Spanish artist Pablo Picasso (1881–1973), is the most famous of the many works that portray the indiscriminate bombing of civilians by the German Luftwaffe in Guernica, Spain, on 26 April 1937, done in support of Francisco Franco's Nationalist uprising.

Commissioned by the Spanish Republican government for 200,000 francs, the 3.49 × 7.77 metre (11 × 25 foot) painting is a chaotic scene in black, white and grey of people and animals enduring terrible suffering. Picasso was inspired by British journalist George Steer's eyewitness reporting of the bombing for the *New York Times* and worked on the canvas at his home in Paris, allowing visitors as he painted to help promote the fight against Franco. He finished the painting on 4 June 1937.

After going on display for the first time at the Paris International Exposition in 1937, to a mixed reception, the painting went on tour around Europe and

America, where it was kept by the Museum of Modern Art, New York on Picasso's request until democracy was restored in Spain. *Guernica* returned to Spain in 1981 (*see* 10 September).

ALSO ON THIS DAY 1798: French painter Eugène Delacroix born · **1859:** English textile designer William Morris marries his model Jane Burden (*see* 1 February) · **1862:** American painter Edmund Tarbell born

27 APRIL

Inigo Jones is appointed Surveyor of the King's Works, 1613

For as outwardly every wyse man carrieth a graviti in Publicke Places, whear ther is nothing els looked for, yet inwardly has his immaginancy set free, and sumtimes licentiously flying out, as nature hirself doeth often tymes stravagantly, to dellight, amase us sometimes moufe us to laughter, sumtimes to contemplation and horror, so in architecture ye outward ornaments oft to be sollid, proporsionabl according to the rules, masculine and unaffected.

Inigo Jones, Roman sketchbook, 1614

Like wise at ye Thearmi at Baia thear ar many wales wth mor courses of Brick and Sum great Bricke amongst for ye Romans varied thes things according to thear Cappriccio minging one wth an other, so yt sheaud well.

Inigo Jones, marginalia of 1613–14, in Andrea Palladio's
***I Quattro libri dell'architettura*, 1601**

English architect and masque-producer Inigo Jones (1573–1652) had built very little before he was engaged as Surveyor of the King's Works on 27 April 1613, but just after his appointment, he took a Grand Tour of Europe and came back a strong convert to the architectural style of Italian architect Andrea Palladio (1508–1580; *see* 3 March). Jones went on to design the Banqueting House in Whitehall and the square of Covent Garden in London.

He travelled with his patron Thomas Howard, 14th Earl of Arundel, through Italy, France and Switzerland, bringing with him Palladio's seminal book about architecture, *Quattro Libri*, which he had bought almost as soon as it was published in Venice in 1601. Inside, Jones added copious annotations, comments and paraphrases, especially about ancient Roman buildings in Italy, in his compact handwriting. His notes fill the margins and even cross over onto the illustrations and plates.

His additions to the book were so useful and important that when it came to be translated into English in 1715, they were included with the text. Jones was very much aware of the value of his thoughts on the book, one of his notes in Book IV pointing out that he is actually writing 'more than is in Palladio'.

ALSO ON THIS DAY 1791: American painter and inventor Samuel Morse born · **1840:** Foundation stone for Palace of Westminster, London (designed by English architect Charles Barry), is laid · **1857:** Norwegian painter Theodor Kittelsen born

28 APRIL

Anthony Blunt is appointed Surveyor of the King's Pictures, 1945

In the early part of last week, Professor Blunt was publicly identified as having been a suspect Soviet agent. This disclosure understandably gave rise to grave concern. Last Thursday, in response to a priority written question from the hon. Member for Hartlepool (Mr Leadbitter), I thought it right to confirm that Professor Blunt had indeed been a Soviet agent and to give the House the salient facts.

**Prime Minister Margaret Thatcher,
House of Commons, London, 21 November 1979**

British art historian Anthony Blunt (1907–1983) held various important positions in the art world, including Professor of the History of Art at the University of London and director of the Courtauld Institute of Art, where he had a long academic career. He published a major work, *Artistic Theory in Italy, 1450–1600*, in 1940 and was a world expert on French painter Nicolas Poussin – his book *Art and Architecture in France, 1500–1700* (1953) was a classic text on the subject.

He became in overall charge of the monarch's art as Surveyor of the King's Pictures in 1945, then until 1972 as Surveyor of the Queen's Pictures for Elizabeth II, who knighted him in 1956. However, despite joining MI5 in

1940, from the early 1930s for about twenty years he was also a spy for the Soviet Union; this was not publicly known until 1979 (*see* 15 November).

Since his death, Blunt has been played by various actors on television and in the theatre – including in *A Question of Attribution* by playwright Alan Bennett, and the Netflix series *The Crown* – often musing about the concept of fakery, fabrication and truth telling.

ALSO ON THIS DAY 1881: Death of French sculptor and photographer Antoine Samuel Adam-Salomon · **1886:** French painter Paul Cézanne marries his model Marie-Hortense Fiquet · **1923:** Wembley Stadium, London, initially known as the Empire Stadium, opens

29 APRIL

Demolition work starts
on the Berlin Wall, 1990

Viele kleine Leute die in vielen
kleinen Orten viele kleine Dinge
tun, können das Gesicht der Welt verändern

Many small people who in many small places do many small things that can alter the face of the world

Graffiti on the Berlin Wall

When the Berlin Wall came down in 1990, a large part of the graffiti art that had been painted onto its West side was also lost (the East side was entirely blank). Happily, some graffiti remains, including that at the East Side Gallery, a 1,300-metre (4,265-foot) stretch of the wall in the Friedrichshain area covered in murals, which is believed to be the largest open-air gallery in the world. It is protected as a heritage site and remains as a testimonial to the history of the wall, attracting millions of visitors every year to its 106 paintings by artists from across the world.

Among the most famous works are East German artist Birgit Kinder's *The Trabant breaking through the wall*, which shows the iconic East German car doing exactly that, and *My God, Help Me to Survive This Fatal Attraction*, also known as the *Fraternal Kiss*, by Russian painter Dmitri Vrubel. This work, painted on the eastern side of the wall in 1990 (and then repainted in 2009), is a reproduction of a photograph from 1979 showing the then leaders of the Soviet Union and the German Democratic Republic, Leonid Brezhnev and Erich Honecker, embracing.

In a 2014 interview for Russian magazine *Kommersant Weekend*, Vrubel said: 'When you paint something large in the open air, you're thinking not only about people's perception but also about their gut reaction. You're expecting everyone to say, "Wow!" I was waiting for this, too. But of course I didn't think that 25 years later my painting would be seen as a symbol of the Berlin Wall.'

ALSO ON THIS DAY 1783: English painter David Cox born · **1848:** Indian painter Raja Ravi Varma born · **1882:** Dutch printer and typographer Hendrik Werkman born

30 APRIL

First Venice Art
Biennale opens, 1895

It's About Time explores the ways in which the archival traces can serve as a means of identifying and unraveling historical narratives built on the absence of women. The project focuses on the public Verbale records of meetings held by the Mayor of Venice Riccardo Selvatico in 1893, which led to the creation of La Biennale two years later. This publication presents a parallel Verbale text generated through a collective endeavor offering an augmented history of the event written by women. The spirit in which the project has been conceived acknowledges the importance of Felicita Bevilacqua La Masa (1822–1899) and her critical position regarding the establishment of the international exhibition in 1895. If we understand the function of archives as sites of contestation, we must accept the challenge they pose to the accepted version of our shared history.

Marysia Lewandowska, 'Introductions',
in *It's About Time* installation catalogue,
Venice Biennale, 2019

The Venice Biennale is a major exhibition of contemporary art that has been held every two years – with some gaps during wartime – since 1895, when a quarter of a million visitors made the event an immediate success.

At the Venice Biennale 2019, women artists accounted for just over half of those showing their work. In a special project for the Biennale, Polish artist Marysia Lewandowska contributed her installation *It's About Time*, which explored the male-dominated establishment of the exhibition through the medium of archives. Her work included a recording of an imagined debate between Italian women discussing founding the Venice Biennale.

This is a far cry from the earliest days of the exhibition to which painters Sir John Everett Millais, Sir Lawrence Alma-Tadema, James McNeill Whistler (who showed his *Symphony in White, No. 2: The Little White Girl*), Sir Edward Burne-Jones and Frederic, Lord Leighton were invited to exhibit their work. At the inaugural show, the most controversial piece was Italian painter Giacomo Grosso's *Il Suprimeo convegno* (Supreme Meeting, or Final Tryst), which depicted the corpse of a man surrounded by five frolicking naked female figures and was strongly criticized by the Patriarch of Venice, Giuseppe Sarto, who later became Pope Pious X. Despite this and other protestations, the painting won a prize for the most popular work voted for by the public attendees.

May

The first Penny Black
stamp is issued, 1840

You always represent me favourably.

Queen Victoria to engraver William Wyon (attributed)

'A bit of paper just large enough to bear the stamp, and covered at the back with a glutinous wash' is how Britain's postal reformer Rowland Hill (1795–1879) described the plans for the world's first pre-paid stamp.

The image of Queen Victoria on the stamp was first produced by the Royal Mint's chief engraver William Wyon (1795–1851) in 1834 when she was fifteen – it was a design she approved of as her remark to Wyon indicates. This image was then sketched by painter and miniaturist Henry Corbould (1787–1844), which in turn was the basis of an engraving by Charles Heath (1785–1848) for the stamp. This became the model for the 1840 Penny Black stamp and remained on all British stamps until the Queen's death in 1901.

As well as the portrait of Queen Victoria (*see* 7 August), the design includes two Maltese crosses in the top left and right corners with radiant solar discs in the middle. Letters in the bottom left- and right-hand corners indicate where an individual stamp lies in the printed sheet of 240, and are particularly meaningful for collectors.

Queen Elizabeth II's stamps from 1952 were initially based on a three-quarter shoulder length profile image from a shot by photographer Dorothy Wilding. Because of design issues, this was changed for a new stamp in 1967 on which artist Arnold Machin and photographer John Hedgecoe collaborated to show the monarch facing left. The first stamp was printed in olive-brown sepia as a hommage to the original Penny Black.

ALSO ON THIS DAY 1848: Norwegian painter Adelsteen Normann born · **1851:** The Great Exhibition opens at the 'Crystal Palace' in Hyde Park, London (*see* 30 November) · **1857:** Dutch art dealer Theo van Gogh born (*see* 23 December)

Proust delights in the
View of Delft, 1921

Since I first saw the *View of Delft* at The Hague Museum, I knew that I had seen the loveliest painting in the world.

**Marcel Proust, letter to friend and art critic Jean-Louis Vaudoyer,
2 May 1921**

French novelist Marcel Proust (1871–1922) first saw *View of Delft* (c. 1660–61) – a depiction by Dutch painter Johannes Vermeer (1632–1675) of a canal in his home town – on a visit to the Netherlands with his friend Bertrand de Fénelon in 1902.

It also features in Proust's most famous work *À la recherche du temps perdu* (In Search of Lost Time), in the death scene of the ageing writer Bergotte who has gone to look at the painting in search of a detail described by an art critic as a patch of yellow wall ('*petit pan de mur jaune*'). Proust describes how Bergotte grows dizzy and fixates on the patch, stimulating him to reconsider how he might have been a better writer, before he then suffers a stroke (which he believes is simply stomach ache caused by undercooked potatoes).

It is not clear exactly where the little patch of yellow wall Bergotte refers to is in the painting, possibly the roof and wall area to the left of the Rotterdam gate with two turrets, or maybe the area of wall on the far right-hand side of the painting. Another theory is that no single detail matching the description exists and it is more of a general impression.

ALSO ON THIS DAY 1519: Death of Italian painter, sculptor and inventor Leonardo da Vinci (*see also* 28 September) · **1695:** Italian painter Giovanni Niccolò Servandoni born · **1904:** German-English photographer Bill Brandt born

Edmonia Lewis enquires about payment for *Forever Free*, 1868

Dear Mrs Chapman,

It seems almost I was going to say, impossible that not one of my many kind friends have not writen to me some word about the group Forever free. Will you be so kind as to let me know what has become of it? And has Mr Sewall got the money for it yet or not. I am in great need of the money. What little money I had I put all in that work with my heart. And I truly hope that the work of two long years has not been lost. Dear Mrs Chapman I been thinking that it may be that you have meet with some who think that it will ruin me to help me – but you may tell them that in giving a little something towards that group – that will not only aid me but will show their good feeling for one who has given all for poor humanity. I have written to Mr Sewall some time ago but as yet I have not heard from him. Will you dear Mrs Chapman be so kind as to see Mr Sewall and if he has been paid the Eaight hundred dollars. Will he be so kind as to send to me the same as I am in need of it very mutch – I have done very little this winter and unless I receive this money from home I will not be able to get on this year. I beg you will excuse the liberty I have taken in sending this letter but my belief that you will receive it without offence.

**Edmonia Lewis, letter to American abolitionist Maria Weston Chapman,
3 May 1868**

Edmonia Lewis (Native American Chippewa name, Wildfire; 1844–1907) was the first professional African American sculptor. She studied initially in America, where she faced considerable hostility, before emigrating to Rome where she lived and worked for most of her life.

Much of her work was Neoclassical in style and as well as producing busts of leading abolitionists, she focused on depicting the struggles of black and indigenous people. *Forever Free* (1867) is one of her finest pieces, a marble statue, 1 metre (3 feet) high, of an African American man and woman enjoying the end of their enslavement. He stands looking up and though he still has a chain on one wrist, it is not holding him back. The woman is kneeling in prayer.

Lewis took something of a gamble when she had finished *Forever Free*, shipping it from Rome to the Boston abolitionist lawyer Samuel Sewall with a bill for $800, without any commission or previous mention of it of any kind. Happily, Sewall was able to find a buyer.

4 MAY

The Monuments Men find looted art in Germany, 1945

SUBJECT: Preservation of Historical Monuments.

1. Shortly we will be fighting our way across the Continent of Europe in battles designed to preserve our civilization. Inevitably, in the path of our advance will be found historical monuments and cultural centers which symbolize to the world all that we are fighting to preserve.

2. It is the responsibility of every commander to protect and respect these symbols whenever possible.

3. In some circumstances the success of the military operation may be prejudiced in our reluctance to destroy these revered objects. Then, as at Cassino, where the enemy relied on our emotional attachments to shield his defense, the lives of our men are paramount. So, when military necessity dictates, commanders may order the required action even though it involves destruction of some honored site.

4. But there are many circumstances in which damage and destruction are not necessary and cannot be justified. In such cases, through the exercise of restraint and discipline, commanders will preserve centers and objects of historical and cultural significance. Civil Affairs Staffs at higher echelons will advise commanders of the locations of historical monuments of this type, both in advance of the front lines and in occupied areas. This information, together with

the necessary instructions, will be passed down through command channels to all echelons.

General Eisenhower, memo to all commanders, second directive on the protection of cultural property, 26 May 1944

The Monuments Men – officially the Monuments, Fine Arts, and Archives Program (MFAA) – was a group set up in 1943 by the Allied Forces to find and protect items of cultural importance during and after the Second World War (*see also* 11 January).

On 4 May 1945, American James Rorimer, who led the MFAA and later became director of the Metropolitan Museum of Art in New York, made a major haul at Neuschwanstein Castle, in Bavaria, Germany, following the previous day's success at a monastery in nearby Buxheim, retrieving work by Reynolds, Gainsborough, Renoir, Watteau, Fragonard, Delacroix and Goya.

As well as simply storing the works of art, a special area of the castle had been set aside for photographing and cataloguing the stolen goods. Delighted to discover this archive of 8,000 negatives and 22,000 catalogue cards, Rorimer locked them away to be investigated properly later. In his 1950 account *Survival: The Salvage and Protection of Art in War*, Rorimer records his amazement at the size of the find, noting that it was obvious it was in the process of being removed before the Nazi troops fled shortly before the arrival of the MFAA men. He estimated it would have taken twenty years to identify everything stored there without the German forces' detailed records of the stolen items.

In the 2014 film *The Monuments Men* based on the work of the MFAA, the 'James Granger' character based on Rorimer was played by American actor Matt Damon.

Coincidentally, on this same day, a Nazi plan to blow up the Altaussee salt mine in Austria, which was also a holding depot for art stolen by Nazi forces, was frustrated by local miners.

ALSO ON THIS DAY 1757: Spanish sculptor and architect Manuel Tolsá born · **1789:** Boydell Shakespeare Gallery opens in London · **1826:** American painter Frederic Edwin Church born

To the Lighthouse is published
with a Vanessa Bell cover, 1927

Quickly, as if she were recalled by something over there, she turned to her canvas. There it was – her picture. Yes, with all its greens and blues, its lines running up and across, its attempt at something. It would be hung in the attics, she thought; it would be destroyed. But what did that matter? she asked herself, taking up her brush again. She looked at the steps; they were empty; she looked at her canvas; it was blurred. With a sudden intensity, as if she saw it clear for a second, she drew a line there, in the centre. It was done; it was finished. Yes, she thought, laying down her brush in extreme fatigue, I have had my vision.

Virginia Woolf, *To the Lighthouse*, 1927

Lily Briscoe and her painting are central characters in *To The Lighthouse*, the fourth novel by English writer Virginia Woolf (1882–1941), the dust jacket for which was designed by her older sister Vanessa Bell (1879–1961). As well as a co-founder of the Omega Workshops design collective with art critic and painter Roger Fry and artist Duncan Grant (*see* 12 June), Bell was a successful artist and produced many book covers, including all but one of her sister's novels. Bell tended not to read the book before starting on her cover designs, most of which were semi-abstract, such as the rose for the first edition of *The Years* (1937) with its background of overlapping circles and cross-hatched border, two of Bell's signature ornamentations.

In these respects, *To the Lighthouse* stands out – the central feature of the cover is a lighthouse made up of three bold blue lines, waves crashing against its base and light beaming out from its peak to support the title of the book. Water and light are given a pointillist treatment, while around the edge is the familiar border of semicircles.

Virginia Woolf valued her sister's book cover artwork. 'Your style is unique, because so truthful and therefore it upsets one completely,' she told her.

ALSO ON THIS DAY 1672: Death of English painter Samuel Cooper · **1869:** Filipino painter Fabián de la Rosa born · **1892:** English archaeologist Dorothy Garrod born

George Cruikshank's
Sales by Auction! is published, 1819

Here are some genuine articles, a present from an Indian prince to the deceased owner & sv'd Entirely for the Moths as they were never worn – poor soul she died very poor having given away all her money in Charity so pray my good people Bid Liberally or the Children will be destitute!!

**Text in 'Auctioneer' Prince Regent's speech bubble,
in George Cruikshank's etching *Sales by Auction!*, 1819**

English caricaturist and illustrator George Cruikshank (1792–1878) was particularly harsh on the royal family and politicians of his day, as were his contemporaries Thomas Rowlandson (*see* 24 April) and James Gillray (*see* 18 May). In *Sales by Auction!*, a hand-coloured etching on paper, he uses the auctions – which were extremely popular among high society on the death of a family member – to attack the Prince Regent (later to become George IV), who is shown selling off the belongings of his recently deceased mother, Queen Charlotte, to the highest bidder. 'Provident Children disposing of their deceased Mother's Effects for the Benefit of the Creditors!!' runs the etching's caption, as the Duke of York and her other children look greedily on. At the top right of the drawing on the four-postered bed is inscribed 'a bribe gift from Governor Hastings', while by the auctioneer's rostrum are a selection of snuff boxes labelled 'Queen's Mixture', 'Prince's Mixture' and 'Strasburg' (a nod to her German heritage).

Queen Charlotte had in fact directed very specifically in her will which of her children was to inhert her property: her jewels, furnishings and fittings, books, art, china and other belongings. In the event, the Prince Regent simply claimed all the jewels for himself and had much of the rest of her belongings auctioned on 7 May 1819, the day after Cruikshank's etching was published.

ALSO ON THIS DAY 1880: South African painter Winifred Brunton born · **1880:** German painter Ernst Kirchner born · **2014:** Death of Austrian painter Maria Lassnig

The Codex Gigas survives
a terrible fire, 1697

KXK Pater Credo. Lord ne ifu
more against fevers
fexes drex artifex master dino
blood you drink and meat you eat and in blood you are washed
but collect 150 claws
and lie down in a place like a yearling lamb.
Sleep now and forever and ever. Amen.

**Spell from Codex Gigas,
early 13th century**

The Codex Gigas is the world's largest surviving medieval illuminated manuscript, known also as the Devil's Bible because it contains a large full-page portrait of the Devil. It measures 92 cm (36 inches) in length, is 50 cm (20 inches) wide and 22 cm (8½ inches) thick, and is bound in wooden boards covered in leather with decorated metal guards and fittings. It weighs nearly 75 kg (165 lb).

The Codex was produced in the early 13th century, probably by a single monk (perhaps called Herman), and first appears in the library of the Benedictine monastery of Podlažice in the Czech Republic, although this small monastery is probably not where it was made. The 310 pages of vellum include a Vulgate Bible, Josephus's *Antiquities of the Jews* and *The Jewish War*, Isidore of Seville's early encyclopaedia *Etymologiae*, various medical treatises including work by Constantine the African, an assortment of spells and a calendar.

As well as the Devil, which is opposite a depiction of a heavenly Jerusalem, illuminations include seventy-seven colourful capital letters at the start of the books of the Bible and the other main texts, six running the height of a whole page. Gold is used only for those at the beginning of the Gospels of Mark and Matthew. Apart from a portrait of Josephus and a squirrel, all the other artwork is geometrical or depicts flora. In addition, there are two images of Heaven and Earth during their creation.

By the mid-17th century after various travels around Europe, the Codex was housed in the Swedish Royal Library in Stockholm, which burned to the ground on 7 May 1697. The Codex was only saved by a quick-thinking librarian who threw it out of the window (an urban legend suggests it injured the person it fell on below).

ALSO ON THIS DAY 558: Dome of the Hagia Sophia, Constantinople, collapses after an earthquake · **1840:** Death of German painter Caspar David Friedrich (*see* 8 February) · **1899:** English sculptor Alfred Gerrard born

8 MAY

Benjamin Haydon enjoys a Reynolds retrospective, 1813

Sir Joshua's exhibition opened. The first impression on my mind was certainly that of flimsiness. They looked faint, notwithstanding the effect was so judiciously arranged. Sir Joshua's modes of conveying ideas were colour & light and shadow; of form, he knew nothing. The consequence was he hinted to his eye & untrained hand, and with great labour & bungling, modelled out his feelings with a floating richness, an harmonious depth, and a gemmy brilliancy that was perhaps encreased by his perpetual repetitions, and which renders him as great a master of colour as ever lived. Of poetical conception of character as it regards portrait, he had a singular share. How delightful are his portraits, their artless simplicity, their unstudied grace, their chaste dignity, their retired sentiment command us, enchant us, subdue us.

The exhibition does great credit to the Directors of the British Gallery. It will have a visible effect on art; it will raise the character of the English School; it will stop that bigotted, deluded, absurd propensity for Leonardo Da Vincis & insipid Correggios, and as men who shared Sir J's friendship and been soothed by his manners, it does credit to their hearts as men.

Benjamin Haydon, diary entry,
8 May 1813

English painter and diarist Benjamin Haydon (1786–1846; *see* 11 July) was in fine company for the preview night of the blockbuster exhibition celebrating the work of portrait painter Sir Joshua Reynolds (1723–1792; *see also* 10 July) at the British Institution in Pall Mall, London. Guest of honour that evening was the Prince Regent and among the famous faces also present were Lord Byron and actress Sarah Siddons whose seated portrait by Reynolds was extremely prominently displayed.

Security was upped for the expected large crowds of visitors over the next three months (including the novelist Jane Austen), including bringing the protective rail 15 cm (6 inches) further into the rooms and raising it to 1 metre (3 feet) high. Opening hours were also extended, lighting was improved and extra attendants employed.

The 141 works by Reynolds were displayed thematically instead of chronologically, his full-length portrait of George III, labelled number 1 in the accompanying one-shilling catalogue, hanging opposite the portrait of Queen Charlotte and next to the popular one of Siddons.

In his preface to the catalogue, art collector and writer Richard Payne Knight said that the Institution's intention was to use Reynolds's art 'to call attention generally to British, in preference to Foreign Art and to oppose the genuine excellence of modern, to the counterfeited semblance of ancient productions, which too frequently usurp its place'.

A painstaking reconstruction of the show is available online at www. whatjanesaw.org.

ALSO ON THIS DAY **1639**: Italian painter Giovanni Battista Gaulli born · **1889**: Vincent van Gogh enters the Saint-Paul asylum in Saint-Rémy-de-Provence (*see* 23 December) · **1903**: Death of French painter Paul Gauguin (*see* 9 June)

9 MAY

Mr Punch is reported in England, 1662

Up and to my office, and so to dinner at home, and then to several places to pay my debts, and then to Westminster to Dr Castle, who discoursed with me about Privy Seal business, which I do not much mind, it being little worth, but by Watkins's late sudden death we are like to lose money. Thence to Mr de Cretz, and there saw some good pieces that he hath copied of the King's pieces, some of Raphael and Michael Angelo [*sic*]; and I have borrowed an Elizabeth of his copying to hang up in my house, and sent it home by Will. Thence with Mr Salisbury, who I met there, into Covent Garden to an ale-house, to see a picture that hangs there, which is offered for 20*s*., and I offered fourteen – but it is worth much more money – but did not buy it, I having no mind to break my oath. Thence to see an Italian puppet play that is within the rayles there, which is very pretty, the best that ever I saw, and great resort of gallants. So to the Temple and by water home, and so walk upon the leads, and in the dark there played upon my flageolette, it being a fine still evening, and so to supper and to bed.

Samuel Pepys, diary entry, 9 May 1662

It was a busy day of art for English diarist Samuel Pepys (1633–1703; *see also* 17 March). As well as calling in on the court painter Emmanuel de Critz (whose father John was serjeant-painter to the king from 1603), he also made the first recorded mention of Mr Punch in England.

Punch evolved from his less violent Italian predecessor Pulcinella who featured in commedia dell'arte theatre. The performance seen by Pepys was by 'Signor Bologna', aka Italian puppeteer Pietro Gimonde, using marionettes rather than the now familiar hand puppets, and its Covent Garden site in London is commemorated by a plaque. The show must have made quite an impact – later that year, Gimonde performed for King Charles II.

Pepys obviously enjoyed the show as he went to another, probably by puppeteer Anthony Devoto, on 10 November with his wife Elisabeth, as he writes: 'Thence to my brother's, and taking my wife up, carried her to Charing Cross, and there showed her the Italian motion, much after the nature of what I showed her a while since in Covent Garden. Their puppets here are somewhat better, but their motions not at all.'

ALSO ON THIS DAY 1825: English painter James Collinson born · **1885:** Maltese painter Gianni Vella born · **1935:** English book illustrator Roger Hargreaves born

10 MAY

London's National Gallery opens to the public, 1824

The Earl of Liverpool acquaints the Board, that his Majesty's Government having deemed it to be highly expedient that an opportunity which presented itself of purchasing the choice collection of pictures belonging to the late Mr Angerstein for the use of the public should not be lost, he had entered into a negotiation with the executors and representatives of that gentleman, and had concluded an agreement for the purchase of the whole collection.... Lord Liverpool further states to the Board, that he has made an arrangement with the executors, and with Mr J. J. Angerstein, for the occupation of the house in Pall Mall where the pictures now are, during the remainder of the term for which it is held by Mr Angerstein, at the rent which he pays for it.

**British government Treasury minute,
23 March 1824**

The art collection of Russian-born businessman and art collector John Julius Angerstein (1735–1823) was so impressive that on his death the British government decided to buy thirty-eight of his paintings for £57,000 and display them in his London house at 100 Pall Mall.

The list of painters represented reads like a Who's Who, including Titian, Van Dyck, Carracci, Poussin, Domenichino, Velázquez, Raphael, Correggio, Cuyp, Reynolds and Rembrandt. Among the works were Flemish painter Sir Peter Paul Rubens's *Rape of the Sabine Women*, Italian painter Sebastiano del Piombo's *Raising of Lazarus*, French artist Claude Lorrain's *Embarkation of the Queen of Sheba*, and English painter and cartoonist William Hogarth's Marriage á-la-Mode series.

The Treasury minute of 23 March 1824 goes on to record that Lord Liverpool stated the new museum would of course need staffing, including a keeper of the gallery, an assistant keeper, 'a respectable person to attend in the two principal rooms during the time of public view, to prevent persons touching or injuring the pictures', another person to attend the lower room, a porter and a housemaid. Other expenses included coals, candles, and 'a small quantity of stationery'.

After its opening on 10 May, the gallery was not an unqualified success because it was too small for the crowds who visited it, among them novelist Anthony Trollope, who called it 'dingy, dull, ill-adapted for the exhibition of the treasures it held'. The gallery moved to a new home in Trafalgar Square in 1838 (*see also* 30 May).

ALSO ON THIS DAY **1818:** Death of American engraver Paul Revere · **1849:** Death of Japanese painter Katsushika Hokusai · **1891:** Egyptian sculptor Mahmoud Mokhtar born

Ottawa's *Man with Two Hats* is unveiled, 2002

During the Second World War, Canadian soldiers played a crucial role in the liberation of the Netherlands. With the donation of this monument – an expression of joy and a celebration of freedom – the Netherlands pays a lasting tribute to Canada.

A statue identical to this one stands in Apeldoorn in the Netherlands. The twin monuments symbolically link Canada and the Netherlands; though separated by an ocean, the two countries will forever be close friends.

Her Royal Highness Princess Margriet of the Netherlands unveiled the monument in Ottawa on May 11, 2002, and the other one in Apeldoorn on May 2, 2000.

Plaque inscription on the Netherlands–Canada Liberation Monument, Commissioners Park, Ottawa

Canadian soldiers played a key part in the defeat of Nazi forces in the Netherlands, particularly from April 1945, when they cleared the cities of Arnhem and Apeldoorn, until the surrender of the enemy forces nationwide the following month. Approximately 7,600 Canadian soldiers were killed in the fighting. During the German occupation, various members of the Dutch royal family escaped to Canada and Princess Margriet was born in Ottawa in 1943.

The two identical bronze *Man with Two Hats* monuments by Dutch sculptor Henk Visch (b. 1950) commemorate this alliance and the ongoing friendship between the two nations. Each man stands 4.6 metres (15 feet) high, his hands reaching up outspread, a hat in each hand. Princess Margriet unveiled the Canadian monument on 11 May 2002, having done the same two years previously in the Netherlands.

ALSO ON THIS DAY 1901: American painter Gladys Davis born · **1918:** English painter Paul Nash's exhibition 'The Void of War' opens at Leicester Galleries, London · **1932:** Italian fashion designer Valentino Garavani born

Dürer keeps his accounts
up to date, 1521

On Sunday after our Lord's Ascension-day Master Dietrich, the Antwerp glasspainter, invited me and asked many others to meet me; and amongst them especially Alexander the goldsmith, a rich, stately man, and we had a costly feast and they did me great honour. I made the portrait in charcoal of Master Marx, the goldsmith who lives at Bruges. I bought a broad cap for 36 stivers. I paid Paul Geiger 1 fl. to take my little box to Nürnberg and 4 stivers. for the letter. I took the portrait of Ambrosius Hochstetter in charcoal and dined with him. I have also eaten with Tomasin at least six times. I bought some wooden dishes and platters for 3 stivers. I paid the apothecary 12 stivers. I gave away two copies of the *Life of our Lady* – the one to the foreign surgeon, the other to Marx's house-servant. I also paid the Doctor 8 stivers. I paid 4 stivers. for cleaning an old cap, lost 4 stivers. at play. I paid 2 fl. for a new cap, and have exchanged the first cap, because it was clumsy, and added 6 stivers. more for another.

I have painted the portrait of a Duke in oils. I have made a very fine and careful portrait in oils of the Treasurer Lorenz Sterk; it was worth 25 fl. I presented it to him and in return he gave me 20 fl. and Susanna 1 fl. *trinkgeld*. Likewise painted the portrait of Jobst my host very finely and carefully in oils. He has now given me his for his. And his wife have I done again and made her portrait in oils.

Albrecht Dürer, diary entry,
12 May 1521

From 1512 until he died in 1519, Holy Roman Emperor Maximilian I was the patron of German painter and printmaker Albrecht Dürer (1471–1528; *see also* 5 August). Worried that Maximilian's death might mean the end of financial support from his successor Charles V, Dürer set off to the Netherlands to meet the new ruler at his coronation in Aachen.

During his journey between 1520 and 1521 (*see also* 27 August) he kept a detailed diary, in which he not only recorded his meetings with the leading artists of their day, but also gave a comprehensive list of his expenses along the way, including the cost of accommodation, his gambling losses and what he paid for works of art (as well as how much he made from the sale of his own) – in effect a ledger. As a result, it provides valuable evidence for the value of art in this period.

ALSO ON THIS DAY **1812:** English painter and illustrator Edward Lear born (*see* 3 February) · **1828:** English painter Dante Gabriel Rossetti born (*see* 30 August) · **1921:** German sculptor and art theorist Joseph Beuys born

13 MAY

John Ruskin writes to his father as his European tour begins, 1858

I mean to write my diary as much as I can by letter; it will amuse mamma and you and be just as useful to me as if in a book.

**John Ruskin, letter to his father,
13 May 1858**

English art critic and author John Ruskin (1819–1900) wrote more than one hundred letters, almost daily, to his father on his four-month tour of France, Switzerland and elsewhere in Europe in 1858. He spent his time drawing and also tracking down some of the locations of J. M. W. Turner's paintings (*see* 16 April) after he had spent the previous year cataloguing the vast collection of work Turner had left to the nation.

Following his letter of 13 May, he wrote to his father seven days later:

Rheinfelden – If you want to see where I am, just call at the National Gallery as soon as you go back to town, and ask Wornum to let you look at the frames Nos. 86, 87, 88, 89, 90; they are all very like, except only that the town, which Mr Turner has made about the size of Strasburg, consists of one street and a few lanes, and what he had drawn as mountains are only the wooded Jura but pretty in shape.... But the most beautiful thing of all is the old moat around the whole town, now filled with the sweetest possible gardens, chiefly in flower with white narcissus and deep red tulips – not striped, but one mass of red, bloomed with blue like a plum, and others purple; the grey walls above covered with ivy, and with all their towers yet unfallen: you will see them in Turner's sketches.

Ruskin was a keen traveller from childhood and kept regular diaries. He visited Europe numerous times, with his family as a young child and again as a teenager, and these inspired his appreciation for art. On his first sight of the Alps in 1833 he noted in his journal: 'They were clear as crystal, sharp on the pure horizon sky, and already tinged with rose by the sinking sun...the seen walls of lost Eden could not have been more beautiful.' He made his final trip to the continent in 1888, aged sixty-nine.

ALSO ON THIS DAY **1835:** Death of English architect John Nash · **1882:** French painter and collagist Georges Braque born · **1922:** German graphic designer Otl Aicher born

14 MAY

Volaire paints Vesuvius while it is erupting, 1771

Eruption of Mt. Vesuvius on 14 May 1771 painted onsite by the Chevalier Volaire.

Inscription on Pierre-Jacques Volaire's *The Eruption of Vesuvius*, 1771

The best-known eruption of Mount Vesuvius in Italy was the AD 79 cataclysm that destroyed Pompeii and Herculaneum. Further eruptions continued sporadically until the 14th century when it became dormant. From the early 17th century, activity recommenced and by the time French landscape artist Pierre-Jacques Volaire (1729–1802) moved to Rome in 1764 and on to Naples in 1769, things were very much hotting up.

Indeed, Volaire was in the right place at the right time when the volcano erupted again in 1771 and his depiction of the event marries the violent drama of the lava flow with the unperturbed air of refined onlookers and their pet dog. Other details include three appearances of Saint Januarius, patron saint of Naples invoked against volcanic eruptions: as a statue on a bridge, as an icon held aloft as a defensive tactic and as a print venerated by women lying on the ground. As the inscription on the painting suggests, Volaire was eager to emphasize that he was working 'live' as the eruption unfolded.

Volaire was best known for his gentle landscapes and seascapes, often set at night, but was so keen on this subject matter that he painted thirty canvases of the volcanic event, which became much in demand from travellers on a Grand Tour of Europe, for whom Naples and the volcano were a major destination.

Volaire's eruption paintings inspired many others, in particular English artist Joseph Wright of Derby (who was unfortunate enough to miss first-hand eruptions himself).

ALSO ON THIS DAY **1727**: English painter Thomas Gainsborough baptized (*see* 10 July) · **1771**: English photography pioneer Thomas Wedgwood born · **1967**: Cathedral of Christ the King, Liverpool, England, is consecrated

15 MAY

Wedgwood's letter marks the start of a friendship, 1762

My much esteemed Friend. If you will give me leave to call you so, and will not think the address too free I shall not care how Quakerish, or otherwise antique, it may sound, as it perfectly corresponds with the sentiments I have, and wish to continue towards you, nor is there a day passes, but I reflect with a pleasing gratitude upon the many kind offices I receiv'd in my confinement at your hospitable town. My good doctor, and you in particular, have my warmest gratitude for the share you had in promoting my recovery, and I know he is too well acquainted with the influence of a good flow of spirits (whatever they are) upon the whole animal economy to refuse you your share of merit in this instance.... Since my return home I have been very busy, but have found time to make an experiment or two upon the aether, the result of which, I have ventured to trouble my good Doctor with; and I can tell you that you, as well as myself, may be thankful if he permits me to write to him on these subjects. You have perhaps this time escaped reading a tedious account of acids and alcalies – precipitation – saturation &c... My respectful compliments wait upon Miss Oats.... Be so kind as to tell Mr Turner I hope to be at Buxton in about three weeks, and should be very glad to see any of my Liverpool friends there.

**Josiah Wedgwood, letter to Thomas Bentley,
15 May 1762**

On a visit to Liverpool in May 1762, English pottery entrepreneur Josiah Wedgwood (1730–1795) had an accident in Warrington and was treated by surgeon Matthew Turner, who introduced him to local businessman Thomas Bentley. Wedgwood wrote the above letter to him soon after returning home and they quickly became very good friends and successful business partners.

Although they were almost exactly the same age, Bentley was rather more cosmopolitan than Wedgwood, who admired and looked up to him. Around nine hundred letters from Wedgwood to Bentley survive, discussing business, local and national stories of the day, family affairs, and issues of mutual interest including the abolition of the slave trade and American independence.

ALSO ON THIS DAY 1930: American painter Jasper Johns born · **1936:** English cartoonist and illustrator Ralph Steadman born · **2019:** American artist Jeff Koons's sculpture *Rabbit* sells for $91.1 million

16 MAY

Grace Pailthorpe paints
May 16th, 1941, 1941

All things considered, I believe in fact that it is better to adopt 'surrealism' than 'supernaturalism' which I had first used. Surrealism does not yet exist in the dictionaries, and it will be more convenient to handle than the supernaturalism already employed by the gentlemen philosophers.

**French writer Guillaume Apollinaire,
letter to the Belgian poet Paul Dermée, March 1917**

Surgeon, art theorist, criminal psychologist and painter Grace Pailthorpe (1883–1971) was the leading British surrealist of her day. Naming her paintings for their day of completion, *May 16th, 1941* is an oil on canvas of what appears to be a lounging foetus and placenta, with a small, red, horse-like figure standing on top of them, all in front of a blue background. The work came during the period in which her art explored the uterus and the baby and their dependency on the mother (the blue in the painting represents amniotic fluid).

Pailthorpe proposed the theory that surrealism was as appropriate a tool to personal understanding of the unconscious mind as psychoanalysis, expounded in depth in her study *The Scientific Aspect of Surrealism* in which she wrote that they both 'strive to free the psychology of the individual from internal conflict so that she or he may function freely'. To this end, she and her partner Reuben Mednikoff (1906–1972) – whom French writer André Breton described as Britain's leading surrealists – would take it in turns to analyse each other's works of art on the basis that every colour and mark had symbolic meaning. They also both contributed work to the 1936 International Surrealist Exhibition in London reviewed by the *Guardian* on 12 June:

> The exhibition of Surrealist art which opens at the Burlington Galleries in London today will no doubt create a stir even among those to whom modern painting usually means nothing. At all events it will give the public something to talk about, for no one can accuse the Surrealists of refusing to deal in definite objects, things that can be described even when they cannot be recognised, things that cast shadows, have weight, volume, and distance; whereas their elder brothers, the abstract painters, deal in nothing more tangible than shape, pattern and colour. The one school uses paint to establish definite references: to the other paint is just paint, a mere means of altering the colour of canvas.

However, Pailthorpe's ideas were controversial and she was expelled from the British Surrealist Group in 1940.

ALSO ON THIS DAY 1827: Dutch architect Pierre Cuypers born · **1906:** German illustrator Margret Rey born · **1959:** The Triton Fountain, Valletta, Malta, is switched on for the first time

17 MAY

Congo the chimpanzee
creates *1st Painting Session*, 1957

It is the work of Congo, not that of the prehistoric cave artists, that can truly be said to represent the birth of art.

**Desmond Morris, in the press release for the
'Ape Artists of the 1950s' exhibition, 2005**

English artist, zoologist, writer and broadcaster Desmond Morris (b. 1928) first began using art in his work with chimpanzees in 1956. From the start, he says it was clear that Congo (1954–1964) had the strongest ability to focus and was the keenest on creating art for art's sake.

Congo made *1st Painting Session* on 17 May 1957 and went on to produce around four hundred drawings and paintings over three years, a high proportion of which depicted an abstract repeating fan pattern rather than anything strongly pictorial. He was so intent on his work that if Morris attempted to stop him before a painting was finished, he would start to scream, but would refuse to continue work on a painting he felt he had already finished. He got no reward for producing any of them.

Sales of Congo's work have been impressive, including exhibitions and an auction in 2005 in which three paintings reached £14,400. Among Congo's fans were Pablo Picasso (who displayed it in his studio), Joan Miró and Salvador Dalí.

ALSO ON THIS DAY **1610:** Italian engraver Stefano della Bella born · **1898:** Canadian painter Alfred Casson born · **1934:** Death of American architect Cass Gilbert

18 MAY

James Gillray on the Princess Royal's bridal evening, 1797

Gillray was marked out and, as it were, predestined for his career by an extraordinary assemblage of qualities: wit, humour, fancy, imagination, boldness of conception and execution, inexhaustible fertility and variety, intuitive knowledge of mankind and unerring quickness of perception, which enabled him to catch the passing follies and fleeting fashions of the gay world as well as the intrigues, corruption and maladministration of the great. He was a painter of manners as well as a political caricaturist, and during the long period covered by his sketches there is hardly a marked step in social progress, hardly a change of costume or national caprice of any kind, that is not fixed and recorded for the amusement of contemporaries and the edification of posterity. The general sense of the value of his works as durable illustrations of our domestic annals, public and private, is shown by the often renewed and constantly increasing demand for copies.

Review of *The Works of James Gillray* in *The Quarterly Review*, 1874

'I will not alter an iota for any Man's opinion upon Earth,' said English caricaturist James Gillray (1756–1815) and he certainly lets everybody have it with both barrels in his work *The Bridal Night*, the third of his coloured etchings focusing on the marriage of Charlotte, Princess Royal (daughter of King George III and his wife, Charlotte; *see also* 6 May) to Frederick, Prince of Württemberg.

Here, Gillray imagines the couple's bridal evening on 18 May 1797 as they are urged towards their bedchamber at Windsor Palace by the great and the good. The thrifty King George carries candles, which have already seen some use, and Prime Minister William Pitt carries a sack of money inscribed £80,000 (the size of the dowry offered by Parliament). Underneath a painting on the wall entitled 'Le Triomphe de l'Amour', which shows a small cupid blowing a trumpet as he sits on an elephant, is a truly obese Prince of Württemberg leading his wife to the nuptial bed (the prince had got increasingly shorter and tubbier in the trilogy of etchings, even though in real life he was a rather tall man). Elsewhere, Gillray shows a tubby Prince of Wales with his mistress the Countess of Jersey rather than the Princess of Wales.

ALSO ON THIS DAY 1822: American photographer Mathew Brady born · **1852:** American photographer Gertrude Käsebier born · **1883:** German architect Walter Gropius born

19 MAY

Magritte explains *Hegel's Holiday*, 1958

When people are asked to apprehend some notion, they often complain that they do not know what they have to think. But the fact is that in a notion there is nothing further to be thought than the notion itself. What the phrase reveals, is a hankering after an image with which we are already familiar. The mind, denied the use of its familiar ideas, feels the ground where it once stood firm and at home taken away from beneath it, and, when transported into the region of pure thought, cannot tell where in the world it is.

Georg Hegel, *Encyclopaedia of the Philosophical Sciences*, 1830

Hegel's Holiday by Belgian artist René Magritte (1898–1967) – a painting of a three-quarter-filled glass of water balanced on top of Magritte's signature motif of an open umbrella – harks back to his early art lessons as a schoolboy when he decorated umbrella stands. In a letter written on 19 May 1958 to his biographer, American artist and writer Suzi Gablik, Magritte includes various sketches indicating his light-hearted train of thought in producing the work, which alludes to the work of the German philospher Georg Hegel (1770–1831). He describes how he wanted to paint a glass of water with genius rather than in a conventional way and his sketches suggested to him the kind of opposing functions – repelling and containing water – that would have appealed to Hegel.

He also wrote to the Greek dealer and collector Alexandre Iolas about the painting in November that year, explaining he had initially decided against including Hegel in the title because of the Nazis interest in him and his theories.

ALSO ON THIS DAY 1593: French painter Claude Vignon born · **1898:** Italian painter Julius Evola born · **1929:** Australian painter Richard Larter born

20 MAY

John Callcott Horsley
attacks the nude in art, 1885

Can any one venture to deny at an exhibition purporting to be for general edification or entertainment, no picture should find place before which a modest woman may not stand hanging on the arm of father, brother or lover without a burning sense of shame.... Women artists as yet seem content to shame their sex by representation of female nudity; it needs but pictures of unclothed men, true to life, executed by the same skilful hands, to complete the degradation of our galleries and walls.

John Callcott Horsley, 'A Woman's Plea',
letter to *The Times*, 20 May 1885

Under the pseudonym of 'British Matron', Royal Academician and Treasurer John Callcott Horsley (1817–1903; *see also* 17 December) stepped up his campaign against nude female models in art by writing a letter to *The Times*, which was printed on 20 May 1885. Horsley had strong views on the matter and the previous year had blackballed a bronze *Dryope* by Robert Barrett Browning, son of the more famous English poets.

That year, there were more nudes than usual featured in the Royal Academy's annual exhibition with various paintings, such as John Collier's *Circe*, causing raised eyebrows due to their realism rather than harking back to classical naked figures. Albert Moore's *White Hydrangea* was deliberately scratched by a member of the public in protest. Horsley went so far as to call for a boycott of galleries that he believed were displaying this offensive material.

Horsley's letter, backed by those who were campaigning for purity in general in public life, precipitated a heated debate about nudes in art.

ALSO ON THIS DAY 1570: The first modern atlas *Theatrum Orbis Terrarum* by Dutch cartographer Abraham Ortelius is first printed · **1726:** English painter Francis Cotes born · **1840:** York Minster sustains significant fire damage

21 MAY

Michelangelo's *Pietà*
is attacked, 1972

To this work let no sculptor, however rare a craftsman, ever think to be able to approach in design or in grace, or ever to be able with all the pains in the world to attain to such delicacy and smoothness or to perforate the marble with such art as Michelangelo did therein, for in it may be seen all the power and worth of art. Among the lovely things to be seen in the work, to say nothing of the divinely beautiful draperies, is the body of Christ; nor let anyone think to see greater beauty of members or more mastery of art in any body, or a nude with more detail in the muscles, veins and nerves over the framework of the bones, nor yet a corpse more similar than this to a real corpse. Here is perfect sweetness in the expression of the head, harmony in the joints and attachments of the arms, legs and trunk, and the pulses and veins so wrought, that in truth Wonder herself must marvel that the hand of a craftsman should have been able to execute so divinely and so perfectly, in so short a time, a work so admirable; and it is certainly a miracle that a stone without any shape at the beginning should ever have been reduced to such perfection as Nature is scarcely able to create in the flesh. Such were Michelangelo's love and zeal together in this work, that he left his name – a thing that he never did again in any other work – written across a girdle that encircles the bosom of Our Lady. And the reason was that one day Michelangelo, entering the place where it was set up, found there a great number of strangers from Lombardy, who were praising it highly, and one of them asked one of the others who had done it, and he answered, 'Our Gobbo from Milan'. Michelangelo stood silent, but thought it something strange that his labours should be attributed to another; and one night he shut himself in there, and, having brought a little light and his chisels, carved his name upon it.

Giorgio Vasari on Michelangelo's *Pietà*,
Lives of the Most Eminent Painters, Sculptors and Architects, **1568**

Italian Renaissance painter and sculptor Michelangelo (1475–1564; *see also* 1 November) carved the *Pietà*, one of his most famous works, out of a single block of Carrara marble following a commission on 27 August 1498. It came from French cardinal Jean de Bilhères who saw it as a way to support a political Franco-Italian marriage. Nearly five hundred years later, unemployed Hungarian geologist Laszlo Toth leapt over an altar railing in St Peter's Basilica in the Vatican City and smashed a hammer into Michelangelo's *Pietà* a dozen times, damaging the Virgin Mary's nose, eyelid and forearm.

Opinions were divided about the restoration of the *Pietà* – including those that argued it should remain entirely unrestored or clearly indicate where work had taken place on the damaged elements. It took five months to simply assemble all the chips and fragments and work out where they all fitted. In the end, the statue underwent 'integral restoration' to return it to its original state as invisibly as possible, before it was then placed in its current position in St Peter's – behind a panel of bulletproof glass.

ALSO ON THIS DAY 1471: German painter and engraver Albrecht Dürer born (*see* 12 May) · **1844:** French painter Henri Rousseau born · **1996:** Death of Estonian art historian and critic Villem Raam

Whistler on the importance
of *Whistler's Mother*, 1878

The vast majority of English folk cannot and will not consider a picture as a picture, apart from any story which it may be supposed to tell.

My picture of a 'Harmony in Grey and Gold' is an illustration of my meaning – a snow scene with a single black figure and a lighted tavern. I care nothing for the past, present or future of the black figure, placed there because the black was wanted at that spot. All that I know is that my combination of grey and gold is the basis of the picture. Now this is precisely what my friends cannot grasp....

As music is the poetry of sound, so is painting the poetry of sight, and the subject matter has nothing to do with harmony of sound or of colour....

Art should be independent of all clap-trap – should stand alone, and appeal to the artistic sense of eye or ear, without confounding this with emotions entirely foreign to it, as devotion, pity, love, patriotism and the like. All these have no kind of concern with it, and that is why I insist on calling my works 'arrangements' and 'harmonies'.

Take the picture of my mother, exhibited at the Royal Academy as an 'Arrangement in Grey and Black'. Now that is what it is. To me it is interesting as a picture of my mother; but what can or ought the public to care about the identity of the portrait?

The imitator is a poor kind of creature. If the man who paints only the tree, or flower, or other surface he sees before him were an artist, the king of artists would be the photographer. It is for the artist to do something beyond this: in portrait painting to put on canvas something more than the face the model wears for that one day; to paint the man, in short, as well as his features; in arrangement of colours to treat a flower as his key, not as his model.

James McNeill Whistler, 'The Red Rag' in 'Celebrities at Home.
No. XCII. Mr Whistler at Cheyne-Walk', *The World* **magazine, 22 May 1878**

The 1871 oil painting *Whistler's Mother* (officially titled *Arrangement in Grey and Black, No. 1*) by American-born artist James McNeill Whistler (1834–1903; *see also* 29 July) became his most famous and gave him the opportunity to expound on his belief in 'art for art's sake'.

23 MAY

Sir William Orpen's 'War' exhibition opens, 1918

I wish to note two things about the exhibition. The first is that it demonstrates an untruth. War is monotonous. It is hellishly monotonous. This is the opinion of all soldiers, and it is the opinion of all artists who have seen the war. It is certainly the opinion of those who, like myself, are engaged in the affair of collocating the war-work of artists with a view to obtaining a more or less complete artistic record of the war. A famous art critic said to me: 'The mischief is that in war there are only six subjects for a painter.' Monotony is therefore inevitable. But William Orpen comes along and brilliantly disproves what everybody else knows in his heart to be a profound truth. So that we are obliged to limit the axiom a little and say: 'War is monotonous – for all men except William Orpen.' He has found, not sixty innumerable different subjects.... These pictures are painted in a new manner – in the artist's 'war' manner – very broadly, very rapidly, sometimes very summarily, perhaps thinly. Their success is largely due, apart from the reality of the inspiration, to an extreme competence in the choice and employment of means.

The second thing I wish to note is the singular freshness of vision, evoking a truly remarkable vivacity of invention, chiefly in the composition. William Orpen, having discovered a new subject, composes it newly. His resourcefulness is as reliable and unerring as that of Mozart. Landscape, shell-holes, ruined trees and buildings, dug-outs, tents, and the tragedy and comedy of human existence – he sees them as though nobody had ever seen them pictorially before; and he arranges them in fresh patterns of contour, colour and plane. His ingenuity in manipulating the material is simply endless, and yet he is never tempted to falsify the material.

English novelist Arnold Bennett,
preface to the 'War' exhibition catalogue, 1918

Irish painter Sir William Orpen (1878–1931) was an official war artist during the First World War, working on the Western Front. His work focused on all aspects of war – the everyday as well as the senior ranks – and on soldiers of both sides.

He donated 138 artworks to the British government and on 23 May 1918, 'War: Paintings and Drawings Executed on the Western Front' opened in London. This exhibition of his works, including *Dead Germans in a Trench*, was very popular, attracting nine thousand visitors in its month-long run. After the war, Orpen concentrated on portraiture, which had been his speciality before 1914.

ALSO ON THIS DAY 1860: English painter Dante Gabriel Rossetti marries his model Elizabeth Siddal in Hastings · **1910:** English architect Hugh Casson born · **2014:** Fire causes major damage to Glasgow School of Art's Charles Rennie Mackintosh building (*see also* 15 December)

24 MAY

Tunnicliffe and Williamson discuss *Tarka the Otter*, 1932

Very many thanks for sending it to me. It has kept me sizzling with joy for three weeks. The best thing I've met for ever so long. Fresh, hopeful, fecund and so, so, careful. It is heartening to see a writer caring much for his words, and chasing and chiselling them with such firmness. I hope he likes it well enough to persevere, for I shall look forward to reading him again – apart from *Tarka*, which I'll read many times yet.

British writer T. E. Lawrence on *Tarka the Otter*, letter to the critic Edward Garnett, 20 January 1928

Early editions of the bestselling nature novel *Tarka the Otter* (1927) by English author Henry Williamson (1895–1977) featured jacket designs by English dancer and artist Hester Sainsbury and Australian artist William Kermode. But the most popular of the book's illustrators was Charles F. Tunnicliffe (1901–1979).

In March 1932, Williamson's publisher Constant Huntington wrote to him to say that he had received out of the blue a bundle of sample illustrations for *Tarka* from the then unknown Tunnicliffe. He was impressed and suggested

Williamson take a look (although he also indicated that Welsh artist Lionel Edwards might be a better bet).

Williamson was indeed interested in the enclosed aquatints of otters and on 24 May Tunnicliffe visited the author at his home in Devon. Over the next few days they explored the area and Tunnicliffe was commissioned to provide wood engravings for an illustrated edition of *Tarka*. He sent early work two weeks later from his home in Macclesfield and over the coming months he and Williamson wrote regularly to each other. Tunnicliffe also made several visits to the area to ensure his work was accurate and by the middle of August he had finished.

The book was published later that year with twenty-three of his full-page woodcuts and sixteen line drawings. It was the first of a long and productive relationship between the two men, with Tunnicliffe illustrating many of Williamson's other works, including *The Old Stag* and *Salar the Salmon*.

Tunnicliffe went on to become particularly famous for his illustrations of wildlife and especially birds. He provided work for Brooke Bond tea cards and reached a wide audience of young readers with his work on *The Farm* and 'What To Look For' series about seasonal flora and fauna for Ladybird Books.

Welsh watercolour artist Lionel Edwards, mentioned by Huntington in his letter, also focused on animal illustration, concentrating on horses and hunting scenes for magazines such as *Country Life* and *The Field* as well as dozens of books.

ALSO ON THIS DAY **1683:** Ashmolean Museum opens in Oxford, England · **1830:** Russian painter Alexei Savrasov born · **1883:** Brooklyn Bridge in New York City opens to traffic

25 MAY

David finishes a second
Napoleon Crossing the Alps, 1801

[NAPOLEON] Sit? What good will that do? Do you believe that the great men of antiquity whose images we had sat?

[JACQUES-LOUIS DAVID] But Citizen First Consul, I shall paint you for your century, for men who have seen you, who know you. They will want a likeness.

[NAPOLEON] A likeness? It's not the accuracy of the features, a wart on the nose that produces a likeness. It is the character that animates the painting. Nobody asks if the portraits of great men are good likenesses, it's enough that their genius is alive.

Antoine-Claire Thibaudeau,
Histoire Générale de Napoléon Bonaparte, **1828**

In May 1800, in a bid to surprise Austrian forces in Italy, Napoleon (1769–1821), now self-appointed First Consul of France, made a successful crossing of the Alps through the Great St Bernard Pass. With his reinforcements, he went on to a famous victory at the Battle of Marengo.

The episode was commemorated in a series of five near-identical oil paintings by French artist Jacques-Louis David (1748–1825) called *Napoleon Crossing the Alps*. A fully uniformed Napoleon is shown in a mountainous scene on his rearing horse, his extended arm and hand gesturing onwards and upwards, looking squarely towards the viewer, his cloak blowing magnificently around him. On the rocks in the foreground is inscribed 'Hannibal'.

Napoleon had strong views not only on how he should be represented but also on how the painting should be completed, and was especially resolute on his insistence not to sit for the portrait as the above exchange reported by French politician Antoine-Claire Thibaudeau indicates. In fact, Napoleon had sat for David for a previous portrait, although only for a couple of hours, which David felt was entirely insufficient. So instead of the great man himself, David used Napoleon's bust, his son as a body model and borrowed Napoleon's uniform. Luckily, Napoleon's horses were more biddable than their master and were happy to sit for David.

On 25 May 1801, David finished the second portrait and Napoleon visited to enjoy the result.

ALSO ON THIS DAY 1869: Canadian art critic Robbie Ross born · **1899:** Death of French painter and sculptor Rosa Bonheur (*see* 30 July) · **1962:** The new Coventry Cathedral is consecrated, designed by Scottish architect Basil Spence and including artwork by painter John Piper (*see* 10 November) and sculptor Sir Jacob Epstein

The Beatles release
their *Sgt. Pepper's* album, 1967

My dealer was a friend of the Beatles and the Stones, and he suggested they used a fine artist. I talked to the Beatles at length about what the cover would be. I worked out it would show the moment after they had played in a bandstand in the park. My big contribution was the life-size cutouts, the magic crowds.

**Sir Peter Blake, Hay Festival,
2 June 2004**

The front-cover image on the album *Sgt. Pepper's Lonely Hearts Club Band* – of the Beatles surrounded by famous faces, mostly from the 20th century – was devised and produced by English artist Sir Peter Blake (b. 1932), his wife American artist Jann Haworth (b. 1942) and British photographer Michael Cooper (1941–1973). The list of who was to appear was put together with input from each of the Beatles (except Ringo who was happy to go with whatever everybody else decided), Blake and Haworth, although it had to be slightly limited to include only those who gave their permission – actress Mae West was among those who required some sweet talking.

There are several artists on the cover in addition to the Fab Four and Stuart Sutcliffe (1940–1962), who left the band to pursue a career as an artist:

- American painter and illustrator Richard Merkin (1938–2009), described by writer Tom Wolfe as 'the greatest of that breed, the Artist Dandy, since Sargent, Whistler and Dali'
- Italian-American Sabato Rodia (1879–1965) who designed the Watts Towers in Los Angeles
- English erotic illustrator and key member of the aesthetic movement Aubrey Beardsley (1872–1898)
- American collagist and filmmaker Wally Berman (1926–1976)
- German-American painter Richard Lindner (1901–1978)
- American sculptor Larry Bell (b. 1939)
- American anti-military printmaker, carpenter and sculptor H. C. 'Cliff' Westermann (1922–1981).

27 MAY

Darwin complains about his photographic look, 1855

You ask about my photograph; I have been done at the [Literary Scientific and Portrait] club; but if I really have as bad an expression as my photograph gives me, how I can have one single friend is surprising. My brother has a large drawing of me, by [Samuel] Lawrence, of which he has had some photographs made & no doubt, if anyone really wished, others could be made.

**Charles Darwin, letter to Sir Joseph Dalton Hooker,
27 May 1855**

English naturalist Charles Darwin (1809–1882; *see also* 10 January) was fascinated by photography, using it not only in his works such as *Expression and Emotions in Man and Animal* (1872) but also exchanging regular photo portraits, or 'cartes de visites', with friends and colleagues, especially botanist Sir Joseph Dalton Hooker.

Indeed, Darwin had numerous photographs taken of him, the earliest a daguerreotype in 1842 (the process had only just been invented) with his son William. However, he did not like them all, including the one taken professionally by Maull and Polyblank, which he mentions in his letter to Hooker on 27 May 1855. 'For Heaven-sake oblige me & burn that now hanging up in your room. It makes me look atrociously wicked,' he later wrote to Hooker on 17 December 1860.

By the 1860s his pictures now included his famous beard and his fame brought many more requests for his photo portrait. Celebrity photographer Julia Margaret Cameron photographed him on a family visit to her home on the Isle of Wight, but by 1869 he had become fed up of the constant demand, which he found overly time-consuming. He wrote to his German translator

Adolph Meyer, 'I cannot endure the thought of sitting again, and I have refused 3 or 4 photographers lately.'

ALSO ON THIS DAY 1849: The Great Hall at Euston railway station in London opens · **1873:** German archaeologist Heinrich Schliemann uncovers the Priam's Treasure hoard in Troy/ Hisarlik, Turkey · **1921:** English animator Bob Godfrey born

28 MAY

A statue of Sir Tim Berners-Lee is unveiled, 2015

Henry was interested in the paradox inherent in the impact of Berners-Lee's invention and his self-effacing demeanour. Henry's sculpted figures are usually anonymous, and in this portrait he has retained the idea of his subject as 'everyman', through the casual pose and clothing. The depiction of his sitter is resolutely contemporary, but the use of bronze has a timeless and permanent quality appropriate for a sitter with such a significant legacy.

Associate Curator Rosie Broadley, National Portrait Gallery, London, in gallery press release announcing the unveiling of Sir Tim Berners-Lee statue, 28 May 2015

The first portrait of Sir Tim Berners-Lee (b. 1955), the English computer scientist and inventor of the World Wide Web, was a painted bronze by sculptor Sean Henry (b. 1965), which was commissioned by the National Portrait Gallery in London and unveiled at the gallery on 28 May 2015.

Berners-Lee, who felt he was too often seen in photographs simply sitting behind a computer, is shown standing at two-thirds life-size, holding a leather rucksack (in which he carries his laptop). Henry commented that: 'Tim is a very dynamic person to sculpt, as he has a very active mind, and is active physically too. Above all what came through was his strong sense of purpose, and it felt important to try to capture this in the work.'

ALSO ON THIS DAY 1837: Irish architect George Ashlin born · **1853:** Swedish painter Carl Larsson born · **1999:** Leonardo da Vinci's *The Last Supper* goes back on display at Santa Maria delle Grazie, Milan, after two decades of restoration

Caravaggio kills
Ranuccio Tomassoni, 1606

Michelangelo Amerigi [Caravaggio's birth name] was a satirical and haughty man; and he sometimes spoke ill of past and present painters, however famous.... Michelangelo, out of an overwhelming daring of spirit and wildness, sometimes sought out occasions which could break his neck or endanger others' lives...confronted with Ranuccio Tomassoni, a young man of great grace, over an argument in the game of ball and rope [a type of tennis], they challenged each other to a duel. Ranuccio fell to the ground, and Michelangelo stabbed him in the thigh with the point of his sword, killing him. Everybody fled from Rome, Michelangelo to Pellestrina.

Giovanni Baglione, 'Life of Caravaggio',
in *The Lives of Painters, Sculptors, Architects and Engravers*, 1642

The account by Italian painter Giovanni Baglione (1566–1643) of his fellow artist and countryman's rather wild life is hardly a hagiographic one – he criticizes Caravaggio (1571–1610) for various artistic failings and concentrates on his various run-ins with authorities around Italy and elsewhere in Europe, including his numerous prison sentences. There was certainly bad blood between the two, following a libel case in which Caravaggio criticized Baglione's work.

However, the actual reason for Caravaggio's assault on Tomassoni is unclear. As well as the tennis theory and another involving gambling debts, art critic Andrew Graham-Dixon has argued that the two men were fighting over the affections of a prostitute and Caravaggio was intending to merely castrate Tomassoni rather than kill him. Whatever the cause, Caravaggio was forced to leave Rome in a hurry to escape a death sentence passed by Pope Paul V.

Caravaggio's own death is similarly murky. Suggested causes include malaria, syphilis, sepsis (via a wound from a fight in Naples), lead poisoning or murder (various candidates include some enemies he made while he was living in Malta).

ALSO ON THIS DAY 1797: French painter Louise-Adéone Drölling born · **1921:** Death of American painter Abbott Thayer · **1970:** Death of German-born American sculptor Eva Hesse

The Prince of Wales makes
his 'carbuncle' speech, 1984

It is hard to imagine that London before the last war must have had one of the most beautiful skylines of any great city, if those who recall it are to be believed. Those who do, say that the affinity between buildings and the earth, in spite of the City's immense size, was so close and organic that the houses looked almost as though they had grown out of the earth and had not been imposed upon it – grown moreover, in such a way that as few trees as possible were thrust out of the way.

Those who knew it then and loved it, as so many British love Venice without concrete stumps and glass towers, and those who can imagine what it was like, must associate with the sentiments in one of Aldous Huxley's earliest and most successful novels, *Antic Hay*, where the main character, an unsuccessful architect, reveals a model of London as Christopher Wren wanted to rebuild it after the Great Fire, and describes how Wren was so obsessed with the opportunity the fire gave the city to rebuild itself into a greater and more glorious vision.

What, then, are we doing to our capital city now? What have we done to it since the bombing during the war? What are we shortly to do to one of its most famous areas – Trafalgar Square? Instead of designing an extension to the elegant facade of the National Gallery which complements it and continues the concept of columns and domes, it looks as if we may be presented with a kind of municipal fire station, complete with the sort of tower that contains the siren. I would understand better this type of high-tech approach if you demolished the whole of Trafalgar Square and started again with a single architect responsible for the entire layout, but what is proposed is like a monstrous carbuncle on the face of a much-loved and elegant friend.

The Prince of Wales, speech to mark the 150th anniversary of the Royal Institute of British Architects, Hampton Court Palace, London, 30 May 1984

The speech made by Charles, Prince of Wales, to the Royal Institute of British Architects in May 1984 was entirely unexpected. Instead of simply handing over the Royal Gold Medal to Indian architect Charles Correa, he took the opportunity to make his feelings known about the direction of modern architectural tastes. Earlier in the speech, he called for a more human approach to take note of ordinary people's likes and needs in designing new projects, but it was the 'carbuncle' comment in relation to the proposed National Gallery extension in London's Trafalgar Square that was highlighted in the media.

After the Prince's intervention – or interference as many architects saw it – the planned extension by British architectural firm Ahrends Burton & Koralek was abandoned, to be replaced by a new approach from American architects Robert Venturi and Denise Scott Brown. The final wing was opened in 1991.

ALSO ON THIS DAY 1640: Death of Flemish painter Sir Peter Paul Rubens (*see 26 February*) · **1959:** Auckland Harbour Bridge opens in Auckland, New Zealand · **1989:** Student protestors unveil an enormous Goddess of Democracy statue in Tiananmen Square, Beijing, during protests

31 MAY

Jaume Plensa's sculpture
Dream is unveiled 2009

If we are to improve arts participation rates in St Helens, a town that does not have a strong history or arts engagement, then we need to find ways to reach out to people to provide opportunities for people that would not under normal circumstances consider taking part in the arts to do so. It has been widely demonstrated locally, nationally and internationally that the arts can provide effective ways to address a range of social, economic and environmental issues and engage positively with a wide range of people and communities, including hard to reach groups or individuals. *Dream* is a strikingly successful example of how the arts can have a significant range of positive outcomes – both arts and non-arts – and play a major strategic part in wider policy and change affecting St Helens. A critical reason for the success of the *Dream* is because it was perceived as relevant – in different ways and for different reasons – to a wide range of people who all had to play an active part if the project was to become a reality. We can learn a great deal from this for future working.

St Helens Council, *Consultation Draft Creative St. Helens, 2011–2016,*
21 September 2011

Sutton Manor Colliery in St Helens in the north-east of England started producing coal in 1910, but the colliery site closed in June 1991. To commemorate its history, local authorities commissioned Catalan sculptor Jaume Plensa (b. 1955) to design a piece of public art. After initial plans for a tall miner's lamp were discarded as being too rooted in the past, Plensa's concept of a monumental elongated head and neck of a nine-year-old girl was accepted, her closed-eye contemplative appearance indicating her thoughts about both the future and the site's previous history.

The sculpture is 20 metres (66 feet) high and weighs 500 tonnes (550 short tons). It is cast in concrete and covered in white Spanish dolomite. Overlooking the M62 motorway, vast numbers of cars drive past *Dream* each year, which has been well received since its unveiling in 2009. It inspired writer Frank Cottrell-Boyce's storyline for the opening ceremony of the 2012 Olympic Games in London and is also seen as a companion piece to Antony Gormley's *Angel of the North* (*see* 15 February 1998).

ALSO ON THIS DAY 1860: English painter Walter Sickert born · **1921:** Anglo-Italian jewelry designer Andrew Grima born · **1923:** American painter and sculptor Ellsworth Kelly born

June

Alfred Stieglitz writes a love letter to Georgia O'Keeffe, 1917

It's queer how fond I am of you. – Not at all as man & woman – something so different – It's very wonderful – & it hurts terribly – Hurts in the same way as it hurts when I look at Kitty – my daughter – You have given me so much – just in being – & doing – & I feel so much liked doing – for you – & for her – & one or two others – & I feel so utterly helpless – paralyzed.

How I wanted to photograph you – the hands – the mouth – & eyes – & the enveloped in black body – the touch of white – & the throat – but I didn't want to break into your time – As I wanted to walk into the night – with you too. – I can tell you now – when it can't be – Others wanted you – & I felt they were nearer life than I was – and I wanted you to be with life –

Alfred Stieglitz, letter to Georgia O'Keeffe, 1 June 1917

American photographer Alfred Stieglitz (1864–1946) came across the charcoal drawings of American painter Georgia O'Keeffe (1887–1986; *see also* 20 November) in early 1916 and was so taken with them that he organized an exhibition without telling the artist. Despite this strange start to their relationship, and the fact that Stieglitz was married, the two began writing each other increasingly passionate love letters.

Things came to a head when his wife Emmy returned unexpectedly to their home and found Stieglitz taking nude photographs of O'Keeffe. The couple moved in together and she quickly became his muse. Stieglitz took hundreds of shots of various parts of O'Keeffe's body and exhibited a large number of them in 1921 in a one-man exhibition in New York, although she was not named as the model.

They married in 1924 and spent the rest of their lives together, despite Stieglitz's serious affair with the photographer Dorothy Norman and often living long distances from each other, O'Keeffe painting in New Mexico and Stieglitz in New York, where he constantly promoted her work.

ALSO ON THIS DAY 1509: Italian mathematician Fra Luca Bartolomeo de Pacioli publishes *De divina proportione* about the 'golden ratio' in art, with illustrations by Leonardo da Vinci · **1822:** English photographer Clementina Maude, Viscountess Hawarden born · **1841:** Death of Scottish painter and engraver Sir David Wilkie (his burial in the Bay of Gibraltar is depicted in J. M. W. Turner's *Peace – Burial at Sea*, 1842)

The Sack of Rome begins, 455

On the third day after the tumult, Genseric boldly advanced from the port of Ostia to the gates of the defenceless city. Instead of a sally of the Roman youth, there issued from the gates an unarmed and venerable procession of the bishop at the head of his clergy. The fearless spirit of Leo, his authority and eloquence, again mitigated the fierceness of a Barbarian conqueror; the king of the Vandals promised to spare the unresisting multitude, to protect the buildings from fire, and to exempt the captives from torture; and although such orders were neither seriously given, nor strictly obeyed, the mediation of Leo was glorious to himself, and in some degree beneficial to his country. But Rome and its inhabitants were delivered to the licentiousness of the Vandals and Moors, whose blind passions revenged the injuries of Carthage. The pillage lasted fourteen days and nights; and all that yet remained of public or private wealth, of sacred or profane treasure, was diligently transported to the vessels of Genseric. Among the spoils, the splendid relics of two temples, or rather of two religions, exhibited a memorable example of the vicissitudes of human and divine things.

Edward Gibbon, *The History of the Decline and Fall of the Roman Empire*, 1776–89

There are no detailed accounts of exactly which treasures were taken or destroyed by the Vandals during the extended sacking of Rome in AD 455, which lasted for longer but was probably less intensive than the previous sack in 410 by the Visigoths. However, it was sufficiently notorious to inspire the term 'vandalism', devised more than a thousand years later as a description of the destruction of art after the French Revolution.

The Sack of Rome in 455 was described by contemporary chronicler Prosper of Aquitaine, who observed that while in the main the Vandals did not go on a burning and slaughtering rampage, they did take all the city's wealth (and enslave many inhabitants). The invading forces also destroyed aqueducts and looted Rome's most important temple, the Temple of Jupiter Optimus Maximus on the Capitoline Hill, especially its gold and bronze roof shingles.

ALSO ON THIS DAY 1889: German animator Lotte Reiniger born · **1918:** American comic book illustrator Ruth Atkinson born · **1951:** American artist Gilbert Baker born

Poussin begins the fifth
of his Seven Sacraments, 1647

I have begun my fifth picture, which is to represent Ordination; if the great heat should not prevent me, and God preserves my health, I flatter myself to have finished your seven pictures, within a year.

**Nicolas Poussin, letter to Paul Fréart de Chantelou,
3 June 1647**

French painter Nicolas Poussin (1594–1665; *see also* 8 September) spent a long period of his early working life in Rome, enjoying the patronage of high-ranking churchmen including Cassiano dal Pozzo, secretary to the Pope's nephew Cardinal Francesco Barberini. It was Cassiano who commissioned the magnificent Seven Sacraments series of paintings, which Poussin completed in the early 1640s: *Baptism*, *Confirmation*, *Marriage*, *Penance*, *Ordination*, *Holy Eucharist* and *Extreme Unction*. *Ordination* shows Christ handing the keys of heaven to Peter, as described in Matthew 16:18–19, surrounded by the other disciples. Described by English painter Sir Joshua Reynolds (*see* 8 May) as Poussin's greatest work, the series has sadly now been dispersed.

One of the visitors who enjoyed the paintings was the French ambassador to the Papal Court, Paul Fréart de Chantelou (1609–1694), who asked Poussin to paint a second series along very similar lines. The artist refers to *Ordination*, the fifth in this series, in his letter to Chantelou on 3 June 1647, adding his thanks for the payment of *Penitence* that he had recently sent. Chantelou became an important patron for Poussin and the two conducted a lengthy correspondence over the next twenty years until Poussin's death. Unlike the first series, the second series is still complete and held on loan by the Scottish National Gallery.

ALSO ON THIS DAY 1819: Dutch painter Johan Jongkind born · **1877:** French painter Raoul Dufy born · **1968:** Valerie Solanas shoots American artist Andy Warhol and art critic Mario Amaya

Goebbels plans for the Degenerate Art exhibition, 1937

Germans, come and judge for yourselves!

**Adolf Ziegler, at the opening of the Degenerate Art exhibition,
19 July 1937**

On 4 June 1937, German Nazi politician Joseph Goebbels (1897–1945; *see also* 20 March) noted in his diary that he had had enough of being shown 'hopeless' works of what he called 'art bolshevism' and had determined to organize an exhibition of examples 'from the era of decay' as soon as possible.

Indeed, 1937 was a bumper year for art in Munich, with two shows opening in July. The first was the official Nazi-sanctioned Great German Art Exhibition, which claimed to offer the best of conventional Aryan art (*see* 18 July). The second, which began the following day at the Archaeological Institute of Munich, was the Degenerate Art (*Entartete Kunst*) exhibition, where about 750 works deemed to be ideologically unsound or dangerously experimental were on show. Adolf Hitler was, to put it mildly, not a fan of abstract or Expressionist works and Goebbels records elsewhere in his diaries that the Führer's reaction to the initial selection for the exhibition by his painting czar Adolf Ziegler was apoplectic.

Paintings and sculpture were brought from collections around the country, including *War Cripples* by Otto Dix, *Descent from the Cross* by Max Beckmann (who, on opening day, permanently left Germany) and Wilhelm Lehmbruck's sculpture *Kneeling Woman*. Work was displayed in a manner that ridiculed it, including the use of anti-Semitic captions, as well as suggesting it was unfit for younger gallery-goers by imposing a minimum-age entry barrier of eighteen. Ziegler referred to the artwork on view as 'monstrosities of madness, impudence, inability and degeneration'. More than two million people came through the doors to judge for themselves, about twice the number that attended the official art exhibition.

A follow-up exhibition went on tour around Germany and Austria and was seen by another million people. After this, works were sold off or burned (*see* 20 March).

5 JUNE

Ferris Bueller visits a gallery on his Day Off, 1985

I have touched with a sense of art some people – they felt the love and the life. Can you offer me anything to compare to that joy for an artist?

Mary Cassatt (attributed)

For a 1980s movie about teenagers skipping off high school and running round their city on 5 June 1985 (dated to this day because of the baseball game they watch), *Ferris Bueller's Day Off* (1986) has a surprisingly long and indeed very important section in which Ferris (Matthew Broderick), his girlfriend Sloane (Mia Sara) and his best friend Cameron (Alan Ruck) visit the Art Institute of Chicago.

This was entirely down to the film's director John Hughes (1950–2009), who grew up in Chicago and visited the Institute regularly while at high school, calling it a place of refuge. The paintings clearly shown in the two-minute sequence are all favourites of Hughes, including five Picassos: *Nude Under a Pine Tree*, *The Old Guitarist*, *The Red Armchair*, *Portrait of Sylvette David* and *Seated Woman*; two Kandinskys: *Improvisation No. 30* (*Cannons*) and *Painting With Green Center*; and works by Giacometti (*L'Homme qui marche*), Hopper (*Nighthawks; see* 21 January), Caillebotte (*Paris Street; Rainy Day*), Modigliani (*Jacques and Berthe Lipchitz*), Gauguin (*Day of the God (Mahana No Atua)*), Pollock (*Greyed Rainbow*), David Smith (*Tanktotem No. 1*), Matisse (*Bathers by a River*), Toulouse-Lautrec (*Equestrienne (At the Cirque Fernando)*), Rodin (*Portrait of Balzac*) and Moore (Maquette for UNESCO *Reclining Figure*).

But three more paintings are particularly important. While Ferris and Sloane kiss in front of Belarussian-French artist Marc Chagall's *America Windows*, Cameron stands fixated by *A Sunday Afternoon on the Island of La Grande Jatte* by French painter Georges Seurat. Hughes has commented on this scene in which the camera alternately focuses increasingly closely on Cameron and the image of a child. Produced in a pointillist style, he says that the closer Cameron looks at the child depicted, the less he actually sees, the very feeling he has about himself.

Similarly, Hughes picked *The Child's Bath* by American artist Mary Cassatt – of whom French painter Edgar Degas said 'no woman has a right to draw like that' – as having special relevance for Cameron because it portrays the kind of tenderness between a mother and a child that Cameron never experienced.

In pre-release testings, audiences disliked the museum scene but once the soundtrack was changed – to the Dream Academy's instrumental cover of the Smiths' 'Please, Please, Please Let Me Get What I Want' – and it was moved to a different part of the film, they loved it.

ALSO ON THIS DAY 1801: English architect William Scamp born · **1894:** Cycloramic painting *Racławice Panorama* (by Polish painters Jan Styka, Wojciech Kossak, Ludwig Boller, Tadeusz Popiel, Zygmunt Rozwadowski, Teodor Axentowicz, Włodzimierz Tetmajer, Wincenty Wodzinowski and Michał Sozański) is unveiled in Lwów, Poland (now Lviv in Ukraine) · **2006:** Death of American sculptor Frederick Franck

6 JUNE

Robert Capa photographs
the D-Day landings, 1944

Under the command of General Eisenhower, Allied naval forces, supported by strong air forces, began landing Allied armies on the northern coast of France.

Supreme Headquarters of the Allied Expeditionary Force, Communique No. 1, 6 June 1944

Hungarian-American photojournalist Robert Capa (born Endre Friedmann, 1913-1954) was a war correspondent in Europe during the Second World War. Covering the D-Day landings of American troops for *Life* magazine, he was among the first to land on the Omaha beachhead in Normandy, attached to the US 16th Infantry Regiment, which saw heavy fighting with losses. Capa claimed he took just over one hundred shots but that less than a dozen survived.

In his 1947 book *Slightly Out of Focus,* he describes himself as a gambler and as such decided to head towards the beaches as part of the first wave of soldiers. He records how he began taking photographs before landing and coming under German machine gun fire. These first images were of the men wading into the water from the boat, rifles at the ready. Capa followed them – saying he was barged into the water by an officer – and headed as fast as possible towards a large steel obstacle behind which he hid while a soldier fired away next to him. After shooting a roll and failing to insert a new one in his camera, he panicked and sprinted back to the safety of the boat. He described the beach, which was covered in barbed wire, as the ugliest in the world.

ALSO ON THIS DAY 1710: Augustus the Strong establishes the Royal Polish and Electoral Saxon Porcelain Manufactory at Meissen, Germany · **1756:** American painter John Trumbull born (*see* 26 December) · **2014:** Death of English illustrator Eric Hill

7 JUNE

Millais buys canvas
for *Ophelia*, 1851

There is a willow grows aslant a brook,
That shows his hoar leaves in the glassy stream;
There with fantastic garlands did she come
Of crow-flowers, nettles, daisies, and long purples
That liberal shepherds give a grosser name,
But our cold maids do dead men's fingers call them:
There, on the pendent boughs her coronet weeds
Clambering to hang, an envious sliver broke;
When down her weedy trophies and herself
Fell in the weeping brook. Her clothes spread wide;
And, mermaid-like, awhile they bore her up:
Which time she chanted snatches of old tunes;
As one incapable of her own distress,
Or like a creature native and indued
Unto that element: but long it could not be
Till that her garments, heavy with their drink,

Pull'd the poor wretch from her melodious lay
To muddy death.

**Queen Gertrude in William Shakespeare's *Hamlet*,
Act IV, Scene VII, 1623**

On 7 June 1851, English painter Sir John Everett Millais (1829–1896; *see also* 13 June) bought two pieces of canvas for 15 shillings from fine art materials supplier C. Roberson to begin work on what was to become his most famous painting, *Ophelia*. Inspired by Gertrude's speech in *Hamlet*, Millais showed Ophelia floating downstream and singing before she drowns, a scene not actually shown in William Shakespeare's play.

Millais started first on the landscape element of the painting along the Hogsmill River at Ewell, Surrey, very close to where painter William Holman Hunt (*see* 30 August) was also at work. The detailed flowers in the painting are named in the play, were growing on the riverbank during the five months Millais was on site or have important symbolism, such as the striking red poppy that in the popular Victorian language of flowers indicated sleep and death.

It was not an entirely enjoyable experience for Millais, who wrote to Hunt of his 'martyrdom' and that, in a separate letter to Mrs Combe, he sat 'tailor-fashion under an umbrella throwing a shadow scarcely larger than a half-penny for eleven hours, with a child's mug within reach to satisfy my thirst from the running stream beside me...I am also in danger of being blown by the wind into the water, and becoming intimate with the feelings of Ophelia when that lady sank to muddy death.' When the weather turned really unpleasant, he had a small hut built for him and worked inside.

Once the landscape was completed, Millais added the figure of Ophelia at his studio in London, using nineteen-year-old Elizabeth Siddal as a model. To achieve the right effect, she wore a silver-embroidered dress and lay in a bath of water, catching a nasty cold in the process.

The finished painting received a mixed reception when it was first shown in 1852 at the Royal Academy exhibition in London but has since been admired as a masterpiece.

ALSO ON THIS DAY 1778: English fashion designer and stylist George 'Beau' Brummell born · **1848:** French painter Paul Gauguin born (*see* 9 June) · **1884:** Swedish landscape architect Ester Claesson born

Dostoyevsky makes a speech at the Pushkin Monument unveiling, 1880

A monument not hand-made I have for me erected;
The path to it well-trodden, will not overgrow;
Risen higher has it with unbending head
Than the monument of Alexander.

Alexander Pushkin, 'My Monument', 1836

A speech made by Russian novelist Fyodor Dostoyevsky at the unveiling of the statue of writer Alexander Pushkin (1799–1837) in Moscow was as much about himself and the state of Russia than it was about Pushkin and rather put sculptor Alexander Opekushin's (1838–1923) state-financed commission into the shade. Opekushin had won through following three competitions to find a suitable design; his statue shows Pushkin in a long frock coat and cape. Excerpts from Pushkin's 'My Monument' poem also featured in the final work.

Opekushin designed several other Pushkin statues around the country and numerous other monuments to prominent Russians, including Tsars Alexander II and III, and writer Mikhail Lermontov. His statue of Pushkin has had a longer life than others in the country and is an iconic meeting place in Pushkinskaya Square, which is also popular with political and environmental protestors. It underwent a major restoration in 2017, including the removal of a flowerbed added during the Soviet era that was badly affecting the monument's foundations.

ALSO ON THIS DAY 1829: English painter Sir John Everett Millais born (*see* 7 June) · **1855:** English painter George Haité born · **1867:** American architect Frank Lloyd Wright born (*see* 18 December)

Gauguin arrives in Papeete, Tahiti, 1891

On the night of 8 June, after 63 days of travelling, 63 days of waiting fever-ishly, we made out odd fires that were zigzagging on the sea...we were dis-covering Tahiti. Dawn broke a few hours later, and, approaching slowly from the reefs, we entered the passage and moored without any damage in the harbour.... Life in Papeete quickly became a burden. It was Europe – Europe from which I'd imagined I was freeing myself – under the maddening grip of colonial snobbery, and the imitation, grotesque to the point of caricature, of our customs, fashions, vices and farces of civilisation. Having come so far, it was exactly what I had been fleeing!

Paul Gauguin, *Noa Noa*, 1901

Tired of a Europe he saw as conventional, corrupt and 'filthy', French painter Paul Gauguin (1848–1903; *see also* 23 December) headed for Tahiti, arriving in Papeete by boat on 9 June 1891 after leaving Marseille sixty-nine days earlier. It was not quite what he had hoped for.

Gauguin kept a written record of his time in Tahiti, partly as a kind of cat-alogue for a planned exhibition of his work there, which included paintings, photographs, drawings and woodcuts. It has been suggested that he was somewhat flexible with the truth in his writings in which he reveals he married a thirteen-year-old girl whom he then left behind – with their baby – when he returned to France two years later (*see also* 28 June 1895).

ALSO ON THIS DAY 1311: Italian painter Duccio di Buoninsegna's Maestà altarpiece in Siena Cathedral, Italy, is unveiled · **1849:** Danish painter Michael Ancher born · **1868:** French model Jane Avril (Jeanne Louise Beaudon) born

Zola describes the ageing Cézanne's working routine, 1861

I rarely see Cézanne. A shame. It is not like it was in Aix when we were eighteen and free from concerns for the future. The weight of our lives, working apart, now push us apart. In the morning, Paul goes to the Swiss's house while I stay to write in my room. At eleven o'clock we have lunch, each on our own. Sometimes at noon I go to his house and then he works on my portrait. Next, he draws the rest of the day at Villevielle. He has supper, goes to bed early, and I don't see him again. Is this what I'd hoped for? Paul is still that fine, fanciful chap I knew at school...to convince Cézanne of anything is like managing to get the towers of Notre-Dame to dance a quadrille.

Émile Zola, letter to Baptistin Baille, 10 June 1861

French novelist Émile Zola (1840–1902) and painter Paul Cézanne (1839–1906; *see also* 19 January) had been close friends since their childhood days together in Aix-en-Provence. Together with a third schoolfriend Baptistin Baille, they were known as 'the three inseparables'. Despite his humble upbringing, Zola became wealthy through his writing and was able to act as the initially wealthier Cézanne's patron when he was making little money from his art.

They wrote to each other regularly throughout their lives and the temperamental Cézanne produced a portrait of Zola in the early 1860s. So when Zola wrote *L'Oeuvre* (The Masterpiece) in 1886, which focuses on the art world, he naturally sent a copy to his friend. Unfortunately, Cézanne believed (probably rightly) that one of the characters was based, unflatteringly, on himself and, while he wrote a final, polite, thank-you letter, he also sent back the novel and ended their friendship: 'I have just received *L'Oeuvre* that you kindly sent me. I thank the author of Rougon-Macquart for this fine testimonial of remembrance, and I ask him to let me shake his hand while reflecting on the past. Yours with the feeling of fleeting time.'

ALSO ON THIS DAY 1819: French painter and sculptor Gustave Courbet born · **1880:** French painter André Derain born · **1911:** Rembrandt House Museum opens in Amsterdam

Painter John Constable
is born, 1776

From his first start in life he was always making some great preparation to render himself worthy of notice: a point from which in his own eyes he seemed always receding. He seemed to think his works would never live: and very few of his brother artists either. He certainly underrated himself. Landscape painters are never popular, and had he carried his own style as far as he was desirous, it is doubtful if he had found more admirers.

It was one of the dicta of that time, that in proportion as you individualized, you lost in general effect. Constable's great aim was breadth, tone and moral sentiment. I suppose he meant by moral sentiment that a good picture is calculated to produce a humanizing effect. It is probable that to these ideas he sacrificed detail and correct drawing. It was Constable's persuasion that you should always work in one material: if a watercolour painter, that you should take Nature in watercolour; if an oil painter, in oil. Not that he rigidly carried out his own views, as he always had a small sketchbook with him in which he noted down anything that struck him; but his sketching, both in watercolour and pencil, was very inferior to his oils.

When a young man in Essex, he did a number of oil sketches, which have much of the fine feeling of Gainsborough, of whom he was an enthusiastic admirer, and at that time an imitator. Later he aimed exclusively at originality. There were a great number of oil sketches sold at his sale, done on the principle that there is no outline in nature. They are full of truth and genius, and possess more variety than his pictures. That such productions did not find admirers was not the fault of the artist; but they required to be seen not simply by the eye, but by the mind.

Reverend Henry Scott Trimmer on Constable,
in Walter Thornbury's *Life of J. M. W. Turner*, 1862

English landscape painter John Constable (1776–1837; *see also* 16 October) was born in East Bergholt, Suffolk, in a manor house built in 1774 over three floors by his father. This was considerably larger than the previous family home of Flatford Mill, and had a stable block and courtyard. An increasingly nostalgic

Constable frequently included East Bergholt House in his work, saying: 'This place was the origin of my Fame.' It was pulled down in the early 1840s.

ALSO ON THIS DAY **1144:** Basilica of St Denis, Paris, is dedicated · **1936:** International Surrealist Exhibition opens in Burlington Galleries, London (*see* 16 May) · **1951:** Japanese painter Yasumasa Morimura born

12 JUNE

The inaugural dinner of Omega Workshops, 1913

Potage Alpha Saumon

Crème de Volaille aux Petits Pois

Côtelettes d'Agneau

Haricots verts

Galantine

Salade Russe

Glaces à l'Oméga

Menu at the Omega Workshops inaugural dinner, 12 June 1913

In July 1913, Omega Workshops Ltd opened its doors at 33 Fitzroy Square, London. The brainchild of English painter and writer Roger Fry (1866–1934), and artists Duncan Grant (1885–1978) and Vanessa Bell (1879–1961; *see* 5 May), it produced a wide range of textiles, furniture, stained glass, murals, pottery and mosaics designed by the owners and a variety of other artists on a commission or part-time basis. Larger commissions to design private homes were also taken. All work was produced anonymously to emphasize its intrinsic beauty rather than celebrity designer, and the manufacture was carried out by professional craftsmen and women.

The designs were lively and colourful, heavily influenced by Cubism and Fauvism. 'It is time that the spirit of fun was introduced into furniture and into fabrics,' said Fry. 'We have suffered too long from the dull and the stupidly serious.'

To launch Omega, a special inaugural dinner was held the night before the workshops were officially launched to attract custom from London's richer literati. 'We should get all your disreputable and some of your aristocratic friends to come,' Vanessa Bell wrote to Roger Fry, 'and after dinner we should repair to Fitzroy Sq. where would be decorated furniture, painted walls etc. Then we should all get drunk and dance and kiss. Orders would flow in and the aristocrats would feel sure they were really in the thick of things.'

The menu for the dinner printed here is described by Jans Ondaatje Rolls, author of *The Bloomsbury Cookbook* (2014), as: 'A delicious six-course menu [that] celebrated the brilliant colours and flavours of Post-Impressionism.'

Omega burned brightly, then fizzled out, closing its doors six years later.

ALSO ON THIS DAY 1580: Flemish painter Adriaen van Stalbemt born · **1863:** The Arts Club, London, is founded to promote all creative arts · **1890:** Austrian painter Egon Schiele born (*see* 27 October)

13 JUNE

Lewis Carroll joins the criticism of a Millais painting, 1862

Saw Millais' 'Carpenter's Shop' at Ryman's. It is certainly full of power, but hideously ugly: the faces of the Virgin and Christ being about the ugliest.

Charles Dodgson (Lewis Carroll),
diary entry, 13 June 1862

Lewis Carroll (1832–1898), the author of the *Alice* books (*see* 16 December), was not alone in his dislike of *Christ in the House of his Parents* ('The Carpenter's Shop') by English painter Sir John Everett Millais (1829–1896; *see also* 7 June). The painting is a revolutionary 1849–50 portrait of the Holy Family, a print of which Carroll saw in the shop of James Ryman, a printseller on the high street in Oxford. The subject matter itself was not controversial – in the carpentry shop of his father who is making a door, a youthful Jesus shows his cut hand (a reference to later stigmata) to his mother, while another boy – who will become John the Baptist – carries water to help wash the injury.

What caused the uproar was the realistic style of the portrayal, which *The Times* described as 'revolting'. The shop was untidy and dirty and the figures look realistic rather than idealized. Indeed, Millais had used an actual carpenter's shop as a model, bought two sheep's heads from a local butcher to copy for the sheep in the painting, and used his father to model Joseph's head and his sister-in-law for Mary's.

Writer Charles Dickens was moved to comment about Millais's portrayal of Mary and the boy Jesus in his magazine *Household Words* on 15 June 1850:

> You behold the interior of a carpenter's shop. In the foreground of that carpenter's shop is a hideous, wry-necked, blubbering, red-headed boy, in a bed-gown, who appears to have received a poke in the hand, from the stick of another boy with whom he has been playing in an adjacent gutter, and to be holding it up for the contemplation of a kneeling woman, so horrible in her ugliness, that (supposing it were possible for any human creature to exist for a moment with that dislocated throat) she would stand out from the rest of the company as a Monster, in the vilest cabaret in France, or the lowest ginshop in England.

The furore over the painting – Queen Victoria asked that it be brought to Buckingham Palace so she could see it first hand – brought considerable attention to the Pre-Raphaelite Brotherhood group of which Millais was a member (*see* 30 August) and more generally galvanized the ongoing debate about realism in the arts.

Although Carroll was not a fan of the painting, when artist Henry Holiday came to illustrate the author's *The Hunting of the Snark*, he appears to have paid homage to various of works by Millais, including the arrangement of Mary and Jesus in his fifth engraving, *The Baker's Tale*.

ALSO ON THIS DAY **1863:** English fashion designer Lucy, Lady Duff-Gordon born · **1935:** Bulgarian installation artist Christo Javacheff born (*see* 24 June) · **2007:** Palacio de Bellas Artes, Mexico City, opens the first major exhibition of work by Mexican artist Frida Kahlo (*see* 20 April)

The Shelley Memorial, University College, Oxford, is unveiled, 1893

The passage connecting the large quadrangle and the new building was practically rebuilt in 1894, in connection with a chamber for the reception of Onslow Ford's pathetic marble statue of the drowned Shelley. This work, exquisite in execution, but in conception almost too true to life for the medium of the sculptor's art, was presented by Lady Shelley. The gift and its acceptance have gracefully marked the restoration of peace between a poet never fitted to endure the discipline of a College and authorities not perhaps altogether qualified to undertake the education of poets.

William Carr, *University College History*, 1902

After an unhappy education at Eton, the English poet Percy Bysshe Shelley (1792–1822) began studying at University College in Oxford in 1810 but was expelled for writing a controversial pamphlet, or as the college authorities put it: 'contumaciously refusing to answer questions proposed and for also repeatedly declining to disavow a publication entitled *The Necessity of Atheism*'.

After his death, Shelley's daughter-in-law Jane dedicated herself to the promotion of his life and work, and commissioned a memorial to him by sculptor Edward Onslow Ford (1852–1901). Too large to be erected in the cemetery in Rome where he was buried, she approached his old college, which agreed to take it.

Ford's memorial is a white marble depiction of a reclining nude Shelley, washed ashore at Viareggio, Italy, after his death (originally, he wore a gilt-bronze laurel wreath but this is no longer on display). It lies on top of a plinth inside a small domed and barred enclosure by architect Basil Champneys (1842–1935), who designed many university buildings in Oxford.

ALSO ON THIS DAY 1777: Congress adopts the Stars and Stripes as the US flag · **1907:** English illustrator Nicolas Bentley born · **1923:** German-English illustrator Judith Kerr born

Muybridge records the first 'moving pictures', 1878

Only photography has been able to divide human life into a series of moments, each of them has the value of a complete existence.

Eadweard Muybridge (attributed)

Although artists traditionally painted galloping horses with all four legs off the ground, there was no definitive proof until horse-racing enthusiast and former California governor Leland Stanford commissioned English photographer Eadweard Muybridge (1830–1904) to look into the matter. Muybridge had already taken a photograph in 1876 that appeared to confirm the theory, but Stanford encouraged him to go further.

On 15 June 1878, Muybridge set up a dozen cameras with fast shutter speeds at a racetrack at Palo Alto, California, in front of a small group of invitees including members of the press. Camera-linked tripwires were set off by a galloping horse and in the twelve shots thus taken, two clearly showed the horse entirely off the ground. His book *The Horse in Motion* (1882) provided a thorough explanation of the experiment and he proceeded to continue his work developing locomotion photos of people and animals, removing the tripwires and increasing the number of cameras. Muybridge used his discovery to invent the 'zoopraxiscope', which built on the concept of the zoetrope to create 'moving pictures'.

Not everybody was delighted with this breakthrough, however, French sculptor Auguste Rodin observing: 'It is the artist who is truthful and it is photography which lies, for in reality time does not stop.'

Muybridge had an intriguing life. After emigrating from England to America to become a bookseller, he developed an interest in photography after sustaining a very serious head injury in a coach accident. He specialized in landscape photography, especially focusing on the country's more remote areas, and of Native Americans. He also stood trial for murder after shooting his wife's lover, though he was acquitted on the grounds of 'justifiable homicide'.

ALSO ON THIS DAY 1618: French architect François Blondel baptized · **1985:** A vandal throws sulphuric acid on Rembrandt's painting *Danaë* and attacks it with a knife · **2018:** Glasgow School of Art, designed by Scottish architect Charles Rennie Mackintosh, is destroyed by fire (*see also* 15 December)

A statue of James Joyce is erected on his grave, 1966

As we, or Mother Dana, weave and unweave our bodies, Stephen said, from day today, their molecules shuttled to and fro, so does the artist weave and unweave his image. And as the mole on my right breast is where it was when I was born, though all my body has been woven of new stuff time after time, so through the ghost of the unquiet father the image of the unliving son looks forth. In the intense instant of imagination, when the mind, Shelley says, is a fading coal, that which I was is that which I am and that which in possibility I may come to be. So in the future, the sister of the past, I may see myself as I sit here now by reflection from that which I then shall be.

James Joyce, *Ulysses*, Ch. 9: Scylla and Charybdis, 1922

When he died in 1941 aged fifty-eight, the Irish writer James Joyce was buried in Zurich's Fluntern Cemetery (later, his wife Nora and their son Giorgio were buried alongside him in 1951 and 1976 respectively). The author of *Ulysses* set the action of his novel on 16 June, a day commemorated each year by numerous celebrations around the world referred to as Bloomsday after the novel's protagonist Leopold Bloom.

On 16 June 1966 a special statue was erected to mark Joyce's grave. The life-size bronze by American sculptor Milton Hebald (1917–2015) shows the writer in his later years, sitting with his legs crossed and a book in his hand, looking over his own gravestone. The commission came via his art dealer friend Lee Nordness, who visited the grave twenty years after Joyce's death and was stunned to find it almost entirely unmarked but for a small plaque. Hebald worked on the head using photographs and drawings of Joyce, then used Giorgio Joyce as a model for the torso.

Hebald produced other literary statuary, including a bust of English writer Anthony Burgess (which featured on the cover of the author's 1987 biography *Little Wilson and Big God*) and depictions of *Romeo and Juliet*, and *The Tempest*, from William Shakespeare, which are located outside the open-air Delacorte Theater in New York. Burgess said Hebald was the finest living sculptor at mediating between the worlds of words and stone and metal.

17 JUNE

Van Gogh sketches
a mudlark, 1888

For ever so long I have been wanting to write to you – but then the work has so taken me up. We have harvest time here at present and I am always in the fields.

And when I sit down to write I am so abstracted by recollections of what I have seen that I leave the letter. For instance at the present occasion I was writing to you and going to say something about Arles as it is – and as it was in the old days of Boccaccio.

Well, instead of continuing the letter I began to draw on the very paper the head of a dirty little girl I saw this afternoon whilst I was painting a view of the river with a greenish yellow sky. This dirty 'mudlark' I thought yet had a vague florentine sort of figure like the heads in the Monticelli pictures.

**Vincent van Gogh, letter to John Peter Russell,
17 June 1888**

Dutch painter Vincent van Gogh (1853–1890; *see also* 9 February) wrote letters mostly in Dutch and French but also five in English, including this one written on 17 June 1888 to his Australian friend and impressionist painter John Peter Russell (1858–1930). With the letter, he also included the sketch of the 'mudlark' (*Head of a Girl*), which is similar to his painting of the same name. The river view he mentions in his letter is *The Trinquetaille Bridge*.

Van Gogh writes of
his 'study of a starry sky', 1889

As for me, it's going well – you'll understand that after almost half a year now of absolute sobriety in eating, drinking, smoking, with two two-hour baths a week recently, this must clearly calm one down a great deal. So it's going very well, and as regards work, it occupies and distracts me – which I need very much – far from wearing me out.... At last I have a landscape with olive trees, and also a new study of a starry sky.

Although I haven't seen the latest canvases either by Gauguin or Bernard, I'm fairly sure that these two studies I speak of are comparable in sentiment. When you've seen these two studies for a while, as well as the one of the ivy, I'll perhaps be able to give you, better than in words, an idea of the things Gauguin, Bernard and I sometimes chatted about and that preoccupied us. It's not a return to the romantic or to religious ideas, no. However, by going the way of Delacroix, more than it seems, by colour and a more determined drawing than *trompe-l'oeil* precision, one might express a country nature that is purer than the suburbs, the bars of Paris.

**Vincent van Gogh, letter to his brother Theo,
18 June 1889**

Six months after his ear self-mutilation (*see* 23 December), Dutch painter Vincent van Gogh (1853–1890) wrote to his brother, art dealer Theo van Gogh, about one of his most famous works, *The Starry Night* (1889).

ALSO ON THIS DAY 1464: Death of Flemish painter Rogier van der Weyden · **1716:** French painter Joseph-Marie Vien born · **1877:** American painter and poster illustrator James Montgomery Flagg born

Manet's *Olympia*
is satirized by Daumier, 1865

[MAN TO WIFE AND SON] Why on earth is this fat, red-faced woman in her nightgown called Olympia?

[WIFE] But my dear, perhaps that's what the black cat is called?

**Honoré Daumier, *Looking at a Manet Painting* caption,
in 'Sketches from the Salon', *Le Charivari* magazine, 19 June 1865**

The print *Looking at a Manet Painting* by French caricaturist, painter and sculptor Honoré-Victorin Daumier (1808–1879) shows a family gazing at the oil painting *Olympia* (1863) by Édouard Manet (1832–1883; *see also* 28 October). Modelled after *Venus of Urbino* by Titian, it shows a naked white woman – various symbolic details including the black cat suggest she is a prostitute – as she lies on a bed, gazing out towards the viewer. To her side, a black servant offers her a bunch of flowers. The painting was exhibited at the 1865 Paris Salon and caused an immediate uproar, not least because the model for *Olympia* was recognizably Victorine Meurent, a painter and well-known figure in Paris society.

The Salon was a series of art fairs and exhibitions held in the French capital every year, visited by numerous visitors interested to see the latest developments in art as well as familiar favourites. As well as the official selections, a fringe version also sprung up for artists such as the Impressionists whose work was less conservative. The contemporary poet Charles Baudelaire said about the Salons that: 'During our time there are only two artists in Paris who are as able as Delacroix: the caricaturist Daumier and the second one is Ingres. All three of them have one thing in common: they express what they mean to say.'

Daumier exhibited at the Salon himself but also produced a series of caricatures for popular magazines such as *Le Charivari* about his fellow Parisians. In prints like the one published on 19 June 1865, he made fun of artists, critics, art lovers and the whole industry of the country's commercial art world.

ALSO ON THIS DAY 1731: Portuguese sculptor Joaquim Machado de Castro born · **1815:** Dutch-Canadian painter Cornelius Krieghoff born · **1903:** American sculptor Mary Callery born

Robert Rauschenberg creates his *First Time Painting*, 1961

oil

paper

fabric

sailcloth

plastic exhaust cap

alarm clock

sheet metal

adhesive tape

metal springs

wire

string on canvas

List of media used by Robert Rauschenberg,
First Time Painting, **1961**

Though he might technically be described as a painter, American Robert Rauschenberg (1925–2008) was an interdisciplinary performer who aimed to combine art and real life in his work. With the viewer constantly in mind, he collaborated with creative colleagues such as dancer and choreographer Merce Cunningham and composer John Cage, who was inspired by Rauschenberg's 'White Paintings' – made to look untouched by human hand and reflecting light on the all-white canvas – to write his piece *4'33"*.

Rauschenberg's 1966 work *Open Score* uses the rackets in a tennis game to transmit sound and activate lights until the end of the game when the audience are left in apparent darkness but are in fact sitting in invisible infrared. He also used a wide range of materials in his work, painting on his own quilt for *Bed*, and for his 1980s series 'Gluts' turned petrol station signs and other car-related scrap metal into sculptures. He argued that it was a time of glut and he hoped his work would help expose the ubiquity of greed to the public.

On 20 June 1961, he produced *First Time Painting* as part of the 'Homage to David Tudor' event at the American Embassy in Paris, which featured other artists including French-American sculptor Niki de Saint Phalle and Rauschenberg's friend, artist Jasper Johns. He created it in front of an audience but with the back of the painting facing them. Although they could not see what he was doing, they could hear his brushes on the canvas via attached microphones. When an alarm clock sounded, he stopped working on it and declared it finished.

ALSO ON THIS DAY 1887: German painter Kurt Schwitters born · **1930:** Polish sculptor Magdalena Abakanowicz born · **2015:** Death of American sculptor and painter Miriam Schapiro

21 JUNE

John Evelyn attends an art auction, 1693

I saw a great auction of pictures in the Banqueting house, Whitehall. They had been my Lord Melfort's, now Ambassador from King James at Rome, and engaged to his creditors here. Lord Mulgrave and Sir Edward Seymour came to my house, and desired me to go with them to the sale. Divers more of the great lords, etc., were there, and bought pictures dear enough. There were some very excellent of Vandyke, Rubens and Bassan. Lord Godolphin bought the picture of the Boys, by Murillo the Spaniard, for 80 guineas, dear enough; my nephew Glanville, the old Earl of Arundel's head by Rubens, for £20. Growing late, I did not stay till all were sold.

John Evelyn, diary entry, 21 June 1693

The first recorded art auction in England took place nineteen years before English diarist John Evelyn (1620–1706; *see also* 24 February) attended an auction in London on 21 June 1693, at which he witnessed the sale of Spanish painter Bartolomé Murillo's *Invitation to the Game of Pelota*, and the portrait of politician and art patron Thomas Howard, 2nd Earl of Arundel, by Flemish artist Sir Peter Paul Rubens (*see* 26 February).

The early auctions from the 1670s onwards were initially set up by booksellers, the most famous of whom was Edward Millington, who then moved into the art market in 1689 and by the early 1690s was holding weekly art auctions in London. The catalogues at this time were not as detailed as their modern-day counterparts, with little emphasis on attribution, provenance or indeed, quality. In his first catalogue, Millington wrote: 'I shall not pretend to commend what I do publickly own, I do not understand.... I shall leave the Gentlemen and Ladies, the Buyers, to approve for themselves; to whose judgment as I ought, so I shall always pay in Matters of this Nature, a suitable veneration.'

Although some works fetched high prices at auctions and some, like the one attended by Evelyn, were not advertised to the public, many were not exclusively aimed at rich collectors and attracted members of the middle classes. Women buyers were also common. Most sales were held in London's coffee houses, but there was some geographic spread to genteel locations such as Bath, Oxford and Tunbridge Wells. At the time of Evelyn's visit there was a boom in art auctions, although this appears to have dropped off towards the end of the 17th century.

ALSO ON THIS DAY 1813: Following his victory at the Battle of Vitoria, the Marquess of Wellington recovers eighty-three paintings stolen by Joseph Bonaparte, from the Spanish Royal Collection · **1858:** Italian sculptor Medardo Rosso born · **1881:** Russian painter and costume designer Natalia Goncharova born

22 JUNE

Anna Rügerin prints
her first book, 1484

Hye endet sich der sachsenspiegel mitt ordnung des rechten den der erwirdig in got vater und herr Theodoricus von bockßdorf bischof zu neünburg säliger gecorrigieret hat. Gedruckt und volendt von Anna Rügerin in der keyserlichen stat Augspurg am aftermontag nächst vor Johannis. do man zalt nach Cristi gepurt/M.CCCC.lxxxiiij.jar./

Colophon in Eike of Repgow,
Sachsenspiegel, **22 June 1484**

Women, and especially nuns, worked as scribes, copyists and illuminators on manuscripts for centuries, and with the advent of printing some also worked in their husbands' printing businesses. Typographer Anna Rügerin, from Augsburg, Germany, is widely accepted as the first woman to include her name as the printer in a book's colophon, the section at the end of the book that includes details about the author and when the title was produced.

In 1484, she printed two books on her own press: the *Sachsenspiegel: Landrecht* (a 13th-century German law handbook by Eike of Repgow), and a manual for editing official documents. Both were set in the Gothic font 1:120G of Johann Schönsperger, who was part of Rügerin's extended family.

ALSO ON THIS DAY **1894:** English art historian and archaeologist Bernard Ashmole born · **1922:** American fashion designer Bill Blass born · **1941:** American historian and professor Paul Kosok watches the sun set along the Nazca Lines

23 JUNE

Hitler takes a tour of Parisian architecture, 1940

The defence of the Paris bridgehead is of vital military and political importance.... Within the city, the most severe measures must be taken against the first signs of rioting, such as blasting of city blocks, public execution of the ringleaders, evacuation of the affected district, as this is the best way to prevent it spreading. The bridges over the Seine are to be prepared for demolition. Paris must not fall into the hands of the enemy, or only as a field of rubble.

Adolf Hitler, telegram to General Dietrich von Choltitz,
23 August 1944

With Paris likely to fall to the advancing Allied Forces in 1944, Adolf Hitler ordered General Dietrich von Choltitz, Nazi Germany's military governor of the city, to destroy it rather than simply capitulate. Choltitz refused to obey the order and instead surrendered to the Free French provisional government.

Hitler, however, had not always been so dismissive of Paris's attractions. In his book *Inside the Third Reich* (1970), the Führer's favoured architect Albert Speer recounted how, shortly after France formally surrendered to Germany, he, Hitler and sculptor Arno Breker (*see* 18 July) had flown to Paris on 23 June 1940 so that Hitler could enjoy a daytrip seeing the sights.

Speer describes how they drove down the Champs-Élysées, stopped to admire the Eiffel Tower, and Napoleon's tomb at the Invalides, then moved on to an inspection of the Pantheon. Their tour concluded at the church of Sacré-Coeur on Montmartre. As they drove back to the airport, Hitler commented that he had now fulfilled a long-standing dream to see Paris. He never returned.

ALSO ON THIS DAY 1902: Monument to Italian opera composer Gioachino Rossini is unveiled in Santa Croce, Florence · **1910:** American photographer Milt Hinton born · **1926:** Italian sculptor Arnaldo Pomodoro born

24 JUNE

Christo and Jeanne-Claude wrap the Reichstag, 1995

The Reichstag stands up in an open, strangely metaphysical area. The building has experienced its own continuous changes and perturbations: built in 1894, burned in 1933, almost destroyed in 1945, it was restored in the sixties, but the Reichstag always remained the symbol of Democracy.

Throughout the history of art, the use of fabric has been a fascination for artists. From the most ancient times to the present, fabric forming folds, pleats and draperies is a significant part of paintings, frescoes, reliefs and sculptures made of wood, stone and bronze. The use of fabric on the Reichstag follows the classical tradition. Fabric, like clothing or skin, is fragile; it translates the unique quality of impermanence.

For a period of two weeks, the richness of the silvery fabric, shaped by the blue ropes, created a sumptuous flow of vertical folds highlighting the features and proportions of the imposing structure, revealing the essence of the Reichstag.

Christo and Jeanne-Claude, artists' statement
'Wrapped Reichstag, Berlin 1971–95'

Husband-and-wife artists Bulgarian Christo Javacheff (1935–2020) and French Jeanne-Claude Denat de Guillebon (1935–2009) produced art on a vast scale, including a 39.4-km (24½-mile) fence in California, which took four years to build, and a similar length of gates along the paths of Central Park, New York.

They were particularly known for their wrapping of objects – the Pont Neuf in Paris, the coast of Little Bay in Sydney, Australia, and the Reichstag in Berlin. For the Reichstag project, they used 100,000 square metres

(1,076,000 square feet) of fireproof polypropylene fabric and 15 km (9 miles) of rope. The wrapping took more than two hundred people a week to put together, and it was unveiled on 24 June 1995 by one hundred rock climbers abseiling down the facade, unfurling the curtain as they went.

Like all their art, once it was removed, there was nothing to show it had ever been there.

ALSO ON THIS DAY 1838: Polish painter Jan Matejko born · **1923:** Australian painter Margaret Olley born · **1991:** Death of Mexican painter Rufino Tamayo

25 JUNE

Hogarth publishes
The Rake's Progress prints, 1735

Madness, Thou Chaos of ye Brain,
What art? That Pleasure giv'st, and Pain?
Tyranny of Fancy's Reign!
Mechanic Fancy; that can build
Vast Labarynths, & Mazes wild,
With Rule disjointed, Shapless Measure,
Fill'd with Horror, fill'd with Pleasure!
Shapes of Horror, that wou'd eaven
Cast Doubt of Mercy upon Heaven.
Shapes of Pleasure, that but Seen
Wou'd spilt the Shaking Sides of Spleen.
O Vanity of Age! here see
The Stamp of Heaven effac'd by Thee –
The headstrong Course of Youth thus run,
What Comfort from this darling Son!
His rattling Chains with Terror hear,
Behold Death grappling with Despaire;
See Him by Thee to Ruin Sold,
And curse thy self, & curse thy Gold.

William Hogarth, caption to Plate 8 of 8,
***The Rake's Progress*, 1735**

English painter and satirical cartoonist William Hogarth (1697–1764) completed various series of works dealing with (im)morality. His first was *A Harlot's Progress* (1731), the cautionary story of a young woman from the country who looks for work in London, becomes a prostitute and dies from syphilis.

He followed this with *The Rake's Progress*, initially a set of eight paintings that he then turned into engravings, which he printed on 25 June 1735, the same day as the Engravers' Copyright Act for which he had lobbied came into force. The eight plates show how the wealthy young man Tom Rakewell descends via gambling and general wild extravagance to imprisonment and finally incarceration in London's Bedlam asylum.

The series has since inspired a 1935 ballet of the same name; an updated film version (1945) set in the Second World War starring English actor Rex Harrison; an opera by Russian-born composer Igor Stravinsky (1951); and a set of tapestries by English artist Grayson Perry called *The Vanity of Small Differences* in which Tom progresses from his working-class upbringing in Sunderland to become a computer millionaire before dying in a car crash.

ALSO ON THIS DAY 1852: Catalan architect Antoni Gaudí born (*see* 19 March) · **1874:** American cartoonist and illustrator Rose O'Neill born · **1929:** American illustrator Eric Carle born (*see* 22 November)

26 JUNE

The Cave of the Golden Calf opens in London, 1912

Our aims have the simplicity of a need: we want a place given up to gaiety, to a gaiety stimulating thought, rather than crushing it. We want a gaiety that does not have to count with midnight. We want surroundings, which after the reality of daily life, reveal the reality of the unreal. We want light and we want song. With these quite modest wishes we desire to harm nobody, unless it be such 'outre-mer' purveyors of entertainment as flourish, not necessarily on their merits so much as on the drastic dullness of our home-life.... Subjoined is, in an approximative and preliminary form, our first week's programme, the character of which can be best suggested by the names of some of the authors and composers under whose banners we range ourselves: Abercrombie, Villiers de l'Isle Adam, John Davidson,

Walter Delamare, Arthur Machen, T. Sturge Moore, Ezra Pound, August Strindberg, Frank Wedekind, Yeats; Granville Bantock, Delius, Holbrooke, Raoul Lapara, Ernest Moret, Florence Schmitt, Dalhousie Young.... Small tables – at which, up to 11, refreshments will be served, after 11, suppers – will be a welcome relief from the disciplinary ranks of theatre seats.

'Aims and Programme' in the promotional brochure
for The Cave of the Golden Calf, May 1912

The Cave of the Golden Calf nightclub in London was set up by the wealthy Austrian heiress Frida Strindberg (1872–1943), the second wife of Swedish playwright August Strindberg. The interior decor was commissioned from young avant-garde British artists, supervised by landscape painter Spencer Gore (1878–1914), to complement its intention to be an avant-garde club. The general theme was the worship of the Golden Calf idol carried out by Israelites while Moses was away on Mount Sinai collecting the Ten Commandments.

Among the works created specifically for the decadent basement club were Gore's deer-hunting mural; painter Charles Ginner's tiger-hunting and chasing monkeys murals; artist and writer Wyndham Lewis's painting *Kermesse*; sculptor and typographer Eric Gill's Golden Calf statue and phallic club sign/motif; and carved columns by sculptor Sir Jacob Epstein.

'The "Troglodytes", or "Cave-dwellers",' the *Observer* newspaper commented 16 June 1912, 'is a singularly appropriate appellation for a coterie of artists, who are not only connected with the "Cave of the Calf", but who aim – most of them – at the primitive simplicity of the days when art was in its infancy. It was, after all, on bones and on the walls of caves, that the artistic instinct found its first expression.'

Although it received positive mentions in the media and was a popular meeting place for artists and other creatives, especially Futurists, it quickly ran into financial problems and closed in 1914. None of the artwork from the club has survived.

ALSO ON THIS DAY 1852: Lebanese painter Daoud Corm born · **1866:** English archaeologist George Herbert, 5th Earl of Carnarvon, born · **1929:** American illustrator and graphic designer Milton Glaser born

Whistler reminds his restorer to care for his pictures, 1892

You have of course had my letter through Mr Kennedy, therefore I need scarcely add more as to the care I trust you are taking with these four pictures. You see the great faith I put in your conscientiousness. I mean that I know you will run me no risks – Now Mr Kennedy wishes you to send over *The Battersea Reach* and the *Balcony* without their frames to me here before you revarnish them – for me to see if I should touch them – you can get them off if possible tomorrow. As to the two there – the cracks if any must be very superficial and you can put them right. Remember there is no 'scumbling' in my painting ever.

**James McNeill Whistler, letter to Stephen Richards,
27 June 1892**

American-born painter James McNeill Whistler (1834–1903; *see also* 25 November) was, understandably, very particular about the appearance of his paintings – how they were hung, how they were framed and how they were varnished – and certainly did not want any 'scumbling' (the use of an opaque glaze for effect).

Whistler's correspondence with the London-based restorer Stephen Richards, including this letter of 27 June 1892, underlines how closely he worked even on reasonably recent works such as *Battersea Reach* (1863) and *Variations in Flesh Colour and Green: The Balcony* (1865), which he sold with two other paintings to New York art dealer Edward Kennedy of Wunderlich & Co. for £650 in June 1892.

In a letter sent earlier in the month, Whistler wrote to Richards that he regarded him as the only man fit to touch his work, a claim he repeated to Kennedy in other letters, pointing out that he not only worked well, but quickly too (a contrast to Whistler's picture framer Frederick H. Grau whom the artist describes in the same letter 'as procrastinating as he is capable').

ALSO ON THIS DAY 1574: Death of Italian painter and art historian Giorgio Vasari (*see* 9 August) · **1892:** French poster artist Paul Colin born · **2001:** Death of Finnish illustrator and painter Tove Jansson

'The Building of Britain'
paintings are unveiled, 1927

It is not easy to account, in a sober history, for the fascination which a hard, masculine old maid exerted for so long over the young and brilliant men about her. But in this picture the feat has been easily achieved. It presents to the eye a spiritual not a material fact. We view a historic scene with the inward vision of the actors in it. We think not at all of dates or details: of a familiar Dover, a risky speculation, a hard mistress; of long years of failure and a death upon the scaffold. We see that which inspired a great generation – we see Elizabeth they saw, their Gloriana, their Semper Eadem, their Faerie Queen; we are conscious of the Court, the Castle, the Ships, the great adventure, only as transfigured into the image of their ideal beauty.

Sir Henry Newbolt, on *Queen Elizabeth Commissions Raleigh to Sail for America, 1584* **by Alfred Kingsley Lawrence, in** *The Building of Britain,* **1927**

There is a prodigious amount of art on display at the Palace of Westminster in London where the members of the House of Commons and House of Lords meet as the UK Parliament. 'The Building of Britain' is one of the most ambitious projects, a series of eight murals commissioned to decorate the palace's St Stephen's Hall.

Historical advice was provided by English poet and scholar Sir Henry Newbolt (1862–1938), while Scottish painter and etcher Sir David Young Cameron (1865–1945) helped to supervise the painters whose work was unveiled on 28 June 1927 by Prime Minister Stanley Baldwin. The subjects were:

- *Richard I Leaving England for the Crusades, 1189* by Glyn Warren Philpot
- *The Parliamentary Union of England and Scotland, 1707* by Walter Thomas Monnington
- *Sir Thomas Roe at the court of Ajmir, 1614* by William Rothenstein
- *Queen Elizabeth Commissions Raleigh to Sail for America, 1584 by* Alfred Kingsley Lawrence
- *The English People Reading Wycliffe's Bible* by Sir George Clausen
- *King John assents to the Magna Carta, 1215* by Charles H. Sims

- *King Alfred's long-ships defeat the Danes, 877* by Colin Gill
- *Sir Thomas More Refusing to Grant Wolsey a Subsidy, 1523* by Vivian Forbes

Former Labour MP Tony Benn was particularly fond of Clausen's mural (he had a copy of it in his home) as he argued it told the story of revolutionary group efforts to resist religious persecution.

ALSO ON THIS DAY 1577: Flemish painter Sir Peter Paul Rubens born (*see* 26 February) · **1895:** French painter Paul Gauguin departs France to go to Tahiti for the second time (*see* 9 June) · **1926:** American cartoonist George Booth born

29 JUNE

The statue of 'Eros' in London is unveiled, 1893

Never having attempted a design of such magnitude, while I was at work upon it I was absolutely studying all the time that part of my art to which I sought to give expression. So the task was doubled from an artistic stand-point, and rendered almost impossible from a financial one. Then there were conditions as to site, and the proper provision for water, and a thousand and one technical questions which I had to master as I went along, the result was what I have always considered an incomplete expression of an enthusiastic intention. Artistically, however, it was more or less a success, financially a great debacle. As the fountain now stands it in no way represents my original design; for the site, although I had it in mind as a hoped-for and possible one, was not actually granted until the work was ready for erection. When, at last, the site was selected, the present surrounding great buildings were not in existence, and the environment was constantly open to alterations.

On the opening day, when the fountain was unveiled, there existed eight drinking-cups of more or less elaborate fashion, attached to the main body of the work, secured by a very carefully hand-wrought chain, specially designed and made for the purpose. The next morning I believe only two of the cups were left, but the fragments of a third were found carefully broken and deposited in one of the basins, carrying clear evidence that the damage had taken some considerable time to effect, and was no doubt meant as a malicious criticism, if not a protest, against the work itself. I believe subsequently the Council recovered much of the missing material a further proof that the damage was not done for the sake of theft.... Then followed a storm of abuse of the work itself, with no attempt at just criticism, but inspired by, and given utterance to, through the grossest form of ignorance.

Alfred Gilbert, interview with Joseph Hatton,
in *The Life and Work of Alfred Gilbert*, 1903

English sculptor Alfred Gilbert (1854–1934) did not have an entirely smooth relationship with the committee that commissioned the Shaftesbury Memorial Foundation, commonly known as 'Eros' (also mistakenly known; it is in fact his more serious brother, Anteros). Cast in aluminium, following the statue's unveiling in London's Piccadilly Circus in 1893 it also had a mixed reception from the public, as Gilbert mentions, and from the press. The *Ilustrated London News* described the 'squirts' from the fountain as 'ludicrous and contemptible', while *The Times* claimed that gusts of wind drenched bystanders and that it was 'a dripping, sickening mess'. Nevertheless, it is now one of the most popular pieces of public art in the capital.

Gilbert's model for Anteros was his assistant, the sixteen-year-old Anglo-Italian Angelo Colarossi whose father had also worked as an artist's model, including for Frederic, Lord Leighton's bronze sculpture *An Athlete Wrestling with a Python*.

ALSO ON THIS DAY 1613: The Globe Theatre in London is destroyed by fire · **1686:** Maltese silversmith and sculptor Pietro Paolo Troisi born · **1940:** Death of Swiss-German painter Paul Klee

30 JUNE

The Statue of Liberty's head
goes on display in Paris, 1878

In regard to the execution of colossal works of art, I think, as I said above, that we find sure principles in the ancient works. The difficulty is to apply them to one's own age, that is to say, without servile imitation of the forms imagined by other epochs and other races. I may cite for example the principle of great simplicity in the movement and in the exterior lines. The gesture ought to be made plain by the profile to all the senses. The details of the lines ought not to arrest the eye. The breaks in the lines should be bold, and such as are suggested by the general design. Beside the work should be as far as possible filled out, and should not present black spots or exaggerated recesses. The surfaces should be broad and simple, defined by a bold and clear design, accentuated in the important places. The enlargement of the details or their multiplicity is to be feared. By exaggerating the forms, in order to render them more clearly visible, or by enriching them with details, we would destroy the proportion of the work. Finally, the model, like the design, should have a summarized character, such as one would give to a rapid sketch. Only it is necessary that this character should be the product of volition and study, and that the artist, concentrating his knowledge, should find the form and the line in its greatest simplicity. These same principles ought to be kept in mind in the construction of the pedestal.

Frédéric-Auguste Bartholdi, *The Statue of Liberty Enlightening the World,* **fundraising pamphlet, 1885**

The goal of French sculptor Frédéric-Auguste Bartholdi (1834–1904) to produce a colossal gift for the United States in celebration of the abolition of slavery took a major step forward on 30 June 1878 when he put on display the completed head of the Statue of Liberty (*see also* 8 October). It was set up in the garden of the Trocadéro palace as part of the Exposition Universelle (the third Paris World's Fair) in a bid to win support, and funding, for the project.

Painter Claude Monet (*see* 13 November) celebrated the exhibition with his eponymous painting of a parade on 30 June, showing La Rue Montorgueil from a high viewpoint, filled with people and red, white and blue flags fluttering from the buildings on the street.

ALSO ON THIS DAY 1649: Death of French painter Simon Vouet · **1789:** French painter Horace Vernet born · **1891:** English painter Stanley Spencer born

July

John Lennon and Yoko Ono's 'You Are Here' exhibition opens, 1968

This exhibit was inadvertently left out.

Note attached to a rusty bicycle donated by Hornsey College of Art students and later added to the 'You Are Here' exhibition, 1968

The art show inspired by the 'You Are Here' arrows on UK street maps and devised by ex-Beatle John Lennon (1940–1980) and multimedia artist Yoko Ono (b. 1933) ran at the Robert Fraser Gallery in London, a space that focused on conceptual and contemporary artists. Both Lennon and Ono wore all white for the opening on 1 July 1968.

As well as a 3-metre (10-foot) circular canvas with 'You Are Here' written on it, the show featured: a jar of 'You Are Here' badges for visitors to take (Lennon reported that some people took them by the handful, not realizing they were being secretly filmed); a white fedora labelled 'For the artist. Thank you'; a dozen charity collection boxes; and Lennon's shoes, labelled 'I take my shoes off to you'. At the opening, Lennon let off 365 white balloons with tags ('I declare these balloons high,' he said at their release), asking for them to be sent back, in return for which he replied to the sender with a short note.

The following month, on broadcaster David Frost's ITV show *Frost on Saturday*, Lennon explained that the artistic element of the exhibition was people's reaction to the items on display.

ALSO ON THIS DAY **1553:** English carpenter and builder Peter Street baptized · **1725:** English painter Rhoda Delaval born · **2000:** Øresund Bridge, which connects Denmark and Sweden, opens for traffic

Méduse runs aground, providing Géricault with inspiration, 1816

Scarcely fifty men had got upon the raft, when it sunk at least seventy centimetres under water; so that to facilitate the embarkation of the other soldiers it was necessary to throw into the sea all the flour barrels, which lifted by the waves, began to float and were violently driven against the men who were at their post; if they had been fixed, perhaps some of them might have been saved: as it was, we saved only the wine and the water, because several persons united to preserve them, and had much difficulty to hinder them from being thrown into the sea like the flour barrels. The raft, lightened by throwing away these barrels, was able to receive more men; we were at length a hundred and fifty. The machine was submerged at least a metre: we were so crowded together that it was impossible to take a single step; at the back and the front, we were in water up to the middle. At the moment that we were putting off from the frigate, a bag with twenty-five pounds of biscuit was thrown us, which fell into the sea; we got it up with difficulty; it was converted into a paste, but we preserved it in that condition.... When tranquillity was a little restored, we began to look upon the raft for the charts, the compass and the anchor, which we presumed had been placed there, from what had been said to us at the time we quitted the frigate. These highly necessary articles had not been put upon our machine.

J. B. Henry Savigny and Alexander Corréard,
***Narrative of a Voyage to Senegal in 1816*, 1818**

When the French frigate *Méduse* foundered off the Mauritanian coast on 2 July 1816, the top-ranking officers took to the ship's lifeboats while the remaining 150 of those aboard climbed aboard a makeshift raft and searched for help. They were, in fact, entirely abandoned by the ship's captain. When they were rescued a fortnight later by chance, there were only fifteen survivors. Because of the ghastly nature of the tragedy – managerial incompetence and cowardice, dehydration, starvation and cannibalism – the incident became notorious.

French artist Théodore Géricault (1791–1824) used survivors' accounts such as that of the ship's surgeon Savigny and passenger Corréard, an engineer and geographer, to ensure his painting of the event, *The Raft of the Medusa*, was as realistic as possible. He also built a miniature version of the raft to help him devise the painting and sketched body parts in a local morgue to guide his work. The painting shows a group of fifteen rather muscular figures on the raft, either in considerable distress or dead. One – a black passenger whose inclusion has been seen as a call from Géricault to end slavery – tries to attract the attention of a distant ship, the *Argos*, which eventually came to their aid. For one of the figures in the foreground, Géricault used his friend the painter Eugène Delacroix as a model and he painted Corréard and Savigny from life. The painting's size – 4.9 × 7.2 metres (16 × 23½ feet) – means the figures are life-size.

The painting, completed by 1819, was the centre of attention at the Paris Salon that year, and made Géricault's reputation.

ALSO ON THIS DAY **1486:** Italian architect and sculptor Jacopo Sansovino born · **1597:** Flemish painter Theodoor Rombouts born · **1900:** English costume and set designer Sophie Harris born

3 JULY

Margaret Thatcher's statue is decapitated, 2002

In the Members' Lobby of the House of Commons there are rightly four principal statues: Lloyd George, who gave us the beginnings of the welfare state; Winston Churchill, who gave us victory in war; Clement Attlee, who gave us the NHS; and Margaret Thatcher, who rescued our country from post-war decline. They say that cometh the hour, cometh the man. Well, in 1979 came the hour, and came the lady. She made the political weather. She made history. And let this be her epitaph: she made our country great again. I commend the motion to the House.

Prime Minister David Cameron, Tributes to Margaret Thatcher, House of Commons, London, 10 April 2013

In May 1998, former UK prime minister Margaret Thatcher (1925–2013) unveiled a 2.4-metre (8-foot) statue of herself carrying a handbag and a House of Commons order paper. Taking eight months of personal sitting, it was made by sculptor Neil Simmons commissioned by the UK Parliament's Speaker's Advisory Committee on Works of Art. At its unveiling, Tony Banks MP, then the chairman of the committee, commented that this was the Marble Lady instead of the Iron Lady.

Four years later, on 3 July 2002, theatre producer Paul Kelleher smuggled a cricket bat into the Guildhall Art Gallery in London where it was on display. He then attacked the statue with the bat and a nearby metal pole, smashing the head clean off. At his trial, in addition to claiming he was simply exercising his right to artistic expression, he also said he had undertaken the move as a protest against the effect Thatcherite policies were having on the world in which his young son Alfie was growing up (inspiring the song 'I Did It For Alfie' by the band Chumbawamba).

Art critic Brian Sewell, writing in London's *Evening Standard* newspaper, argued that while the sculpture was not an especially notable work, the attack had in fact turned it into a contemporary work of art and that Kelleher should only be fined a farthing.

At the trial, in reply to Kelleher's claims that the attack was not a case of criminal damage, prosecuting barrister John Hardy said that being a man of principle did not allow anyone to commit wanton destruction. Kelleher was found guilty and sentenced to three months in prison.

After a successful repair, the statue went on long-term loan to the Corporation of London and is on public display at the Guildhall Art Gallery.

4 JULY

Henry David Thoreau moves into his Walden Pond cabin, 1845

So I went on for some days cutting and hewing timber, and also studs and rafters, all with my narrow axe, not having many communicable or scholar-like thoughts, singing to myself.... I hewed the main timbers six inches square, most of the studs on two sides only, and the rafters and floor timbers on one side, leaving the rest of the bark on, so that they were just as straight and much stronger than sawed ones. Each stick was carefully mortised or tenoned by its stump, for I had borrowed other tools by this time. My days in the woods were not very long ones; yet I usually carried my dinner of bread and butter, and read the newspaper in which it was wrapped, at noon, sitting amid the green pine boughs which I had cut off, and to my bread was imparted some of their fragrance, for my hands were covered with a thick coat of pitch. Before I had done I was more the friend than the foe of the pine tree, though I had cut down some of them, having become better acquainted with it.

Henry David Thoreau,
Walden; or, Life in the Woods, **1854**

Not all notable works of architecture are on a grand scale or include trailblazing features. One building that has had a long-lasting impact on society is the one-room cabin that American writer and philospher Henry David Thoreau (1817–1862) built at Walden Pond in Concord, Massachusetts, and lived in for the following two years, choosing Independence Day 1845 to begin his experiment.

'I went to the woods because I wished to live deliberately,' he wrote, 'to front only the essential facts of life, and see if I could not learn what it had to teach, and not, when I came to die, discover that I had not lived.' Thoreau wanted to experiment with cutting himself off from the everyday life of Concord in order to discover the inner truths of being. His cabin lifestyle was relatively cheap and he lived simply so that earning money could become a less important part of his life. It also gave him a spiritual retreat in which to be alone with his thoughts (as well as a place to work).

Thoreau's book about his life at Walden Pond received a mixed reception on its publication in 1854, but in more recent times has become a key text in the environmental movement and even regarded as an example of performance art. 'A century and a half after its publication,' wrote novelist John Updike in his introduction to the 150th anniversary edition of the book, '*Walden* has become such a totem of the back-to-nature, preservationist, anti-business, civil-disobedience mindset, and Thoreau so vivid a protester, so perfect a crank and hermit saint, that the book risks being as revered and unread as the Bible.'

The cabin is no longer standing although a replica has been erected close to its original location.

ALSO ON THIS DAY **1821:** Death of English painter Richard Cosway · **1883:** American cartoonist Rube Goldberg born · **1970:** Death of American painter Barnett Newman

D. H. Lawrence's paintings are confiscated for indecency, 1929

The reason the English produce so few painters is not that they are, as a nation, devoid of a genuine feeling for visual art: though to look at their productions, and to look at the mess which has been made of actual English landscape, one might really conclude that they were, and leave it at that. But it is not the fault of the God that made them. They are made with aesthetic sensibilities the same as anybody else. The fault lies in the English attitude to life.

The English, and the Americans following them, are paralysed by fear. That is what thwarts and distorts the Anglo-Saxon existence, this paralysis of fear. It thwarts life, it distorts vision, and it strangles impulse: this over-mastering fear. And fear of what, in heaven's name? We have to answer that before we can understand the English failure in the visual arts: for, on the whole, it is a failure.

D. H. Lawrence, 'Introduction to These Paintings', 1929

Fresh from the hullabaloo over his novel *Lady Chatterley's Lover*, English writer D. H. Lawrence (1885–1930) again courted controversy with the opening of a one-man exhibition of about twenty of his oils and watercolour paintings at the Warren Gallery in London on 15 June 1929. Lawrence was particularly inspired by another writer-artist, William Blake (*see* 28 November), who he felt was an imaginative exception to what he saw as an English failure in art.

While his work is not regarded as especially impressive, even by himself, his subject matter – erotic portrayals of nude men and women with often biblical or classical themes, such as *Leda and the Swan* – meant that more than twelve thousand people came to view the exhibition, including critics from the national press ('disgusting', the *Observer*; 'gross', the *Daily Telegraph*; 'repellent', *Daily Express*).

On 5 July, the police were moved to intervene, entering the gallery and confiscating thirteen paintings, which were then placed under lock and key in a cell. Lawrence was horrified, even though the action seemed to confirm his theory about art in England. The magistrate presiding on the case when it came to court on 9 August, Justice Frederick Mead, said: 'It is utterly immaterial whether they are works of art or not.... The most splendidly painted picture in the universe might be obscene [and therefore should] be put an end to, like any wild animal which is dangerous.' Rather than escalate the situation, Lawrence paid the five guineas costs and promised never to show them again in Britain. Consequently the paintings have been widely dispersed.

ALSO ON THIS DAY 1549: Italian art collector Cardinal Francesco Maria del Monte born · **1631:** Work begins on St Paul's in Covent Garden, London, designed by English architect Inigo Jones (*see* 27 April) · **2012:** The Shard in London is inaugurated as Europe's tallest building (310 m/1,016 ft)

6 JULY

Lewis Carroll buys Sophie Anderson's
Girl with Lilac, 1865

Paid another visit to the Royal Academy, then to the Andersons, where I saw several beautiful pictures, and gave Mr Anderson some hints on the perspective of a picture of his, which will lead to his altering it a good deal. I bought a little picture by Mrs Anderson, of a child's head in profile: the original was in the house, and was called into the room, a beautiful child about 12, Elizabeth Turnbull by name. I intend taking a photograph of her in the same attitude as the picture.

Charles Dodgson (Lewis Carroll), diary entry, 6 July 1865

English mathematician Charles Dodgson (1832–1898), better known as the writer Lewis Carroll, was a keen lover of art and indeed was the first illustrator of his *Alice's Adventures in Wonderland* (*see* 16 December). Among his favourite artists was Anglo-French painter Sophie Anderson (1823–1903); two of her pictures – *Minie Morton* (1864) and the one he bought on 6 July, *Girl with Lilac* (1865) – had pride of place over the mantlepiece in his sitting room.

Anderson specialized in portraits and paintings of young girls, as well as classical and oriental subjects featuring young women (she never painted adult men). She had a cosmopolitan upbringing and lived and worked in a number of countries around Europe, and was associated with the Pre-Raphaelites.

In 1871, her painting *Elaine* (1870), based on a poem by Alfred, Lord Tennyson, was the first work by a female artist to be bought for the Walker

Art Gallery in Liverpool. Although less well known today than during her lifetime when she exhibited widely, her *No Walk Today* fetched £1 million at auction in November 2008.

ALSO ON THIS DAY 1840: Mexican painter José María Velasco Gómez born · **1887:** Belarussian-French painter Marc Chagall born · **1907:** Mexican painter Frida Kahlo born (*see* 20 April)

7 JULY

Unveiling of the 7 July Memorial to the London bombing victims, 2009

Through the language of abstract architecture, the memorial is intended to be a symbol of reconciliation for the families, as well as a permanent reminder for generations to come of the devastating effects of the bombings.

Carmody Groarke architectural practice, project statement

The 7 July Memorial in Hyde Park, London, is in remembrance of the fifty-two people who were killed in terrorist bombings in the city on 7 July 2005. Designed by architects Carmody Groarke and engineering specialists Arup, with advice from sculptor Antony Gormley (*see* 15 February 1998), it was unveiled on 7 July four years later by the Prince of Wales and the Duchess of Cornwall.

It is made up of fifty-two stainless steel stelae, or pillars, 3.5 metres (11½ feet) tall, one for each of the victims, and grouped in four linked sections to represent the four locations of the bombings: Tavistock Square, Edgware Road, King's Cross and Aldgate East Underground station. The pillars were cast by Norton Cast Products in Sheffield and each has a unique grain and texture. They carry information about the time, date and locations of the bombings, but no names – these are listed in alphabetical order on a nearby stainless steel plaque.

ALSO ON THIS DAY 1531: Death of German sculptor Tilman Riemenschneider · **1833:** Belgian painter Félicien Rops born · **1863:** Death of Irish painter William Mulready

Ian Breakwell works
on his diary art, 1973

Breakwell was as much a verbal as a visual artist, and a large part of his creative life was taken up with the diary he kept for more than 40 years, a mere fraction of which has been published. He sought an art of recurring epiphany, to be captured either visually or verbally. A diary entry dated 8 July 1973 gives the flavour: 'The 18.30 train from London to Plymouth. In the dining car the fat businessman farts loudly and unexpectedly, and simultaneously by the side of the railway track, a racehorse falls down.'

Nick Kimberley, obituary of Ian Breakwell,
***Guardian*, 21 October 2005**

English multimedia artist Ian Breakwell (1943–2005) worked in almost every conceivable medium, with painting and sculpture relegated to a very minor role in favour of documentation. His own wide-ranging list mentions collage, texts, theatre performances, illustrations, video and audio installations.

At the centre of his work was his *Continuous Diary* (1965–85), which chronicled the everyday details of life, and *The Walking Man Diary* (1975–78) that features shadowy photographs and written observations about a man who seemed to drift in and out of the Smithfield area of London where Breakwell lived, which he turned into an eleven-panel collage. Among his other works is *Auditorium* (1994) in which the viewer is only shown the audience's reactions at a theatre rather than the show itself.

ALSO ON THIS DAY **1593:** Italian painter Artemisia Gentileschi born · **1867:** German artist Käthe Kollwitz born (*see* 20 August) · **1917:** Death of Canadian painter Tom Thomson

Warhol first exhibits
Campbell's Soup Cans, 1962

NEW CONCENTRATED SOUP
The new Concentrated Soup now being demonstrated in our Canned Goods Department is a great boon to the modern housekeeper. Ready for use excepting the addition of a little water and season to suit the taste. Once used will always be kept in the house.
TRY A SAMPLE CUP FREE
It's wonderful how they can produce such a fine quality at the low price of $1.10 Per Dozen Cans.
Advertisement for Campbell's Soup, 1898

Campbell's produced its first condensed soup cans with orange and blue labels. When it brought out its first range of condensed soups in 1898, the labels changed to the now familiar red and white design on the suggestion of employee Herberton Williams, later to become the company's treasurer. The cursive script was used to suggest a feeling that the soup was home-made. The soup was a success, but the design was to find unexpected fame, too.

American painter, photographer, printmaker, commercial illustrator and filmmaker Andy Warhol (1928–1987) produced one of his most iconic Pop works by sketching each of thirty-two Campbell's cans on canvas with a pencil, painting it and the label, then projecting lettering onto the canvas, which he traced around. There is only very minor variation in the lettering. His intention was to emphasize the idea of uniformity and mass production rather than originality (the label had remained unchanged for the previous half a century) and the work was exhibited on narrow ledges, shelved as if in a supermarket, with each can depicting a different variety. The one-man exhibition at the Ferus Gallery in Los Angeles on 9 July 1962, his first Pop art show, made his name, although there was a decidedly mixed reception to the cans. Among the first buyers was the actor Dennis Hopper.

The initial inspiration for the work is unclear. Warhol's simple explanation was that he had it for lunch every day for twenty years so it became extremely familiar to him, but his friend the artist and curator Muriel Latow appears to have also suggested both the approach and the specific idea of the Campbell's cans (Warhol indeed sent her a cheque for $50).

Warhol worked on the soup cans from November 1961 and came back to the soup can theme repeatedly during his career, as well as using a multiple-image approach of the same subject.

ALSO ON THIS DAY **1441:** Death of Dutch painter Jan van Eyck · **1853:** American painter William Turner Dannat born · **1911:** English illustrator Mervyn Peake born

10 JULY

Reynolds offers to swap
a Gainsborough for a Titian, 1786

My Lord,

After a carfull examination of the picture I am sorry to confirm Roma's opinion that it has been much damaged and painted upon, and that too in places which can never be successfully repaired particularly in the back of the Venus. I am at a loss what to advise, the Picture cleaner will only make it ten times worse.

The best advice I can give is that we make an exchange, by which each of us may have a bargain. If there ever was an instance where an exchange may be made by which both parties may be benefitted, it is the present.

The picture is a copy by Titian himself from that in the Colonna palace. I am confident I see the true Titian tint through the yellow dirty paint and varnish with which the picture is coverd. If it was mine I should try to get this off, or ruin the picture in the attempt. It is the colour alone that can make it valuable. The Venus is not handsome and the Adonis is wretchedly disproportioned with an immense long body & short legs. The sky and trees have been painted over and must be repainted which I have the vanity to think nobody can do but myself – at any rate it is better to let it remain at my house till your Lordship comes to town.

PS I am thinking what picture to offer in exchange – what if I give Gainsborough's *Pigs* for it? It is by far the best picture he ever painted or perhaps ever will.

Sir Joshua Reynolds, letter to Lord Ossory, 10 July 1786

English painter Sir Joshua Reynolds (1723–1792; *see also* 8 May) was particularly interested in the construction and restoration of paintings, experimenting with his own paints to such a degree that many of them rapidly degraded during his own lifetime, and restoring or advising on restoration of other artists' work. Indeed, he did this to such an extent that the *Guardian* newspaper's art critic Jonathan Jones has described him as 'a kind of mad scientist, a would-be alchemist of art'.

Girl with Pigs (1782) by painter Thomas Gainsborough (1727–1788) is the subject of one of the odes composed by satirical poet John Wolcot (who wrote as 'Peter Pindar'), 'The Lyric Bard commendeth Mr Gainsborough's Pig – Recommendeth Landscape to the Artist':

> AND now, O Muse, with song so big,
> Turn round to Gainsb'rough's Girl and Pig,
> Or Pig and Girl I rather should have said:
> The Pig in white, I must allow,
> Is really a well painted Sow:
> I wish to say the same thing of the Maid.

In the end, Reynolds decided against making the swap he suggested to Lord Ossory on 10 July 1786 and instead sold Gainsborough's painting in 1790 for 300 guineas.

Benjamin Haydon observes galloping horses, 1810

In passing Piccadilly I observed in some horses galloping the various positions of their limbs – what was the position of the fore legs when the hind legs were in such a position, &c – it is astonishing how truly you get at their motions by thus scrutinizing; I made some sketches, after I arrived home, and they seemed to spring and had all the variety I could possibly wish – and such a look of Nature and activity!

**Benjamin Haydon, diary entry,
11 July 1810**

Known today as much for his diaries as his artistic work, English painter Benjamin Haydon (1786–1846; *see also* 28 December) concentrated on contemporary portraits and historical subjects. He also took an interest in horses as shown in his diary entry for 11 July 1810. This interest was partly anatomical as he felt it was a key but under-appreciated element of an artist's education. He collected his own drawings of people and animals in an album that he used to teach his students, including Edwin Landseer (*see* 17 April) who produced many notable paintings of animals.

Other horse-related works include a sketch of the Horse of Selene from the Elgin Marbles before they were bought by the British government, and *Gentleman with a Horse* (1844) to which he refers in his diary on 25 October ('Worked & rubbed in a Horse & Man.') and 1 November ('Worked hard & finished a horse in a Portrait.') in 1844.

ALSO ON THIS DAY 1593: Death of Italian painter Giuseppe Arcimboldo · **1834:** American-born painter James Abbott McNeill Whistler born (*see also* 22 May) · **1875:** English illustrator Henry Matthew Brock born

Van Dyck sketches an elderly Sofonisba Anguissola, 1624

Portrait of the painter Signora Sofonisba, painter, done from life in Palermo in the year 1624, on 12 July, her age being 96, still having her memory, with her brain most alert, being most courteous; and though through old age she had lost her sight, she still took much pleasure in putting pictures before her, and then by constantly putting her nose to the picture, managed to discern some little of it, and took great pleasure in doing this. As I was making her portrait, she gave me many hints, such as not to take the light from too high in case the shadows in the wrinkles of old age should become too strong, and many other good sayings, as she went on telling me parts of her life, by which I knew that she was a painter by nature and wonderful, and the greatest trouble she had was that from lack of sight she could paint no more, though her hand was firm without tremor of any sort.

Anthony van Dyck, sketchbook note, 1624

Italian painter Sofonisba Anguissola (c. 1532–1625) had a long and successful international career. Her work was appreciated by Michelangelo and described by art historian Giorgio Vasari in his *Lives of the Artists* as showing 'greater application and better grace than any other woman of our age'. She became an official court painter at the Spanish court of Philip II, becoming close to him and his queen, Elisabeth of Valois, and produced a series of highly regarded portraits of the royal family, as well as a range of other paintings, including *The Chess Game* (1555), which depicts her sisters playing in their home garden.

In her old age, when she was ninety-two, the Flemish painter Anthony van Dyck (1599–1641) – aged twenty-five and himself later to become a royal favourite at the court of Charles I – visited her at her home in Palermo, Italy. He made a sketch of her in his notebook and wrote up some of the advice she gave him at that meeting (although he was slightly out in assuming her age).

Van Dyck's portrait of Anguissola is part of the National Trust's collection at Knole country house in Kent, England.

ALSO ON THIS DAY 1730: Pottery entrepreneur Josiah Wedgwood born (*see* 15 May) · **1857:** American potter George E. Ohr born · **1960:** Etch A Sketch is produced by Ohio Art Company

William Hodges joins Captain Cook's second voyage, 1772

Whereas we have engaged Mr William Hodges, a lanskip painter to proceed in his Majesty's Sloop under your Command on her present intended voyage in order to make drawings and paintings of such places in the countries you may touch at in the course of the said voyage as may be proper to give a more perfect idea thereof than can be formed from written descriptions only; You are hereby required and directed to receive the said Mr William Hodges on board giving him all proper accommodation and assistance, victualling him as the ship's company and taking care that he does diligently employ himself in making drawings or paintings of such places as you may touch at that may be worthy of notice in the course of your voyage as also of such other objects and things as may fall within the compass of his abilities.

Admiralty letter to Captain Cook, 30 June 1772

English painter William Hodges (1744–1797) was a supernumerary member of the *Resolution*'s crew on Captain James Cook's second Pacific Ocean expedition of 1772–75, travelling aboard as the ship's artist. Although known as a landscape painter, Hodges also paid particular attention to the flora and fauna of the new lands they visited, as well as the people they met and what they wore, and the geographical features that were of special interest to the Admiralty. This was all done with a sense of the importance of light and meteorological elements that were well ahead of his time, as was his open-air approach to his subjects.

Although he completed much of his work when he had returned to England, among Hodges's 'firsts' were: the first visual images of the Antarctic, including a painting of an iceberg, and the first painting of Easter Island (*see also* 10 April).

Hodges also travelled through India but gave up painting following a disastrous exhibition and died soon after a catastrophic banking venture. For many years he was largely forgotten until a retrospective of his work in 2004 at the National Maritime Museum brought him to 21st-century attention. In the catalogue's foreword, Sir David Attenborough described him as 'the most unjustly neglected British painter of the eighteenth century' and art critic Andrew Graham-Dixon said of Hodges's *A View of Matavai Bay* (1776) that 'the palette of this picture, and others in the same vein, is unlike anything in earlier European landscape painting'.

Contemporary writer William Haley's epitaph on Hodges in 1809 included the lines:

> To active Hodges, who with zeal sublime,
> Pursued the art, he lov'd in every clime;
> Who early traversing the globe with Cook,
> Painted new life from Nature's book.

14 JULY

The Bayeux Tapestry is (probably) first used, 1077

HIC. HAROLD. REX. INTERFECTVS. EST.
Matthew Paris, and another English author, say he was slain by an arrow, and that a soldier of duke William's cut him in the thigh. This is confirmed by the tapestry, where one sees a man on horseback, cutting the thigh of Harold; which so much displeased duke William, that he degraded the soldier who did it. The remaining part of the tapestry is so defaced, that hardly any thing is to be distinguished: the inscriptions are intirely obliterated. In some bits, one may perceive the French pursuing and slaying the English. This battle was one of the longest and best-disputed of any recorded in history. The tapestry, as it now remains, comes only to this period; but there is no doubt but it went at least as far as duke William's coronation; and it is even to be admired, that so much of it should have endured now upwards of seven hundred years.

Smart Lethieullier, appendix in Andrew Ducarel's
***Anglo-Norman Antiquities Considered*, 1767**

English antiquary Smart Lethieullier (1701–1760) wrote the first detailed account in English of the Bayeux Tapestry (which is in fact an embroidery), published posthumously. Although there is no conclusive evidence about when and for what reason the 68-metre (224-foot) tapestry was commissioned, it seems most likely that it was done on the order of Bishop Odo, William the Conqueror's half-brother and regent of England, to be used perhaps as decoration for the cathedral during its consecration on 14 July 1077.

Anglo-Saxon elements in the Latin titles that accompany the images suggest it may have been made in England, possibly under the supervision of Abbot Scolland of St Augustine's Abbey, Canterbury. Notable features include the earliest illustration of a harrow and the first image of Halley's Comet. The end of the tapestry, likely to have shown William's coronation, has never been found.

ALSO ON THIS DAY **1862:** Austrian painter Gustav Klimt born · **1872:** French doll maker Albert Marque born · **1910:** American animator William Hanna born

15 JULY

Florence Wyman Ivins exhibition at the Met, New York, 1921

The work of Florence Wyman Ivins cannot be unknown to Museum visitors of recent years; for the poster advertising the Story-Hours for Children which has stood for several seasons in the Fifth Avenue Hall was designed by her, as were the covers of the *Children's Bulletin*. These have occasioned many expressions of delight and many queries as to the artist who executed them. An opportunity to know the notable character of the contribution that Mrs Ivins has made to American art will be afforded at the Museum during the next few months in Class Room B, where an exhibition of a collection of her watercolor drawings, woodcuts and drawings in black and white will be on view from 15 July through the month of October. Admirable in draughtsmanship and skilful in design, these have a special charm of subject in that with a spontaneous gaiety of treatment they portray various episodes of childhood experience.

'The Work of Florence Wyman Ivins',
***The Metropolitan Museum of Art Bulletin*, 1921**

American artist Florence Wyman Ivins (1881–1948) studied at the Art Students League in New York, and was a professional portrait painter and book illustrator by the time she married Williams Ivins (who went on to become assistant then acting director at the Metropolitan Museum of Art in New York). Florence Ivins regularly designed posters for the Met's children's activities, in a style compared to British illustrators Kate Greenaway and Randolph Caldecott, before she became the first female artist to hold a solo exhibition of work at the museum on 15 July 1921.

'The Children's World: Drawings' featured 122 of her watercolours, woodcuts and black and white drawings, and came shortly after years of suffragette campaigning, which resulted in the passing of the Nineteenth Amendment and the enfranchisement of millions of women in America in time for the 1920 presidential election won by Republican Warren Harding.

ALSO ON THIS DAY 1149: Church of the Holy Sepulchre, Jerusalem, is consecrated (*see* 18 October) · **1573**: English architect Inigo Jones born (*see* 27 April) · **1799**: Rosetta Stone is uncovered by Captain Pierre-François Bouchard in Egypt

16 JULY

Arshile Gorky chases Roberto Matta in New York, 1948

Mural painting does not serve only in a decorative capacity, but an intellectual one as well. By education I do not mean in a descriptive sense, portraying cinema-like the suffering or progress of humanity, but as to the plastic forms and treatments in the art of painting. since many workers, school children or patients in hospitals (as the case may be, depending on the type of institution) have little or no opportunity to visit museums, mural painting could and would open up new visas to their neglected knowledge of a far too-little popularized Art.

Rimbaud has epitomized for me the true function of the artist when he wrote: 'The poet should define the quantity of the unknown which awakes in his time, in the universal soul. He should give more than the formula of his thought, than the annotation of his march toward progress. The enormous becoming the normal, when absorbed by everyone, he would really be a multiplication of progress.'

Arshile Gorky, 'My Murals for the Newark Airport: An Interpretation', 1936

Although the reputation of Armenian-American Abstract Expressionist painter Arshile Gorky (1904–1948) is firmly established, many of his works were accidentally destroyed in a series of fires, while his Newark murals were also destroyed or painted over. He was similarly unlucky in love. His wife Agnes Magruder was rather lukewarm towards Chilean surrealist painter Roberto Matta (1911–2002) in her diary entry of 7 June 1948. She wrote that she found him stimulating but rather self-centred and superficial, and essentially did not trust him. Nevertheless, the following week she began an affair with him.

When Gorky found out he first angrily confronted Magruder (or 'Mougouch' as he called his muse) and then 'visited' Matta on 16 July. Extremely upset, he chased Matta through Central Park in New York in an unsuccessful attempt to attack him with a walking cane, comparing him unfavourably to Soviet dictator Joseph Stalin. When Matta told Magruder about the incident, she took the children and left her husband.

Less than a week later, on 21 July, Gorky took his own life.

17 JULY

Audubon requests payment
for *Birds of America*, 1830

I have been in London a fortnight and am yet without any answer to my last letter sent to you from Liverpool about a month ago, in which I desire you to collect the money due to me by Miss Harriet Douglas of New York. I am extremely anxious to have your answer and some money from you and I again ask you to send in a regular list of my Subscribers with you and their respective residence to have the whole engraved in the sheets of my 1st Jany next plates of frontispieces. I hope you received the 19th number in good order.

John James Audubon, letter to Alexander Hill, 17 July 1830

American ornithologist and painter John James Audubon (1785–1851; *see also* 27 January) wrote to Alexander Hill, a bookseller in Edinburgh, asking him to collect payment for his book *The Birds of America*, which was issued in parts between 1827 and 1838. The money was due from Harriet Douglas in New York, the first subscriber to it in America; it was a sum well worth chasing – a volume of loose prints was priced at $189, a half-bound one at $225 and a full-bound one at $234. Audubon had many problems with subscribers who failed to pay promptly or simply went back on their pledge.

Audubon's diary contains another reference to Harriet Douglas, on 21 March 1827:

> Called on Miss D–, the fair American. To my surprise I saw the prints she had received the evening before quite abused and tumbled. This, however, was not my concern, and I regretted it only on her account, that so little care should be taken of a book that in fifty years will be sold at immense prices because of its rarity. The wind blew great guns all morning.

ALSO ON THIS DAY **1797:** French painter Paul Delaroche born · **1871:** German-American painter Lyonel Feininger born · **1998:** Death of American book illustrator Lillian Hoban

18 JULY

Hitler opens the House of German Art, 1937

When the laying ceremony of the foundation stone of this building was held four years ago, we all knew that it was important not just to erect a a new house, but also a foundation for a new and true German art. The task was to generate a turning point in the progress of German cultural creation...now the exhibition itself must result in a sea change in relation to the decay of art, sculpture and painting we have experienced.... We do not believe that the time of individual creativity ended with the great men in previous centuries.... No! We believe that today, when the highest individual achievements are apparent in so many areas, the highest value of personality will again emerge victoriously in the field of art.

**Adolf Hitler, speech at the opening of
the House of German Art, Munich, 18 July 1937**

On 18 July 1937, the day before the Degenerate Art exhibition opened (*see* 4 June), Adolf Hitler gave a speech to officially open the House of German

Art in Munich. The inaugural exhibition at the new museum, which was designed by one of Hitler's favourite architects Paul Troost (1878–1934), was the Great German Art Exhibition that the Führer intended would be a key part of Germany's post-First World War cultural renewal.

It was hard to pin down exactly what this renewal entailed, and indeed some artists initially held up as shining exemplars, such as the Reich's favoured sculptors Arno Breker (1900–1991) and Josef Thorak (1889–1952), later fell foul of the regime's arbitrariness, but essentially work had to be optimistic and conspicuously pro-German. Those who toured the Great Exhibition would have seen pieces such as Breker's 3-metre (10-foot)-high, classically proportioned bronze figures *Decathlete* and *Victory*, looking expressionlessly ahead. However, even Hitler was disappointed with the standard of the fifteen thousand works submitted for the exhibition.

ALSO ON THIS DAY 1573: The Roman Catholic Inquisition questions Italian painter Paolo Veronese about some of the details in his *Last Supper* (Veronese renames it *The Feast in the House of Levi* to avoid further problems) · **1610:** Death of Italian painter Caravaggio (*see* 29 May) · **1721:** Death of French painter Jean-Antoine Watteau

19 JULY

New stamps celebrate the Apollo 11 moon landing, 2019

CAPSULE COMMUNICATOR (CAPCOM): Man, we're getting a picture on the TV.

ALDRIN: Oh, you got a good picture. Huh?

CAPCOM: There's a great deal of contrast in it, and currently it's upside-down on our monitor, but we can make out a fair amount of detail.

ALDRIN: Okay, will you verify the position, the opening I ought to have on the camera.

CAPCOM: Stand by.

CAPCOM: Okay, Neil, we can see you coming down the ladder now.

ARMSTRONG: Okay, I just checked – getting back up to that first step, Buzz, it's not even collapsed too far, but it's adequate to get back up.

CAPCOM: Roger, we copy.

ARMSTRONG: It takes a pretty good little jump.

CAPCOM: Buzz, this is Houston. F 2 1/160th second for shadow photography on the sequence camera.

ALDRIN: Okay.

ARMSTRONG: I'm at the foot of the ladder. The LM foot pads are only depressed in the surface about 1 or 2 inches. Although the surface appears to be very, very fine grained, as you get close to it. It's almost like a powder. Now and then, it's very fine.

ARMSTRONG: I'm going to step off the LM now.

ARMSTRONG: That's one small step for a man. One giant leap for mankind.

Transcript of Apollo 11 moon landing, 20 July 1969

The US Postal Service (USPS) issued special stamps on 19 July 2019 to celebrate the anniversary of the first moon landing fifty years previously (although Apollo 11 in fact landed on 20 July). The first stamp depicts Neil Armstrong's iconic moon walk photograph of Buzz Aldrin (*see also* 12 November), which includes his own reflection. The second is a photograph of the moon taken by lawyer and amateur astrophotographer Gregory Revera from his home in Madison, Alabama, with a yellow dot indicating the spot in the Sea of Tranquility where the *Eagle* landed.

The stamps were designed by Antonio Alcalá, the USPS's art director, who also designed the service's solar eclipse stamp that used temperature-sensitive ink. The moon landing stamps – offset-printed in cyan, magenta, yellow and black inks – have an unusual silvery shimmer from the metallic chrome paper stock they were printed on.

ALSO ON THIS DAY 1789: English painter, illustrator and engraver John Martin born · **1834:** French painter and sculptor Edgar Degas born · **1883:** Austrian-American animator Max Fleischer born

Land artist Robert Smithson dies in a plane crash, 1973

This little theory is tentative and could be abandoned at any time. Theories like things are also abandoned. That theories are eternal is doubtful. Vanished theories compose the strata of many forgotten books.

Robert Smithson, 'A Provisional Theory of Nonsites', 1968

American land and multimedia artist Robert Smithson (1938–1973) was a founder of the land art movement. Smithson was interested in the relationship between works of art and the environment in which they were observed. He developed the concept of site-specific work as opposed to non-sites (works that gather earth and minerals from one location and are then set up in a gallery as sculptures).

His best-known work is *Spiral Jetty* (1970), a swirling sculpture 457 metres (1,500 feet) long, constructed out of mud, salt crystals and basalt rocks. It is so close to Utah's Great Salt Lake that it is often submerged due to fluctuating water levels. This was the first in a kind of land art triptych and was followed by *The Broken Circle* (The Netherlands, 1971); it would have been completed by a final artwork on the artificial Tecovas Lake, near Amarillo, Texas.

However, Smithson's plane crashed as he reconnoitered the site on 20 July 1973; after his death, *Amarillo Ramp* was finished by other artists: his widow, Nancy Holt, and colleagues Richard Serra and Tony Shafrazi. Built out of sandstone, the 42.7-metre (140-foot)-diameter ramp stretched 120 metres (400 feet) from the shore into the lake, but now that the lake is dried up, at 4.6 metres (15 feet) high, the ramp stands proud and is slowly eroding. The work is on private land, so visitors must book timeslots a week in advance to view the artwork.

ALSO ON THIS DAY 1895: Hungarian painter and photographer László Moholy-Nagy born · **1939:** American painter and sculptor Judy Chicago born (*see* 14 March) · **2011:** Death of German-born British painter Lucian Freud

Herostratus burns down
the Temple of Artemis, 356 BC

The iniquity of oblivion blindly scattereth her poppy, and deals with the memory of men without distinction to merit of perpetuity. Who can but pity the founder of the Pyramids? Herostratus lives that burnt the Temple of Diana, he is almost lost that built it. Time hath spared the Epitaph of Adrian's horse, confounded that of himself. In vain we compute our felicities by the advantage of our good names, since bad have equal durations; and Thersites is like to live as long as Agamemnon. Who knows whether the best of men be known? Or whether there be not more remarkable persons forgot, than any that stand remembred in the known account of time?

English author Sir Thomas Browne,
Hydriotaphia, **1658**

The Temple of Artemis, also known as the Temple of Diana, at Ephesus in Turkey enjoyed three incarnations. The first was destroyed by a flood in the 7th century AD and the second (paid for by Croesus *c.* AD 550) by Herostratus, a low-born or possible slave, who burnt down the structure in a bid for fame. To ensure his plan came to nothing, the local authorities not only executed him but also passed a law banning any mention of his name, either in speech or in writing. However, his name was recorded by his contemporary, historian Theopompus, and details of his infamy continued through the ages – the term 'herostratic fame' became a term to describe anybody who went to extreme lengths to ensure their name lived on after them.

In its pre-Herostratian heyday, the marble temple was 115 metres (377 feet) long and 46 metres (150 feet) wide, with a statue of Artemis in the centre, and it boasted double rows of pillars that were 12 metres (40 feet) high, most of which had life-size relief carvings. It was regarded as a place of sanctuary.

The third temple – which had fallen into disrepair by AD 401 – was the building regarded as one of the Seven Wonders of the World.

ALSO ON THIS DAY 1858: German painter Lovis Corinth born · **1866:** Swiss painter Carlos Schwabe born · **1897:** The Tate Gallery opens in London

Nude models become canvases for NYC Bodypainting Day, 2017

If I ventured to describe that attitude there would be a fine howl – but there the Venus lies for anybody to gloat over that wants to – and there she has a right to lie, for she is a work of art, and art has its privileges. I saw a young girl stealing furtive glances at her; I saw young men gazing long and absorbedly at her, I saw aged infirm men hang upon her charms with a pathetic interest. How I should like to describe her – just to see what a holy indignation I could stir up in the world...yet the world is willing to let its sons and its daughters and itself look at Titian's beast, but won't stand a description of it in words. Which shows that the world is not as consistent as it might be.

Mark Twain on Titian's *Venus of Urbino*, in *A Tramp Abroad*, 1880

Bodypainting Day was founded by American artist Andy Golub, who had painted a wide range of objects, including cars and hats, before he decided to paint naked bodies in 2007 and thereby extend the concept of a canvas and collaborate on a personal level with the subject. Two years later he was arrested while painting two almost naked female and male models in Times Square, New York, and also in 2011 when, for the first time, his two models were fully nude (he was warned by the city authorities this could only be done during the night).

On 22 July 2014, he established NYC Bodypainting Day to explore the idea of public art, the human form and freedom of artistic experession, which attracted thirty artists from around America and forty entirely nude models who were painted at Columbus Circle. Since then, the event has been held in Amsterdam, Berlin, Brussels and San Francisco.

The 2017 event was the first run by Golub's non-profit organization Human Connection Arts, which now supervises all Bodypainting Day events, and involved one hundred nude models. It aims to help artists share their work with the public and give models of any age, size and gender the chance to use their bodies to become living art.

ALSO ON THIS DAY 1632: Foundation stone of the Buen Retiro Palace, Madrid, is laid · **1882:** American painter Edward Hopper born (*see* 21 January) · **1971:** The Lady of Baza, a 4th-century AD sculpture, is uncovered near Granada, Spain

The first graphic novel is nominated for the Booker Prize, 2018

Given the changing shape of fiction, it was only a matter of time before a graphic novel was included on the Man Booker longlist. *Sabrina* makes demands on the reader in precisely the way all good fiction does. Oblique, subtle, minimal, unmanipulative: the style of the pictures is the book's worldview. Drnaso uses images to express an idea about what's invisible – an idea about uncertainty, and the different kinds of holes that missing people leave in our lives.

**Booker Prize judges' comment on Nick Drnaso *Sabrina*,
in the longlist announcement, 23 July 2018**

American writer Nick Drnaso (b. 1989) became the first graphic novelist whose work appeared on the longlist of the Booker Prize when *Sabrina* was nominated in 2018. Published by Drawn & Quarterly, it tells the story of the fallout after the murder of a young woman named Sabrina. In particular, it concentrates on the conspiracy theories and fake news surrounding her death and its impact on her boyfriend Teddy and other friends and family. Chris Ware, reviewing it for the *Guardian* newspaper on 2 June 2018 wrote: 'What's most curious and, ultimately, valuable about this book is that it is not a crime story; it's a perspicacious and chilling analysis of the nature of trust and truth and the erosion of both in the age of the internet – and especially, in the age of Trump.'

ALSO ON THIS DAY 1599: Flemish painter Bonaventura Peeters the Elder born · **1777:** German painter Philipp Otto Runge born · **1933:** English-Italian architect Richard Rogers born

The unveiling of the
Menin Gate Memorial, 1927

Our hearts are stirred by feelings of deep emotion as we stand here to pay a Nation's tribute to the memory of the great army of men whose names are inscribed on this beautiful Memorial, who have no known graves.

One of the most tragic features of the Great War was the number of casualties reported as 'Missing, believed killed'.

To their relatives there must have been added to their grief a tinge of bitterness and a feeling that everything possible had not been done to recover their loved ones' bodies and give them reverent burial. That feeling no longer exists; it ceased to exist when the conditions under which the fighting was being carried out was realised.

But when peace came and the last ray of hope had been extinguished, the void seemed deeper and the outlook more forlorn for those who had no graves to visit, no place where they could lay tokens of loving remembrance.

The hearts of the people throughout the Empire went out to them and it was resolved that here at Ypres, where so many of the missing are known to have fallen, there should be erected a Memorial worthy of them which should give expression to the Nation's gratitude for their sacrifice and their sympathy with those who mourned them.

A Memorial has been erected which, in its simple grandeur, fulfils this object, and now it can be said of each one in whose honour we are assembled here today:

'He is not missing: he is here!'

Field Marshal Lord Plumer, speech at the
memorial unveiling ceremony, Belgium, 24 July 1927

Permanently open, the Menin Gate Memorial to the Missing in Ypres, Belgium, commemorates nearly 54,000 soldiers from the UK, India, Australia, Canada and South Africa who died unidentified in the area and who have no known grave. Their names are inscribed on panels inside the monument.

The concrete, Euville stone and red-brick memorial was designed by English architect Sir Reginald Blomfield (1856–1942) as both a hall and triumphal arch. Decorative features including the lion on the top of the monument were made by Scottish sculptor Sir William Reid Dick (1879–1961). When it suffered major damage during the Second World War, Blomfield's architect son Austin (1895–1967) supervised the restoration work.

Although generally the memorial has received a positive reception, English poet and soldier Siegfried Sassoon was less happy with its construction and in his poem 'On Passing the New Menin Gate' described it as a 'sepulchre of crime' that failed to celebrate those who died in the conflict.

25 JULY

Rembrandt goes bankrupt and makes an inventory, 1656

Weapons
Indian fans
Giant's head
Cuirasses [armour]
Wooden trumpet
Coral
Lion's skin
Deer horns
Casts of body parts
Crossbows
Antique helmets
Gourds
Bird of Paradise
Shield decorated with figures
Box of medals
Several globes

Extracts from the inventory of Rembrandt's effects, 25 July 1656

He used to say, he aimed at nothing more than to imitate living Nature, making that Nature consist only in things created, such as they appear. he had old pieces of armour, old instruments, old head-dresses and abundance of old clothes of divers sorts hanging up in his workhouse, which he said were his antiques.

Roger de Piles, *The Art of Painting and the Lives of the Painters*, 1699

Dutch painter Rembrandt van Rijn (1606–1669; *see also* 31 January) was not marvellous with money and in 1656 had no option but to declare himself bankrupt. In so doing, he was forced to make an inventory of his possessions. Naturally there was plenty of art – one of the reasons he had fallen so heavily into debt was his buying habit, although as he also worked as an art dealer this is understandable. Among the artists whose works are mentioned in the inventory are the rather wild Flemish painter Adriaen Brouwer, Dutch painters Pieter Lastman (Rembrandt's teacher), Jacob Pynas (who also taught Rembrandt) and Jan Lievens (who shared a studio with Rembrandt for five years), and printmaker/landscapist Hercules Seghers, as well as work by the likes of Raphael, Titian and Michelangelo.

The intriguing list not only featured his own works, etchings and scrapbooks, as well as twenty-two books, but also included all the paraphenalia of a working artist as can be seen in the extracts above. In particular, there were dozens of Roman busts (stone originals and plaster copies), and plaster casts of hands, which he used for his own paintings as well as instructional tools for his students.

ALSO ON THIS DAY **1905:** English illustrator Denys Watkins-Pitchford ('BB') born · **1918:** American mixed-media artist Jane Frank born · **2013:** German artist Katharina Fritsch's sculpture *Hahn/ Cock* is unveiled on the Fourth Plinth, Trafalgar Square, London

26 JULY

Ryde pier opens to the public, 1814

THE TOWN REGATTA – On Tuesday and Wednesday next our time-honoured regatta will take place off the pier with promises of more than usual *éclat* and spirit. The programme issued by the committee promises fair to give two good days' sport and enjoyment to the sight-seeing public. There is something of one sort or another which cannot fail to please the most fastidious. There is sailing, rowing, sculling, canoeing, aquatic Derby and mortal combat carried out in true martial style, and the everlasting pig hunt, which never fails to cause endless amusement. The committee promise a grand display of fireworks, and we only need a recurrence of the splendid weather to ensure a successful regatta. Great praise is due to the active committee and their indefatigable assistants for the strenuous labours which they have exerted to provide entertainment for our visitors and amusement for all.

Isle of Wight Observer, 29 August 1874

Ryde's 703-metre (2,305-foot)-long pier on the Isle of Wight is regarded as the first seaside pleasure pier and has been a Grade II listed building since 1976. It was designed by Southampton architect John Kent (d. 1837), better known for his domestic commissions. The foundation stone was laid on 29 June 1813 and the pier opened to the public on 26 July the following year. Although Kent was forced to sell off his goods and stock when he was declared bankrupt in 1811 and spent some time in Marshalsea debtors' prison, he was still chosen for the pier work – he designed and built it at a cost of £12,000 while under bankruptcy restrictions. Kent was also interested in perpetual motion and submitted two patents for such machines.

Although it has always provided entertainment for the general public, it was originally commissioned by local businessmen who wanted a secure location where ships could dock whatever the tide rather than force passengers to disembark into sandbanks or water. The pier had the desired effect, helping to turn Ryde into a popular resort as well as becoming popular for promenaders. In his memoir *Babycham Night* (2003), Philip Norman gives an account of living on the pier in the 1950s, and describes it as 'a serious industrial artefact' and a key part of the island's tourist trade. It remains a working pier with regular ferry crossings to the UK mainland and has its own railway stations at its sea and land ends.

At the start of the First World War, there were more than one hundred piers around the UK. About half that number still remain.

ALSO ON THIS DAY 1796: American painter George Catlin born · **1908:** Luxembourger sculptor Lucien Wercollier born · **1971:** Death of American photographer Diane Arbus

Bells celebrate the first day
of the Olympic Games, 2012

I don't think making these works is any different from trying to decide on buying a pair of trousers.... It's all trying to live, you know.... I'm not saying the art is superfluous crap, but that [everything is] really important. It's all profound. Everything you do affects other people, and might have a terrible or an amazing effect. Not just paintings in a gallery. I find it difficult to draw a line.

Martin Creed, interview with Charlotte Higgins,
***Guardian*, 30 May 2012**

British performance artist Martin Creed (b. 1968) won the 2001 Turner Prize (*see* 6 November) for his installation *Work No. 227: The lights going on and off*. His *Work No. 1197: All the Bells* was a three-minute chorus of bells that was rung out across Britain at 8 a.m. on 27 July by a wide variety of local groups to signal the start of the first day of the London 2012 Olympic Games and Paralympic Games (though some ringers performed it a few minutes later).

Creed was keen to include as many bells as possible, listing a selection of possibilities: 'Hand bells, door bells, bicycle bells, church bells, town hall bells, sleigh bells, cow bells, school bells, last orders bells, dinner bells...where there is a bell, we need someone to ring it!' His instructions to all those taking part were simply: 'All the bells in a country rung as quickly and as loudly as possible for three minutes.' The work was re-commissioned as part of the London 2012 Festival with slightly revised instructions from its first performance six years earlier in San Juan, Puerto Rico.

ALSO ON THIS DAY 1768: Austrian painter Joseph Koch born · **1942:** Death of Estonian painter Karl Pärsimägi · **1992:** Death of Australian photographer Max Dupain

Ohio State University decides not to give Lichtenstein tenure, 1950

Dorothy Lichtenstein and the Board of the Roy Lichtenstein Foundation, in partnership with The Ohio State University, are pleased to announce that the Roy Lichtenstein Foundation has permanently endowed two high-level named chairs at the university. Two $3 million endowments will support the Roy Lichtenstein Foundation Endowed Chair of Art History and the Roy Lichtenstein Endowed Chair of Studio Art. 'We are delighted and honored to carry forward the creative spirit and intellectual inquiry of alumnus and world-renowned artist Roy Lichtenstein', said Ohio State President Michael V. Drake. 'These complementary chairs will elevate the arts and humanities across the university, broadening horizons for students and faculty for years to come.'

**Ohio State University press release,
30 January 2017**

On 28 July 1950, Frank Siberling Jr, Professor of Art History at the Ohio State University, wrote a polite letter to American artist Roy Lichtenstein (1923–1997; *see also* 10 February) informing him that, after consulting senior members of staff, the decision had been taken not to offer him tenure. Siberling added that not only did Lichtenstein's promise appear insufficient, the chance of promotion within the department was also very small. Happily, the Roy Lichtenstein Foundation of New York did not turn this decision into a grudge, with the establishment in 2017 of two endowed professorships at the university.

ALSO ON THIS DAY **1609:** Dutch painter Judith Leyster born · **1866:** English book illustrator Beatrix Potter born (*see* 4 March) · **1887:** French-American painter and sculptor Marcel Duchamp born (*see* 2 September)

Carlyle sits for a portrait
by Whistler, 1873

Carlyle tells me he is 'sitting' to Whistler. If C. makes signs of changing his position W. screams out in an agonised tone, 'For God's sake, don't move!' C. afterwards said that all W.'s anxiety seemed to be to get the coat painted to ideal perfection; the face went for little. He had begun by asking two or three sittings, but managed to get a great many. At last C. flatly rebelled. He used to define W. as the most absurd creature on the face of the earth.

William Allingham, diary entry,
29 July 1873

There are numerous portraits of Scottish philosopher, historian and mathematician Thomas Carlyle (1795–1881), but not all of them were to his taste. Of the one produced in 1869 by George Frederic Watts (*see* 20 February), he said it made him look like a 'mad labourer'. Writing to his brother he called it: 'Decidedly the most insufferable picture that has yet been made of me, a delirious-looking mountebank full of violence, awkwardness, atrocity and stupidity, without recognizable likeness to anything I have ever known in any feature of me.' Indeed, when in 1872 he arranged to sit for American-born painter and his neighbour in Chelsea, James McNeill Whistler (1834–1903; *see also* 11 August), Carlyle remarked of this portrait: 'I've been painted by a man of note – Watts, his name...and he painted my shirt-collar as if I'd never had a laundress.'

As his friend the Irish writer William Allingham (1824–1889; author of 'The Fairies' poem) recounted in his diary, the sittings were not very relaxing and went on far longer than initially suggested by Whistler, who was known as something of a tyrant in terms of requesting no movement. Scottish watercolourist Hugh Cameron also stepped in to watch the work in progress, writing: 'It was the funniest thing I ever saw. There was Carlyle sitting motionless, like a Heathen God or Oriental sage, and Whistler hopping about like a sparrow.' The result was a painting that Whistler called *Arrangement in Grey and Black, No. 2: Portrait of Thomas Carlyle*, along similar lines to his 1871 *Arrangement in Grey and Black, No. 1: Portrait of the Artist's Mother*, or *Whistler's Mother* (see 22 May), which Carlyle liked.

The portrait of Carlyle was offered to the National Portrait Gallery in London but the director Sir George Scharf refused it, asking rhetorically 'Has painting come to this?' and mocking the idea that 'such work should pass for painting'.

ALSO ON THIS DAY 1801: English cartographer George Bradshaw born · **1836:** Inauguration of the Arc de Triomphe in Paris · **1890:** Death of Dutch painter Vincent van Gogh (*see* 17 June)

30 JULY

Rosa Bonheur declares her feelings to Anna Klumpke, 1898

Quite late this afternoon [30 July 1898], Rosa Bonheur entered the studio where I am working on the accessories of the large canvas; she cast an eye over her portrait and said a few nice things. Then, turning to me, she put her hands on my shoulders, and as I look at her with a little bewilderment, she said, in a voice mixing tenderness with supplication: 'Anna, will you stay with me and share my existence? I am so attached to you. Life would seem very sad if you are no longer here. I'll be all alone'. 'You rejuvenate my heart', she continued, 'you give me energy to work.... Wouldn't you like to stay with your old friend, who will adopt you as if you were her child, and who would help you to do beautiful things in painting?'

Anna Klumpke, *Rosa Bonheur*, 1908

French painter and sculptor Rosa Bonheur (1822–1899) was arguably the leading female painter of the 19th century and the first female artist to be made Officer of the French Legion of Honour. She was known particularly for her depictions of animals – especially *Ploughing in the Nivernais* (1849) and *The Horse Fair* (1855) – which she had begun painting since the start of her teenage years, going on to study animal anatomy at Paris's main veterinary college and the city's abbatoirs.

As well as her artistic success, she was famous for wearing men's clothing and enjoyed 'men's' sports such as hunting. She lived openly as a lesbian with her partner and schoolfriend Nathalie Micas for forty years, and then, after Micas's death, with American artist Anna Klumpke (1856–1942) after

Klumpke had travelled to her home in France to paint her portrait. All three are buried together at the Père Lachaise Cemetery, Paris.

ALSO ON THIS DAY 1511: Italian painter and art historian Giorgio Vasari born · **1898:** English sculptor Henry Moore born (*see* 15 September) · **1938:** English photographer Terry O'Neill born

31 JULY

Ranger 7 sends the first close-up photographs of the moon, 1964

There is no difficulty in procuring impressions of the moon by the Daguerreotype, beyond that which arises from her motion. By the aid of a lens and a heliostat, I caused the moonbeams to converge on a plate, the lens being three inches in diameter. In half an hour a very strong impression was obtained. With another arrangement of lenses I obtained a stain nearly an inch in diameter, and of the general figure of the moon, in which the places of the dark spots might be indistinctly traced. An iodized plate, being exposed for fifteen seconds only close to the flame of a gas light, was very distinctly stained; in one minute there was a very strong impression.

John Draper, 'On the Process of Daguerreotype',
September 1840

The surface of the moon was a virtually closed book only five years before the first human landing, opinion even divided about whether it was sufficiently solid to land on. NASA's Ranger series of spacecrafts were tasked with taking the first close-up photographs, but it was not until *Ranger 7* – launched on 28 July 1964 – that this was achieved (although slightly blurry images of the far side had been sent back by the *Luna 3* spacecraft in 1959). *Ranger 7* reached the moon on 31 July and sent back more than four thousand images of the surface in its last quarter of an hour of existence before crashing into it.

Although French inventor Nicéphore Niépce took a photo of the moon in 1826 or 1827, it was barely recognizable, and French painter and photography pioneer Louis Daguerre managed one of the crescent phase only. The honour of the first detailed shot of the full moon goes to the English-born scientist John W. Draper (1811–1882). His astrophotograph of 23 March 1840 was the first to show mountains, craters and other geographic features. Draper also took the first sharp photograph of a female face, about the same time.

ALSO ON THIS DAY 1598: Italian sculptor Alessandro Algardi born · **1860:** American botanical artist Mary Walcott born · **1947:** English illustrator Ian Beck born

August

The first work of art
is left on the moon, 1971

Bassett, Charles A. II
Belyayev, Pavel I.
Chaffee, Roger B.
Dobrovolsky, Georgi T.
Freeman, Theodore C.
Gagarin, Yuri A.
Givens, Edward G., Jr.
Grissom, Virgil I.
Komarov, Vladimir M.
Patsayev, Viktor I.
See, Elliot M., Jr.
Volkov, Vladislav N.
White, Edward H. II
Williams, Clifton C. Jr.

**Inscription on the plaque left by David R. Scott
alongside artwork on the moon, 1 August 1971**

Unbeknown to NASA, when the astronauts on board Apollo 15 landed on the moon on 30 July 1971, they were carrying with them a 9-cm (3½-inch) sculpture by Belgian artist Paul Van Hoeydonck (b. 1925). Somehow the crew had managed to smuggle it aboard and during a quiet moment during their lunar exploration, mission commander David R. Scott and lunar module pilot James Irwin planted it in the soil of a crater. Next to it they left a plaque that memorialized in alphabetical order the fourteen American and Russian astronauts and cosmonauts who had died in service. The existence of *Fallen Astronaut* was not revealed until the mission was completed.

The plaque is made of an incredibly durable and lightweight anodized aluminium product called Metalphoto, while the figure is made of aluminium. It does not depict any race or gender.

ALSO ON THIS DAY 1714: Welsh painter Richard Wilson born · **1865:** English painter Isobel Gloag born · **1910:** German photojournalist Gerda Taro born

The Saint Petersburg Union of Artists
is founded, 1932

The Central Committee declares that in recent years, on the basis of significant successes in socialist construction, there has been a considerable growth, qualitatively and quantitatively, in literature and art.

Several years ago, when literature was still significantly influenced by alien elements, especially in the early years of NEP, and the teams of proletarian literature were still weak, the party did everything possible to help create and strengthen special proletarian organizations in the fields of literature and other arts in order to strengthen the position of proletarian writers and artists.

At the present time, when the teams have managed to grow and new writers and artists have emerged from factories and collective farms, the framework of existing proletarian literary and artistic organizations has become too narrow and is slowing down the scope of artistic creation.

This position creates the danger of turning these organizations from the means of the greatest mobilization of Soviet writers and artists around the tasks of socialist construction into a means of cultivating group isolation and separation from the political tasks of our time and from significant groups of writers and artists supporting socialist construction.

Hence the need for a corresponding restructuring of the literary and artistic organizations and an expansion of their base work. Consequently, the Central Committee of the CPSU decides to:

1. Liquidate the Association of Proletarian Writers;
2. Unite all writers supporting the platform of Soviet power and who aspire to participate in socialist construction in a single Union of Soviet Writers with a communist faction in it;
3. To carry out a similar change for other art forms;
4. To instruct the Organization Bureau to develop practical measures for carrying out this decision.

Resolution of the Central Committee of the All-Union Communist Party on the Restructuring of Literary Artistic Organizations, 23 April 1932

The formation of the Saint Petersburg Union of Artists on 2 August 1932 marked the start of Soviet era art under Joseph Stalin (*see also* 3 December) when every previous art and literature organization was dissolved to form one mighty monolith that supervised all creative production. Soviet Realism became the order of the day as part of a thoroughly traditional system of artistic education.

Its first chairman was the painter Kuzma Petrov-Vodkin (1878–1939), one of a select group of artists allowed to sketch Vladimir Lenin lying in state in his coffin eight years earlier.

ALSO ON THIS DAY 1612: Dutch model (and wife) of Rembrandt, Saskia van Uylenburgh born · **1834:** French sculptor Frédéric-Auguste Bartholdi born (*see* 8 October) · **1973:** Catalan artist Joan Miró paints *Femmes, Oiseaux* (Women, Birds)

3 AUGUST

Sky Tower opens to the public, 1997

This is quite a moment. An event of this size doesn't come along all that often. In fact it is reasonable to suggest that another Sky Tower will never be built in New Zealand. So this is it – warts and all – critics and all. In construction terms it's a great achievement and a great credit to New Zealand's construction industry, and in particular a credit to those who actually built it. Your business is getting more sophisticated all the time. And this Tower proves that. The materials get better, the equipment gets better, and everything gets more high-powered and more automated.

But there's one thing that'll never change. And that's the old rule that the equipment is only ever as good as the person who's using it. In the end, the building you get depends on the ability of the people who design and build it. So you have a lot to be proud of...I know having been part of the team that built the Sky Tower will be an ongoing source of pride for you all. I say that knowing it has many critics and they, like the Tower, won't go away. So, well done, and good luck. This Tower is a credit to you.

Jim Bolger, prime minister of New Zealand,
speech at topping off ceremony of the Sky Tower, 18 April 1997

The telecommunications and observation Sky Tower in Auckland, New Zealand, is 328 metres (1,076 feet) high, and the tallest free-standing structure in the southern hemisphere as well as a popular tourist attraction. Designed by architect Gordon Moller (b. 1940), the tower is built from reinforced concrete on eight legs and can withstand earthquakes up to magnitude 8.0 and winds of 193 kmph (120 mph) – it is designed to sway slightly in very high winds, when its elevators automatically descend until safe to continue. It took nearly three years to build and opened to the public on 3 August 1997.

ALSO ON THIS DAY **1778:** La Scala opera house opens (first production is *Europa Riconosciuta* by Antonio Salieri) · **1803:** English architect Joseph Paxton born (*see* 30 November) · **1879:** Death of English painter Joseph Severn

4 AUGUST

The *Lady of Elche* is discovered in Spain, 1897

Hannibal marched down the road to Rome, and the Romans who rushed to war with him felt as if they were fighting with a magician.... It was no mere military defeat, it was certainly no mere mercantile rivalry, that filled the Roman imagination with such hideous omens of nature herself becoming unnatural. It was Moloch upon the mountain of the Latins, looking with his appalling face across the plain; it was Baal who trampled the vineyards with his feet of stone; it was the voice of Tanit the invisible, behind her trailing veils, whispering of the love that is more horrible than hate.

G. K. Chesterton, *The Everlasting Man*, 1925

Dating from about the 4th century AD and discovered in 1897 in a field in L'Alcúdia, near Elche, Spain, the *Lady of Elche* limestone bust depicts a woman – perhaps a priestess – wearing a complex headdress and ornate neck-laces, with two large coils or 'rodetes' on the left and right side of her head (along the lines of Princess Leia in the *Star Wars* movies). Traces of red, blue and white paint were found on it when excavated.

It is not fully clear exactly what the bust represents, but the most accepted theory is that it is connected to Tanit, the leading goddess of Carthage, who was also worshipped in this region, and it may have been used as a funerary urn and was part of a larger statue. Suggestions that it is a forgery have been generally dismissed. English writer G. K. Chesterton (1874–1936) used the reference to Tanit in his Christian-themed history of the world when describing the immense impact Hannibal's armies had on local forces as they invaded Italy over the Alps in AD 218.

ALSO ON THIS DAY **1463:** Arts patron Lorenzo di Pierfrancesco de' Medici born · **1821:** French fashion designer Louis Vuitton born · **1836:** Danish architect Jens Vilhelm Dahlerup born

5 AUGUST

Dürer paints his *Dream Vision*, 1525

In 1525, in the night between Wednesday and Thursday after Whitsuntide, I had a vision in my sleep, and saw many great waters falling from heaven. The first hit the ground four miles away from me with such a cruel force, enormous noise and splashing that it drowned the whole countryside. I was so hugely frightened at this that I woke up before the cloudburst. And the subsequent downpour was massive. Some waters fell a distance away and some near by. And they came from such a height that they seemed to fall equally slowly. But the very first water that hit the ground fell at such velocity, and was accompanied by wind and roaring so frightening, that when I woke up my whole body was shaking and I could not recover for a long time. When I got up in the morning, I painted the above as I had seen it. May God turn all things to the best.

Albrecht Dürer, caption to *Dream Vision*, 1525

On the night of 7 June 1525, German painter and engraver Albrecht Dürer (1471–1528; *see also* 12 May) had a very unsettling dream. Three months later on 5 August, he decided to reproduce it in *Dream Vision*, a watercolour that shows a landscape of trees and houses being flooded via an apocalyptic spout of water falling from above, accompanied by text detailing his recollections of the dream.

He had noted previously that he often dreamed about art, although usually forgot it when he awoke (a dream also inspired American artist Jasper

Johns's iconic painting *Flag*, 1955). *Dream Vision* is part of Dürer's Kunstbuch (Art Book) collection of woodcuts, drawings and prints.

ALSO ON THIS DAY 1844: Russian painter and sculptor Ilya Repin born · **1882:** Irish sculptor Anne Acheson born · **1890:** Russian sculptor Naum Gabo born

6 AUGUST

'Lovely Lucy' statue of Lucille Ball replaces 'Scary Lucy', 2016

Herennius Severus, a man of great learning, is anxious to place in his library portraits of your fellow-townsmen, Cornelius Nepos and Titus Catius, and he asks me to get them copied and painted if there are any such portraits in their native place, as there probably are. I am laying this commission upon you rather than on any one else, first, because you are always kind enough to grant any favour I ask; secondly, because I know your reverence for literary studies and your love of literary men; and, lastly, because you love and reverence your native place, and entertain the same feelings for those who have helped to make its name famous. So I beg you to find as careful a painter as you can, for while it is hard to paint a portrait from an original, it is far more difficult to make a good imitation of an imitation. Moreover, please do not let the painter you choose make any variations from his copy, even though they are for the better. Farewell.

Pliny the Younger, letter to Vibius Severus,
c. **1st/early 2nd century** AD

American sculptor David Poulin (1961–2020) unfortunately hit the headlines when his life-size statue of the television comedian Lucille Ball – originally a private commission – was donated to her hometown of Celoron, New York. Not universally popular, it attracted the local nickname of 'Scary Lucy' because of its unconventionally confrontational depiction, which then hit international media headlines in 2015.

In a letter to the *Hollywood Reporter* published on 6 April 2015, Poulin said he had been inundated with unflattering comments from around the world about his statue, saying that while he took responsibility for the work, which he admitted was 'unsettling', his intention had not been to ridicule Lucille Ball.

It was replaced on 6 August 2016 – which would have been Ball's 105th birthday – with one by sculptor Carolyn Palmer, who took a more conventional approach with the star wearing pearls and carrying a handbag. Palmer said she was keen to emphasize Ball's playful side as well as her glamorous one, and hoped all Lucy fans would be pleased with it. The 'Scary Lucy' statue was moved 70 metres (75 yards) from its original spot.

7 AUGUST

Queen Victoria and Prince Albert sign the Book of Kells, 1849

Its weird and commanding beauty; its subdued and goldless colouring; the baffling intricacy of its fearless designs; the clean, unwavering sweep of rounded spiral; the creeping undulations of serpentine forms, that writhe in artistic profusion throughout the mazes of its decorations; the strong and legible minuscule of its text; the quaintness of its striking portraiture; the unwearied reverence and patient labour that brought it into being; all of which combined go to make up the Book of Kells, have raised this ancient Irish volume to a position of abiding pre-eminence amongst the illuminated manuscripts of the world.... Unhappily, what Norseman and Dane had failed to effect in early and wilder centuries was accomplished by an ignorant and mischievous bookbinder, some hundred years ago; and under the barbarous hands of this craftsman many of the outer margins of its priceless illuminations have been 'trimmed' out of existence.

Sir Edward Sullivan, *The Book of Kells,* **1920**

The illustrated Book of Kells manuscript of the New Testament's four gospels was produced about AD 800 in the eponymous abbey. The book has not remained untouched over the last twelve hundred years, however, with chapter numbering added in the 16th century and rebinding work carried out in the 19th and 20th centuries.

One of the most startling additions came when Queen Victoria and Prince Albert were asked to sign the manuscript on a trip to Ireland, although this was not such a heinous act as it sounds – they added their names to a modern flyleaf that was quietly removed during a later rebinding.

ALSO ON THIS DAY **1867**: German-Danish painter Emil Nolde born · **1916**: American puppet maker Kermit Love born · **1928**: English architect Owen Luder born

8 AUGUST

The Beatles cross Abbey Road
in London, 1969

The world-famous zebra crossing near Abbey Road Studios in London has been listed Grade II.

Following expert advice from English Heritage, the crossing becomes the first of its kind ever to be listed, reflecting its cultural and historical importance. The Abbey Road studios themselves were listed in February.

John Penrose said: 'It is a fantastic testimony to the international fame of The Beatles that – more than 40 years on – this crossing continues to attract thousands of visitors each year, trying to mimic their iconic Abbey Road album cover.'

Paul McCartney added 'It's been a great year for me and a great year for The Beatles and hearing that the Abbey Road crossing is to be preserved is the icing on the cake.'

John Penrose continued 'This London zebra crossing is no castle or cathedral but, thanks to The Beatles and a ten minute photo-shoot one August morning in 1969, it has just as strong a claim as any to be seen as part of our heritage. And as such it merits the extra protection that Grade II listing provides.'

UK government and MP John Penrose,
press release, 22 December 2010

Perhaps the most famous photograph of the Beatles is the cover shot of the group's final album taken on 8 August 1969 by Scottish photographer Iain

Macmillan (1938–2006). It shows them walking across a pedestrian crossing near the Abbey Road recording studios (then the EMI studios) in London's St John's Wood. John Lennon leads Ringo Starr and Paul McCartney (all dressed in Welsh designer Tommy Nutter's suits) across the road in single file, with George Harrison (in double denim) at the rear.

From 11.35 a.m. that morning, Macmillan spent just ten minutes taking photographs with his Hasselblad camera. The album cover was designed by John Kosh, creative director at Apple Records, who insisted that neither the album nor the group's names should appear on it despite strong opposition from EMI. The image was a key element in the 'Paul is dead' conspiracy theory that argued that McCartney had died and had been replaced by a lookalike. 'Clues' included McCartney not wearing shoes and the 28IF numberplate of a Volkswagen in the shot apparently referencing his age.

The pedestrian crossing was awarded Grade II listed status in December 2010.

ALSO ON THIS DAY **1646:** German painter Sir Godfrey Kneller (Gottfried Kniller) born · **1919:** English animator John Wilson born · **1936:** Polish illustrator Jan Pieńkowski born

9 AUGUST

Foundation work starts on the Leaning Tower of Pisa, 1173

Guglielmo, so it is said, in the year 1174, together with Bonanno a sculptor, founded in Pisa, the Campanile of the Duomo where there are certain words carved that say: A.D. MCLXXIV, CAMPANILE HOC FUIT FUNDATUM, MENSE AUG. But these two architects not having much practice of founding in Pisa and therefore not supporting the platform with piles, as they ought, before they had gone halfway with that building it inclined to one side and bent over to the weakest part, in a manner that the said campanile leans six and a half braccia out of the straight, according as the foundation sank on this side; and although in the lower part this is not much, up above it shows clear enough to make men stand fast in a marvel how it can be that it has not fallen down and has not thrown out cracks.

The reason is that this edifice is round both without and within and built in the shape of a hollow well, and bound together with the stones in a manner that it is well-nigh impossible that it should fall; and it is assisted, above all, by the foundations, which have an outwork three braccia wide outside the tower, made, as it is seen, after the sinking of the campanile, in order to support it. I am convinced that if it had been square it would not have been standing today, for the reason that the corner stones of the square sides, as is often seen to happen, would have forced them out in a manner that it would have fallen down. And if the Garisenda, a tower in Bologna, although square, leans and does not fall, that comes to pass because it is slender and does not lean so much, not being burdened by so great a weight, by a great measure, as is this campanile, which is praised, not because it has in it any design or beautiful manner, but simply for its extravagance, it appearing impossible to anyone who sees it that it can in any wise keep standing.

Giorgio Vasari, *Lives of the Most Eminent Painters, Sculptors and Architects*, 1568

The famous campanile bell tower in Pisa, Italy, 56 metres (184 feet) in height, started to subside and tilt even as it was being built in 1178. The 4-degree tilt from the vertical was reduced from 5.5 degrees during restoration work in the 1990s. Italian painter and writer Giorgio Vasari (1511–1574) was probably wrong about the architects – as it is now thought that it was built by the 12th-century architect Diotisalvi who designed other buildings in the city.

ALSO ON THIS DAY 1516: Death of Dutch painter Hieronymus Bosch (*see* 17 January) · **1757:** Scottish engineer Thomas Telford born (*see* 26 November) · **1945:** English cartoonist and illustrator Posy Simmonds born

The Musée du Louvre opens in Paris, 1793

The Louvre is the book where we learn to read. We should not nevertheless be happy to retain the beautiful formulas of our illustrious predecessors. Let us go out and study beautiful nature, aim to capture its spirit, let us try to express ourselves according to our personal temperament. Time and reflection gradually changes our vision and finally understanding comes to us.

**Paul Cézanne, letter to French painter
Émile Bernard, 1905**

The Louvre art museum in Paris is located in the Louvre Palace, which was built in the late 12th century by Philip II of France. When it opened on 10 August 1793, 537 paintings were put on display, a number that has risen - Napoleon's looting of Europe was a major boost to acquisitions - to the point where it is now the world's largest art museum.

ALSO ON THIS DAY 1675: Foundation stone is laid of the Royal Greenwich Observatory, London · **1737:** Russian painter Anton Losenko born · **1960:** Scottish National Gallery of Modern Art opens in Edinburgh

Beatrice Birnie Philip marries James McNeill Whistler, 1888

Chinkie I am having a nice long talk with you – this Sunday afternoon – and yet I shall have scarcely time to tell you half – not that so much has happened – but I miss you so continually – without you I am forlorn – and you know it – and you are my own dear sweet bad Wam! – How can you leave me like this without your daily little letters! – They are delightful when they come – the last so charming – so dear to me – and so encouraging to the poor grinder – exiled with his big black mangle! – We are much to be envied though I know – for I look round and I see no others so happy as we two are in each other. – I suppose we are even a little spoilt in the luxury of this knowledge – and so the Wam bullies her man and says he is cross and beats him!

Beatrice Birnie Philip (also Beatrix, 'Trixie, 'Luck', 'Chinkie' and 'Wam'; 1857–1896) studied under and posed for American-born painter James McNeill Whistler (1834–1903; *see also* 29 July) – she was the model for his *Harmony in Red: Lamplight* (1886). They married in 1888 after her separation from the English architect Edward Godwin.

She was also a notable artist herself, painting mostly flowers, and women in oils (some of her work has been misattributed to her husband) and water-colour, as well as designing jewelry, tiles, wallpaper, stained glass and furniture.

It was a very happy marriage, with Beatrice acting as a kind of studio manager for her husband. Whistler was distraught at her death after a long period of ill health.

ALSO ON THIS DAY 1494: Death of German painter Hans Memling · **1614:** Death of Italian painter Lavinia Fontana · **1956:** Death of American painter Jackson Pollock (*see* 30 October)

12 AUGUST

Tutankhamun's beard accidentally snaps off, 2014

A very neatly wrapped mummy of the young king, with golden mask of sad but tranquil expression, symbolizing Osiris. The similitude of the youthful Tut.Ankh.Amen, until now known only by name, amid that sepulchral silence, made us realize the past. By this bespangled mummy as it lies in the coffin, he must have been a tall youth – from the top of the headdress of the mask to the feet it measures 6 feet. The mask has fallen slightly back, thus its gaze is straight up to the heavens....

All the moveable objects upon the exterior of the mummy were removed today. I then attempted to remove the mummy and mask from the coffin, but found that unfortunately both were stuck fast to the bottom of the coffin, and could not be under the present conditions raised out without using great force, endangering both the royal remains and the finely wrought mask. The libation that was poured over the body had consolidated at the bottom and stuck them fast.

**Howard Carter, excavation journal entries,
28 and 31 October 1925**

From the first moments of its discovery by English archaeologist Howard Carter (1874–1939; *see also* 16 February), Tutankhamun's mask proved problematic as the entries in his journal indicate. At this point, the mask's beard – which helped rulers such as Tutankhamun identify with the under-world god Osiris – had come away and was not reattached until 1946. The slim, gold beard itself weighs 2.5 kg (5½ lb) and is inlaid with lapis lazuli.

On 12 August 2014, restoration workers at the Egyptian Museum in Cairo, Egypt, accidentally snapped off the beard from the mask while lifting it up and then hurriedly tried to glue it back on using epoxy adhesive, not an officially recommended restoration technique. It went unnoticed for several months until traces of the glue were spotted.

Expert restorers removed the new glue and then reattached the beard using natural beeswax, commonly used in ancient Egypt and less likely to damage the mask. During their work, they discovered that when the beard had first been reattached, soft solder had been used.

ALSO ON THIS DAY 1870: Swedish-American painter Henry Reuterdahl born · **1940:** Death of Estonian painter and illustrator Nikolai Triik · **1943:** Death of Italian photographer Vittorio Sella

13 AUGUST

A visitor falls into an Anish Kapoor installation, 2018

True is it, that upon the verge I found me
Of the abysmal valley dolorous,
That gathers thunder of infinite ululations.
Obscure, profound it was, and nebulous,
So that by fixing on its depths my sight
Nothing whatever I discerned therein.

'Let us descend now into the blind world',
Began the Poet, pallid utterly;
'I will be first, and thou shalt second be.'...
Great grief seized on my heart when this I heard,
Because some people of much worthiness
I knew, who in that Limbo were suspended.

Dante Alighieri, Canto IV,
The Divine Comedy, c. **1308–21**

Descent into Limbo (1992) by British-Indian sculptor Anish Kapoor (b. 1954) was described by the Serralves Museum of Contemporary Art in Porto, Portugal, as 'an expression of Kapoor's interests in the formal and metaphoric play between light and darkness, inside and outside, the contained and the infinite, which underpins his sculptural oeuvre' when it put the work on show in 2018.

It consisted of a large concrete and stucco cubed-room structure at the middle of which was a circular pit with its sides painted black, making it unclear whether it was merely a circle or actually an infinitely deep hole – the black used was Kapoor's trademark Vantablack material, which blocks 99.8 per cent of light. It was, in fact, a hole 2.5 metres (8 feet) deep, although Kapoor has described it as a 'space full of darkness'.

Around it were signs warning of the hole and an attendant was on hand as an added safety precaution. Visitors also signed disclaimer forms that set out the risks of viewing the work. Unfortunately, on 13 August, a sixty-year-old Italian man fell into the hole and was slightly injured, forcing a temporary closure of the installation. Happily, after a trip to hospital, he made a full recovery.

Descent into Limbo takes its name from a 1492 painting, and earlier works on a similar theme, by Italian painter Andrea Mantegna (1431–1506) showing Christ's post-death journey into limbo before his resurrection, a story that does not feature in the New Testament.

ALSO ON THIS DAY 1756: English caricaturist James Gillray born (*see* 18 May) · **1867:** American painter George Luks born · **1907:** Scottish architect Basil Spence born

Alfred Eisenstaedt photographs
a sailor kissing a nurse, 1945

OFFICIAL *** TRUMAN ANNOUNCES JAPANESE SURRENDER ***

News Ticker, One Times Square,
7.03 p.m., 14 August 1945

German-born American photographer Alfred Eisenstaedt (1898–1995) took his shot *V-J Day in Times Square* on what was effectively the final day of the Second World War, the day on which Japan formally surrendered. As crowds swarmed around Times Square in New York at 5.51 p.m., he captured the moment near 45th Street when a uniformed sailor kissed a nurse while she held her purse. He took just four shots.

Eisenstaedt did not have time to ask the couple their names, which has led to a long and still not entirely conclusive search for their identities. The woman was almost certainly Greta Friedman, a dental hygienist. She pointed out that while it may have been a spontaneous act of jubilation and the sailor was expressing his thanks to all the nurses who had helped the armed forces: 'It wasn't my choice to be kissed. The guy just came over and grabbed.... That man was very strong. I wasn't kissing him. He was kissing me.' Indeed, when *Life* magazine printed the photo, the caption described the sailor as 'uninhibited' and in his book *Eisenstaedt on Eisenstaedt* (1985), the photographer described how he saw the sailor grabbing any female in sight as he ran along the street.

As a result, the incident has also been seen as a sexual assault, part of a now forgotten three-day series of drunken riots in the city following the announcement of the surrender, which left more than one thousand people injured, a dozen killed and six women raped.

The man has never been definitively identified, but shortly after one of the strongest candidates died, a statue of the moment by sculptor Seward Johnson (1930–2020) called *Unconditional Surrender* was attacked with paint and marked #metoo.

ALSO ON THIS DAY **1875**: Lithuanian painter Mstislav Dobuzhinsky born · **1926**: French writer René Goscinny born (*see* 29 October) · **1950**: American cartoonist Gary Larson born

Skolnick's poster advertises
the Woodstock festival, 1969

Art Show – Paintings and sculptures on trees, on grass, surrounded by the Hudson valley, will be displayed. Accomplished artists, 'Ghetto' artists, and would-be artists will be glad to discuss their work, or the unspoiled splendor of the surroundings, or anything else that might be on your mind. If you're an artist, and you want to display, write for information.

Crafts Bazaar – If you like creative knickknacks and old junk you'll love roaming around our bazaar. You'll see imaginative leather, ceramic, bead, and silver creations, as well as Zodiac Charts, camp clothes, and worn out shoes.

Work Shops – If you like playing with beads, or improvising on a guitar, or writing poetry, or molding clay, stop by one of our work shops and see what you can give; and take.

Woodstock music festival poster text, 1969

Billed as 'An Aquarian Exposition – 3 Days of Peace & Music', the Woodstock music festival ran from 15 to 18 August (on a farm in Bethel, New York State, rather than nearby Woodstock itself) and featured musicians such as Janis Joplin, the Who, Jimi Hendrix and Ravi Shankar.

The original poster for the event was designed by David Byrd, who came up with an elaborately floral pattern inspired by the painting *La Source* (1856) by French artist Jean-Auguste-Dominique Ingres, which shows Aphrodite pouring water out of a large jar, a water carrier like Aquarius. Byrd's poster similarly featured a naked woman, although one surrounded by hearts and cupids, but none of the names of the groups booked to play.

When a sudden venue change required a new poster and Byrd was on holiday and uncontactable, the festival organizers turned to American graphic designer Arnold Skolnick (b. 1937) and asked him to take a different approach as the previous poster had received a mixed reception. Skolnick had recently been to the French painter Henri Matisse's exhibition at the Museum of Modern Art in New York so experimented by making paper cut-outs of a white catbird and a flute on a red background (which later became a stylised blue and green guitar and something more like a dove).

Skolnick went to the first day of the festival but then left because an enormous downpour of rain was forecast and he had no tent. Byrd also went to Woodstock and worked as part of the production crew.

16 AUGUST

Michelangelo signs a contract to work on *David*, 1501

The Consuls of the Arte della Lana and the Lords Overseers [of the Cathedral] being met together in joint assembly within the hall of the said Overseers, have chosen as sculptor to the said Cathedral the worthy master, Michelangelo, the son of Lodovico Buonarrotti, a citizen of Florence, to the end that he may make, finish and bring to perfection the male figure known as the Giant, nine braccia in height, already blocked out in marble by Maestro Agostino grande, of Florence, and badly blocked; and now stored in the workshops of the Cathedral. The work shall be completed within the period and term of two years next ensuing, beginning from the first day of September next ensuing, with a salary and payment together in joint assembly within the hall of the said of six broad florins of gold in gold for every month. And for all other works that shall be required about the said building (edificium) the said Overseers bind themselves to supply and provide both men and scaffolding from their office and all else that may be necessary. When the said work and the said male figure of marble shall be finished, then the Consuls and Overseers who shall at that time be in authority shall judge whether it merits a higher reward, being guided therein by the dictates of their own consciences.

Contract for the statue of *David*,
16 August 1501

The statue of *David* by Italian painter and sculptor Michelangelo (full name Michelangelo di Lodovico Buonarroti Simoni; 1475–1564) was a long time in the making. Initially, it was to have been one of a dozen sculptural buttresses of Old Testament figures for the Cathedral of Santa Maria del Fiore in Florence (*see* 19 August), the first of which was produced by the sculptor Donatello in 1410. *David* was the third in this long drawn-out schedule and the block of Carrara marble was first worked on by Italian sculptors Agostino di Duccio in 1464 and then Antonio Gamberelli.

Known as the Giant, the 5-metre (17-foot) block was finally handed over to the twenty-six-year-old Michelangelo, who was awarded the contract on 16 August 1501 and began carving in September (*see* 13 September). The statue was finished in 1504.

ALSO ON THIS DAY **1557:** Italian painter Agostino Carracci born · **c. 1735:** The Feast Day of Saint Roch, an annual event in Venice, depicted by Canaletto in a painting of the same name · **2012:** Death of Belgian photographer Martine Franck

17 AUGUST

Prince William qualifies to study history of art, 2000

We have no certain knowledge as to the commencement of the art of painting, nor does this enquiry fall under our consideration. The Egyptians assert that it was invented among themselves, six thousand years before it passed into Greece; a vain boast, it is very evident. As to the Greeks, some say that it was invented at Sicyon, others at Corinth; but they all agree that it originated in tracing lines round the human shadow. The first stage of the art, they say, was this, the second stage being the employment of single colours; a process known as 'monochromaton', after it had become more complicated, and which is still in use at the present day. The invention of line-drawing has been assigned to Philocles, the Egyptian, or to Cleanthes of Corinth. The first who practised this line-drawing were Aridices, the Corinthian, and Telephanes, the Sicyonian, artists who, without making use of any colours, shaded the interior of the outline by drawing lines; hence, it was the custom with them to add to the picture the name of the person represented. Ecphantus, the Corinthian, was the first to employ colours upon these pictures, made, it is said, of broken earthenware, reduced to powder.

Pliny the Elder on the history of art,
***Natural History,* 1st century** AD

Like thousands of other teenagers across the UK, eighteen-year-old Prince William received his A-level exam results on 17 August in 2000 and his A in geography, B in history of art and C in biology were good enough to claim his place on a history of art degree course at his first choice, the prestigious University of St Andrews in Scotland. He then took a gap year and in fact later changed to study geography instead. William's brother Harry also studied art, and was awarded a B grade, although he dropped history of art after AS level.

ALSO ON THIS DAY **1920:** American photographer Lida Moser born · **1923:** Venezuelan painter, sculptor and installation artist Carlos Cruz-Diez born · **1932:** French cartoonist Jean-Jacques Sempé born

18 AUGUST

Monet seeks a green light for his water garden, 1901

Mister Prefect,
I am pleased to ask for permission to change the course of a stream of the Epte river called the 'bras communal' into a property that I own, which is situated in the town of Giverny once the administrative procedures such a scheme may need have been fulfilled.
Sincerely,
Claude Monet

> **Claude Monet, letter to the prefect of Eure,**
> **18 August 1901**

By 1901, French painter Claude Monet (1840–1926) was already settled at his home, the 'Pressoir' in Giverny (*see* 3 May 1883). He had established a garden around a pond, overcoming the fears of locals who were worried his planting would somehow poison the river water that irrigated it. Keen to enlarge the pond, on 18 August, he asked the authorities for permission to do so and was successful (again, with the caveat that he was not to endanger public health – happily, the water lilies, irises and wisteria had not poisoned anybody in the previous eight years).

He cultivated the water garden for the rest of his life and it provided him with constant inspiration as well as a spot for entertaining visitors. Although he had gardeners, Monet took an extremely active interest in horticulture, reflected in the many gardening books and journals he kept in his library. 'I love water but I also love flowers,' he told writer Marc Elder in 1924 for his book *À Giverny, chez Claude Monet*. 'That is why, with the pond filled, I thought of planting it. I took a catalogue and I made a choice at random, that's all.'

Monet focused exclusively on the water garden in his later years, starting work from dawn and working throughout the day, admitting that it had become an obsession. His 'Water Landscapes' series of paintings produced in the first decade of the 20th century were immediately praised when first exhibited in 1909.

ALSO ON THIS DAY **1855:** English painter Alfred Wallis born · **1869:** German painter Carl Rungius born · **2012:** Death of Native American painter Harrison Begay

19 AUGUST

Florence's cathedral dome competition is launched, 1418

This remarkable temple demonstrates the success of Filippo the architect in the arts of Daedalus and many other inventions devised by his divine genius.

Memorial plaque inscription for Filippo Brunelleschi, the Duomo, Florence

By the time Italian architect Filippo Brunelleschi (1377–1446) was born, building work on Florence's Cathedral of Santa Maria del Fiore (known as the Duomo) had been ongoing for almost a century. Its first stone was laid on 9 September 1296, and the final element of its facade was completed in 1887.

On 19 August 1418, the Arte della Lana wool merchants guild launched a competition to design and build a dome on the cathedral, which essentially became a straight race between Brunelleschi and his main rival of the day, Lorenzo Ghiberti (1378–1455) who had made his name with the design for the bronze doors of the Florence Baptistery. At stake were 200 florins, not to mention the chance of artistic immortality.

As the winner, although initially he was obliged to work with Ghiberti on the build, Brunelleschi faced a major challenge – the cathedral required a record-breaking octagonal dome in terms of height and width with the added problem that no flying buttresses could be used. His solution was a herringbone brickwork dome and a double shell of marble and sandstone, using a series of iron and stone chains to keep everything in shape. In his initial submission for the competition, he refused to go into too much detail about exactly how this would be achieved, concerned that rivals would steal his plans. Along the way, he also invented a new hoisting system required to move the incredibly heavy materials around the site.

Construction work started in 1420 and, without the use of free-standing scaffolding, the Duomo was finished in 1436, consecrated on 25 March by Pope Eugenius IV. It remains the largest masonry dome on the planet.

20 AUGUST

Käthe Kollwitz unveils a monument to her son, 1932

The artist is mostly a child of their time, especially when their own period of development falls into the time of early socialism. My development occurred during the time of early socialism. This grabbed me completely. At that time there was no question of conscious work in the service of the proletariat. But what did I care about the concepts of beauty, such as those of the Greeks, which were not my own and felt by me? The proletariat was just beautiful for me.

Käthe Kollwitz, reply to a questionnaire
sent to prominent artists, 1942

German sculptor, painter and printmaker Käthe Kollwitz (1867–1945) began working on a memorial to her teenage son Peter and other German soldiers soon after he died in October 1914 while serving in the First World War. An early monument was abandoned after the end of the war; the second, *The Grieving Parents*, was erected on 20 August 1932 in the cemetery of Roggevelde, Belgium (later moved to the Vladslo German war cemetery, also in Belgium, where there are 25,000 graves of German soldiers). It shows Kollwitz and her husband Karl kneeling in front of numerous marked grave memorials, Karl looking at the one bearing Peter's name.

A politically inspired artist who felt strongly about issues of poverty, Kollwitz continued to produce anti-war art for the rest of her life. Constantly outspoken, she was persecuted by the Nazis who categorized her work as 'degenerate' (*see* 4 June) and threatened her with removal to a concentration camp. However, her international fame saved her from such a fate.

Kollwitz died in April 1945, a fortnight before the end of the Second World War. 'War accompanies me to the end,' she wrote in her final letter.

ALSO ON THIS DAY **1785:** Death of French sculptor Jean-Baptiste Pigalle · **1910:** Finnish-American architect Eero Saarinen born · **1947:** English book illustrator Alan Lee born

21 AUGUST

The *Mona Lisa* is stolen, 1911

60 DETECTIVES SEEK
STOLEN 'MONA LISA'
But No Clue Has Yet Been Discovered to Whereabouts
of Lionardo's Masterpiece.
FRENCH PUBLIC INDIGNANT
Affair Regarded as National Scandal Investigators
Believe the Picture Is Still In the Louvre
Headline in the *New York Times*, 24 August 1911

Painted by Italian Renaissance artist Leonardo da Vinci (1452–1519) in the early 16th century. Owned by Francis I of France after Leonardo's death. Hung in Napoleon's bedroom in the early 1800s. Stolen by museum employee Vincenzo Peruggia in 1911.

Today, the *Mona Lisa* is the world's most famous painting; in 1911, it was certainly popular but not nearly as iconic. Which is why it was only noticed as missing from its home in the Louvre hours after it was snatched, and only then because an amateur painter casually wondered why it was not on show and a guard was wrong when he assumed it had been taken out to be photographed.

The police wasted no time in rounding up the usual suspects, which in this case rather remarkably included the famous French poet and critic Guillaume Apollinaire (*see* 7 September) as well as Pablo Picasso, neither of whom were at all guilty. When the Picasso trail led them nowhere, the police were stumped...

It is now known what happened that night: in a fit of what he later claimed to be patriotic fervour, Louvre employee Vincenzo Peruggia, keen that Leonardo's painting should be on show in Italy, simply waited until the gallery was empty, lifted it off the wall, hid it under his coat and hightailed it back to his flat. Here it stayed for the next two years in a trunk while he pondered his next move. As he waited, the authorities at the museum simply left the wall blank, which attracted enormous crowds, among them a curious Franz Kafka.

Increasingly unsure what his next move should be, Peruggia eventually took the painting to an art dealer in Italy who clearly felt it was being offered to him for sale, although the thief said he was simply returning it to the motherland. Whatever his true motive, half an hour later, the Italian police were knocking on Peruggia's front door.

The recovered painting went back on show in January 1914 and became a sensation worldwide; Peruggia went to prison for six months. When he was released, and the First World War was over, he began a career as a painter and decorator.

Since then, the *Mona Lisa* has been much better protected, surviving an acid attack and a rock being hurled at it in 1956 (the latter nearly damaging her elbow), red spray paint in 1974, and finally in 2009 emerging unscathed when a ceramic teacup lobbed at the painting got no further than the bullet-proof glass that now protects it.

ALSO ON THIS DAY 1872: English illustrator Aubrey Beardsley born · **1906:** American animator Isadore 'Friz' Freleng born · **1978:** Death of American architect and furniture designer Charles Eames

The Scream by Munch is stolen...again, 2004

A digitized version of 'Scream' by Edvard Munch was Thursday deposited in the Arctic World Archive by the National Museum of Norway.... 'The Scream' by Edvard Munch, one of the world's most iconic paintings, is fragile and vulnerable. It is therefore important for the National Museum to preserve all knowledge about the painting. Future generations will have access to a digitized version of the artwork and related research material as the National Museum today deposited 'Scream' in the Arctic World Archive.... 'Located far away from instabilities in the rest of the world, we believe the Arctic World Archive is the safest place on the planet for storing irreplaceable information. We are honored to be trusted with protecting national treasures for various countries,' comments Rune Bjerkestrand, CEO of Piql.

**Piql press release, 'Edvard Munch's "Scream"
stored in Arctic World Archive', 22 February 2018**

While the Ghent Altarpiece by Dutch painter Jan van Eyck (*c.* 1390–1441) is generally regarded as the most stolen work of art in history, *The Scream* by Norwegian painter Edvard Munch (1863–1944) is also starting to climb the rankings.

Munch's original 1893 painting of *The Scream* was stolen and recovered in 1994 (*see* 12 February). A decade later, at 11 a.m. on 22 August 2004, two masked and armed men simply wandered up to the 1910 version at the Munch Museum in Oslo and ripped it off the wall using a wire cutter. As they ran out, they also snatched a *Madonna* by Munch, then leapt into a waiting car outside. No alarms went off.

The first arrest came six months later but even though three men were convicted of the crime in May 2006, it took two years until the paintings were recovered in August 2006, both in good though not perfect condition despite rumours that they had been burned. The police have never revealed how they tracked them down or where they found them other than 'in the Oslo area', although it is believed a serving prisoner helped with a tip-off. One theory is that the theft was merely a distraction from an armed robbery that was taking place at exactly the same time elsewhere. At least it is now safe and sound forever in the Arctic World Archive. Hopefully.

ALSO ON THIS DAY **1764:** French architect and designer Charles Percier born · **1891:** Lithuanian sculptor Jacques Lipchitz born · **1908:** French photographer Henri Cartier-Bresson born

23 AUGUST

The National Gallery begins its wartime evacuation of paintings, 1939

Hide them in caves and cellars, but not one picture shall leave this island.

Winston Churchill, directive to Kenneth Clark,
1940 (attributed)

With the outbreak of war looming, on 23 August 1939 the National Gallery in London began to ensure the survival of its collection in case of bombing by evacuating much of it to locations in Wales (in fact, fifty works had already been temporarily transported to Bangor in Wales when the Munich crisis blew up in September 1938). With the possibility of invasion looming in the summer of 1940, a more secure location was needed, but the National Gallery's director Sir Kenneth Clark (*see* 7 November) was told in no uncertain terms by Winston Churchill that it should not be risked by transporting it to Canada.

By the summer of 1941, an isolated and disused slate mine in Manod in North Wales thus became the main temporary home for about two thousand pieces of art, including those by Rembrandt, Claude Monet, William Hogarth and many other masters. Here they were hidden once the tiny entrance had been dynamited to allow them to be carried inside. During a nine-month building programme, six underground brick storerooms with individual air-conditioning systems to keep temperature and humidity under control were constructed in 30-metre (100-foot)-high man-made chambers – which were in effect a dry run for similar measures that were installed at the renovated gallery after the war. Special arrangements were needed to bring Sir Anthony van Dyck's *Equestrian Portrait of Charles I* and Sebastiano del Piombo's *Raising of Lazarus* to safety, including lowering the road surface under a local bridge by 60 cm (2 feet) to accommodate the massive packing cases.

Other galleries took similar precautions. In Paris, the Louvre shut on 25 August 1939 for 'repairs', a cover story for the removal of its art to a place of greater safety, and at the same time art from the Tate Gallery in London was packed up and sent to country houses in England for safekeeping, while some stayed in London in the disused tunnels of the Underground network.

The evacuation was a wise move – the National Gallery was bombed nine times during the war.

ALSO ON THIS DAY 1846: Scottish-American sculptor Alexander Milne Calder born · **1908:** Scottish sculptor and illustrator Hannah Frank born · **1913:** *Little Mermaid* statue by Danish sculptor Edvard Eriksen is unveiled in Copenhagen (*see* 6 January)

24 AUGUST

Eugène Delacroix
sketches a dying horse, 1854

Today, I finally took out a novel by Dumas, to get out of the boredom that the absence of occupation gives me. Every previous day, walks, drawings from photographs by Durieu. Found today, before dinner, coming back from Pollet, the poor horse stretched out on the ground and whom I thought was dead. He was indeed dying.

Eugène Delacroix, diary entry,
24 August 1854

Like his friend Théodore Géricault (*see* 2 July), French painter and lithographer Eugène Delacroix (1798–1863) was especially inspired by the exotic and the concept of the sublime, with a particular interest in wild animals, seen in works such as *A Young Tiger Playing with its Mother* (1830).

Horses often featured in his works and Delacroix was keen from a young age to add an understanding of horse anatomy to his skills as a painter. Sometimes they featured alone, as in the dramatic *Horse Frightened by a Thunderstorm* (1824) where a terrified white horse rears up on a seashore, a work he gave to his friend the painter Louis-Auguste Schwiter. At about the same time, he sketched and made lithographs of the horses on the Elgin Marbles in the British Museum, but frequently they were part of a more savage ensemble, as in *Tiger attacking a Wild Horse* (1829) – which echoes English painter George Stubbs's earlier *Horse Attacked by a Lion* (1769) – and *Lion Hunt* (1855), in which horses play a colourfully central role.

ALSO ON THIS DAY 1552: Italian painter Lavinia Fontana born · **1872:** English caricaturist Max Beerbohm born · **1926:** American painter and mixed-media artist Nancy Spero born

25 AUGUST

German troops destroy a university library, 1914

The Germans sentenced Louvain [Leuven] on Wednesday to become a wilderness and with the German system and love of thoroughness they left Louvain an empty and blackened shell....

At Louvain it was war upon the defenseless, war upon churches, colleges, shops of milliners and lacemakers; war brought to the bedside and fireside; against women harvesting in the fields, against children in wooden shoes at play in the streets. At Louvain that night the Germans were like men after an orgy....

It was all like a scene upon the stage, so unreal, so inhuman, you felt that it could not be true, that the curtain of fire, purring and crackling and sending up hot sparks to meet the kind, calm stars, was only a painted backdrop; that the reports of rifles from the dark rooms came from blank cartridges, and that these trembling shopkeepers and peasants ringed in bayonets would not in a few minutes really die, but that they themselves and their homes would be restored to their wives and children. You felt it was only a nightmare, cruel and uncivilized. And then you remembered that the German Emperor has told us what it is. It is his Holy War.

Richard Harding Davis,
***New York Tribune*, 31 August 1914**

When invading German soldiers massacred and looted Leuven in Belgium during the early days of the First World War, they destroyed a vast swathe of the city, including burning the Catholic University of Leuven's prestigious library collection, even though it served no military purpose. About 300,000 books and 800 incunabula went up in flames, as well as a large number of manuscripts. Among the items lost were the Rongorongo text E tablet from Easter Island and the Leskovec-Dresden Bible, the oldest Bible in Czech, written in the mid-14th century.

A campaign to restock the library was led by the John Rylands Library in Manchester, England, and although this was well supported by other libraries around the world, the Leuven library was destroyed again by Nazi forces in May 1940 during the Second World War.

The international 1954 Hague Convention for the Protection of Cultural Property in the Event of Armed Conflict has now technically outlawed destruction of this kind.

ALSO ON THIS DAY 1724: English painter George Stubbs born · **1814:** British soldiers burn the White House, Capitol and Library of Congress, Washington DC · **1856:** English painter Dante Gabriel Rossetti meets model Fanny Cornforth (born Sarah Cox) for the first time; she later becomes his mistress, muse and housekeeper

26 AUGUST

Pierre-Auguste Renoir
joins the French army, 1870

Bazille, after having been so promising, died very young at the first battle of 1870. It is hardly possible to begin to do him justice. The first buyers of 'Impressionism' did not take his painting seriously, doubtless because Bazille was rich.

Ambroise Vollard, *La Vie & L'Oeuvre*
***de Pierre-Auguste Renoir*, 1919**

French Impressionist painter Pierre-Auguste Renoir (1841–1919) started his mandatory reservist duty for the French army with a three-month stint in 1862, another in 1864 and a final stretch in 1868. He reported for duty on 26 August 1870 at Libourne in southwestern France where, despite his lack of knowledge about horses, he joined the 10th Light Cavalry (*'chasseurs à cheval'*) Regiment, 4th platoon.

Although he served during the Franco-Prussian War (1870–71), during which Paris was under siege, he never saw action and mentions his boredom and frustration in a letter to his friend, architect Charles Le Coeur. He caught dysentery and was given up by his fellow soldiers for dead, but recovered and spent some time convalescing at his uncle's home in Bordeaux.

Fit again, he spent the rest of his time in the army in Tarbes at the luxurious home of his commander, undertaking some light horse grooming, painting his wife Marie-Octavie Bernier and giving his daughter painting lessons. Renoir was discharged from the army on 10 March 1871 and avoided being called up again later that year while living in Paris, maybe by going into hiding, although he was nearly thrown in the Seine by the city's Communards who misguidedly thought he was a spy.

Other French painters involved in the conflict included Edgar Degas and Claude Monet, who volunteered for the National Guard. Meanwhile, Paul Cézanne lay low in a fishing village, and Camille Pissarro did the same in London. Not all were so lucky. Renoir's close friend the painter Frédéric Bazille (1841–1870), mentioned by the art dealer Ambroise Vollard (*see* 30 March), joined an elite Zouave regiment and died in combat in November 1870.

ALSO ON THIS DAY 1666: Death of Dutch painter Franz Hals · **1898:** American art collector Peggy Guggenheim born (*see* 20 October) · **1992:** Death of Belgian comics illustrator Bob de Moor

27 AUGUST

Dürer sees Aztec gold displayed in Brussels, 1520

I saw the things brought to the King from the new gold-country (Mexico): a sun, entirely of gold, a whole fathom broad, and a moon all of silver quite as large; two rooms full of the armour worn by the people there; likewise all kinds of wonderful arms, harness, weapons, very quaint clothing, bedding, and all sorts of strange objects of common use, which are as interesting as they are strange. These things are all so costly, that they are valued at a hundred thousand florins. But I never before in all my life saw what delighted me so much, for I perceived among them marvellously artistic objects, and I was amazed at the subtle *ingenia* of the people in foreign countries. Indeed, I cannot say enough about everything that I had before me there.

Albrecht Dürer, diary entry,
27 August 1520

German printmaker and painter Albrecht Dürer (1471–1528) spent a year travelling around the Netherlands from July 1520 to July 1521 (*see* 12 May). As well as networking, painting and doing a lot of shopping, in 1520 he also visited the town hall in Brussels to see the display of Aztec gold offered to the Spanish invaders in Mexico and sent back to Europe to Charles V, king of Spain. It was later melted down and none of the pieces survives.

ALSO ON THIS DAY **1576:** Death of Italian painter Titian (Tiziano Vecelli) · **1664:** Death of Spainish painter Francisco de Zurbarán · **1890:** American photographer Man Ray (Emmanuel Radnitzky) born

28 AUGUST

President Erdoğan's statue is removed from Wiesbaden, 2018

We are inundated with real news, fake news and bad news: the world is changing, and not always for the better. Populism has re-entered the mainstream, holding court everywhere from barstool discussions, to parliamentary sessions, to newspaper headlines. In keeping with this phenomenon, the second Wiesbaden Biennale for Performing Arts, which will be held this summer in the Staatstheater Wiesbaden, has chosen 'Bad News' as its theme. To announce the occasion, we designed a newspaper that evokes the style of the tabloid press, with large, flashy fonts communicating the highlights of this year's event.

**German graphic designer Fons Hickmann,
artistic statement for *Bad News* newspaper, 2018**

In 2018, the erection of a statue of Turkish president Recep Tayyip Erdoğan in a central square in Wiesbaden, Germany, as part of its biennial arts festival (with the theme of 'Bad News') was, to put it mildly, controversial. By an anonymous artist, the President was shown with his right arm aloft in a similar pose to the statue of Saddam Hussein, which was famously toppled in 2003 (*see* 9 April). The 2-tonne (2.2-short ton), 4-metre (13-foot)-high mock-gold statue – daubed with graffiti, including 'Turkish Hitler' – was the location of violent clashes between those with differing views of the politician. When the local police said it could no longer provide security for the statue, it was craned out by local firefighters on 28 August.

29 AUGUST

The Federal Art Project begins operation in America, 1935

The Federal Government must and shall quit this business of relief. I am not willing that the vitality of our people be further sapped by the giving of cash, of market baskets, or of a few hours of weekly work cutting grass, raking leaves or picking up papers in public parks. We must preserve not only the bodies of the unemployed from destruction but also their self-respect, their self-reliance and courage and determination.

**US President Franklin D. Roosevelt,
State of the Union Address, 4 January 1935**

President Franklin D. Roosevelt (1882–1945; *see also* 12 April) established the Federal Art Project in 1935 as part of the New Deal initiative. The project ran until 1943 and funded visual arts across America. It was supervised by writer and art curator Holger Cahill (1887–1960) and paid artists across all disciplines to produce work, among them photographer Berenice Abbott, collagist Lee Krasner, and painters Willem de Kooning, Mark Rothko and Jackson Pollock. It helped more than 10,000 artists, set up over 100 community art centres, and was directly responsible for the creation of more than 200,000 artworks, including many in public spaces.

There is no definitive list of art produced under the project's auspices, but among the works it funded were Arshile Gorky's *Aerial Map* mural (1937) for Newark Airport's administration building, Charles Alston's large-scale painting *Magic and Medicine* (1940) and John Sloan's New York street scene painting *Fourteenth Street at Sixth Avenue* (1935).

Writing in the *New York Times* of 19 December 1937, Cahill wrote that for too long people had not regarded works of art as an honourable and vital part of everyday life, treating them simply as something to be accumulated as a snobbish or economic investment, and that with the arrival of the Great Depression in 1929, even this demand had almost stopped.

ALSO ON THIS DAY 1009: Mainz Cathedral, Germany, inauguration and badly damaged by fire · **1780:** French painter Jean-Auguste-Dominique Ingres born · **1780:** Death of French architect Jacques-Germain Soufflot

30 AUGUST

Rossetti and Hunt put together a list of 'Immortals', 1848

Apropos of death, Hunt and I are going to get up among our acquaintance a Mutual Suicide Association, by the regulations whereof any member, being weary of life, may call at any time upon another to cut his throat for him. It is all of course to be done very quietly, without weeping or gnashing of teeth. I, for instance, am to go in and say, 'I say, Hunt, just stop painting that head a minute, and cut my throat'; to which he will respond by telling the model to keep the position as he shall only be a moment, and having done his duty, will proceed with the painting....

Hunt and I have prepared a list of Immortals, forming our creed, and to be pasted up in our study for the affixing of all decent fellows' signatures. It has already caused considerable horror among our acquaintance. I suppose we shall have to keep a hair-brush. The list contains four distinct classes of Immortality; in the first of which three stars are attached to each name, in the second two, in the third one, and in the fourth none. The first class consists only of Jesus Christ and Shakespear [*sic*]. We are also about to transcribe various passages from our poets, together with forcible and correct sentiments, to be stuck up about the walls.

> **Dante Gabriel Rossetti, letter to his brother William Michael Rossetti, 30 August 1848**

The list of inspirational figures prepared by English painters Dante Gabriel Rossetti (1828–1882) and William Holman Hunt (1827–1910) on 30 August 1848 was presented to the first meeting of the Pre-Raphaelite Brotherhood in September and was signed by them and the other five members – painters Sir John Everett Millais and James Collinson, art critics Frederic George Stephens and William Michael Rossetti, and sculptor Thomas Woolner. The statement read 'We, the undersigned, declare that the following list of Immortals constitutes the whole of our Creed, and that there exists no other Immortality than what is centred in their names and in the names of their contemporaries, in whom this list is reflected.'

The list comprised a wide range of artists and writers; when Hunt included the list in his memoir of the group, only Jesus got four stars. William Shakespeare and 'The Author of Job' got three stars. Two stars went to Homer, Dante, Chaucer, Leonardo da Vinci, Goethe, Keats, Shelley, King Alfred, Landor, Thackeray, Washington and Browning.

A single star was awarded to Boccaccio, Fra Angelico, Elizabeth Barrett Browning, Patmore, Raphael, Longfellow, Tennyson and the 'Author of Stories after Nature' (aka Charles Jeremiah Wells). On the list but not meriting a star were Pheidias, Early Gothic architects, Cavalier Pugliesi, Rienzi, Ghiberti, Spenser, Hogarth, Flaxman, Hilton, Kosciusko, Byron, Wordsworth, Haydon, Cervantes, Isaiah, Joan of Arc, Michelangelo, Early English balladists, Giovanni Bellini, Giorgioni, Titian, Tintoretto, Poussin, Milton, Cromwell, Hampden, Bacon, Newton, Poe, Hood, Emerson, Leigh Hunt, Wilkie and Columbus.

Rossetti suggested the need for a hairbrush because the list was intended to make people's hair stand on end…

ALSO ON THIS DAY 1716: English landscape architect Lancelot 'Capability' Brown baptized (*see* 6 February) · **1748:** French painter Jacques-Louis David born (*see* 25 May) · **1998:** A stick figure representing the Burning Man event, Nevada, becomes the first Google Doodle

Thomas Cobden-Sanderson begins to destroy his Doves typeface, 1916

The Doves Press type was designed after that of Jensen; this evening I began its destruction. I threw three pages into the Thames from Hammersmith Bridge. I had gone for a stroll on the Mall, when it occurred to me that it was a suitable night and time; so I went indoors, and taking first one page and then two, succeeded in destroying three. I will now go on till I have destroyed the whole of it.

Thomas Cobden-Sanderson, diary entry, 31 August 1916

In 1893, English artist and bookbinder Thomas Cobden-Sanderson (1840–1922) set up his Doves Bindery at 15, Upper Mall, Hammersmith, London, not far from textile designer William Morris's Kelmscott House. Credited with coining the phrase 'Arts and Crafts' to describe the 19th-century artistic movement (*see* 1 October), Cobden-Sanderson went into partnership in 1900 with printer Emery Walker to found the Doves Press. Together they produced high-quality works including a Bible and an edition of *Paradise Lost*, all in its signature Doves Press typeface designed by Walker.

Unfortunately, the relationship between the two men broke down irretrievably and Cobden-Sanderson took decisive action to prevent further debate about the future of the typeface, as he noted in his diary on 31 August 1916. By January 1917, entirely unknown to Emery, he had gradually thrown all 500,000 pieces of the 16-point type into the river.

Long thought lost, the typeface was recreated digitally and then partially retrieved by designer Robert Green in 2014, and lives again, most recently in Lara Maiklem's 2019 book *Mudlarking*. The title of the book on the front jacket is in Doves Type, as are the running heads at the top of each page, the epigraphs and the first letter of every chapter.

ALSO ON THIS DAY 1913: American photographer Helen Levitt born · **1935:** English painter Bryan Organ born · **2019:** The first edition of the Urban Morphogenesis street art festival in Moscow ends

September

War artist Eric Ravilious arrives at RAF Kaldardarnes, 1942

Would you believe I've been made an honorary captain in the Royal Marines. I expect they'll be issuing me with my own Brigade and paint brushes before the day is out. It's a far cry from my days on the observation post on Sudbury Hill. It was more lovely than words can say, flying over the moors and the coast today in an open plane, just floating on great curly clouds, perfectly still and cool.

Eric Ravilious, letter to his wife and artist Tirzah Garwood, 1940

English painter and wood engraver Eric Ravilious (1903–1942) produced a wide range of work, from watercolours and murals to ceramic designs and book illustrations, including the shop-front lithographs for *High Street* (1938). He was also a strong supporter of anti-fascist causes, backing the Republican forces in the Spanish Civil War and displaying work in the 1937 'Artists Against Fascism' exhibition in London.

In 1939 he became an official war artist and was assigned to the navy, with postings to Norway, Portsmouth and Scotland. He wrote to his wife Tirzah in 1940 that he was enjoying working on deck in the Arctic Circle well after midnight in the sunshine. He was made an honorary captain the same year, based initially at Chatham Dockyard, from where he wrote the letter above, and then in Norway.

On 1 September 1942, Ravilious flew to RAF Kaldardarnes in Iceland. 'We flew over that mountain country that looks like craters on the moon,' he wrote to Tirzah, 'and it looked just like those photographs the Ministry of Information gave me, with shadows very dark and striped like leaves.' The following day he joined a crew on a search and rescue mission. His plane was never seen again and he was declared lost in action.

Two other artists were also killed during their work as part of the war artists' scheme (*see* 7 November): rural landscape painter Thomas Hennell in Java, and painter Albert Richards, the youngest official war artist, in Germany after driving over a landmine.

ALSO ON THIS DAY 1608: Italian stage designer Giacomo Torelli born · **1715:** Death of French sculptor François Girardon · **1884:** Australian painter Hilda Nicholas born

Marcel Duchamp enters a chess championship, 1925

The standard chess sets now in use, the FRENCH Set and the STAUNTON, are both somewhat confusing in the similarity and intricacy of their forms. In the French Set for example, the Bishop is a little Queen and the pawn a little Bishop. Cannot a new set be designed, that is, without too radical a departure from the traditional figures, at once more harmonious and more agreeable to the touch and to the sight, and above all, more adequate to the role the figure has to play in the struggle? Thus, at any moment of the drama its optical aspect would represent (by the shape of the actors) a clear incisive image of its inner conflicts. In the complicated modern game the figures should inspire the player instead of confusing him. They should whisper to him at the right moment: 'Move now to QB4.... Break through the center.... Pin the Knight.... Let me win a piece.... We can exchange Queens, the pawn will be metamorphosed into a new Queen.... to mate the King.'

**Anon., 'On Designing Chessmen',
in Imagery of Chess exhibition brochure, 1944**

French-American artist Marcel Duchamp (1887–1968) experimented in the fields of painting and sculpture, producing Cubist works early in his career and going on to his 'readymade' installations of 'found' art, coining the term 'mobiles' for his kinetic art, and using random methods to compose music.

By the 1920s he had become engrossed in the world of chess, carving his own sets and moving away from the established art world. 'It's a long time that I've been wanting to write you,' he wrote in a letter to his friends, the Stettheimer sisters, on 3 May 1919. 'But I haven't been able to find the time: my attention is so completely absorbed by chess. I play night and day and nothing in the world interests me more than finding the right move.... I like painting less and less.'

In 1925, he designed the poster for the 3rd French Chess Championship in Nice and also took part, winning three, losing three and drawing two. Eventually coming sixth, at one point it appeared he might win. In the following decade he played for the French team in various chess olympiads and became a very strong correspondence chess player as well as a respected chess journalist.

His love of chess and art was celebrated in 1944 when, with his friend the German painter Max Ernst, he co-organized the 'Imagery of Chess' exhibition at the Julien Levy Gallery in New York. He invited thirty-two artists and musicians – one per chess board square – to either design a chess set or produce a chess-related work (American composer John Cage wrote a piece for solo piano called *Chess Pieces*).

Duchamp regarded chess as very much an artistic calling, describing it as 'very plastic' and a 'mechanical sculpture'. In a speech to the New York State Chess Association annual meeting in 1952, he opined that chess was like a 'pen and ink drawing' and that experience had taught him that although all artists are not chess players, all chess players are artists.

3 SEPTEMBER

The Great Fire of London destroys St Paul's Cathedral, 1666

I went to the royal bridge in the New Palace [Yard] at Westminster, to take a fuller view of the fire. The people who lived contiguous to St Paul's church raised their expectations greatly concerting the absolute security of that place upon account of the immense thickness of its walls and its situation; built in a large piece of ground, on every side remote from houses. Upon this account they filled it with all sorts of goods; and besides, in the church of St Faith, under that of St Paul's, they deposited libraries of books because it was entirely arched all over; and with great caution and prudence even the least avenue through which the smallest spark might penetrate was stopped up. But this precaution availed them little.

As I stood upon the bridge among many others, I could not but observe the gradual approaches of the fire towards that venerable fabric. About eight o'clock it broke out on the top of St Paul's Church, already scorched up by the violent heat of the air, and lightning too, and before nine blazed so conspicuous as to enable me to read very clearly a 16mo. edition of Terence which I carried in my pocket. On Thursday soon after sunrising, I endeavoured to reach St Paul's. The ground so hot as almost to scorch my shoes; and the air so intensely warm that unless I had stopped some time upon Fleet Bridge to rest myself I most have fainted under the extreme languor of my spirits. After giving myself a little time to breathe I made the best of my way to St. Paul's. And now let any person judge of the violent emotion I was in when I perceived the metal belonging to the bells melting; the condition of its walls; whole heaps of stone of a large circumference tumbling down with a great noise just upon my feet, ready to crush me to death. I prepared myself for returning back again, having first loaded my pockets with several pieces of bell metal.

**William Taswell, 'Autobiography and Anecdotes,
AD 1651–1682'**

As a young boy, English parish priest Dr William Taswell (1652–1731) was an eyewitness to the Great Fire of London that broke out in the city on 2 September 1666 and reached St Paul's Cathedral later that evening. Over the following forty-eight hours, the flames gutted the building, as diarists John Evelyn and Samuel Pepys also noted. Once the fire was out, it was decided to knock down what remained and build an entirely new cathedral, designed by architect Sir Christopher Wren (1632–1723).

ALSO ON THIS DAY 1810: Irish painter Paul Kane born · **1842:** Queen Victoria paints Scottish fisherwomen in her personal journal · **1919:** American photographer Phil Stern born

4 SEPTEMBER

Laurence Broderick's 'The Bull' is unveiled, 2003

A John Cooper, the same person who stands in the list of donors in St Martin's church...for some services rendered to the lord of the manor, obtained three privileges, that of regulating the goodness and price of beer, consequently he stands in the front of the whole liquid race of high tasters; that he should, whenever he pleased, beat a bull in the Bullring, whence arises the name; and, that he should be allowed interment in the south porch of St Martin's church. His memory ought to be transmitted with honour, to posterity, for promoting the harmony of his neighbourhood, but he ought to have been buried in a dunghill, for punishing an innocent animal.

English historian and poet William Hutton,
***An History of Birmingham*, 1781**

British sculptor and teacher Laurence Broderick (b. 1935) produced his 6-tonne (6.6-short ton), twice life-size bronze of a turning bull for the Bullring in Birmingham to commemorate the city's history and its 21st-century rejuvenation. He said his goal was to make it 'powerful and strong' to reflect the city itself. Modelled on the Hereford Bull, it was instantly popular and has become one of the most photographed works of art in the UK, as well as subject to numerous attacks by vandals. It is often dressed up in appropriate attire for important events. Although commonly referred to as 'The Bull', the 2.2-metre (7¼-foot)-high sculpture is officially called *The Guardian*.

ALSO ON THIS DAY 1676: Death of Scottish cartographer John Ogilby · **1888:** German painter and sculptor Oskar Schlemmer born · **1982:** Death of Polish-born American painter Jack Tworkov

5 SEPTEMBER

'Your Country Needs You'
image first appears, 1914

Posters appealing to recruits are to be seen on every hoarding, in most windows, in omnibuses, tramcars and commercial vans. The great base of Nelson's Column is covered with them. Their number and variety are remarkable. Everywhere Lord Kitchener sternly points a monstrously big finger, exclaiming 'I Want You'. Another bill says 'Lord Kitchener wants another 100,000 men.'

***The Times*, 3 January 1915**

On 5 September 1914, the *London Opinion* magazine ran on its cover an advertisement – later to become a poster – designed by English graphic artist and cartoonist Alfred Leete (1882–1933) to encourage men to enlist in the army as it embarked upon the First World War. It featured Lord Kitchener, secretary of state for war, with the words 'Your Country Needs You', and followed a far more pedestrian attempt with a straightforward image of Kitchener and a text that read: 'Men, materials & money are the immediate necessities. Does the call of duty find no response in you until reinforced – let us rather say superseded – by the call of compulsion? Enlist today.' Leete's design was copied for a similar recruitment drive in the United States with the Kitchener image substituted with one of Uncle Sam.

Leete contributed comic work to many magazines, including *Punch* and *Tatler*, and designed posters and advertisements for clients as varied as Guinness and the London Underground. During the war he was also a member of the Artists Rifles (*see* 28 February) and produced art during this time, including *Sanctuary or the Ever Open Door* (1914), which shows Belgian refugees arriving in England from the fighting in Flanders.

ALSO ON THIS DAY 1774: German painter Caspar David Friedrich born (*see* 8 February) · **1914:** English make-up artist Stuart Freeborn born · **2019:** Death of Mexican painter and sculptor Francisco Toledo

6 SEPTEMBER

The Fighting Temeraire
takes its final voyage, 1838

It is absurd, you will say (and with a great deal of reason), for Titmarsh, or any other Briton, to grow so politically enthusiastic about a four-foot canvas, representing a ship, a steamer, a river and a sunset. But herein surely lies the power of the great artist. He makes you see and think of a great deal more than the objects before you; he knows how to soothe or intoxicate, to fire or to depress, by a few notes, or forms, or colours, of which we cannot trace the effect to the source, but only acknowledge the power. I recollect some years ago, at the theatre at Weimar, hearing Beethoven's 'Battle of Vittoria', in which, amidst a storm of glorious music, the air of 'God save the King' was introduced. The very instant it began, every Englishman in the house was bolt upright, and so stood reverently until the air was played out. Why so? From some such thrill of excitement as makes us glow and rejoice over Mr Turner and his *Fighting Téméraire* which I am sure, when the art of translating colours into music or poetry shall be discovered, will be found to be a magnificent national ode or piece of music.

William Makepeace Thackeray,
***Ballads and Miscellanies*, 1899**

This famous painting (full title: *The Fighting Temeraire tugged to her last berth to be broken up*) of the ninety-eight-gun, three-decked ship is a glorious but inaccurate portrait of its final journey to Rotherhithe on 6 September 1838 – there's no evidence the artist actually watched it happen at all. English painter J. M. W. Turner (in full Joseph Mallord William Turner; 1775–1851) wanted to celebrate the ship's impressive history but in truth HMS *Temeraire* had not seen action for more than a decade and its masts had been removed, a far cry from its defence of Nelson's flagship HMS *Victory* at the Battle of Trafalgar in 1805.

Turner used less experimental materials for the painting than on many of his other works and as a result it has survived particularly well. It was hailed as a triumph by the media and the Royal Academy, where it was exhibited in 1839, and was voted Britain's favourite painting in a poll run by BBC Radio 4 in 2005. It now hangs in the National Gallery in London.

However, not everybody has been as enthused as author William Makepeace Thackeray (1811–1863; *see also* 11 March). In the 2012 film *Skyfall*, Q shows James Bond the painting, pointedly saying: 'Always makes me feel a little melancholy. Grand old war ship, being ignominiously hauled away for scrap.... The inevitability of time, don't you think? What do you see?' Bond replies: 'A bloody big ship.'

ALSO ON THIS DAY **1517:** Portuguese artist and architect Francisco de Holanda born · **1877:** Walker Art Gallery, Liverpool, England, opens · **1939:** Death of English illustrator Arthur Rackham

Guillaume Apollinaire is detained for supsected art theft, 1911

Before entering my cell
I had to be naked
Then a sinister voice hooted
'Guillaume what have you become'...
No, I don't feel like myself in here
I am just the fifteenth of the eleventh row...
In a pit like a bear
Every morning I walk
Around, around, around, around.
The sky is blue like a chain
In a pit like a bear
Every morning I walk

**Guillaume Apollinaire,
'In the Santé', 1911**

When Leonardo da Vinci's *Mona Lisa* was stolen from the Louvre in 1911 (*see* 21 August), suspicion initially fell on the French writer and inventor of the term 'surrealism', Guillaume Apollinaire (1880–1918; *see also* 27 February). Not only was he arrested for the theft, but the police also collared him for the disappearance of several Egyptian statuettes. Blameless for the first, certainly implicated in the second (although charges were later dropped), Apollinaire spent a week in the cells of La Santé prison in Paris and wrote about his experiences in one of his finest poems before he was released.

ALSO ON THIS DAY 1705: German painter Matthäus Günther born · **1855:** English photography pioneer William Friese-Greene born · **1925:** Welsh fashion designer Laura Ashley born

Edgar Deacon finally achieves fame in a last novel, 1975

Things of perfection must not be looked at in a hurry, but with time, judgment and intelligence. We must use the same process to judge them as to make them.

**Nicolas Poussin, letter to Paul Fréart de Chantelou,
French ambassador to the Papal Court, 20 March 1642**

A keen collagist, the twelve-novel sequence 'A Dance to the Music of Time' by English writer Anthony Powell (1905–2000) was not only inspired by the painting of the same name by French artist Nicolas Poussin (1594–1665; *see* 3 June), but it also contains an immense number of detailed descriptions of art, real and ficitonal, throughout. The narrator's closest school friend is compared to Italian painter Paolo Veronese's depiction of Alexander in his *The Family of Darius before Alexander* (1565–67), an unidentified Modigliani pops up enigmatically throughout the cycle, and a set of 16th-century tapestries depicting the seven deadly sins play an important role in the main characters' developments.

We first encounter the fictional painter Edgar Deacon (1871–1928) in *A Buyer's Market*, the second of the twelve books. His works include his notable *Boyhood of Cyrus*, *Pupils of Socrates* and *By the Will of Diocletian*. Nick Jenkins, the narrator of the books, meets Deacon as a young boy and receives a wooden paintbox from him as a gift. Jenkins then bumps into him again as a young man when Deacon has become a slightly dubious antiques dealer, dying from injuries shortly after falling down the stairs of a nightclub at his birthday party.

Portrayed as essentially a minor painter for most of the 'Dance', in the final volume – *Hearing Secret Harmonies*, published on 8 September 1975 – his reputation is very much on the up and Jenkins is amused to attend a centenary exhibition celebrating his work, the final set-piece scene in the narrative.

ALSO ON THIS DAY 1504: Michelangelo's statue *David* is unveiled (*see* 13 September) · **1924:** Canadian artist Mimi Parent born · **1997:** English painter Marcus Harvey's painting of Myra Hindley goes on display at the Royal Academy of Art, London, and is vandalized twice immediately

Van Gogh plans
his studio in Arles, 1888

Now yesterday I worked at furnishing the house.... One of these days you'll see a painting of the little house itself, in full sunshine or else with the window lit and the starry sky.

Then you'll be able to believe you own your country house here in Arles. Because I myself am enthusiastic about the idea of arranging it in such a way that you'll like it, and that it'll be a studio in a style absolutely meant to be that way. And the studio — the red floor-tiles, the white walls and ceiling, the rustic chairs, the deal table, with, I hope, decoration of portraits. That will have character à la Daumier — and it won't, I dare predict, be commonplace.

Now I'm going to ask you to look for some Daumier lithographs for the studio, and some Japanese prints, but it's not at all urgent, and only when you find duplicates of them.

And some Delacroixs too, ordinary lithographs by modern artists.

It's not the least little bit urgent, but I have my idea. I really want to make of it — an artist's house but not precious, on the contrary, nothing precious, but everything from the chair to the painting having character.

**Vincent van Gogh, letter to his brother Theo,
9 September 1888**

Dutch painter Vincent van Gogh (1853–1890; *see also* 17 June) rented what became known as the Yellow House in Arles, France, at the beginning of May 1888, but did not start living there until September after furnishing and decorating it; he made it his official address on 16 October 1888. In his 9 September letter to his brother Theo van Gogh, he talks enthusiastically about all his purchases for the house and exactly how everything was to be arranged.

In the same letter, he tells his brother, who was an art dealer, that he has just sent him a drawing of his famous painting *The Night Café* (1888), an interior of the Café de la Gare in Arles where the painter spent many hours. 'In my painting of the night café I've tried to express the idea that the café is a place where you can ruin yourself, go mad, commit crimes,' he wrote. 'Anyway, I tried with contrasts of delicate pink and blood-red and wine-red. Soft Louis XV and Veronese green contrasting with yellow greens and hard blue greens.'

10 SEPTEMBER

Picasso's *Guernica* returns to Spain, 1981

We are fighting for the essential unity of Spain.
We are fighting for the integrity of Spanish soil.
We are fighting for the independence of our country and for
the right of the Spanish people to determine their own destiny.

**Text at the entrance to the Spanish Pavilion,
Paris International Exposition, 1937**

The first public sight of the painting *Guernica* by Pablo Picasso (1881–1973) came at its unveiling in the Spanish pavilion at the Paris International Exposition in July 1937 (*see* 26 April). Organized by the Spanish Republican government during the civil war, the entrance to the pavilion was decorated with a large mural of Republican soldiers and the words above.

When the world collapsed into the Second World War, Picasso suggested that *Guernica* be held on loan at the Museum of Modern Art in New York until the death of Spain's dictator Francisco Franco and the restoration of civil liberties in the country.

On 10 September 1981, after decades in its temporary home in New York and with no fanfare, *Guernica* was rolled up and left the museum to make the journey to Spain, boarding an Iberia plane at 7 p.m.

More than a million people came to view *Guernica* in the first year it was exhibited in Madrid.

The attacks on New York's World Trade Center destroy art, 2001

O happy friends! for, if my verse can give
Immortal life, your fame shall ever live,
Fix'd as the Capitol's foundation lies,
And spread, where'er the Roman eagle flies!

Virgil, *The Aeneid, Book IX, c.* 19 BC

A quote from this section of Virgil's poem – 'No Day Shall Erase You from the Memory of Time' – is on display at the 9/11 Memorial & Museum in New York. The letters, 38 cm (15 inches) high and stretching 18 metres (60 feet), were forged by New Mexico artist Tom Joyce (b. 1956) using steel found at the site.

In addition to the nearly three thousand people who died in the 9/11 attacks in 2001, art worth more than $100 million was also destroyed. Some of this was public art on display, but most was in the offices of the businesses located in the towers, much of it not insured for its full value. Among works lost were:

- an unspecified number of sculptures by French sculptor Auguste Rodin in the Cantor Fitzgerald offices, including a cast of *The Thinker* that appeared to have survived the attack only to be stolen
- photographs by American artist Cindy Sherman in the Fred Alger offices
- American sculptor Elyn Zimmerman's fountain memorial to the people killed in the 1993 World Trade Center bombing
- *Sky Gate New York*, a wood relief wall-hanging by American sculptor Louise Nevelson
- *World Trade Center Stabile*, or *Bent Propeller*, a 7.6-metre (25-foot)-high red steel abstract sculpture by American artist Alexander Calder (this was partially recovered but not enough for proper restoration)
- a large tapestry by Catalan artist Joan Miró
- American artist Roy Lichtenstein's 'Entablature' series.

More than a dozen artists' studios in the trade centre were also destroyed and sculptor Michael Richards died during the attack while he was at work.

One piece that survived, although by no means intact, was the rotating metal sculpture *The Sphere* by German artist Fritz Koenig, a symbol of world peace. It is now installed in Liberty Park, overlooking the 9/11 Memorial & Museum.

ALSO ON THIS DAY 100: Claudia Severa's birthday invitation date on a Vindolanda tablet · **1470:** German mapmaker Martin Waldseemüller born · **1917:** French art dealer Daniel Wildenstein born

The entrance to the Lascaux Cave is discovered, 1940

We have invented nothing.

**Pablo Picasso, on seeing the rock art
at Lascaux, France (attributed)**

The Lascaux complex of caves near Montignac in France's Dordogne region was uncovered by chance when eighteen-year-old Marcel Ravidat's dog Robot fell into a hole. When Ravidat and his friends Simon Coencas, Georges Agnel and Jacques Marsal investigated further, they discovered a long shaft leading to various caverns. These have now been named according to the art discovered in each one, including the Hall of the Bulls and the Feline Diverticulum.

Hundreds of wall paintings cover the ceilings and walls of the caves, featuring large animals (including a rhinocerous) and humans of the era, painted by generations of people, about 17,000 years ago. There are also what appear to be abstract signs, but no depictions of flora. The caves were opened to the public in 1948 but the very great number of visitors contributed to a deterioration in the paintings and the caves were closed again in 1963. Replicas have since been made and put on general display.

ALSO ON THIS DAY 1829: German painter Anselm Feuerbach born · **1862:** German-American painter Carl Eytel born · **1921:** Turkish architect Turgut Cansever born

Michelangelo starts to create his *David*, 1501

The Board of Works at S. Maria del Fiore owned a piece of marble nine cubits in height, which had been brought from Carrara some hundred years before by a sculptor insufficiently acquainted with his art. This was evident, inasmuch as, wishing to convey it more conveniently and with less labour, he had it blocked out in the quarry, but in such a manner that neither he nor any one else was capable of extracting a statue from the block, either of the same size, or even on a much smaller scale. The marble being, then, useless for any good purpose, Andrea del Monte San Savino thought that he might get possession of it from the Board, and begged them to make him a present of it, promising that he would add certain pieces of stone and carve a statue from it. Before they made up their minds to give it, they sent for Michelangelo; then, after explaining the wishes and the views of Andrea, and considering his own opinion that it would be possible to extract a good thing from the block, they finally offered it to him. Michelangelo accepted, added no pieces, and got the statue out so exactly, that, as any one may see, in the top of the head and at the base some vestiges of the rough surface of the marble still remain.

English writer John Addington Symonds, *The Life of Michelangelo Buonarroti*, 1893

Italian painter and sculptor Michelangelo (1475–1564) was still only twenty-six when he won the commission to produce his *David* in 1501 (*see* 16 August). He began working on it nearly a month later on 13 September and spent the next two years devoted to its completion. Unlike previous renditions of David, Michelangelo presents him without the giant and before the fight with Goliath.

Among the many replicas of *David* was one that was a gift to Queen Victoria in 1857 from Leopold II, the Grand Duke of Tuscany. Unfortunately, the monarch was so taken aback by David's nudity that a plaster fig leaf had to be hurriedly produced to cover his genitalia. No longer in use, it is still part of the Victoria and Albert Museum's holdings.

ALSO ON THIS DAY 1506: Death of Italian painter Andrea Mantegna · **1931:** Death of Danish model and painter Lili Elbe · **1944:** Death of English cartoonist W. Heath Robinson

Rembrandt's *The Night Watch* is vandalized, 1975

As time went on and he became more firmly established in popular estimation as the leading painter of his day, he released himself from the self-imposed duty of thinking as much of his sitters as of his art, and treated natural data in the sovereign fashion which suited his genius. It was this emancipated Rembrandt to whom there came in 1641–2 the commission to paint another of the corporation pieces, in which he had achieved success in the earlier period of comparative self-restraint.

The result was the so-called 'Night Watch', which, by the very fact that it has received this title, an entirely misleading one, betrays its specific character. It is not a night-piece at all, but represents an open-air scene illumined by a sun that is still high in the heavens, yet the effect of chiaroscuro is so forced that at the end of the eighteenth century it was supposed to be a scene in an interior artificially illumined. It is true that the picture had already by that time been considerably darkened both by the smoke and dirt of the shooting-company's hall where it was hung and by successive coats of varnish, so that to Reynolds it appeared 'to have been much damaged', and he writes of it, 'it was with difficulty I could persuade myself that it was painted by Rembrandt'. That it was a dark picture from the first is however proved by Rembrandt's own pupil Hoogstraten, who ends an appreciative notice of it with the words 'yet I wish he had put more light into it'.

Professor Gerard Baldwin Brown,
Rembrandt: A Study of His Life and Work, 1907

Samuel van Hoogstraten, the pupil of Dutch painter Rembrandt (1606–1669; *see also* 2 November), was right to claim that *The Night Watch* (1642) – officially, *Militia Company of District II under the Command of Captain Frans Banninck Cocq*, but also known as *The Shooting Company of Frans Banning Cocq and Willem van Ruytenburch* – would achieve lasting fame. It is the centrepiece of the Rijksmuseum in Amsterdam, on display in a gallery specifically designed for it. The huge painting, which shows the almost life-size figures of the company on the move, has also unfortunately been vandalized numerous times.

Arguably the first was in 1715 when it was moved to Amsterdam's City Hall to be exhibited. To fit the space allocated, the painting was trimmed by 60 cm (2 feet) on the top and left, and 5 cm (a couple of inches) from the bottom and right, losing two figures and some of the buildings, and radically altering its compositional integrity.

In the 20th century it has been the subject of an attemped knife slashing in 1911 (largely ineffectual thanks to the protective thick coat of varnish) and a further slashing with a bread knife by an unemployed school teacher on 14 September 1975, which required four years of restoration. In 1990 there was yet another attack, this time with acid, but again only the varnish was damaged thanks to the swift thinking of a security guard who sprayed the area with water.

ALSO ON THIS DAY 1643: American silversmith Jeremiah Dummer born · **1883:** Austrian painter Richard Gerstl born · **1923:** Greek painter Nicholas Georgiadis born

15 SEPTEMBER

Henry Moore muses on Stonehenge and sculpture, 1933

When any work seems to have required immense force and labour to effect it, the idea is grand. Stonehenge, neither for disposition nor ornament, has anything admirable; but those huge rude masses of stone, set on end, and piled each on other, turn the mind on the immense force necessary for such a work. Nay, the rudeness of the work increases this cause of grandeur, as it excludes the idea of art and contrivance; for dexterity produces another sort of effect, which is different enough from this.

British philosopher Edmund Burke, *A Philosophical Enquiry into the Origin of Our Ideas of the Sublime and Beautiful*, 1757

English artist and sculptor Henry Moore (1898–1986) visited Stonehenge in 1921 and the sight of the stones in the moonlight had an immediate and lasting impact on him. On 15 September 1933, he wrote a letter to his friend the artist Paul Nash in which he remarks on the sense of 'immense power' he felt about the roughly fashioned stones. Moore added that he was keen to sculpt his own massive standing stone in his studio as a kind of inspiration for his work.

Moore returned to Stonehenge many times. Between 1971 and 1973 he produced fifteen lithographs and several etchings of the site, concentrating on the textures of individual formations from very close up rather than of Stonehenge as a whole. In 1979, he gave a complete set of the artwork to Wakefield Art Gallery (he grew up in nearby Castleford) and drove them to the gallery to deliver them by hand.

ALSO ON THIS DAY 1644-1913: Feast day of the portrait *Saint Dominic in Soriano*, which 'miraculously appeared' at the Dominican friary, Soriano Calabro, Italy· **1892:** Italian-born Thai sculptor Silpa Bhirasri born · **1991:** Michelangelo's *David* is attacked with a hammer and one of the toes is broken off (*see* 13 September)

16 SEPTEMBER

Jane Austen shops
for Wedgwood, 1813

Thank you, my dearest Cassandra, for the nice long letter I sent off this morning. I hope you have had it by this time, and that it has found you all well, and my mother no more in need of leeches.... The poor girls and their teeth! I have not mentioned them yet, but we were a whole hour at Spence's, and Lizzy's were filed and lamented over again, and poor Marianne had two taken out after all, the two just beyond the eye teeth, to make room for those in front. When her doom was fixed, Fanny, Lizzy and I walked into the next room, where we heard each of the two sharp and hasty screams...

We then went to Wedgwood's, where my brother and Fanny chose a dinner-set. I believe the pattern is a small lozenge in purple, between lines of narrow gold, and it is to have the crest.

**Jane Austen, letter to her sister Cassandra,
16 September 1813**

English novelist Jane Austen (1775–1817) never namechecks Wedgwood china in her novels but General Tilney's breakfast set described in *Northanger Abbey* – 'neat and simple...well flavoured from the clay of Staffordshire' – is probably Wedgwood (*see* 15 May).

The Austen family had plenty of Wedgwood pieces in their house and her letter of 16 September 1813 describes a visit to buy a set for her brother Edward Knight. Austen would have used this on visits to his house and parts of it are on display at the Jane Austen House Museum in Chawton, Hampshire.

Widely used though not regarded as remarkable by Jane Austen's peers, the earlier arrival of new Wedgwood at her home in 1811 still provided entertainment, as she recounts in another letter to Cassandra on 6 June that year:

> On Monday I had the pleasure of receiving, unpacking and approving our Wedgwood ware. It all came very safely and upon the whole is a good match, tho' I think they might have allowed us rather larger leaves, especially in such a year of fine foliage as this. One is apt to suppose that the woods about Birmingham must be blighted.

ALSO ON THIS DAY 1886: German-French painter and sculptor Jean Arp born · **1956:** Belgian painter René Magritte completes his painting *The Sixteenth of September* · **1965:** Death of American animator Fred Quimby

17 SEPTEMBER

Baroness Elsa von Freytag-Loringhoven is arrested for wearing men's clothes, 1910

Mrs Elsie Greve, recently of New York, but formerly of Berlin, was arrested in crowded Fifth Avenue this forenoon while walking by the side of her husband, F. P. Greve of New York, dressed in men's clothes and puffing a cigarette. Both Mrs Greve and her husband were taken, protesting, to the central police station and locked up as suspicious persons.

Both Greve and his wife asserted that they were subjects of Germany, had done no wrong, and intended no wrong. If they were not released speedily, they would appeal to the German Ambassador at Washington tomorrow morning, they said. Whether this threat was considered or not is not known, but this evening it was announced at Police Headquarters that Mrs Greve and her husband had been allowed to leave the police station and go on their way, and that Supt of Police McQuaide issued a letter to the pair setting forth that Mrs Greve and her husband were all right and that the woman was wearing men's clothes only because she could walk better and keep up with her husband, who was walking out his vacation.

**Report in the *New York Times*,
17 September 1910**

As well as her arrest in New York for wearing men's clothes on 17 September 1910 while out walking with her husband (at that time writer Felix Paul Greve), German Dadaist artist Baroness Elsa von Freytag-Loringhoven (1874–1927) was also later known for her extraordinary clothing combinations. In an undated letter to her friend the American artist Djuna Barnes, the Baroness describes going to a party wearing a large birthday cake on her head complete with lit candles, matchboxes as earrings and with postage stamps on her beauty spots, lamenting that she did not have enough money to buy the multicoloured rubber boots and gold paper skirt to match the cake that she wanted.

The Baroness wrote poetry, too, but concentrated on body-related art, often making her costumes from items she found on the street as well as household items such as spoons. She may also have provided the creative inspiration for Marcel Duchamp's 1917 urinal sculpture, *Fountain*.

ALSO ON THIS DAY 1877: Death of English photography pioneer William Henry Fox Talbot · **1915:** Indian painter Maqbool Fida Husain born · **1925:** A road accident causes Mexican painter Frida Kahlo life-changing injuries (*see* 20 April)

18 SEPTEMBER

Cecil Beaton photographs
Queen Elizabeth II, 1968

The Photographic Institution, Brighton, 57, Marine Parade

The Proprietor of this Establishment respectfully announces that it is now open to the public. He feels it to be necessary on this occasion to correct an erroneous but very current opinion, that the photographic art cannot be practised successfully except by means of direct sunshine...the only difference between the effect of a bright sunshine and of a clouded sky being that the time required for the sitting in the latter case is protracted a few seconds beyond that of the former. The charge for a portrait in a plain morocco case is One Guinea. Frames and Cases of a more ornamental kind may be had upon moderate additional charges.

Advert, *Brighton Guardian*,
10 November 1841

The advert in the *Brighton Guardian* was placed by English photographer William Constable (1783–1861); six months later he took what was the first (surviving) photograph of a member of the British royal family – a shot of Prince Albert, Queen Victoria's husband, who visited Constable's Brighton studio for a head and shoulders daguerreotype portrait. Now badly faded, Queen Victoria noted her appoval of the results in her diary.

Victoria's great-great granddaughter Queen Elizabeth II was chronicled photographically, most memorably by photographer and stage designer Sir Cecil Beaton (1904–1980) throughout the 20th century. The first sitting was in 1942 when Elizabeth was still a princess, and later shoots followed the births of her children and included her Coronation Day in 1953.

Early shoots were extremely picturesque with a strong pastoral feel enhanced by flowers picked by Beaton from his own garden. For the 1968 session on 18 September, however, Beaton was keen to avoid the traditional tiara and crinoline approach. Instead, they agreed on a navy blue serge Admiral's Boat cloak and Beaton notes in his diary that the Queen was in quite a giggly mood. While Beaton was not pleased with the results, which he felt failed to gloss over any imperfections, Tom Blau who founded the Camera Press agency that distributed Beaton's photographs told him that it was an honest portrait of the Queen.

By the time he came to photograph the Queen for this last time in 1968, he used simple plain backgrounds of blue and white and had definitively replaced the sumptuous gowns and regalia of previous shots with a cloak. Although the two had a friendly working relationship, Beaton was still nervous for this final session, noting in his diary that their points of view and tastes were very different.

ALSO ON THIS DAY 1914: English cinematographer Jack Cardiff born · **1939:** Death of Polish painter and photographer Stanisław Witkiewicz ('Witkacy') · **1958:** Death of Norwegian painter and caricaturist Olaf Gulbransson

Scott Fahlman proposes the first internet emoticons, 1982

:-)

:-(

**Scott Fahlman, post on the Carnegie Mellon University
bulletin board system, 19 September 1982**

Using punctuation to indicate emotion has a long history that arguably dates back to the 17th century; Morse Code also uses numbers as shorthand expressions of feelings. But American computer scientist Scott Fahlman (b. 1948) was the first to come up with the smiley emoticon, which uses several combined punctuation marks and allowed those posting on the Carnegie Mellon University online bulletin board to make clear that their comment was humorous (or not humorous, with the sad version).

Other posters on the original thread of 19 September 1982 took to the idea with glee and added their own suggestions, which included using:

* or % in the subject field to indicate a joke
* for good jokes and % for bad jokes or *% for jokes 'that are so bad, they're funny'
& 'as it looks funny (like a jolly fat man in convulsions of laughter)'
{#} 'because it looks like two lips with teeth showing between them'

These are all 'Western style' emoticons; 'Eastern' and '2channel' emoticons developed in Japan are also in widespread general use.

ALSO ON THIS DAY **1865:** American photographer Frank Eugene born · **1867:** English illustrator Arthur Rackham born · **1930:** American photographer Bettye Lane born

A family friend diagnoses the cause of Richard Dadd's collapse, 1843

Accept my best thanks for returning me poor Dadd's letters which I have just rec'd and with this I send for your perusal an earlier one dated Athens in which you will find his remarks upon first seeing the Pictures of the Great Italian Masters particularly those of Venice – as also, his first impressions, on landing in Greece – and the overpowering affect it had upon his excitable imagination...after reading those letters together with those to his Father (which were of the most affectionate nature) it is not difficult to see – that unfortunately from the rapidity with which they traversed those countreys – the continual succession of objects every one partaking of a deeper interest than another the contemplation of which upon a young and sensitive mind – reason was at last overpowered, and hence the mental powers, although in themselves strong, by overoperation became at last a total wreck – whether this (had the journey been less rapid) could have been avoided, is not for us now to say – one thing is evident it was on the voyage homewards from Egypt that the change first became sensible to himself as also to his companion. He never wrote to me again after the one written at Malta, probably his reflexions on coming home, as to what he had to show, the hurridness of the journey admitting of his making little more than pencil sketches – may have had its effect in hurr[y]ing on the catastrophe.

David Roberts, letter to Samuel Carter Hall, 20 September 1843

English painter Richard Dadd (1817–1886) was an exceptional young artist who was starting to make a name for himself when he accompanied businessman Sir Thomas Phillips on a tour of Europe and the Middle East in 1842. On the way home, Dadd suffered a serious bout of schizophrenic mental illness. When it was clear the situation was grave, Scottish painter David Roberts (1796–1864), a friend of Dadd's father, wrote to Samuel Carter Hall, the writer and journalist who had commissioned Dadd to illustrate his *Book of British Ballads*.

Shortly after Dadd's return to England in 1843, he murdered his father whom he believed to be the devil. Committed to Bethlem and Broadmoor psychiatric hospitals, he was allowed his own studio and continued painting, focusing on landscapes and ships, as well as fantasy subjects with miniature detailing. His most famous work is *The Fairy Feller's Master-Stroke* (1855–64), which is now in the Tate's collection, and other works that are still on display at Broadmoor.

ALSO ON THIS DAY **1844:** English photographer William Illingworth born · **1941:** American glass sculptor Dale Chihuly born · **1946:** Cannes Film Festival launches

21 SEPTEMBER

The BBC launch
The Shock of the New, 1980

The Shock of the New

Eight films on modern art and a century of change.

Robert Hughes looks at the past 100 years through the lens of its art, from the Impressionists to the present day.

'Centuries don't start neatly on cue. Ours began around 1880 and it is finishing its run now, leaving behind it – in my view – some of the most challenging, intelligent and beautiful works of art ever made by man, along with a mass of superfluity and rubbish.'
1: The Mechanical Paradise

In 1913 a French writer remarked 'the world has changed less since the time of Jesus Christ than it has in the last 30 years'. This was a widespread feeling. Rapid advances in science and technology, radically changed man's view of himself and the world in which he lived. And artists responded with radical new approaches to the new world.

This film shows the optimism with which people in general, and artists in particular, reacted to the machine age.

Radio Times, 18 September 1980

The Shock of the New, the BBC television series (and accompanying book) by Australian art critic Robert Hughes (1938–2012) began on 21 September 1980

and ran over eight one-hour episodes. It became a popular and critically acclaimed guide to the development of modern art from 1880 and the arrival of Cubism and Futurism, to its growing commercialization and interest in land art, body art and performance art.

Hughes was a less patrician presenter than art historian Sir Kenneth Clark whose *Civilisation* series aired in the previous decade (*see* 23 February), and his straightforward if sometimes rather conservative approach was a contrast to what he described in his 2006 autobiography *Things I Didn't Know* as the 'airy-fairy, metaphor-ridden kind of pseudo-poetry' art criticism, which he said was too widespread.

ALSO ON THIS DAY **1552:** Italian painter Barbara Longhi born · **1915:** English barrister Cecil Chubb buys Stonehenge at an auction in Salisbury, England, for £6,600 (*see* 26 October) · **1937:** *The Hobbit*, written and illustrated by English author J. R. R. Tolkien, is first published

22 SEPTEMBER

The Duke of York's Picturehouse
opens in Brighton, 1910

I want an Electric Theatre!

Violet Melnotte Wyatt to her husband Frank Wyatt (attributed)

Bring her to the Duke's, it is fit for a Duchess.

Original marketing slogan for the picturehouse

Opened in 1910 and regarded as the oldest cinema in continuous use in Britain, the Duke of York's in Brighton was the vision of actress and theatrical entrepreneur Violet Melnotte Wyatt (1855–1935). It cost £3,000 to build on the site of a former brewery and was named after the theatre she owned in London. Its impressive Edwardian baroque-style exterior was designed by local architects Clayton and Black, while inside audiences of up to eight hundred could enjoy the white heat of technology, electrically run rather than hand-cranked projectors.

The interior was overhauled in 1937 to include state-of-the-art interior lighting, and the 4.6-metre (15-foot) screen was replaced by one that was 8.5 metres (28 feet) in 1956. The major change outside was the addition to the outer balcony of a 6-metre (20-foot)-high can-can dancer's legs sculpture, which was transferred from the Not the Moulin Rouge cinema in Oxford in 1991. The Brighton cinema received Grade II listed building status three years later.

Joseph Farington visits
two Scottish painters, 1801

After breakfast I called at Mr Nasmith's, who is in high reputation as a landscape painter. I saw 2 views of Rosslin Castle painted for Sir James Erskine Sinclair, the proprietor of it, a view of a waterfall belonging to Mr Drummond near Perth. A view of Corrie Lynn. A view of Cullen Castle, and some others. On first seeing them I thought them much inferior to what I expected, being defficient in style & in colouring & executed in a puerile & feeble manner. There is a purplish tint prevailing over them. He does not appear to feel the points on which the effect of a picture shd. rest and which denote the master. In short they do not look like the works of a master learned in the art, but are likely enough to please people not conversant with superior art and to be esteemed by such as pleasing furniture. I cannot but think if such pictures were sent to a London Exhibition they wd. be thought very indifferent by the professors....

I next went to Mr Raeburn the portrait painter most esteemed here, who lives in the same street, York-Place, New Town. The House is excellent & built by Himself. His show room is lighted from the top. His painting room commands a view of the Forth and the distant mountains. Here I found pictures of a much superior kind to those I saw at Mr Nasmiths. Some of Mr Raeburn's portraits have an uncommonly true appearance of nature and are painted with much firmness, but there is great inequality in his works. That which strikes the eye is a kind of Camera Obscura effect, and from those pictures which seem to be his best, I should conclude he has looked very much at nature, reflected in a camera.... The Servant who shewed me

Mr Raeburn's pictures told me when I enquired what other artists there were in Edinburgh that there was Mr Nasmith, who was a great landscape painter, the best in Scotland and superior to any in England.

English landscape painter Joseph Farington (1747–1821) kept an almost daily diary from 13 July 1793 until his death, which chronicled his life and times in the art world and had particularly intriguing details about the Royal Academy. In this entry for 23 September 1801, he compares and contrasts the work of two of the leading lights of the day in Scotland: Alexander Nasmyth (1758–1840) was a portrait and landscape painter, while the prolific Sir Henry Raeburn (1756–1823) was a portrait painter to King George IV in Scotland.

ALSO ON THIS DAY 1865: Finnish painter Pekka Halonen born · **1865:** French painter and model Suzanne Valadon born (*see* 2 April) · **1971:** *The Love Letter* by Dutch painter Johannes Vermeer is stolen from the Centre for Fine Arts, Brussels

24 SEPTEMBER

Mondrian sets sail for New York, 1940

I would like to try to go to America. But everything is very expensive there, and it is a long way away. I am also thinking of London, although there will be bombs. I could settle for a while in London and think afterwards of moving from there to New York.

Piet Mondrian, letter to Ben Nicholson, 7 September 1938

Dutch abstract painter Piet Mondrian (1872–1944) had spent two decades living in Paris before he felt that it would be safer for him to relocate in 1938 – his work had been included in the Nazis' Degenerate Art exhibition in 1937 (*see* 4 June).

His first move, organized by his friend the English artist Ben Nicholson (1894–1982), was to Belsize Park in London where he continued to work, enjoy visits to the cinema and go dancing at nightclubs. It was Nicholson who left the capital first, in 1939, and tried to persuade Mondrian to come with him to his new home in St Ives, Cornwall. Mondrian, who preferred urban to rural life, instead followed through on his original plan to move to America, a decision probably hastened by the German invasion of the Netherlands in May 1940, the fall of Paris and his narrow escape from being killed in a bomb attack, which blasted out the windows of his London flat.

He bought a ticket to travel to New York from Liverpool and left on 24 September on the ocean liner RMS *Samaria*, now transformed into a troop carrier and for child evacuation. This too was dangerous – the ship was nearly bombed during the sea voyage and other vessels were destroyed. Mondrian arrived safely, however, and lived in New York for the rest of his life, continuing to develop his aesthetic with works including *Broadway Boogie-Woogie* (1942–43) and the unfinished *Victory Boogie Woogie* (1942–44).

ALSO ON THIS DAY 1795: French sculptor Antoine-Louis Barye born · **1899:** Australian painter William Dobell born · **1936:** American puppeteer Jim Henson born

25 SEPTEMBER

UK Parliament publishes a list of art with links to the slave trade, 2020

In response to the Black Lives Matter movement, the Parliamentary Art Collection is being reviewed to identify depictions of individuals and activities related to the British slave trade and the use of forced labour of enslaved Africans and others in British colonies and beyond.

British involvement in the transatlantic slave trade began in 1562, and by the 1730s Britain was the biggest slave-trading nation in the world. The abolition movement in Britain, and the acts of resistance and rebellion by enslaved Africans in the Colonies, led to the abolition of first the trade, and then the use of enslaved labour in British colonies by Acts of Parliament in 1807 and 1833. However, many British people continued to have direct financial gain from the trading and use of enslaved labour and indentured labour in the West Indies, America, India and elsewhere....

The Parliamentary Art Collection documents the history and work of Parliament, and includes works featuring 17th, 18th and 19th century parliamentarians. As many were wealthy landowners and businessmen, they or their families were often directly involved in, and profited from, the forced labour of enslaved peoples and the trading of those people. Today this is recognised as abhorrent.

The intention of the Parliamentary Art Collection is not to venerate people who have supported and committed acts of atrocity, but to truthfully reflect the history of Parliament, our democracy and the people who played a part in it. The interpretation of these artworks is constantly under review. We will continue to explore ways to better explain and contextualise works in the Collection through our website and in other interpretive material.

The following list of artworks [given in the document] is not comprehensive, and this document will be updated as new research is undertaken, becomes available or acquistions are made. There is no definitive list of MPs with close connections to the transatlantic trade, or those who had financial interests in the use of enslaved labour and indentured labour in the West Indies, America, India and elsewhere. However, they will be numerous, and some will be included in artworks on display in Parliament. There are also instances of MPs whose views changed over their time in Parliament, for example those with economic interests in the use of enslaved peoples and the slave trade who later fought for abolition.

UK Parliament, Speaker's Advisory Committee for Works of Art,
statement, 25 September 2020

On 25 September 2020, following greater awareness of the Black Lives Matter campaign earlier in the year, the UK Parliament released a document providing an analysis of the links between its art collection and the transatlantic slave trade, which included a list of works depicting people who supported or benefited from slavery. Although the list is not definitive, it is being continually updated.

ALSO ON THIS DAY 1903: Latvian-born American painter Mark Rothko born · **1906:** English painter and cartographer Phyllis Pearsall born · **1967:** Gilbert and George meet at Saint Martin's School of Art, London

Jeff Koons updates classic art
for Florence Biennale, 2015

Gazing Ball takes its name from the mirrored spherical ornaments frequently found on lawns, gardens and patios around Koons's childhood home in Pennsylvania. Their unique visual qualities allow viewers to see around corners while absorbing them and their entire surroundings within one image.... Hand-blown from glass, the blue gazing balls have been placed on white plaster sculptures depicting signature examples of antique statues from the Greco-Roman era along with everyday utilitarian objects encountered in today's suburban and rural landscape, such as mailboxes and a birdbath....

In *Gazing Ball*, the pristine whiteness of the sculptures stands in stark contrast to the brightly colored spheres, which subtly alter their appearance based on available lighting and nearby elements. Yet, the gazing balls' seriality throughout the exhibition creates an element of continuity across stylistic genres and epochs that inspires a dialogue between old and new, classical and commonplace.

**Press release for Jeff Koons's 'Gazing Ball' exhibition, New York,
8 May–29 June 2013**

American sculptural artist Jeff Koons (b. 1955) provided two works for the 2015 International Biennale of Antiques (BIAF) in Florence. His 3.3-metre (10¾-foot)-tall, acidic yellow, polished stainless steel statue *Pluto and Proserpina* was erected on Piazza della Signoria, next to a marble copy of Michelangelo's *David* (*see* 13 September). Koons's sculpture, which included live flowering plants, was his contemporary take on *The Rape of Proserpina* by Gian Lorenzo Bernini (*see* 22 February).

The second work, *Gazing Ball (Barberini Faun)*, was postioned inside the city's Palazzo Vecchio in the Room of the Lilies alongside the bronze *Judith and Holofernes* by Italian sculptor Donatello.

ALSO ON THIS DAY 1637: French painter Sébastien Leclerc baptized · **1687:** The Parthenon in Athens is blown up in a siege by Venetian soldiers during the Great Turkish War · **1791:** French painter Théodore Géricault born (*see* 2 July)

Geoffrey Rose sketches poplars
on the front line, 1917

Capt. Geoffrey Keith Rose, M.C., Oxf. & Bucks. L. I. For conspicuous gallantry and devotion to duty. When in command of a raid on the enemy's trenches, he displayed the greatest skill and energy. He organised an effective resistance to the enemy counter-attack, and conducted a masterly withdrawal under heavy machine gun and rifle fire.

Military Cross citation for Geoffrey Rose, award gazetted 14 January 1916

Sketched on 27 September 1917, *The 'Six' Poplars Between the British and German Front Lines East of Hebuterne* by Geoffrey Rose (1889–1959) shows three war-torn poplar tree stumps and was made in the area where the Somme and Artois battles were fought (he made another on the same day of trees damaged by bombs called *Gommecourt Wood from Old German Front Line*). Rose regularly turned to his sketchbook over the three years he served in the Oxford and Buckinghamshire Light Infantry on the Western Front and more than 150 examples of his work are held today by the Imperial War Museum. He was among many artists of the war who regularly returned to the motif of an avenue in his work, whether as a path towards freedom or as a symbol of destruction. He made his final sketch, of the devastated landscape around Bourlon Wood in France, in October 1918.

ALSO ON THIS DAY **1840:** German-American cartoonist Thomas Nast born · **1906:** Russian art collector Sergei Varshavsky born · **1927:** Italian illustrator Romano Scarpa born

Leonardo receives final payment
for *The Adoration of the Magi*, 1481

Certainly while a man is painting he ought not to shrink from hearing every opinion. For we know very well that a man, though he may not be a painter, is familiar with the forms of other men and very capable of judging whether they are hump backed, or have one shoulder higher or lower than the other, or too big a mouth or nose, and other defects; and, as we know that men are competent to judge of the works of nature, how much more ought we to admit that they can judge of our errors; since you know how much a man may be deceived in his own work. And if you are not conscious of this in yourself study it in others and profit by their faults. Therefore be curious to hear with patience the opinions of others, consider and weigh well whether those who find fault have ground or not for blame, and, if so amend; but, if not make as though you had not heard, or if he should be a man you esteem show him by argument the cause of his mistake.

Leonardo da Vinci, notebooks, c. 1478–1518

The contract that Italian artist Leonardo da Vinci (1452–1519; *see also* 6 October) made with the Augustinian monks of San Donato in Scopeto, Florence, for his *The Adoration of the Magi* was rather unusual. It stipulated that he was to be paid not in money but in land (which he could sell back after three years), and required him to fund a dowry for the relation of one of the friars, as well as pay for all his own paints and gold. As it turned out, the monastery relaxed both of the latter stipulations.

Leonardo never finished the oil on wood painting and the final recorded payment was made on 28 September 1481 – a shipment of red vermilion wine from the monastery's vineyard. Leonardo then left the city to travel to Milan and did not return for eighteen years.

The painting that today hangs in the Uffizi Gallery in Florence is essentially an unfinished draft, which includes all the usual elements of the scene but in a very busy and unconventional setting and combination of figures, and was almost certainly not what the monks had in mind. They gave the commission instead to Italian painter Filippino Lippi who completed it in 1496.

ALSO ON THIS DAY 1909: American cartoonist Al Capp born · **1913:** Swiss book illustrator Warja Honegger-Lavater born · **1933:** Spanish sculptor Miguel Ortiz Berrocal born

The *Angels Unawares* sculpture is unveiled, 2019

Do not neglect to show hospitality to strangers, for thereby some have entertained angels unawares.

Hebrews 13:2

Canadian sculptor Timothy Schmalz (b. 1969) frequently produces public work with a religious or social theme, including his *Homeless Jesus* (2013), which shows Jesus sleeping rough on a park bench. Schmalz calls his sculptures 'visual prayers' that give Christianity 'visual dignity' and make the Christian message alive and relevant in the 21st century.

Commissioned in 2016, his life-size bronze and clay *Angels Unawares*, 6 metres (20 feet) in length, was inspired by Hebrews 13:2 and shows a group of refugees and migrants from various racial and cultural backgrounds tightly standing together on a simple raft, including a Jew escaping Nazi Germany and·a Syrian leaving his country behind because of civil war. In the middle are angel's wings. The sculpture was installed in St Peter's Square in the Vatican City to commemorate the 105th World Day of Migrants and Refugees in 2019.

Before more than 40,000 people, Pope Francis said in his homily at the unveiling that he wanted Schmalz's sculpture to 'remind everyone of the evangelical challenge of welcoming' and that nobody should be left behind. He was aided in the unveiling by several migrants, including twenty-five-year-old Henrica from the Democratic Republic of Congo, and Gift, aged nineteen, from Nigeria.

ALSO ON THIS DAY 1640: French sculptor Antoine Coysevox born · **1703:** French painter and theatrical designer François Boucher born · **1923:** American book illustrator Stan Berenstain born

Cartoons of Muhammad
are published in Denmark, 2005

Islam has never welcomed painting as a handmaid of religion as both Buddhism and Christianity have done. Mosques have never been decorated with religious pictures, nor has a pictorial art been employed for the instruction of the heathen or for the edification of the faithful.... Accordingly, there has never been any historical tradition in the religious painting of Islam – no artistic development in the representation of accepted types – no schools of painters of religious subjects; least of all has there been any guidance on the part of leaders of religious thought corresponding to that of ecclesiastical authorities in the Christian Church.

Thomas Walker Arnold,
Painting in Islam, 1928

On 30 September 2005, the Danish newspaper *Jyllands-Posten* published a dozen cartoons by Danish cartoonists featuring Muhammad as part of an ongoing debate about Islam and free speech/censorship. It provoked immediate outrage within some of the country's Muslim communities and in others around the world, as well as demonstrations and violent riots.

Although it was widely reported in the international media, many outlets did not reproduce the cartoons. Among those that did was the French satirical magazine *Charlie Hebdo*, which itself printed cartoons of Muhammad in 2011 and was the subject of a murderous attack on its staff in 2015.

On 8 February 2006, *Jyllands-Posten* printed an open letter 'to the honourable fellow citizens of the Muslim world' in which the editor-in-chief Carsten Juste wrote that the newspaper believed the twelve drawings were 'sober', not intended to be offensive and not illegal, but that he apologized that they had certainly offended many Muslims.

ALSO ON THIS DAY **1800:** English architect Decimus Burton born · **1840:** Foundation for Nelson's Column, London, is laid · **1910:** Death of American painter Winslow Homer

October

The first Arts and Crafts Exhibition Society exhibition opens, 1888

The decorative artist and the handicraftsman have hitherto had but little opportunity of displaying their work in the public eye, or rather of appealing to it upon strictly artistic grounds in the same sense as the pictorial artist; and it is a somewhat singular state of things that at a time when the Arts are perhaps more looked after, and certainly more talked about, than they have ever been before, and the beautifying of houses, to those to whom it is possible, has become in some cases almost a religion, so little is known of the actual designer and maker (as distinct from the proprietary manufacturer or middleman) of those familiar things which contribute so much to the comfort and refinement of life –of our chairs and cabinets, our chintzes and wallpapers, our lamps and pitchers – the Lares and Penates of our households, which with the touch of time and association often come to be regarded with so peculiar an affection...

It will readily be understood that the organization of an exhibition of this character, and with such objects as we have in view, is a far less simple matter than a picture exhibition. Instead of having an array of artists whose names and addresses are in every catalogue, our constituency, as it were, outside the personal knowledge of the Committee, has had to be discovered. Under the designation of So-and-so and Co. many a skilful designer and craftsman may be concealed; and individual and independent artists in design and handicraft are as yet few and far between. However, in the belief, as elsewhere expressed, that it is little good nourishing the tree at the head if it is dying at the root, and that, living or dying, the desirability of an accurate diagnosis while there is any doubt of our artistic health will at once be admitted, the Society open their first Exhibition.

English book illustrator Walter Crane, preface in the society's *Catalogue of the First Exhibition*, 1888

The Arts and Crafts Exhibition Society, founded in London in 1887, aimed to promote the decorative arts – such as textiles, ceramics and furniture – to emphasize its artistic importance, provide dedicated exhibition space and improve the market for the decorative artists who produced such pieces (initially the exhibition catalogues did not contain prices; Honorary Secretary Thomas Cobden-Sanderson (*see* 31 August) was most put out when they did start to include them).

The society held its first exhibition in October 1888 at the New Gallery in Regent Street, London, and then regularly until 1960 when a name change turned it into the Society of Designer Craftsmen, now the largest multi-craft society in the UK. Strangely, textile designer William Morris (*see* 1 February), who is regarded as the founder of the Arts and Crafts movement but was very cool about the idea and did not think it would succeed, wrote in a letter that: 'I rather dread the said exhibition.' However, he later changed his mind, becoming the society's president in 1891.

ALSO ON THIS DAY 1507: Italian architect Giacomo Barozzi da Vignola born · **1929:** Death of French sculptor Antoine Bourdelle · **1939:** English sculptor Henry Moore writes to Sir Kenneth Clark enquiring about a scheme for war artists (*see* 7 November)

2 OCTOBER

The Tale of Peter Rabbit is published, 1902

My dear Noel,
I don't know what to write to you, so I shall tell you a story about four little rabbits whose names were – Flopsy, Mopsy, Cottontail and Peter.

Beatrix Potter, letter to Noel Moore, 4 September 1893

Throughout her life, English illustrator Beatrix Potter (1866–1943) loved animals and natural history. There were several inspirations for the famous Peter, including her first pet rabbit Benjamin Bouncer (who sometimes ate her paints) and then Peter Piper, who she claimed could play the tambourine. This letter, written in 1893 to the young son of her former governess Annie Moore (*see also* 4 March), was the birth of Peter Rabbit; later letters featured Squirrel Nutkin and Jeremy Fisher.

The first trade edition of *The Tale of Peter Rabbit* was published on 2 October 1902 and was such a success that it enabled her to buy the 17th-century house Hill Top in Near Sawrey, Cumbria, which is now run by the National Trust.

Potter was a canny businesswoman as well as an excellent artist, proving the appeal of the book by privately printing the first edition herself in 1901, and then insisting that the books be small enough so that a child could hold them when publisher Frederick Warne wanted something larger. Indeed, she insisted on being involved in every part of the production process and then created a brand for her art by designing a Peter Rabbit doll in 1903 and subsequently wallpaper, tea sets and numerous other Potter products.

ALSO ON THIS DAY **1909:** American cartoonist Alex Raymond born · **1949:** American photographer Annie Leibovitz born · **1950:** The first *Peanuts* comic strip by Charles M. Schulz appears

3 OCTOBER

President Theodore Roosevelt sends his son a self-portrait, 1907

Darling Quentin, this is a funny steamboat, there is no hold; simply a flat bottom, on deck; the engine room right on top of this, and open at both sides. We 'run her nozzle agin the bank' wherever we want to land. At St. Louis we were caught in a drenching rain; the chairman of the reception committee minded it more than I did. I can't make the water running down off our faces. The farmers drive down to the bank to see us in funny old rigs. One, with a large family of children, had a mule and a horse in his wagon. Your loving father.

US President Theodore Roosevelt,
letter to his son Quentin, 3 October 1907

President Theodore Roosevelt (1858–1919; *see also* 17 February) had strong views on art, believing that it had a key part in maintaining the virtues of the American way by expressing the soul of the nation (he was far less enthusiastic about the modernist movement).

In his private life, he often dotted his many letters to his children with doodles illustrating what he was up to when he was away from them. These charming picture letters include the one sent on 3 October 1907 to his youngest son Quentin about a trip down the Mississippi, which features a smiling self-portrait of himself braving the rain, as well as a farmer and his family in a wagon.

ALSO ON THIS DAY 1875: Mexican painter Dr Atl (Gerardo Cornado) born · **1882:** Canadian painter Alexander Young Jackson born · **1934:** Colombian-Dutch painter and video artist Miguel-Ángel Cárdenas born

4 OCTOBER

Work begins on Mount Rushmore National Memorial, 1927

On many occasions, when a new project is presented to you on paper, and, later on you see the accomplishment, you are disappointed; but just the opposite is the fact in what we are looking at now. I had seen photographs, I had seen the drawings and I had talked with those who are responsible for this great work. Yet I had had no conception until about ten minutes ago, not only of its magnitude, but of its permanent beauty and of its permanent importance.

Mr Borglum has well said that this can be a monument and an inspiration for the continuance of the Democratic-Republican form of government, not only in our own beloved country, but, we hope, throughout the world.

This is the second dedication. There will be others by other presidents in other years. When we get through, there will be something for the American people that will last not merely through generations but for thousands and thousands of years.

I think that we can perhaps meditate a little on those Americans ten thousand years from now, when the weathering on the faces of Washington and Jefferson and Lincoln shall have proceeded to perhaps the depth of a tenth of an inch – meditate and wonder what our descendants, and I think they will still be here, will think about us.

Let us hope that at least they will give us the benefit of the doubt, that they will believe we have honestly striven every day and generation to preserve for our descendants a decent land to live in and a decent form of government to operate under.

US President Franklin D. Roosevelt, speech at the unveiling
of the Thomas Jefferson sculpture, Mount Rushmore, 30 August 1936

America's Mount Rushmore National Memorial in South Dakota features a vast sculpture carved in the mountain's granite face of four heads, 18 metres (60 feet) high, of presidents George Washington, Thomas Jefferson, Theodore Roosevelt and Abraham Lincoln. American sculptor Gutzon Borglum (1867–1941) began the project on 4 October 1927 – using dynamite as a sculpting tool – and finished it in 1941. As well as overseeing the work, he also worked extremely hard on raising funds for it around the world.

ALSO ON THIS DAY 1720: Italian etcher Giovanni Battista Piranesi born · **1814:** French painter Jean-François Millet born · **1861:** American painter and sculptor Frederic Remington born (*see* 11 April)

5 OCTOBER

Banksy's *Girl with Balloon* becomes *Love Is in the Bin*, 2018

In rehearsals it worked every time...
Banksy, *Shredding the Girl and Balloon*
– *The Director's half cut*, 17 October 2018

The framed copy of street artist Banksy's *Girl with Balloon* based on his 2002 mural was the subject of competitive bidding when it came up for auction on 5 October 2018 at Sotheby's in London, selling eventually for just over £1 million. A few seconds after the hammer came down on the winning bid, the artwork began to shred using a mechanism hidden in the bottom of the frame. However, only the lower portion of the print was shredded. Sotheby's hailed it as the first work of art to have been created live during an auction when Banksy changed its name to *Love Is in the Bin*.

A video posted on YouTube by the artist later in October showed how the contraption was built and ended with the words above.

ALSO ON THIS DAY 1712: Italian painter Francesco Guardi born · **1817:** Japanese artist Katsushika Hokusai paints *Big Daruma* · **1869:** English painter and model Elizabeth Siddal exhumed

Invading soldiers destroy Leonardo's Horse, 1499

Most Illustrious Lord, Having now sufficiently considered the specimens of all those who proclaim themselves skilled contrivers of instruments of war, and that the invention and operation of the said instruments are nothing different from those in common use: I shall endeavor, without prejudice to any one else, to explain myself to your Excellency, showing your Lordship my secret, and then offering them to your best pleasure and approbation to work with effect at opportune moments on all those things which, in part, shall be briefly noted below....

In times of peace I believe I can give perfect satisfaction and to the equal of any other in architecture and the composition of buildings public and private; and in guiding water from one place to another.

I can carry out sculpture in marble, bronze or clay, and also I can do in painting whatever may be done, as well as any other, be he who he may.

Again, the bronze horse may be taken in hand, which is to be to the immortal glory and eternal honour of the prince your father of happy memory, and of the illustrious house of Sforza.

Leonardo da Vinci, letter to Ludovico Sforza, Duke of Milan, 1482

When Italian Renaissance artist Leonardo da Vinci (1452–1519; *see also* 29 December) wrote to the Duke of Milan in 1482 outlining his many skills in war, he also included how useful he could be during less bellicose times, including artistically. Among the projects he mentioned in his letter was a colossal 8-metre (26-foot) bronze statue of a horse, *Il Gran Cavallo* (also known as Leonardo's Horse). He was indeed commissioned to make it and after studying horses and writing a treatise on their anatomy, he initally built a clay prototype 7.3 metres (24 feet) tall, while accumulating 70 tons of bronze.

On 6 October 1499, when Milan was invaded by French forces and fell immediately, the occupying archers decided to use this clay model for their target practice, destroying it in the process.

In 1977, American amateur artist Charles Dent (1917–1994) established a project to reconstruct Leonardo's Horse, which was eventually finished by Japanese American sculptor Nina Akamu and unveiled in Milan on 10 September 1999.

7 OCTOBER

The film *The Agony and the Ecstasy* is released, 1965

I would ride post haste to you this coming week, although it would be a very great inconvenience to me – for this reason, that I am due to receive five hundred ducats which I have earned according to my agreement, while the Pope ought to have given me another five hundred for undertaking the other part of the work [The Sistine Chapel]. He has now gone away from here without leaving me any instructions, so that I am without money and do not know what I ought to do. I might go away, but I do not want him to be angry, nor do I want to lose my money: on the other hand, it will be difficult for me to stay here. I have written to him and am waiting for the reply.

Michelangelo, letter to his father, 5 September 1510

The 1965 film *The Agony and the Ecstasy* was made by English director Carol Reed (1906–1976) and starred actors Charlton Heston as Michelangelo and Rex Harrison as Pope Julius II. Based on a section in American writer Irving Stone's novel of the same name, it covers the conception and completion of the artist's Sistine Chapel ceiling in the Vatican City in Rome (*see* 1 November). 'A raging era of titans, popes and princes', as the film's tagline put it, the rivalry between Michelangelo and Raphael (played by Tomas Milian) is also featured, with Raphael pointing out to a disgruntled Michelangelo – who is reluctant to be continually on the search for patronage ('harlots always peddling beauty at the doorsteps of the mighty') – that there is no choice because he will always be an artist.

As the Sistine Chapel was unavailable as a shooting location, a replica set was built at the Cinecittà Studios in Rome, although the actual platform

Michelangelo worked from allowed him to stand and work rather than lying down as is shown in the film. Anachronistically, two frescoes shown in the film were in fact painted thirty years after the film is set in the early 16th century. However, when Michelangelo is shown heading to the famous Carrara quarry, the marble quarry itself was used as the location.

ALSO ON THIS DAY 1635: French painter and art theorist Roger de Piles born · **1910:** American art collector Henry Plumer McIlhenny born · **1990:** Death of Australian architect Beatrice Hutton

8 OCTOBER

Bartholdi sends an invitation to the Statue of Liberty unveiling, 1886

You are invited to be present on the occasion of the inauguration by the President of the United States, of the Statue of Liberty Enlightening the World.

Having been authorized by the American Committee to extend a few personal invitations to the inaugural celebration of the Statue of Liberty, I beg you to do me the pleasure joining this group.

I have sent your name to the Committee so that it might added in advance to my lists.

You will receive in New York the special invitations relative to the celebrations that will take place; in the meantime please keep the present letter which will be useful to you on that occasion.

Frédéric-Auguste Bartholdi, invitation to the Statue of Liberty inauguration with accompanying letter, sent to Alphonse Buhot de Kersers, 8 October 1886

French sculptor Frédéric-Auguste Bartholdi (1834–1904) had waited a long time to see his greatest work, the Statue of Liberty, come to fruition from the moment he first heard the idea floated at a dinner party in 1865 (*see also* 30 June). In early October 1886, he sent out invitations to the official dedication and unveiling ceremony on 28 October – with an accompanying personal letter to French historian, archaeologist and numismatist Alphonse Buhot de Kersers, who also had a particular interest in monuments and modern sculpture.

342

The inaugural celebration in New York led by US president Grover Cleveland was a great success, with a vast procession through Manhattan (the occasion of the world's first ticker-tape parade courtesy of the city's stock market workers) and another on the Hudson River. The actual ceremony was closed to uninvited members of the public and Bartholdi's wife was one of only two women allowed access.

ALSO ON THIS DAY 1779: English illustrator William Blake starts studying at the Royal Academy, London · **1864:** Canadian painter Ozias Leduc born · **1873:** Russian architect Alexey Shchusev born

9 OCTOBER

Weegee's photograph *Their First Murder* is published, 1941

School Children See Street Killing

Varying reactions are mirrored in the faces of these Brooklyn school children who saw Peter Mancuso, 23, shot to death in a busy street. The killer, darting into the group of children, escaped pursuing police. In the rear, weeping, is Mrs Angelina Derazio, aunt of the victim, attempting to push her way through the crowd.

Hudson Register, picture caption, 10 October 1941

American photojournalist Arthur Fellig (1899–1968), better known as Weegee, made a point of trailing emergency services as they rushed to incidents and taking emotional and gritty photographs of crime scenes. *Their First Murder* shows the varying reactions of a crowd of people to the afternoon murder in 1941 of small-time racketeer and gambler Peter Mancuso in Brooklyn, some laughing, some staring, some looking into camera, and one woman crying. The photo was taken while Weegee was standing over the corpse as a priest gave the last rites and was published on 9 October in the daily *PM* newspaper before other titles also carried the story and picture. It was later printed in Weegee's first book collection *Naked City* (1945), with the shot of the dead body on the opposite page.

ALSO ON THIS DAY 1840: English painter Simeon Solomon born · **1874:** Russian painter Nicholas Roerich born · **1939:** English architect Nicholas Grimshaw born

Anne Frank pastes a photo of herself into her diary, 1942

Love of tender girlhood! Passionate deeds of heroes! A rushing, leaping drama of charm and excitement!

Tagline for the film release of *America*, 1924

Diarist Anne Frank (1929–1945), a young German-born Jewish girl in hiding from the Nazis in Amsterdam during the occupation of the Netherlands, was attracted by the glitz, glamour and hyperbole of publicity for films such as D. W. Griffith's blockbuster war romance *America*. On 10 October 1942, she added a photograph of herself into her diary and remarked that she wished she looked like that all the time so that she might have a crack at getting into Hollywood.

Anne Frank decorated the walls of the room in which she hid during the occupation with a collage of numerous postcards – including one of chimpanzees having a meal sat at a table – and pictures of film stars. Among the actors featured were Rudy Vallee, Sonja Henie, Deanna Durbin, Greta Garbo (as Ninotchka) and Ginger Rogers. She had already been collecting these before her enforced life in the concealed room, as she explains in her diary entry for 11 July 1942: 'Thanks to Father, who had brought my whole collection of picture postcards and movie stars here beforehand, I have been able to treat the walls with a pot of glue and a brush and so turn the entire room into one big picture.'

She also put up photos of the UK's future Queen Elizabeth II and her sister Margaret, and the Dutch royal family in exile in Canada (*see* 11 May). Art images included a picture of an ancient statue of Hermes and a Medici Society postcard of *The Lark's Song* by English illustrator Margaret Tarrant showing two girls picking primroses, as well as a self-portrait by Leonardo da Vinci, Rembrandt's *Portrait of an Old Man* and Michelangelo's *Pietà* (*see* 21 May).

After Anne's death in the Bergen-Belsen concentration camp some of the pictures were lost. Others were even stolen by visitors to the house when it opened as a museum after the war. Ongoing restoration work from the 1950s onwards has seen many returned and others put back in their original positions.

ALSO ON THIS DAY 1656: French painter Nicolas de Largillière born · **1858:** American painter Maurice Prendergast born · **1901:** Swiss sculptor Alberto Giacometti born

The AIDS Memorial Quilt
goes on display, 1987

The work of the National AIDS Memorial helps ensure that the lives of people who died from AIDS are never forgotten and the story of AIDS is known by future generations – so that never again will a community be harmed because of fear, silence, discrimination or stigma.

US National AIDS Memorial, mission statement

On a candlelight San Francisco march in 1985 to commemorate the lives of all those who had died of AIDS, LGBT rights activist Cleve Jones was inspired by the many names that people had posted in the streets of loved ones who had died. He decided that a quilt would provide a permanent reminder of the terrible effects of the AIDS pandemic and began organizing production of the panels, individually or in special groups around America.

The completed quilt, which weighs 50 tonnes (54 short tons), was displayed in public for the first time on 11 October 1987 on the National Mall in Washington DC during a march for lesbian and gay rights. As well as raising money for AIDS organizations, it is probably the largest community art project ever completed and was nominated for the Nobel Peace Prize in 1989.

The quilt is made up of more than 50,000 panels celebrating the lives of 105,000 friends, family and lovers who have died from AIDS. These include musician Freddie Mercury and actor Rock Hudson. Each one measures 90 × 180 cm (3 × 6 feet), the approximate size of a grave. They come in many different types of fabric (including bubble wrap), use a wide range of techniques in addition to traditional embroidery, and are decorated with sequins, wedding rings, records and hair.

ALSO ON THIS DAY 1913: American comic book artist Joe Simon born · **1945:** English sculptor Andrew Logan born · **1965:** Death of American photographer Dorothea Lange (*see* 24 January)

Carel Fabritius dies in an explosion in Delft, 1654

So, to our loss, did this Phoenix die
In the middle and height of his powers
Yet, happily from the flames came
Vermeer, who skilfully walked the same road.

Arnold Bon on Carel Fabritius, in *A Description of the City of Delft* by Dirk van Bleyswijck, 1667

Dutch painter Carel Fabritius (1622–1654) studied under Rembrandt in the early 1640s, developed his own much lighter style and opened his own studio in Amsterdam, then moved to Delft in about 1650. He was regarded as one of the brightest new stars in the artistic firmament with a particular interest in *trompe-l'oeil* wall paintings.

Sadly, Fabritius's life was cut short when about 30 tonnes (33 short tons) of gunpowder exploded in an old convent in Delft. The event became known as The Delft Thunderclap and destroyed about a quarter of the city, including Fabritius's studio where he was working and many of his paintings. The event is portrayed in the topographically accurate *A View of Delft after the Explosion of 1654* by Dutch artist Egbert van der Poel and in the tribute above by contemporary publisher Arnold Bon, in which he describes Fabritius as a phoenix who died at the height of his career, but in his place, phoenix-like, arrived the Dutch Golden Age painter Johannes Vermeer (*see* 2 May), who may have been Fabritius's pupil.

Little remains of Fabritius's work today. The most famous piece is *The Goldfinch* (1654), which depicts a bird tethered to a wall. It is the centrepiece of American author Donna Tartt's 2013 novel of the same name (*see* 31 January) and is stolen by the narrator during an explosion set off by terrorists in the Metropolitan Museum of Art in New York. During the attack, his mother dies and her final words to him are 'Anything we manage to save from history is a miracle.'

ALSO ON THIS DAY 1492: Death of Italian painter Piero della Francesca · **1590:** Death of Japanese painter Kanō Eitoku · **1930:** Canadian photographer Denis Brodeur born

Scientific dating techniques disprove the Turin Shroud theory, 1988

And when Joseph had taken the body, he wrapped it in a clean linen cloth, And laid it in his own new tomb, which he had hewn out in the rock: and he rolled a great stone to the door of the sepulchre, and departed.

Matthew 27:59–60

And he bought fine linen, and took him down, and wrapped him in the linen, and laid him in a sepulchre which was hewn out of a rock, and rolled a stone unto the door of the sepulchre.

Mark 15:46

And, behold, there was a man named Joseph, a counseller; and he was a good man, and a just: (The same had not consented to the counsel and deed of them;) he was of Arimathaea, a city of the Jews: who also himself waited for the kingdom of God. This man went unto Pilate, and begged the body of Jesus. And he took it down, and wrapped it in linen, and laid it in a sepulchre that was hewn in stone, wherein never man before was laid.

Luke 23:50–53

The Turin Shroud is a piece of cloth, about life-size, with the image of a naked man with his arms folded across his groin imprinted on it. For centuries, it was said to be the burial shroud of Jesus Christ but a report released on 13 October 1988 by independent testers at the universities of Oxford and Arizona, and the Swiss Federal Institute of Technology, show that it in fact dates to the period c. AD 1390 (about the time of its first recorded appearance in history).

Pope John Paul II, in an address on his visit to Turin on 24 May 1998, said the Church has no scientific expertise to decide on the Shroud's authenticity, but did say that it was a reminder of humans' ability to cause suffering and kill, and as such a spur to try to end such acts of selfish violence.

ALSO ON THIS DAY 1269: Henry III's rebuilt Westminster Abbey, London, is consecrated · **1713:** Scottish painter Allan Ramsay born · **1792:** Cornerstone for the White House, Washington, laid

E. H. Shepard's illustrations appear in *Winnie-the-Pooh*, 1926

Pooh Bear – A Delightful Milne Fantasy
Quality not quantity is the motto of Mr A. A. Milne and his artist friend, Mr E. H. Shepard, who supplies the decorations to his Christmassy fantasy. Compared with the bulky gaudiness of the annuals, in many a case too big and heavy for little hands to hold, 7s 6d seems a lot to ask for *Winnie-the-Pooh* (Methuen), Mr Milne's latest delightful creation. As a matter of fact it is cheap at three half-crowns, a book that all children will adore, and that their elders will pick up by stealth and read zestfully to the very end.
Aberdeen Journal, 9 December 1926

It is almost impossible to imagine the *Winnie-the-Pooh* stories by English author A. A. Milne (1882–1956) without the original accompanying illustrations by English painter, cartoonist and book illustrator Ernest H. Shepard (1879–1976). After studying art and exhibiting, Shepard had a busy war – he was awarded the Military Cross in 1917 and began to contribute cartoons to *Punch* magazine.

He and Milne first worked together on the author's book of poems, *When We Were Very Young* (1924). They collaborated again two years later to produce *Winnie-the-Pooh*, which was published on 14 October 1926, Milne sending his work to Shepard chapter by chapter to illustrate. It was a happy and successful working relationship, Shepard especially enjoying the free hand he was given with the illustrations.

The inspiration for the main characters was the two men's families' toys. Pooh was modelled on Shepard's son Graham's teddy bear, Growler, but most of the others belonged to Christopher Robin Milne (Eeyore was a 1921 Christmas present); Owl and Rabbit were entirely made up. Graham himself was a model for the sketches of Christopher Robin. Almost as important as the characters was Shepard's depiction of the locations mentioned in the text. He visited the Milnes, who lived near Ashdown Forest in Sussex, to sketch the scenery, which became the fictitious, but topographically accurate and detailed, Hundred Acre Wood in the book.

So integral to the success of *Winnie-the-Pooh* was Shepard that Milne acknowledged his contribution by offering him an exceptional 20 per cent of the royalties, before later going a stage further and suggesting the figure of 50 per cent for a forthcoming version of Mother Goose (which never saw the light of day).

15 OCTOBER

Lincoln is advised his portrait would look better with a beard, 1860

Dear Sir

My father has just home from the fair and brought home your picture and Mr Hamlin's. I am a little girl only 11 years old, but want you should be President of the United States very much so I hope you wont think me very bold to write to such a great man as you are.... I have yet got four brothers and part of them will vote for you any way and if you let your whiskers grow I will try and get the rest of them to vote for you you would look a great deal better for your face is so thin. All the ladies like whiskers and they would tease their husbands to vote for you and then you would be President.

Grace Bedell, letter to Abraham Lincoln, 15 October 1860

Among my sitters during these dreadful years, I counted many of our most celebrated generals – Grant, Sherman, McClellan, Admiral Porter, and many others. I also had sittings from Abraham Lincoln. These I particularly enjoyed. So much has been said about that great and good man that it seems almost presumptuous to add to the numberless anecdotes of his humor and genial temper. During one of the sittings, as he was glancing at his letters, he burst into a hearty laugh, and exclaimed: 'As a painter, Mr Healy, you shall be a judge between this unknown correspondent and me. She complains of my ugliness. It is allowed to be ugly in this world, but not as ugly as I am. She wishes me to put on false whiskers, to hide my horrible lantern jaws. Will you paint me with false whiskers? No? I thought not. I tell you what I shall do: give permission to this lover of the beautiful to set up a barber's shop at the White House!' And he laughed again with perfect delight.

George Healy, *Reminiscences of a Portrait Painter***, 1894**

American artist George Healy (1813–1894), when painting a portrait of Abraham Lincoln in 1860, was put on the spot when the then whiskerless Abraham Lincoln read out the letter he had received from the young Grace Bedell on 15 October. Grace and US president Lincoln met the following year at a train station when he had indeed grown a beard, an encounter celebrated in 1999 by a life-size statue by local sculptor Don Sottile in Westfield, New York, where Grace lived.

ALSO ON THIS DAY 1690: Death of Spanish painter Juan de Valdés Leal · **1836:** French painter Jacques 'James' Tissot born · **1938:** American painter Brice Marden born

16 OCTOBER

Artists watch the Houses of Parliament destroyed by fire, 1834

On the 16th of October the Houses of Parliament were burnt; and Constable witnessed the scene from a hackney coach, in which, with his two eldest sons, he took a station on Westminster Bridge. The evening of the 31st he spent with me; and while describing the fire, he drew with a pen, on half a sheet of letter paper, Westminster Hall, as it showed itself during the conflagration; blotting the light and shade with ink, which he rubbed with his finger where he wished it to be lightest. He then, on another half sheet, added the towers of the Abbey and that of St Margaret's Church – and the papers, being joined, form a very grand sketch of the whole scene.

Charles Robert Leslie, *Memoirs of the Life of John Constable***, 1843**

In 1834, the fire that broke out accidentally in the Palace of Westminster, London, on the evening of 16 October was the city's largest since 1666. As *The Times* reported the next day: 'Shortly before 7 o'clock last night the inhabitants of Westminster, and of the districts on the opposite bank of the river, were thrown into the utmost confusion and alarm by the sudden breaking out of one of the most terrific conflagrations that has been witnessed for many years past.'

Among those on the scene were the English painters John Constable (*see* 11 June) and J. M. W. Turner (*see* 6 September). As the painter Charles Robert Leslie (1794–1859) recorded in his biography, Constable sketched the fire from where he stood on the bridge but did not go on to produce a painting from this beginning.

Turner, however, from the many sketches he made, produced two paintings of the fire, one directly across Westminster Bridge, the other downriver, from the river's south bank. While Constable's sketches are quite sober, Turner's paintings are brilliantly colourful, exaggerating the height of the flames and showing the boats that charged members of the public for trips to get a better view. Among those who paid was Turner.

ALSO ON THIS DAY 1553: Death of German painter and printmaker Lucas Cranach the Elder · **1620:** French painter and sculptor Pierre Puget born · **1847:** *The History of British Birds, illustrated* by wood engraver Thomas Bewick, provides comfort and imagery in Charlotte Brontë's *Jane Eyre,* which is first published today (*see* 11 March)

17 OCTOBER

Matisse's *Le Bateau*
is hung upside down, 1961

You don't know what's up and you don't know what's down and neither do we.

**Museum attendant, reported comment to Genevieve Habert,
3 December 1961**

Final preparations for an exhibition of works by French painter Henri Matisse (1869–1954), 'The Last Works of Matisse: Large Cut Gouaches' at the Museum of Modern Art, New York, went well on 17 October 1961. The groundwork had taken place so that all was ready in time for that evening's press night before the exhibition opened to the public the following day.... The only fly in the ointment was that among the forty works from the 1940s and 1950s, the paper-cut *Le Bateau* (The Boat, 1953) – a sailing boat reflected in water – was hung upside down.

Nobody noticed for forty-seven days – not the 120,000 visitors, not the museum's staff, not even Matisse's art dealer son, Pierre.

The mistake was finally pointed out by stockbroker Genevieve Habert, who had felt there was something odd about the work when she first visited the exhibition; she took another look on 3 December and also scrutinized the catalogue. She mentioned the error to a museum attendant but he dismissed her advice, so Habert then contacted the *New York Times* who passed on her comments to the red-faced museum staff. When the back of the picture was examined, the placement of the labels suggested this was not the first time that it had been shown upside down...

ALSO ON THIS DAY **1759:** Russian painter and architect Andrey Voronikhin born · **1817:** Pharaoh Seti I's tomb is uncovered · **1969:** *Nativity with St Francis and St Lawrence*, a painting by Italian artist Caravaggio, is stolen from the Oratory of Saint Lawrence, Palermo, Italy

18 OCTOBER

The Church of the Holy Sepulchre is destroyed, 1009

Let the deeds of your ancestors move you and incite your minds to manly achievements; the glory and greatness of king Charles the Great, and of his son Louis, and of your other kings, who have destroyed the kingdoms of the pagans, and have extended in these lands the territory of the holy church. Let the holy sepulchre of the Lord our Saviour, which is possessed by unclean nations, especially incite you, and the holy places which are now treated with ignominy and irreverently polluted with their filthiness. Oh, most valiant soldiers and descendants of invincible ancestors, be not degenerate, but recall the valour of your progenitors....

Let therefore hatred depart from among you, let your quarrels end, let wars cease, and let all dissensions and controversies slumber. Enter upon the road to the Holy Sepulchre; wrest that land from the wicked race and subject it to yourselves. That land which as the Scripture says 'floweth with milk and honey', was given by God into the possession of the children of Israel.

Jerusalem is the navel of the world; the land is fruitful above others, like another paradise of delights.... This royal city, therefore, situated at the centre of the world, is now held captive by His enemies, and is in subjection to those who do not know God, to the worship of the heathens. She seeks therefore and desires to be liberated, and does not cease to implore you to come to her aid. From you especially she asks succour, because, as we have already said, God has conferred upon you above all nations great glory in arms. Accordingly undertake this journey for the remission of your sins, with the assurance of the imperishable glory of the kingdom of heaven.

On 18 October 1009, the riot of destruction decreed for no obvious reason by the Fatimid caliph Al-Hakim bi-Amr Allah saw the total demolition of the Church of the Holy Sepulchre in Jerusalem down to its foundations, as well as numerous associated religious objects such as the Torah scrolls. Understandably, it caused an uproar in Christian Europe where Pope Sergius IV and later Pope Urban II (c. 1035–1099) called for a crusade in retaliation, although the speech made by Urban II as reported by contemporary chronicler Robert the Monk, a French prior, is almost certainly dramatized rather than strictly accurate. The church was fully rebuilt forty years after its destruction.

ALSO ON THIS DAY 1678: Death of Flemish painter and tapestry designer Jacob Jordaens · **1906:** American painter James Brooks born · **1956:** The Museum of Modern Art, New York, writes to artist Andy Warhol rejecting his *Shoe* drawing

19 OCTOBER

Henry Ossawa Tanner
wins a medal in Paris, 1900

In his personal life Mr Tanner has had many things to contend with. Ill-health, poverty and race prejudice, always strong against a negro, have made the way hard for him. But he has come unspoiled alike through these early struggles and through his later successes.

Dear Mrs Tietjens

Your good note & very appreciative article to hand I have read it & except it is more than I deserve, it is exceptionally good.... The only thing I take exception to is the inference in your last paragraph....

Now am I a Negro? Does not the 3/4 of English blood in my veins, which when it flowed in 'pure' Anglo-Saxon men & which has done in the past, effective & distinguished work in the U.S. – does this not count for anything? Does the 1/4 or 1/8 of 'pure' Negro blood in my veins count for all? I believe it (the Negro blood) counts & counts to my advantage – though it has caused me at times a life of great humiliations & sorrow – unlimited 'kicks' & 'cuffs' but that it is the source of all my talents (if I have any) I do not believe, any more than I believe it all comes from my English ancestors.

**Henry Ossawa Tanner's letter to Eunice Tietjens in reply,
25 May 1914**

Although he preferred to concentrate on his work, especially those with religious subjects, African American painter Henry Ossawa Tanner (1859–1937) was forced to deal with questions of race throughout his life. To escape the racial abuse he endured as a child and young struggling artist in Philadelphia (where the high standard of his work was noted by his teacher Thomas Eakins; *see* 13 February), he moved to Paris where the quality of his work was recognized and he was more readily accepted socially. Tanner's painting *Daniel in the Lions' Den* (1895) was exhibited at the city's 1896 Salon and went on to win the Silver Medal at the Paris Exposition four years later on 19 October 1900.

The exchange between the American poet and art critic Eunice Tietjens (1884–1944) and Tanner in 1914 was the result of a magazine article she planned to write.

ALSO ON THIS DAY 1814: Greek painter Theodorus Vryzakis born · **1882:** Italian painter and sculptor Umberto Boccioni born (*see* 5 February) · **1928:** American animator Lou Scheimer born

Peggy Guggenheim's Art of This Century gallery opens, 1942

Miss Guggenheim established an Art Gallery in London and began to collect modern works of art. Towards the end of 1939 she went to Paris where she decided to save as many paintings and sculptures as possible from the threatening Germans and bring them to America.... After long and careful preparations and necessary research work, the collection will now be shown at Art of this Century where it will serve as a basis as well as a background for changing exhibitions of individuals and groups.... Miss Guggenheim hopes that Art of this Century will become a center where artists will be welome and where they can feel that they are co-operating in establishing a research laboratory for new ideas.

**Press release for the opening of
Art of This Century gallery, 20 October 1942**

The Art of This Century gallery was opened in New York by American art collector Peggy Guggenheim (1898–1979), who divided it into four sections: the Abstract Gallery, the Surrealist Gallery, the Kinetic Gallery and the Daylight Gallery. This last was a commercial space where dozens of temporary exhibitions – including 'Exhibition by 31 Women' featuring work by Mexican painter Frida Kahlo (*see* 20 April) – were held until Art of This Century closed in 1947.

The gallery was designed by Austrian architect Frederick Kiesler (1890–1965) and had concave walls and a hanging mechanism so that the paintings appeared to be suspended in mid-air. Some of the items on show were interactive, with visitors looking through peepholes and winding handles or a ship's wheel to reveal works by Paul Klee, and there was a rotating presentation of reproductions of everything on display. Every two minutes, lights would go on and off at either end of the gallery while the roar of an approaching train was played over loudspeakers.

ALSO ON THIS DAY **1632:** English architect Sir Christopher Wren born · **1847:** Norwegian painter Frits Thaulow born · **1973:** Sydney Opera House is officially opened

Paula Modersohn-Becker
plans to start art lessons, 1892

I'll start with the newest news. Aunt Marie and I have just come back from a school of art that I will be attending from Monday. I will have lessons there daily from 10 am to 4 pm. At first I will only draw, do very simple arabesques, etc. If I make progress in this, I will draw Greek plaster casts in charcoal. I have seen some Venuses and I tell you they are quite enchanting, the shadows so soft. Should I get any further, I will draw and paint from live models. But I am not thinking that far ahead, I'm just happy to draw the Greek works in chalk. We will be about 50 to 70 ladies and gentlemen in the studio, most of us training to be artists. I think I am the youngest, and don't really fit into the company of such talented people. But it will be good if I seem to be the furthest behind and how far I might progress; that also spurs my ambition. Lessons start on Monday, I'm so grateful to Uncle Charles for this chance.

**Paula Modersohn-Becker, letter to her parents,
21 October 1892**

German Expressionist painter Paula Modersohn-Becker (1876–1907), commonly acknowledged to be the first woman to paint a full-length nude self-portrait, had her first art lessons at St John's Wood Art School in London in 1892. Although her parents were quite encouraging on seeing her work, they were not entirely sure if a career in the world of art was quite suitable for their daughter. On 14 January the following year, Modersohn-Becker wrote to her Aunt Marie:

> I waited always for a conclusion of my parents, whether I am to remain here or whether to come over. Today Papa told me, that Mama thought it best I should remain here and learn busily in the household, to learn cooking and so on. I think I don't quite agree with their resolution. Here I am my own mistress, I can do what I like and leave off what I don't like. There is a great temptation in it...

ALSO ON THIS DAY 1581: Italian painter Domenichino (Domenico Zampieri) born · **1959:** American architect Frank Lloyd Wright's Guggenheim Museum opens in New York · **1992:** American singer Madonna's illustrated photography book *Sex* goes on sale

The design of the official flag of Canada is chosen, 1964

Principles to be followed in the selection of a Canadian Flag
(a) simplicity – it should be clean cut and not cluttered.
(b) easily recognizable.
(c) use traditional colours and traditional emblems.
(d) serve as a rallying symbol and hence to be a unifying force.

Application of the above principles to a Canadian flag
(a) The Canadian flag should avoid the over-use of heraldic devices such as are to be found on coats of arms....
(b) There should be no question of confusing the flag of one country with that of another. In selecting a Canadian flag, therefore, every effort should be made to avoid including on it symbols more properly associated with another country, i.e., stripes, stars. A Canadian flag must be sufficiently Canadian that it can be easily recognized at a distance as being Canadian....
(c) The colours now associated with Canada are Red and White. These are traditional colours in the sense that they are usually looked upon as representing Great Britain and France....
(d) The traditional heraldic device or emblem of Canada is the maple leaf. This emblem has official sanction by its inclusion in two provincial coats of arms and in the official coat of arms of Canada. It has been used by Canadian troops in two world wars, and by Canadian Olympic teams (including the colours red and white)...
(e) If the flag is to be a unifying symbol it must avoid the use of national or racial symbols that are of a divisive nature. It is clearly inadvisable in a purely Canadian flag to include such obvious national symbols as the Union Jack or the Fleur de Lys. Racial feelings should be content with the use of the colours red and white, if it is essential to read these in such a light.

Suggestions
(a) The flag which would meet most of the requirements mentioned above

would be a simple red and white flag bearing a stylized maple leaf on it.

George F. G. Stanley's flag memo in a letter to MP John Matheson, 23 March 1964

There was an ongoing debate in 1963 and 1964 about the design of a new national flag for Canada, which became particularly vitriolic in the Canadian parliament. The special flag committee made its final, unanimous decision on 22 October 1964, following the guidelines suggested by historian George Stanley (1907–2002), then Dean of Arts at the Royal Military College of Canada. However, the selection was still held up by parliamentary objections and was even the subject of an unsuccessful filibuster. The flag was inaugurated on 15 February 1965.

ALSO ON THIS DAY 1865: Estonian painter Kristjan Raud born · **1882:** French-English illustrator Edmund Dulac born · **1882:** American painter and book illustrator Newell Convers Wyeth born

23 OCTOBER

Jervis McEntee struggles to concentrate on his painting, 1884

Have been painting all day in my studio, but do not get on as well as I could wish. Am painting a picture 15x18 from one of my studies of this fall. The Autumn color is fine now but I have not been off the hill. Gertrudes tree is rapidly changing to its splendid yellow. I am not in the mood for producing, there are so many anxious things in my mind. My father seems to get stronger but he does not like us to say he is improving. He seems not to want to recover and keeps saying he wants to die. I think he is lonely and dull as we are so quiet here and he can do nothing to occupy his mind. He still wishes me to help him dress and undress although today he went down to the wood shed and got a great piece of wood and split it up for kindling wood. I have a constant apprehensive dread of I know not what and cannot get into a quiet frame of mind. This is fatal to an artist. I must and do try to overcome it.

Jervis McEntee, diary entry, 23 October 1884

358

American painter Jervis McEntee (1828–1891) was friends with many of the Hudson River School artists in New York and also ran a popular artistic salon with his wife, but his diaries are also revealing about the daily and working life of a painter in the late 19th century. Strongly opposed to avant-garde painting, he specialized in sensitive landscapes with cloudy skies.

'Some people call my landscapes gloomy and disagreeable,' he wrote in his diary. 'They say that I paint the sorrowful side of Nature, that I am attracted by the shadows more than by the sunshine. But this is a mistake. I would not reproduce a late November scene if it saddened me or seemed sad to me. In that season of the year Nature is not sad to me, but quiet, pensive, restful. She is not dying, but resting. Mere sadness, unless it had the dramatic element in it, I would not attempt to paint.'

ALSO ON THIS DAY 1857: Filipino painter and sculptor Juan Luna born · **1880:** German architect Dominikus Böhm born · **1986:** American artist Keith Haring paints a mural on the Berlin Wall (*see also* 29 April)

24 OCTOBER

A ceiling fresco by Giovanni Battista Tiepolo is destroyed, 1915

The destruction of this world-known ceiling decoration is thus described by Sir Claude Phillips: 'A single bomb from an ordinary Austrian aeroplane, dropped on the roof of the Church of S. Maria dei Scalzi, at Venice, has irretrievably shattered and ruined one of the most famous works of Giovanni Battista Tiepolo, the great master of monumental decoration that the eighteenth century produced. The great ceiling decoration by Tiepolo, now lost to the world, was a commission entrusted to him by the Carmelite friars in 1743.'

Sydney Morning Herald,
29 December 1915

In 1745, Italian painter Giovanni Battista Tiepolo (1696–1770) completed his depiction of the legendary transportation of the Virgin Mary's house from Nazareth to Loreto in Italy in 1294. The fresco, *The Translation of the House of Loreto*, covered the ceiling of the Scalzi church in Venice. During the First

World War, on 24 October 1915, it was destroyed in a two-hour bombing raid by Austro-Hungarian forces aiming at the railway station next door. Other bombs fell in the Piazzetta di San Marco and in the water. Happily, some of Tiepolo's sketches for the fresco still survive, as well as a copy by Spanish artist Mariano Fortuny y Madrazo and some good black and white photographs.

ALSO ON THIS DAY 1260: Dedication of Chartres Cathedral, France · **1881:** US ambassador to France Levi Morton drives home the first rivet in the Statue of Liberty (*see* 30 June) · **1942:** Fashion illustrator Brian Stonehouse, working as a spy in France, is captured

25 OCTOBER

The first auction of AI art, 2018

Edmond de Belamy, from La Famille de Belamy
Price realised: $432,500
Estimate: $7,000–$10,000
Edmond de Belamy, from La Famille de Belamy Generative Adversarial Network print, on canvas, 2018, signed with GAN model loss function in ink by the publisher, from a series of eleven unique images, published by Obvious Art, Paris, with original gilded wood frame
S. 27½ × 27½ in (700 × 700 mm.)

> **Auction lot details for *Edmond de Belamy*,**
> **Christie's, New York, 25 October 2018**

The portrait *Edmond de Belamy* shows a slightly rotund Frenchman in a dark frockcoat and white collar, with a slightly blurred face and untouched areas of canvas.

It was produced by artificial intelligence (AI) via an algorithm using an algebraic formula, which is in the place of a signature in the corner of the work. About fifteen thousand portraits produced between the 14th and 20th centuries were uploaded from WikiArt and then AI was tasked with making its own image based on these works.

The humans behind the programming are Hugo Caselles-Dupré, Pierre Fautrel and Gauthier Vernier, working together as an art collective called Obvious that explores the meeting point of art and AI, which they call GAN (generative adversarial network). Their website opens with the maxim:

'"Computers are useless. They can only gives answers." Well Picasso (1881–1973), it's a disagreement.'

26 OCTOBER

Cecil Chubb gives Stonehenge to the nation, 1918

There are four things in England which are very remarkable. One is that the winds issue with such great violence from certain caverns in a mountain called the Peak, that it ejects matters thrown into them, and whirling them about in the air carries them to a great distance. The second is at Stonehenge, where stones of extraordinary dimensions are raised as columns, and others are fixed above, like lintels of immense portals; and no one has been able to discover by what mechanism such vast masses of stone were elevated, nor for what purpose they were designed. The third is at Chedder-hole, where there is a cavern which many persons have entered, and have traversed a great distance under ground, crossing subterraneous streams, without finding any end of the cavern. The fourth wonder is this, that in some parts of the country the rain is seen to gather about the tops of the hills, and forthwith to fall on the plains.

Henry of Huntingdon, *Historia Anglorum*, c. 1129

The first recorded mention of Stonehenge in England was in the history written by Henry of Huntingdon (c. 1088–c. 1157). Ownership of the monument passed through a series of noble and private hands until it was bought in 1915 by lawyer Cecil Chubb (1876–1934; *see* 21 September 1915). It cost him £6,600, or about £500,000 in today's money. Two weeks before the end of the First World War, Chubb put it into public ownership, an act for which he was knighted the following year to become the First Baronet of Stonehenge (his new coat of arms featured druids' mistletoe branches and the motto *Saxis Condita* or 'Founded on stones'). One condition of the gift, now operated by English Heritage, was that the entrance fee should not exceed a shilling.

ALSO ON THIS DAY 1764: Death of English painter William Hogarth (*see* 25 June) · **1794:** Russian architect Konstantin Thon born · **2006:** Death of Swedish art director and collector Pontus Hultén

27 OCTOBER

Egon Schiele draws his wife, his final work of art, 1918

I am a human, I love
Death and I love
Life

> **Egon Schiele,**
> **'A Self-Portrait', 1910**

Austrian painter Egon Schiele (1890–1918) drew his pregnant wife Edith Schiele for the final time on the evening of 27 October 1918 while she was very ill in bed. She died the following morning, and Schiele three days later, both of the Spanish flu, which killed 20 million people in Europe during the 1918–20 pandemic.

ALSO ON THIS DAY 1885: Swedish painter Sigrid Hjertén born · **1923:** American painter Roy Lichtenstein born (*see* 10 February) · **1930:** English cartoonist Leo Baxendale born

28 OCTOBER

Édouard Manet marries Suzanne Leenhoff, 1863

My dear Suzon,

I still cannot, despite it going on for so long, get used to coming back to this sad apartment at night. When will all this end? And we still have to be patient. We are really suffering here, it is freezing cold and we're out of fuel. I will not talk about food, we just sit down to eat out of habit. Despite all this, we are all doing well. Stock up on health, because the air in Paris is

and will be infected for a long time. However, I hope to see you again soon.
I can't wait to see you and kiss you. I think about you ceaselessly. If I heard
from you I would be consoled, for many people are falling ill and will not
be able to endure the last hardships of the siege. What an end of the year!...

Goodbye my dear Suzanne, I have a portrait of you in every corner of
my room so I see you morning and evening. See you soon. How I long to be
able to stay by the fireside at home! It has been three months now.

Édouard Manet, letter to Suzanne Leenhoff,
25 December 1870

Dutch-born pianist Suzanne Leenhoff (1829–1906) first met the French
painter Édouard Manet (1832–1883) when she became his piano teacher.
They grew fond of each other, started a relationship and then married on
28 October 1863, a year after Manet's authoritarian father died. Leenhoff
modelled for Manet's paintings, including for his works *Le Déjeuner sur l'herbe*
and *Olympia* (*see* 19 June), and later became a well-regarded painter in her
own right.

At the time Manet wrote this letter in 1870, Paris was under siege as
France continued to fight against Prussia. He had stayed in the city and joined
the National Guard, as did other artists such as Edgar Degas, while his wife
and son were sent to safety in the Pyrenees. Manet mentions the problem
of food – the issue became so acute that the capital's residents ate all the
animals in the city, including those in the zoo.

ALSO ON THIS DAY 1897: American film costume designer Edith Head born · **1909:** Irish painter
Francis Bacon born · **2011:** ArcelorMittal *Orbit* sculpture tower designed by British-Indian
sculptor Sir Anish Kapoor (*see* 13 August) unveiled in London

29 OCTOBER

Asterix the Gaul first appears
in *Pilote* magazine, 1959

Immediately after midnight, the cavalry are sent out and overtake the rear,
a great number are taken or cut to pieces, the rest by flight escape in different directions to their respective states. Vercingetorix, having convened a
council the following day, declares, 'That he had undertaken that war, not

on account of his own exigencies, but on account of the general freedom; and since he must yield to fortune, he offered himself to them for either purpose, whether they should wish to atone to the Romans by his death, or surrender him alive.' Ambassadors are sent to Caesar on this subject. He orders their arms to be surrendered, and their chieftains delivered up. He seated himself at the head of the lines in front of the camp, the Gallic chieftains are brought before him. They surrender Vercingetorix, and lay down their arms. Reserving the Aedui and Arverni, [to try] if he could gain over, through their influence, their respective states, he distributes one of the remaining captives to each soldier, throughout the entire army, as plunder.

Caius Julius Caesar, *The Gallic Wars*, Book VII, *c.* 52 BC

Asterix, the hero of a village of indomitable Gauls resisting ancient Roman invasion, was co-created by French writer René Goscinny (1926–1977) and illustrator Albert Uderzo (1927–2020), who was colour blind. The couple had been working together for several years beforehand on a range of other characters, including the Native American Ompa-pa (*Oumpah-pah* in the original French) before Asterix first appeared in issue one of their new comic *Pilote* – a counterpoint to American superheroes and *Tintin*, it was an immediate success. This story was then published as *Asterix the Gaul* in 1961.

The book begins with the surrender of Vercingetorix, who had led a united Gaulish revolt against Roman rule in AD 52, and the action of the story unfolds two years later. Vercingetorix is a running theme in the series, the surrender cropping up again in *Asterix and the Chieftain's Shield* and *The Mansions of the Gods*, while the thirty-eighth book *Asterix and the Chieftain's Daughter* focuses on Vercingetorix's daughter Adrenalin. Caesar's book about the Gallic Wars is the central element of the thirty-sixth book, *Asterix and the Missing Scroll*, with the story suggesting that there was a missing censored chapter in *Gallic Wars* called 'Defeats at the Hands of the Indomitable Gauls of Armorica'.

When Goscinny died, Uderzo wrote as well as illustrated subsequent adventures. He bowed out in 2009, although officially sanctioned new books have continued to appear regularly written by Jean-Yves Ferri and illustrated by Didier Conrad.

ALSO ON THIS DAY 1837: American quilter Harriet Powers born · **1930:** French-American sculptor Niki de Saint Phalle born · **1947:** Trial begins in Amsterdam of Dutch art forger Han van Meegeren

Scientists prove Pollock avoided hydrodynamic instabilities, 2019

Jackson Pollock's most celebrated abstract paintings were produced with the so-called dripping technique. By pouring liquid paint with the help of a stick or from a can, Pollock deposited viscous fluid filaments on a horizontal canvas, rhythmically moving around it. The intricate webs of lines, ubiquitous in his compositions, have fascinated art historians and scientists. Based on image analysis of historical video recordings, we experimentally reproduced the painting process. We conclude that Pollock avoided the appearance of the hydrodynamic instabilities, contrary to what was argued by previous studies. Pollock selected the physical properties of the paint to prevent filament fragmentation before deposition, and applied it while moving his hand sufficiently fast and at certain heights to avoid fluid filaments from coiling into themselves. An understanding of the physical conditions at which these patterns were created is important to further art research and it can be used as a tool in the authentication of paintings.

Bernardo Palacios et al., abstract in 'Pollock Avoided Hydrodynamic Instabilities to Paint with His Dripping Technique', *PLOS ONE* journal, 30 October 2019

American painter Jackson Pollock (1912–1956) produced many of his celebrated paintings without using a brush but instead poured paint onto canvases, sometimes along a stick. Published on 30 October 2019, the abstract above summarized a scientific investigation into exactly how he created his works, the authors arguing that Pollock had an impressive understanding of a relevant aspect of fluid dynamics.

The researchers recreated his set-up and technique using a rotating mounted syringe, moving at various heights and speeds. What is commonly referred to as Pollock's 'drip technique' is actually not quite right in terms of fluid mechanics as dripping produces droplets, while Pollock was looking for long unbroken filaments. In short, they found that Pollock deliberately avoided 'coiling instability', the tendency of a viscous fluid to produce curls or coils when poured onto a surface.

ALSO ON THIS DAY **1466:** Death of German printing pioneer Johann Fust · **1839:** French-English painter Alfred Sisley born · **1861:** French sculptor Antoine Bourdelle born

The Statue of Unity is unveiled in India, 2018

I remember that when this idea was placed, there were doubts and apprehensions and I wish to reveal something today. When this idea came up in my mind, I was looking for a massive hillock from where Sardar Saheb's statue could be carved out. After a lot of assessment, it came out that it was not possible to get such a massive rock or even if such a rock was available, the carved-out statue wouldn't have been strong enough. So I had to change my mind and whatever you are witnessing today was born out of that....

This is the tallest statue of the world. It will keep reminding our future generations of that personality's courage, abilities and resolutions; about the one who thwarted the conspiracy of disintegrating Mother India into pieces; about the great personality who ended such desires forever, something that the world was expecting about the future of India. I salute such a Man of Steel Sardar Vallabh Bhai Patel....

This statue is an auspicious manifestation of Sardar Patel's love, talent, foresight and spirituality. This statue is not only a token of respect for his strength and dedication, but is also an expression of New India's new self-confidence. This statue is also a reminder to those who questioned the existence of India that India had always been eternal; India is eternal and India will always be eternal.

It is a symbol of self-respect for all those farmers who donated the soil of their fields and also the iron from their tool and equipment, from which the foundation of this statue was built and the soul of this statue was from their expressions of producing food grains by fighting against all odds. This statue is also the contribution of those tribal brothers and sisters who had made their contribution since the freedom movement up to the journey of development. These great heights are to remind the country's youth that the India of the future is like your towering dreams and aspirations. It is massive.

India's prime minister Narendra Modi,
speech at the dedication of the Statue of Unity, Gujarat, 31 October 2018

The Statue of Unity in Gujarat, India, the world's tallest statue at 182 metres (597 feet) high, depicts statesman and independence campaigner Sardar Vallabhbhai Patel (1875–1950). Work on the bronze statue designed by Indian sculptor Ram Sutar (b. 1925) began in October 2013 and shows Patel standing, wearing a dhoti and sandals. More than three thousand workers were involved in its construction.

ALSO ON THIS DAY **1541:** Michelangelo finishes *The Last Judgment* in the Sistine Chapel (*see* 1 November) · **1920:** German-Australian photographer Helmut Newton born · **1941:** Work on Mount Rushmore ends (*see* 4 October)

November

The Sistine Chapel ceiling opens to the public, 1512

Michelangelo complained that from the haste of the Pope he could not finish it as he would, for the Pope constantly asked him when it would be finished. 'Well, and this chapel, when will it be finished?' 'When I can, Holy Father.' The Pope having a stick in his hand struck Michelangelo, saying, 'When I can! when I can! I will make you finish it!'

Once he answered, 'It will be finished when I have satisfied myself.' 'But we will,' replied the Pope 'that you should satisfy us in our desire to have it quickly.' And he added that if it was not done soon he would have him thrown from his scaffold.

The work was done in great discomfort from constantly looking up, and it so injured his sight that he could only read or look at drawings in the same position, an effect which lasted many months. But in the ardour of labour he felt no fatigue and cared for no discomfort. The work has been, indeed, a light of our art, illuminating the world which had been so many centuries in darkness. Oh, truly happy age, and oh, blessed artists, who at such a fountain can purge away the dark films from your eyes. Give thanks to Heaven, and imitate Michelangelo in all things.

Giorgio Vasari, *Lives of the Most Eminent Painters, Sculptors and Architects*, 1568

At the start of the 16th century a crack appeared in the ceiling of the Sistine Chapel in the Vatican City in Rome. Quickly repaired, it nevertheless damaged Piero Matteo d'Amelia's pleasant but simple painting of a blue sky dotted with golden stars that covered it. Sensing an opportunity to replace this design with something rather more spectacular by a fresh artist, Pope Julius II put together a shortlist of one. Michelangelo.

The Italian artist and architect who is the embodiment of the Renaissance was at first reluctant to accept the commission as he had made his name as a sculptor rather than a painter, but the Pope was very persuasive and eventually Michelangelo (1475–1564; *see also* 21 May) began work on it in 1508. Initially, Julius II – nephew of Pope Sixtus IV who had built the chapel thirty years previously – intended that the 40 × 14-metre (130 × 46-foot) artwork would feature a dozen apostles, but Michelangelo in turn persuaded him to think much bigger.

There is still much discussion about the exact theological message contained in the ceiling and there are various theories about secret messages concealed by Michelangelo in his frescoes, including hidden allusions to female anatomy and reproduction, the structure of the brain, and human consciousness. Whatever his intentions, the main section focuses on nine scenes from the book of Genesis of which the best known is *The Creation of Adam* with its iconic image of God reaching out to animate Adam. In addition, there are depictions of the prophets, the ancestors of Christ and a range of biblical scenes including David and Goliath. In total there are 343 figures on the ceiling, as well as a scattering of acorns, the symbol of the Pope's family.

It was hard work. Unlike American actor Charlton Heston who played Michelangelo in the film *The Agony and the Ecstasy* (*see* 7 October), the artist did not paint it lying on his back. Instead, he worked from a movable platform. As his friend and biographer Giorgio Vasari (1511–1574) recounted: 'The work was carried out in extremely uncomfortable conditions, from his having to work with his head tilted upwards'. Or as Michelangelo poetically put it himself in a letter to a friend: 'I've already grown a goitre from this torture, hunched up here like a cat in Lombardy.'

Four years after Michelangelo first picked up his brushes, the ceiling was officially unveiled on All Saints Day, 1512. Half a millennium later, this is where papal conclaves are held to elect a new pope, and around 25,000 tourists a day crane their own necks, while attendants do their best to enforce the no talking and no photographs rules. As German writer Johann Wolfgang von Goethe said in 1787: 'Without having seen the Sistine Chapel one can form no appreciable idea of what one man is capable of achieving.'

ALSO ON THIS DAY 1755: Paintings by Titian, Rubens and Correggio in the Royal Ribeira Palace are destroyed in the Lisbon earthquake · **1887:** English painter Laurence Stephen 'L. S.' Lowry born (*see* 17 November) · **1889:** German photomontagist Hannah Höch born

Peter Greenaway's *Nightwatching* is released, 2007

The vigour of the work is beyond all praise, and every spectator will understand the exclamation of Hoogstraten that it was so powerful that it made all other pictures look like painted cards! A certain air of strain and effort is however unmistakeable, and is to be seen in the actions, motives and costumes, some of which are forced and even theatrical, as well as in the light-and-shade that is too pronounced for a scene in the open air. It is the greatest effort of the master, but few would single it out as the most perfect expression of his artistic ideal.

Professor Gerard Baldwin Brown on *The Night Watch*, in *Rembrandt: A Study of His Life and Work*, 1907

The film *Nightwatching* by British director Peter Greenaway (b. 1942) follows Dutch painter Rembrandt (*see* 25 July) as he produces his painting *The Night Watch* and navigates his complicated love life. Greenaway said the aim of the film was to show Rembrandt as a social moralist and his painting as a kind of precursor to cinema (*see also* 14 September).

It was followed by his equally graphic life of Dutch printer and publisher Hendrik Goltzius, *Goltzius and the Pelican Company* (2012). Greenaway has also produced a multimedia series of installations called *Nine Classical Paintings Revisited* in which he analysed famous works such as *The Night Watch*, Leonardo da Vinci's *The Last Supper* and Paolo Veronese's *The Wedding at Cana*.

ALSO ON THIS DAY 1799: American scientific illustrator Titian Peale born · **1927:** American comic book artist Steve Ditko born · **2015:** Death of Polish art dealer and collector Andrzej Ciechanowiecki

The Robespierre Monument
is unveiled in Moscow, 1918

The art of any propagandist and agitator consists in his ability to find the best means of influencing any given audience, by presenting a definite truth, in such a way as to make it most convincing, most easy to digest, most graphic and most strongly impressive.

**Vladimir Lenin, 'The Slogans and Organisation of Social-Democratic Work',
Sotsial-Demokrat newspaper, 8 December 1911**

A key strand in the campaign of Soviet leader Vladimir Lenin (1871–1924) to win hearts and minds was his Plan of Monumental Propaganda, which he officially put into action in April 1918 soon after taking control of Russia. An early example of using statues as mind tools was the Robespierre Monument, commissioned by Lenin and designed by sculptor Beatrice Sandomierz. The work was a life-size representation of the French revolutionary Maximilien de Robespierre, described by Lenin as a '*Bolshevik avant la lettre*', and was to have been the first of a series featuring other French revolutionaries.

Unfortunately, as the country was still suffering from civil war, materials for large works of art were difficult to obtain and the concrete statue was unsteady from the start. Unveiled in Moscow on 3 November, by the 7th, it had disintegrated (maybe with a helping hand from opponents of Lenin's Bolsheviks). While this particular example was not long-lasting, the overall plan was far more successful and provided much work for sculptors across the country. A wide range of revolutionary and famous figures were celebrated, including composer Frédéric Chopin and Russian painter Mikhail Vrubel, as well as theorists Karl Marx and Friedrich Engels.

ALSO ON THIS DAY 1500: Italian sculptor Benvenuto Cellini born (*see* 28 January) · **1560:** Italian painter Annibale Carracci born · **2014:** One World Trade Center opens in New York, replacing the Twin Towers destroyed in the 9/11 attack (*see* 11 September).

The River Arno floods Florence and destroys art, 1966

In the said year 1269, on the night of the first of October, there was so great a flood of rain and waters from heaven, raining down continually for two nights and one day, that all the rivers of Italy increased more than had ever been known before; and the river of Arno overflowed its borders so beyond measure that a great part of the city of Florence became a lake, and this was by reason of much wood which the rivers brought down, which was caught and lay across at the foot of the Santa Trinita Bridge in such wise, that the water of the river was so stopped up that it spread through the city, whence many persons were drowned and many houses ruined. At last so great was the force of the river that it tore down the said bridge of Santa Trinita, and again by the disgorging thereof the rush of the water and of the timber struck and destroyed the Carraia Bridge; and when they were destroyed and cast down the height of the river, which had been kept up by the said retention and damming of the river, went down, and the fulness of the water ceased which had spread through the city.

Giovanni Villani, *Nuova Cronica*, 1346

When the Arno burst its banks – 633 years to the day since its first catastrophic flood and 400 years since the huge deluge recorded by Italian banker and chronicler Giovanni Villani (*c.* 1275–1348) – it killed more than 100 people and made thousands homeless as 600,000 tons of mud and stone smashed through Florence. Estimates suggest up to four million manscripts and books were damaged, as were fourteen thousand artworks, including sculptor Donatello's *Penitent Magdalene*, painter Cimabue's *Crucifix* from Santa Croce and artist Giorgio Vasari's 2.4 × 6.4 metre (8 × 21 foot) five-panel painting *The Last Supper*, which was later restored despite floating in water for twelve hours. As well as water, oil slicks covered and damaged marble sculptures.

The conservation work after the flood brought together experts from around the world and marked a turning point in international cooperation and knowledge sharing. Much of the reclamation and restoration work was undertaken by volunteers, many of them young travellers, who became known as the Mud Angels (*angeli del fango*). Among their jobs was carrying works of art out of the city's Uffizi galleries.

Meanwhile, an international network of female artists known as the Flood Ladies sprang into action and contributed works of art. A huge fund-raising campaign included the auction of Pablo Picasso's *Femme couchée lisant* (Reclining Woman Reading) donated by the Spanish artist, and a documentary of the disaster produced by Italian director Franco Zeffirelli called *Florence: Days of Destruction*, narrated by the Welsh actor Richard Burton. A second film made in 2015, *When the World Answered*, also chronicled the flood.

ALSO ON THIS DAY 1592: Dutch painter Gerard van Honthorst born · **1856:** Death of French painter Paul Delaroche · **1948:** New Zealand painter and photographer Alexis Hunter born

5 NOVEMBER

Effegies at Bonfire Night celebrations in Lewes, England, 1679

Lewes in Sussex, 5 Nov. This day was celebrated here with extraordinary solemnity, there being a procession not unworthy taking notice of. In the first place went a company of young men armed with swords and muskets, pikes &c. like a company of soldiers.... Just before the Pope marched Guy Faux with his dark Lanthorn, being booted and spurred after the Old Fashion, and wearing a vizrd with a wonderful long nose. Next comes the Pope with his Cross Keys, Crosier Staff and other Fopperies.... There were between twenty and thirty boys with vizards, and two or three who had their faces painted after an antick manner, one whereof carried Holy Water in a tin pot, sprinkling the people with a bottlebrush. In this manner they having carried his Holiness through the Town and Streets adjacent, at night, after they had first degraded him, they committed him to the flames.

Benjamin Harris, *Domestick Intelligence* news-sheet, no. 39, 18 November 1679

English publisher Benjamin Harris (*c.* 1647–1716) provides the first record of the bonfire celebrations in Lewes, England, where every year the failed Gunpowder Plot to blow up King James I and Parliament in 1605 is commemorated. As well as numerous processions and firework displays organized by the town's various bonfire societies, it is also the occasion for a major display of public art – many large and complex effigies of notable figures who have made the news in the preceding year, often for the wrong reasons, are built out of combustible materials, filled with fireworks and then burnt. This has naturally caused some controversy, particularly the regular burning of Pope Paul V, who was in office in 1605. Recent figures who have gone on the pyre include Osama bin Laden, former first minister of Scotland Alex Salmond, English broadcaster Jeremy Clarkson and UK prime minister Boris Johnson (whose effigy was shown urinating on newspapers).

ALSO ON THIS DAY **1607:** Dutch engraver Anna Maria van Schurman born · **1742:** English painter Richard Cosway born · **1955:** Vienna State Opera reopens (with Beethoven's *Fidelio*) after destruction during the Second World War

6 NOVEMBER

Malcolm Morley wins the inaugural Turner Prize, 1984

By his will, after leaving some small annuities to his relations, he gave the bulk of his property, sworn as under £140,000, for the benefit of art and artists; but his will, drawn by himself, was so unskilfully framed and so vague, that after four years' litigation, by the advice of the Lord Chancellor a compromise was arranged. The Royal Academy received £20,000, his pictures and drawings were assigned to the National Gallery, his real estate to the heir-at-law, and his large collection of prints, with other property, to the next of kin. The Academy set aside the sum adjudged to them as 'The Turner Fund', for the relief of distressed artists, not members of their body, and to perpetuate his memory founded a Turner gold medal to be awarded biennially in competition for the best landscape painting.

Samuel Redgrave, on J. M. W. Turner's plan to fund a prize, in *A Dictionary of Artists of the English School*, 1878

Photorealist Malcolm Morley (1931–2018) was the first winner of the often controversial Turner Prize, awarded annually to an artist who is either British or working mainly in Britain for their recent work, rather than their lifetime achievement. The most high-profile art award in the UK, it is named after J. M. W. Turner (*see* 6 September) who was himself a controversial artist and intended to found a prize for younger artists (although there is now no upper age limit, between 1991 and 2016 artists over fifty were not eligible).

Morley's winning work was an installation of two oil paintings depicting a visit to Greece. Later winners include Gilbert & George (in 1986; *see also* 25 September 1967) and Damien Hirst (in 1995; *see also* 1 March). In his Dimbleby Lecture in 2000, Nicholas Serota, former chairman of the Turner Prize jury, pondered the negative headlines that the prize often provokes in the media, but argued that part of art's appeal is its ability to provoke shock and disgust, and that art should be transgressive.

ALSO ON THIS DAY 1753: Russian sculptor Mikhail Kozlovsky born · **1974:** Russian composer Dmitri Shostakovich finishes his song cycle *Suite on Verses of Michelangelo Buonarroti* using poems by Michelangelo · **2017:** A grasshopper is found embedded in Vincent van Gogh's painting *Olive Trees*

7 NOVEMBER

The UK's War Artists' Advisory Committee is appointed, 1939

To draw up a list of artists qualified to record the war at home and abroad. In co-operation with the Services Departments, and other Government Departments, as may be desirable, to advise on the selection of artists on this list for war purposes and on the arrangements for their employment.

British government, War Artists Advisory Committee brief, 1939

Headed by director of the National Gallery in London, Sir Kenneth Clark (*see* 23 August), the War Artists Advisory Committee (WAAC) was formed in the UK to provide work for artists whose livelihoods were damaged by the Second World War, to make a pictorial record of both the home front and the front line, and also to preserve the lives of artists who might otherwise have been killed in fighting. Artists who lived and worked with their units in the army, navy and air force wore official uniforms and often went into action with their units (*see* 1 September). Others worked on the home front. The 'Britain at War' exhibition at the Museum of Modern Art in New York, which showed some of the war artists' early work, was held in a bid to encourage America to enter the war. A similar organization had been set up during the First World War (*see* 23 May).

About four hundred artists, including Dame Laura Knight, Edward Ardizzone and Barnett Freedman, were offered either full-time contracts or short-term commissions, while others produced work that was then bought by the committee. By the end of the war, more than 5,500 works of art had been created as part of the scheme.

ALSO ON THIS DAY 1687: English archaeology pioneer William Stukeley born · **1815:** German sculptor Christian Rauch begins work on a bust of Tsar Alexander I of Russia · **1860:** Canadian painter Paul Peel born

8 NOVEMBER

Camille Claudel works on *Sakuntala*, 1889

My dear Florence

I have been so busy that I didn't have time to write you a single word. I am now working on my two larger than life-size figures and have two models every day: a woman in the morning and a man in the evening. You can guess how exhausted I am; I usually work 12 hours a day, from 7 a.m. to 7 p.m., and back home I can barely stand up so I go to bed straight away. I'm in a lot of trouble of all kinds and I'm very discouraged.

**Camille Claudel, letter to her friend English sculptor Florence Jeans,
8 November 1889**

In November 1889, French sculptor Camille Claudel (1864–1943) began work on her first major solo project *Sakuntala*, depicting a life-size kneeling young man embracing his wife as she leans into him, inspired by a passage from the play of the same name by the 5th-century Indian poet and playwright Kalidasa. Claudel produced various versions in marble, bronze and terracotta, some with retitled names including *Vertumnus and Pomona* (marble; 1905) and *The Abandonment* (bronze; 1905). *Sakuntala* pictures the moment when the naked couple is reunited after a long separation.

By 1888, Claudel had lived in Paris for half a dozen years, studying under and collaborating with sculptor Auguste Rodin (1840–1917) for four. They became lovers but despite Claudel's hopes that he would leave his partner Rose Beuret and marry her, they gradually became more distant. Rodin was inspired by *Sakuntala* to produce *The Eternal Idol* (c. 1890–93).

9 NOVEMBER

Auschwitz prisoner Josef Dziura writes an illustrated letter, 1941

Each prisoner may receive and send two letters or two cards a month from his relatives. Letters to prisoners must be legible, in ink, and contain only 15 lines on a page. Only normal sized letterheads are allowed. Envelopes must be unlined. Only 5 stamps of 12 Pfg. may be included in a letter. Anything else is forbidden and subject to seizure. Postcards have 10 lines. Photographs cannot be used as postcards.

**Extract from Nazi regulations regarding letters in and
out of concentration camps in the Second World War**

In the Second World War, prisoners in Nazi concentration camps in Germany were allowed to send letters. They had to be written on pre-printed forms, were rigorously scrutinized and censored, and subject to all kinds of prohibitions. Their entitlement could be ended for no reason and with immediate effect.

Some professional and amateur artists held in Auschwitz were allowed some leeway in producing art and including artwork in their letters, even though this was technically not allowed. Several examples of botanical drawings and paintings in letters by a prisoner named Josef Dziura survived the war, including one done on 9 November 1941 of trees, fields and a path. Dziura was released from the camp in January 1942, not long after his letter was sent.

John Piper dithers over a London Transport poster, 1948

Over the hills and over the meadows
Gay is my way till day be done
Blue as the heaven are all the shadows
And every light is gold in the sun.

**Robert Bridges, 'Septuagesima' poem text
quoted on *Pinner, via Bakerloo* poster, 1916**

London Transport publicity officer Harold Hutchinson was intent on commissioning artist John Piper (1903–1992) for a London Transport poster and the two exchanged numerous pleasant letters but unfortunately this did not lead to Piper finally producing the poster discussed.

14 October 1948 – Hutchinson writes to confirm conversation agreeing 150 guineas for a pair of posters about London architecture. Asks for roughs by mid-November.

10 November 1948 – Piper replies that he has been entirely taken up with hanging an exhibition of his work at the Leicester Galleries in London but could perhaps produce a rough at the beginning of December. He thanks Hutchinson for helping him get some extra petrol for his car.

10 January 1949 – Any news yet? writes Hutchinson.

16 February 1949 – Hutchinson says he is becoming anxious that he hasn't heard from Piper and asks when roughs might be ready.

27 February 1949 – Piper apologizes for his long silence, blaming recent gastric flu, but says he hopes to catch up on work for the poster soon.

27 April 1949 – 'The year marches on,' observes Hutchinson and wonders how things are progressing and if not fast then could Piper let him know.

26 November 1949 – Hutchinson tries to appeal to Piper by saying that in 1950 they will be focusing on the rural attractions around London and in 1951 on London as part of the Festival of Britain. He suggests maybe something on the capital's architecture, its statues, parks or heaths and commons.

4 April 1968 – Publicity officer Bryce Beaumont responds to a query letter to say that, as far as he knows, Piper has never worked for London Transport.

The poster that carried the lines from 'Septuagesima' by Poet Laureate Robert Bridges (1844–1930) was designed by artist Nancy Smith (1881–1962), who produced several for London Transport.

ALSO ON THIS DAY 1544: Flemish painter Jan Matsys accused of heresy and banished from Antwerp · **1697:** English painter William Hogarth born (*see 25 June*) · **1954:** Marine Corps War Memorial unveiled in Arlington, Virginia, inspired by the photograph of US servicemen raising the flag at Iwo Jima in 1945 (*see 23 February 1945*)

11 NOVEMBER

The Cenotaph war memorial is unveiled in London, 1920

We shall build the Cenotaph: Victory, winged, with Peace, winged too, at the column's head.
And over the stairway, at the foot – oh! here, leave desolate, passionate hands to spread
Violets, roses, and laurel with the small sweet twinkling country things
Speaking so wistfully of other Springs
From the little gardens of little places where son or sweetheart was born and bred.
In splendid sleep, with a thousand brothers
    To lovers – to mothers
    Here, too, lies he:
Under the purple, the green, the red,
It is all young life: it must break some women's hearts to see
Such a brave, gay coverlet to such a bed!
Only, when all is done and said,
God is not mocked and neither are the dead.

    English poet Charlotte Mew, 'The Cenotaph',
    ***Westminster Gazette*, 7 September 1919**

The Cenotaph war memorial in Whitehall, London, was designed by English architect Sir Edwin Lutyens (1869–1944) and is the focal point of an annual Service of Remembrance. The 11-metre (35-foot)-tall construction is built from Portland stone, a rectangular pylon with slightly curved rather than parallel sides, rising in stepped tiers to an empty tomb at the top. There are many other cenotaphs and memorials around the world that honour those who have died during conflict.

ALSO ON THIS DAY **1921:** Tomb of the Unknown Soldier, Arlington Cemetery, Virginia, USA, is dedicated · **1993:** Vietnam Women's Memorial, Washington DC, is dedicated · **2004:** Tomb of the Unknown Warrior, Wellington, New Zealand, is dedicated

12 NOVEMBER

Buzz Aldrin takes the first 'selfie' in space, 1966

Now let me raise my visor and I'll smile.

Buzz Aldrin, space,
12 November 1966

The first photographic self-portrait was taken in 1839 by American photography pioneer and shop owner Robert Cornelius who simply set up his camera and then ran into view. The result, thanks to the necessarily long exposure time at that point in the photographic process, was surprisingly good and he noted the occasion of this landmark selfie on its reverse. While this was the first selfie on Earth, American astronaut Buzz Aldrin (b. 1930) took the first 'selfie' in space on 12 November 1966 during a spacewalk, or EVA (extra-vehicular activity), on the four-day Gemini 12 mission.

The camera, firmly mounted on the spacecraft, had been packed for ultraviolet astronomical photography and taking pictures of Earth. It was a Hasselblad, a make that became the standard on early space missions, adapted to be used with the thick gloves worn by astronauts.

Aldrin told Mission Control to tell everyone on Earth to smile for a photo, then raised his visor and smiled himself. He took the shot, which also includes the blue curve of the Earth in the background, a boom antenna and, in the foreground, the Maurer 16mm sequence camera that was being used to film the EVA. A 20 × 25-cm (8 × 10-inch) print of the image sold for £6,000 at auction in London in 2015.

Aldrin tweeted about the experience in 2014, describing it as the 'best selfie ever'.

13 NOVEMBER

Claude Monet paints
Impression, Sunrise, 1872

I took a quick look at Bertin's pupil: his face was turning dark red. An upheaval seemed imminent to me, and it was reserved for M. Monet to give it the final push. – Ah! here it is, here it is! he exclaimed in front of number 98. I recognize him Papa Vincent's favourite! What does this painting represent? Check the catalogue. – 'Impression, Sunrise.' – Impression, I was sure. I was just saying to myself that since I am impressed there must be an impression there...and what freedom, what ease in the style! The wallpaper in its early state is more complete than this seascape!

Louis Leroy, 'The Exhibition of the Impressionists',
***Le Charivari* magazine, 25 April 1874**

At precisely 7.35 a.m. on 13 November 1872, French painter Claude Monet (1840–1926; *see also* 18 August) began work on *Impression, Sunrise* and it is this painting that was among those singled out for criticism by contemporary art writer Louis Leroy (1812–1885) when it was first exhibited in 1874 (*see* 15 April). It shows the sun above Le Havre port in France, with various fishing and row boats in the harbour, and other larger ships in the distance.

It was Texas State University astronomer and physics professor Donald Olson who managed to drill down to determine not only the date on which it was painted but also the exact time, describing it as: 'an accurate representation of a sparkling glitter path extending across the waters of the harbor, beneath a solar disk seen through the mist accompanying a late fall or winter sunrise'.

With the help of 19th-century maps and old photographs of Le Havre, Olson was able to pinpoint the exact hotel room from where Monet painted. He used the view from the room to calculate the sun's position over the harbour, 20–30 minutes before sunrise. Additionally, he calculated tides to narrow down the times and dates on which the larger sailing ships pictured would have been able to enter the harbour, then checked on meteorological reports to discount days where there was windy, stormy or rainy weather, and which days had an east wind (to match the appearance of the columns of smoke to the left of the painting).

His findings were published in the catalogue for the exhibition 'Monet's Impression Sunrise: The Biography of a Painting' at the Musée Marmottan Monet in Paris in 2014.

ALSO ON THIS DAY 1906: Hungarian-American ceramicist Eva Zeisel born · **1909:** Maltese sculptor Vincent Apap born · **1940:** Walt Disney animated musical *Fantasia* released

14 NOVEMBER

Statue of Mahatma Gandhi is unveiled in Geneva, 2007

I do not want a single soldier, after having taken an oath to serve the army, to mislead the people by shooting in the air. I regard myself as a soldier, as a soldier of peace. I know the value of discipline and truth and I would consider it unmanly for a soldier who has taken an oath to deny himself the consequences when he defies the order by shooting in the air. In my opinion, when a soldier comes to the conclusion that it is inhuman and beneath the dignity of man, he should lay down arms and pay the penalty of insubordination.

Meanwhile I must ask you to believe me when I say that I never made the statement that masses would, if necessary, resort to violence. I regard myself in my lucid moments as incapable of making a statement of that character. Nonviolence is not a policy but a creed. I would pray to God that He may give me faith to lay down my life rather than countenance violence in any shape or form.

Mahatma Gandhi, speech to Women's International League for Peace and Freedom, Geneva, 10 December 1931

When Indian civil rights campaigner Mahatma Gandhi (1869–1948) visited Geneva, Switzerland, in 1931, he gave one of his most important speeches in the city's Victoria Hall, talking about his belief in non-violent action and describing himself memorably as 'a soldier of peace'.

The bust of Gandhi sitting and reading a book that was unveiled in Geneva's Ariana Park on 14 November 2007, inscribed 'My life is my message', was a present from the Indian government to the city as a mark of its efforts in encouraging non-violence and to mark sixty years of friendship between the two countries.

ALSO ON THIS DAY **1691:** Death of Japanese painter Tosa Mitsuoki · **1840:** French painter Claude Monet born (*see* 13 November) · **2018:** French queen Marie Antoinette's jewelry is auctioned after being unseen for two centuries

15 NOVEMBER

Margaret Thatcher reveals Anthony Blunt as a spy, 1979

In April 1964 art historian Sir Anthony Blunt admitted to the security authorities that he had been recruited by and had acted as a talent-spotter for Russian intelligence before the war, when he was a don at Cambridge, and had passed information regularly to the Russians while he was a member of the Security Service between 1940 and 1945. He made this admission after being given an undertaking that he would not be prosecuted if he confessed.

Inquiries were of course made before Blunt joined the Security Service in 1940, and he was judged a fit person. He was known to have held Marxist views at Cambridge, but the security authorities had no reason either in 1940 or at any time during his service to doubt his loyalty to his country.

On leaving the Security Service in 1945 Blunt reverted to his profession as an art historian. He held a number of academic appointments. He was also appointed as Surveyor of The King's Pictures in 1945, and as Surveyor of The Queen's Pictures in 1952. He was given a KCVO in 1956. On his retirement as Surveyor, he was appointed as an Adviser for The Queen's Pictures and Drawings in 1972, and he retired from his appointment in 1978.

Prime Minister Margaret Thatcher,
written statement to the House of Commons, London,
15 November 1979

British art historian Anthony Blunt (1907–1983), a reputed academic and Surveyor of the King's/Queen's Pictures between 1945 and 1972 (*see* 28 April), was recruited into Russian espionage in the early 1930s. In 1940, he joined the British intelligence agency MI5 and later admitted to the Service in 1964 that from 1940 to 1945 he regularly passed on information he thought would be of interest to the Russian intelligence services. It is not clear exactly what this was but, although damaging, it is thought unlikely that British military operations or lives were put at risk. After the war, he returned to life as an art critic and claimed that he passed no more information to Russia from this point.

Blunt's confession in 1964 was in return for full immunity from prosecution, and the information about him was not made public until the media began publishing material about his position in 1979.

ALSO ON THIS DAY 1887: American painter Georgia O'Keeffe born (*see* 20 November) · **1951:** Death of American painter Frank Weston Benson · **1966:** Death of Lithuanian-born American painter and sculptor William Zorach

16 NOVEMBER

A metal detectorist
uncovers the Hoxne Hoard, 1992

Meaning of 'treasure'.

(1) Treasure is – (a) any object at least 300 years old when found which – is not a coin but has metallic content of which at least 10 per cent by weight is precious metal;

when found, is one of at least two coins in the same find which are at least 300 years old at that time and have that percentage of precious metal; or

when found, is one of at least ten coins in the same find which are at least 300 years old at that time;

(b) any object at least 200 years old when found which belongs to a class designated under section 2 (1);

(c) any object which would have been treasure trove if found before the commencement of section 4;

(d) any object which, when found, is part of the same find as – an object within paragraph (a), (b) or (c) found at the same time or earlier; or an object found earlier which would be within paragraph (a) or (b) if it had been found at the same time.

UK Treasure Act, 1996

In the 2014–17 BBC comedy series *Detectorists*, Lance (played by English actor Toby Jones) describes metal detecting as the nearest you can get to time travel, and that archaeologists are interested in facts while metal detectorists are putting together stories.

When farmer Peter Whatling lost a hammer in one of his fields near the village of Hoxne, Suffolk, he asked his friend Eric Lawes, who was a keen metal detectorist, to try and locate it. Although Lawes did not find the hammer, he did come across numerous gold and silver coins, gold jewelry and silver spoons. He immediately contacted the local council and archaeologists from the Suffolk Archaeological Unit moved in – Lawes's action helped to warm a relationship between archaeologists and detectorists that had become decidedly frosty over the previous decade.

They immediately uncovered what became known as the Hoxne Hoard, the largest late Roman hoard in Britain and the finest collection of late Roman gold and silver coins in the empire (they also found the hammer). Within what remained of a wooden chest they found nearly fifteen thousand coins and around two hundred pieces of jewelry and tableware, sorted and stacked, dating from the early fifth century AD but with no evidence suggesting the identity of the owner.

Among the most important objects in the hoard were a rare gold body chain and several silver pepper pots, including the Empress, which shows a woman with elaborate black hair, almond-shaped earrings and a necklace wearing an ornate tunic and holding a gilded scroll. The entire hoard is now in the British Museum, London.

ALSO ON THIS DAY 1625: Death of Italian painter Sofonisba Anguissola (see 12 July) · **1643:** French jeweller Jean Chardin born · **2008:** Death of Polish art dealer Jan Krugier

Bury Council sells Lowry's
A River Bank, 2006

By conferring on me the freedom of the borough of Bury – a sign of kindliness and esteem from my fellow townsmen which I know is meant to embrace all the members of the Wrigley family. I feel it to include my father...of whose memory we are all proud. It includes my brother and sister, by whose aid it has been possible to give to our native town the collection of pictures which my father brought together at Timberhurst, and which we have been delighted to present in his memory. I am to lay the foundation stone of their new home today and I hope that the pictures may be of use and enjoyment to those who come after us.

**Oswald Wrigley, speech at the laying of
the Bury Art Gallery and Public Library foundation stone,
Bury Guardian, 29 April 1899**

Lancashire paper manufacturer and mill owner Thomas Wrigley (1808–1880) was also a keen art collector. After his death, his children gave his art collection to the local town of Bury in England to start its own art gallery if money to build one could be found. As thanks, the children were given the freedom of the town.

A century later, facing a £10 million budget deficit for 2006/2007, Bury Metropolitan Borough Council took the controversial decision to auction *A River Bank*, a 1947 painting by English artist L. S. Lowry (1887–1976) of factories at the edge of the River Irwell, which hung in Bury Art Gallery. The council had bought it in 1951 for £175 and hoped to realize around £500,000. In the event, Christie's – which described it as 'one of the finest examples of Lowry's industrial landscapes, a theme that provided a constant, binding thread throughout his life' – sold the painting for £1.4 million on 17 November 2006.

The decision was criticized by arts organizations and as a result the council was severely sanctioned by the Museums Association – Caitlin Griffiths, advisor on professional issues at the Museums Association, described it as a dark day for museums. However, the council claimed it had no alternative following the drop in funding from central government, and that the painting was not central to its collection.

Although Lowry is traditionally most associated with Salford, he was also the president of Bury Art Society.

18 NOVEMBER

Raja Ravi Varma works on a new commission, 1903

This morning I was engaged in painting the body and sari of Dr Dawar's wife while Brother painted his mother's head.

> **Raja Raja Varma (brother of Raja Ravi Varma), diary entry, 18 November 1903**

India's leading 19th-century painter Raja Ravi Varma (1848–1906) was particularly known for a style that synthesized Indian subjects and European techniques, and in 1904 he received the Kaisar-i-Hind Gold Medal for his dedication to the country. He also ran a pioneering and successful lithographic printing press. Indeed Ravi Varma took on a wide range of commissions and spent most of November 1903 working on the picture his brother mentions in the diary entry for the 18th. Here is how work progressed, recorded by Raja Varma in these brief entries in his diary:

> 4 November: The orders that we have now in hand are two and both are from Dr E. E. Dawar. One bust is of his deceased mother and the other of his late wife.
>
> 7 November: We paid a visit to Dr Dawar at his house on the Wandley Road to select a suitable sari for his wife's portrait. Poor man, his eyes filled with tears when he unpacked along with his late wife's clothes, a lock of hair and he could not speak for some time. We were moved too.
>
> 26 November: I am almost relieved of my health and feverishness and I have commenced today my daily baths. This morning I worked on Dr Dawar's wife's portrait.
>
> 27 November: This morning Dr Dawar came and had a look at his wife's portrait and said that he could not recognize her. Though it requires

improvements we did not think it was so great a failure. These are the difficulties of portrait painting especially from photographs.

ALSO ON THIS DAY **1626:** St Peter's Basilica in the Vatican City is completed · **1785:** Scottish painter David Wilkie born · **1882:** English painter Wyndham Lewis born

Tracey Emin's first solo exhibition opens, 1993

Emin's is an art that tells plain truths, unalloyed, of her life and opinions. But does she really deserve all this attention, culminating in a mid-career retrospective at the Stedelijk Museum in Amsterdam and MAO [Modern Art Oxford] concurrently? In our almost entirely relativistic and voyeuristic celebrity culture, this is probably the wrong question. A more realistic question might be whether her art can really sustain all this attention on its own. Its value is almost – if not entirely – an adjunct to personality, the public persona that may well be her only genuine artwork.

Adrian Searle, *Guardian*, 12 November 2002

In her wittily titled first major exhibition, 'My Major Retrospective 1963–1993', English artist Tracey Emin (b. 1963) filled the newly opened White Cube gallery in London with a vast physical collage of more than a hundred personal objects. The confessional works included her teenage diaries as well as photographs, toys and a patchwork quilt covered with the names of her family. 'A brilliantly simple idea,' ran the *TimeOut* magazine review, 'which takes one step further the fashion for bringing real-life into the galleries.'

Highlights included *My Abortion*, which featured a bottle of pills and hospital wrist tags, and *My Uncle Colin*, a tribute to her uncle who was killed in a car accident, with the Benson and Hedges cigarette pack that he was holding when he died and a newspaper cutting reporting on the crash. Among the numerous texts on display were letters to former boyfriends and family, and diary entries about sexual experiences.

Emin has continued to draw on her personal life for later works including her 1995 *Tent: Everyone I Have Ever Slept With (1963–1995)*, which gives the names of everybody she has slept with (sexually and non-sexually) appliquéd onto a tent, and *My Bed* (1998), her unmade double bed complete with empty vodka bottles, underwear and dirtied sheets.

ALSO ON THIS DAY 1617: French painter Eustache le Sueur born · **1665:** Death of French painter Nicolas Poussin (*see* 3 June) · **1770:** Danish sculptor and medallist Bertel Thorvaldsen born

20 NOVEMBER

A Georgia O'Keeffe painting sells for $44.4 million, 2014

A flower is relatively small. Everyone has many associations with a flower – the idea of flowers. You put out your hand to touch the flower – lean forward to smell it – maybe touch it with your lips almost without thinking – or give it to someone to please them. Still – in a way – nobody sees a flower – really – it is so small – we haven't time – and to see takes time, like to have a friend takes time. If I could paint the flower exactly as I see it no one would see what I see because I would paint it small like the flower is small.

So I said to myself – I'll paint what I see – what the flower is to me but I'll paint it big and they will be surprised into taking time to look at it – I will make even busy New-Yorkers take time to see what I see of flowers.

Well – I made you take time to look at what I saw and when you took time to really notice my flower, you hung all your own associations with flowers on my flower and you write about my flower as if I think and see what you think and see of the flower – and I don't.

Georgia O'Keeffe,
***Exhibition of Oils and Pastels* catalogue, 1939**

American painter Georgia O'Keeffe (1887–1986; *see* 1 June) started painting flowers in 1924 and produced various magnified versions of the large jimson weed blossoms that grew around her home in Abiquiu, New Mexico, including one for the exercise room at Elizabeth Arden's Fifth Avenue Salon, New York. Her *Jimson Weed/White Flower No. 1* (1932) became the most expensive painting by a woman sold at auction on 20 November 2014 when it went for $44,405,000 at Sotheby's, New York.

21 NOVEMBER

The Piltdown Man skull
is exposed as a hoax, 1953

Several years ago I was walking along a farm-road close to Piltdown Common, Fletching (Sussex), when I noticed that the road had been mended with some peculiar brown flints, not usual in the district. On inquiry, I was astonished to learn that they were dug from a gravel bed on the farm, and shortly afterwards I visited the place where two labourers were at work digging the gravel for small repairs to the roads. As this excavation was situated four miles north of the limit where the occurrence of flints overlying the Wealden strata is recorded, I was much interested and made a close examination of the bed. I asked the workmen if they had found bones or other fossils there. As they did not appear to have noticed anything of the sort, I urged them to preserve anything that they might find. Upon one of my subsequent visits to the pit, one of the men handed to me a small portion of an unusually thick human parietal bone. I immediately made a search, but could find nothing more; nor had the men noticed anything else. The bed is full of tabular pieces of iron-stone closely resembling this piece of skull in colour and thickness; and although I made many subsequent searches, I could not hear of any further find nor discover anything – in fact, the bed seemed to be quite unfossiliferous.

Charles Dawson, statement to a Geological Society of London meeting, 18 December 1912

The 'missing link' skull of a supposed early human – 'Piltdown Man' – found by amateur archaeologist Charles Dawson (1864–1916) in Sussex, England, was anything but. In fact, it was a remarkable artistic fake put together using a variety of human and orangutan bone fragments. Although doubts were raised from the very beginning of the 'find', it was not until 21 November 1953 that it was internationally exposed in the press following tests by the Natural History

Museum. Although various suspects have been suggested as responsible for the deception, it is now commonly agreed that Dawson – who falsified other pieces – was solely responsible.

Among those who helped to uncover the truth about Piltdown Man was archaeologist and art historian Professor Edward Hall who contributed to the development of archaeometry that uses carbon-dating to establish the age of objects. He used X-ray fluorescence to prove the skull was a fake and was also part of the team that definitively pronounced on the age of the Turin Shroud (*see* 13 October).

Discussion on the Piltdown Skull, a 1913 painting by John Cooke depicting a meeting of scientists discussing the skull, still hangs at the Geological Society's headquarters in London.

ALSO ON THIS DAY 1874: Death of Spanish painter Mariano Fortuny · **1898:** Belgian painter René Magritte born (*see* 19 May) · **1907:** Death of German painter Paula Modersohn-Becker (*see* 21 October)

22 NOVEMBER

The Eric Carle Museum of Picture Book Art opens, 2002

My wife Barbara and I share a vision of 'giving back'. And from this feeling and from our love for picture books and wanting others to experience the wonder and joy that we felt when we looked at books, came the impetus to build the museum. It came from a shared amazement as we looked at a framed original illustration versus the printed book, and watching others look carefully and begin to inquire about the process, technique and the feelings a single illustration evoked. It came from the joy we felt when we visited other artists in their studios and when we looked and talked with them about their work. It came from an absolute conviction that picture book art is precious and deserves a home of its own and an honored place among the arts.

It is the first museum of picture book art on this scale in this country and I think the presence the museum now has is raising up the work of illustrators from all around the world and saying, this is art, this is important and meaningful, for people of all ages. and for some young visitors, it is their first visit to a museum. and so it is an introduction to that experience of visiting a museum, learning to appreciate art and books, too.

Although American writer and illustrator Eric Carle (1929–2021) has illustrated more than seventy books, he is best known for *The Very Hungry Caterpillar* (1969), which features his trademarks of nature themes, colourful collage technique and die-cut pages. In 2002, he opened his own museum in Amherst, Massachusetts, which has three art galleries, and runs educational programmes for children and training for those working in education.

ALSO ON THIS DAY 1904: Mexican painter and caricaturist Miguel Covarrubias born · **1995:** *Toy Story*, the first full-length computer-generated animated film, is released · **2018:** Leaning Tower of Pisa in Italy has its tilt reduced to help safeguard it (*see* 9 August)

23 NOVEMBER

Dame Rachel Whiteread wins the Turner Prize and one other..., 1993

That this House congratulates Rachel Whiteread on winning the Turner Prize as best modern artist of the year; recognises that good art is often challenging and controversial; believes it would be an act of intolerance and philistinism to destroy her sculpture in Grove Road, Bow before more people have had the opportunity to see it; and calls upon Tower Hamlets Council to allow it to remain for three months and during that time to consult local people about whether or not it should be destroyed.

English sculptor Dame Rachel Whiteread (b. 1963) had made numerous casts of objects, such as living room walls, baths and dolls' houses, and even voids under staircases, before she attempted to cast an entire Victorian terraced house – 193 Grove Road in Mile End, London. The concrete cast of *House* (1993) was exhibited where the original house had stood before it was demolished and went on to win the Turner Prize, making Whiteread the first female winner.

On the same day, Whiteread was also presented with the K Foundation art award for the work – at £40,000, worth double the amount of the Turner – for the worst piece of British art. Initially reluctant to receive it, Whiteread relented when the K Foundation, formed by musicians and artists Bill Drummond and Jimmy Cauty, threatened to burn the money. She donated £10,000 to the housing charity Shelter and the rest to other artists, and took out an advertisement in *Art Monthly* magazine, saying that she did not agree with the K Foundation's aims or methods.

Tower Hamlets London Borough Council demolished *House* on 11 January 1994.

ALSO ON THIS DAY 1868: American painter Mary Brewster Hazelton born · **1883:** Mexican muralist José Clemente Orozco born · **1936:** *Life* magazine rebranded as a photographic title

24 NOVEMBER

Robert Jackson photographs Jack Ruby shooting Lee Harvey Oswald, 1963

I had the gun in my right hip pocket, and impulsively, if that is the correct word here, I saw him, and that is all I can say. And I didn't care what happened to me.

I think I used the words, 'You killed my President, you rat.' The next thing, I was down on the floor.

I said, 'I am Jack Ruby. You all know me.'

I never used anything malicious, nothing like s.o.b. I never said that I wanted to get three more off, as they stated.

The only words, and I was highly emotional; to Ray Hall – he interrogated more than any other person down there – all I believe I said to him was, 'I didn't want Mrs Kennedy to come back to trial.'

And I forget what else. And I used a little expression like being of the Jewish faith, I wanted to show that we love our President, even though we are not of the same faith.

**Jack Ruby, testimony to the Warren Commission,
7 June 1964**

On 22 November 1963, *Dallas Times Herald* photographer Robert Jackson (b. 1934) had travelled several cars behind US president John F. Kennedy as he was driven from the airport through the city. When the president was assassinated, Jackson was in the process of changing the film in his camera and so was unable to document the moment. When JFK's killer Lee Harvey Oswald was being led out of the police station on 24 November, Jackson was again on the spot. Fortunately for him, his Nikon S3 35mm camera was this time fully loaded as Jack Ruby, a Dallas nightclub owner, stepped forward and shot Oswald.

The unlucky photographer on this occasion was Jack Beers who was working for the *Dallas Morning News*. He had noticed Ruby move in before Jackson and taken a shot a split second earlier, but this lacked Oswald's pained expression and the surprise of those around him.

Jackson's photograph was published the following day in the *Herald* and in 1964 it won him the Pulitzer Prize for Photography.

ALSO ON THIS DAY **1472:** Italian sculptor Pietro Torrigiano born · **1859:** American architect Cass Gilbert born · **1864:** French painter Henri de Toulouse-Lautrec born

25 NOVEMBER

Whistler's libel trial
against Ruskin opens, 1878

For Mr Whistler's own sake, no less than for the protection of the purchaser, Sir Coutts Lindsay ought not to have admitted works into the gallery in which the ill-educated conceit of the artist so nearly approached the aspect of wilful imposture. I have seen, and heard, much of cockney impudence before now; but never expected to hear a coxcomb ask two hundred guineas for flinging a pot of paint in the public's face.

John Ruskin, *Fors Clavigera* pamphlet, no. 79, June 1877

Now, Mr. Whistler. Can you tell me how long it took you to knock off that nocturne?... I beg your pardon? (Laughter.)

Oh! I am afraid that I am using a term that applies rather perhaps to my own work. I should have said, 'How long did you take to paint that picture?'

Oh, no! permit me, I am too greatly flattered to think that you apply, to work of mine, any term that you are in the habit of using with reference to your own. Let us say then how long did I take to – 'knock off', I think that is it – to knock off that nocturne; well, as well as I remember, about a day.

Only a day?

Well, I won't be quite positive; I may have still put a few more touches to it the next day if the painting were not dry. I had better say then, that I was two days at work on it.

Oh, two days! The labour of two days, then, is that for which you ask two hundred guineas!

No; – I ask it for the knowledge of a lifetime. (Applause.)

Trial transcript, in James McNeill Whistler,
***The Gentle Art of Making Enemies,* 1890**

American-born painter James McNeill Whistler (1834–1903; *see also* 22 May) took strong exception to the comments of English art critic John Ruskin (1819–1900; *see also* 13 May) about his *Nocturne in Black and Gold: The Falling Rocket* (1875), which was exhibited at the Grosvenor Gallery, London, in 1877. Whistler sued Ruskin – who had been a strong critic of Whistler's for several years – for libel and over two days the court was treated to an intriguing debate about the value of art. Technically, Whistler won, but was only awarded a farthing in damages and the court costs bankrupted him.

ALSO ON THIS DAY 1870: French painter Maurice Denis born · **1873:** American painter Albert Krehbiel born · **1909:** American book illustrator and animator Philip Eastman born

26 NOVEMBER

Telford's Pontcysyllte Aqueduct opens, 1805

The nobility and gentry, the adjacent counties having united their efforts with the great commercial interests of this country. In creating an intercourse and union between England and North Wales by a navigable communication of the three Rivers, Severne, Dee and Mersey for the mutual benefit of agriculture and trades, caused the first stone of this aqueduct of Pontcysyllty [*sic*], to be laid on the 25th day of July MDCCXCV. When Richard Myddelton of Chirk, Esq, M.P. one of the original patrons of the Ellesmere Canal was Lord of this manor, and in the reign of our Sovereign George the Third. When the equity of the laws, and the security of property, promoted the general welfare of the nation. While the arts and sciences flourished by his patronage and the conduct of civil life was improved by his example.

Pontcysyllte Aqueduct inauguration plaque inscription

The Pontcysyllte Aqueduct, designed by Scottish civil engineer Thomas Telford (1757–1834; *see also* 30 January) is one of the greatest architectural achievements of the canal age, at 307 metres (1,007 feet) long and 38 metres (126 feet) high. A stone and cast iron navigable aqueduct that is still in use today across the River Dee in Wales, it carries the Llangollen branch of the Ellesmere Canal. Made up of nineteen arches, it is the longest aqueduct in Britain, the highest canal aqueduct in the world and a UNESCO World Heritage Site since 2009. As well as the canal, there is a towpath for pedestrians.

This was the first time that Telford worked with the group of people who went on to become a team for his future structures, including civil engineers William Jessop and Matthew Davidson, ironmaster William Hazeldine, and master masons John Wilson and John Simpson. The foundation stone was laid on 25 July 1795, and the project's final cost was £47,000.

Although the aqueduct was a success, commercial use fell away gradually until it was closed in 1944, but in recent years it has become a popular holiday route because of its history and picturesque surroundings.

ALSO ON THIS DAY **1915:** German-Australian sculptor Inge King born · **1922:** American cartoonist Charles M. Schulz born (*see* 2 October 1950) · **1994:** The body of Polish painter Stanisław Witkiewicz ('Witkacy') is exhumed; later tests showing it to be that of an unknown woman

Sir John Tenniel's cartoon *The Tempter* is published, 1886

SPIRIT OF ANARCHY: 'What! No work! Come and enlist with me – I'll find work for you!'
[Spirit of Anarchy/Death to unemployed man in threadbare clothes and carrying a hammer just about to jump off the edge of a cliff]

**Sir John Tenniel, *The Tempter* cartoon caption,
Punch magazine, 27 November 1886**

Best known today for illustrating the *Alice* books by Lewis Carroll (*see* 16 December), English illustrator Sir John Tenniel (1820–1914) was a political cartoonist at the popular magazine *Punch* for half a century, retiring at the age of eighty-one when he was going blind. Often given a full page for a single work, Tenniel's drawings regularly carried important social messages about the need for the reform of poor working conditions and the problems of bureaucracy (although his portrayal of Irishmen as a kind of missing link has not aged well). Ghosts and spectres such as in *The Tempter*, published in the magazine on 27 November 1886, were regular devices. His coverage of the Jack the Ripper murders focused on the appalling living conditions in the areas where the women were murdered rather than on gory details of the killings.

He drew well over two thousand cartoons for *Punch* and its spin-off publications, as well as providing illustrations for books such as *The Ingoldsby Legends*, which the *Illustrated London News* of October 1863 described as 'masterly handiwork'.

Tenniel's work was celebrated in a Google Doodle featuring the Cheshire Cat on 28 February 2020.

ALSO ON THIS DAY 1570: Death of Italian architect and sculptor Jacopo Sansovino · **1853**: English painter Frank Dicksee born · **1859**: American painter William Bliss Baker born

Blake's *Ancient of Days* is projected onto St Paul's Cathedral, 2019

The frontispiece represents the 'Ancient of Days', as shadowed forth in Proverbs viii. 27: 'when he set a compass upon the face of the earth'; and again, as described in *Paradise Lost*, Book vii. line 236: a grand figure, 'in an orb of light surrounded by dark clouds, is stooping down, with an enormous pair of compasses, to describe the world's destined orb'; Blake adopting with childlike fidelity, but in a truly sublime spirit, the image of the Hebrew and English poets. This composition was an especial favourite with its designer. When colouring it by hand, he 'always bestowed more time,' says Smith*, 'and enjoyed greater pleasure in the task, than from anything else he produced'. The process of colouring his designs was never to him, however, a mechanical or irksome one. Very different feelings were his from those of a mere copyist. Throughout life, whenever for his few patrons filling in the colour to his engraved books, he lived anew the first fresh, happy experiences of conception, as in the high hour of inspiration.

Smith tells us that Blake 'was inspired with the splendid grandeur of this figure, "The Ancient of Days", by the vision which he declared hovered over his head at the top of his staircase' in No. 13, Hercules Buildings, and that he has been frequently heard to say that it made a more powerful impression upon his mind than all he had ever been visited by.

Alexander Gilchrist, *Life of William Blake*, 1863

*1828, John Thomas Smith, Keeper of the Prints and Drawings at the British Museum and early biographer of Blake

To celebrate the birthday of English artist and writer William Blake, who was born on 28 November 1757 (*see also* 18 January), Tate Britain projected one of his favourite works, and one he was working on in 1827 at the end of his life, onto the dome of St Paul's Cathedral in London. Blake's hope for his work to be seen at the largest possible scale was never achieved in his lifetime.

He initially produced *The Ancient of Days* for the frontispiece of the book *Europe a Prophecy, Ancient of Days* (1794) and then worked on various versions for the rest of his life. It was inspired by a name for God in the Book of Daniel and shows Blake's bearded wise old man Urizen crouching down in front of a golden disc and clouds while holding a compass into the darkness below.

ALSO ON THIS DAY 1680: Death of Italian architect and sculptor Gian Lorenzo Bernini (*see 22 February*) · **1870:** Death of French painter Frédéric Bazille at the Battle of Beaune-la-Rolande, France (*see 26 August*) · **2019:** At a political debate about the climate crisis on Channel 4 in the UK, Prime Minister Boris Johnson fails to appear and is replaced by a melting ice sculpture

29 NOVEMBER

The *Knife Angel* is unveiled in Liverpool, 2018

Sadly scarcely a day goes by without hearing another tragic story of knife crime. Through hosting the *Knife Angel* at Liverpool Cathedral we want to show solidarity with the victims of this crime and make a powerful statement to everyone who comes to visit.

As people encounter the artwork, we hope this helps them make sense of the issues it raises by coming in, lighting a candle or reflecting in one of our chapels. We will continue to pray for peace in our city and beyond.

As well as standing alongside all those affected by knife crime we want to urge those who carry knives to recognise the pain they cause themselves and others as we work to a day when we truly see peace in our streets.

Dean of Liverpool, Dr Sue Jones, statement in Liverpool Cathedral press release, 27 November 2018

English stone carver and sculptor Alfie Bradley (b. 1990) had already produced *Spoon Gorilla* (2014) using 40,000 welded spoons before he began work on *Knife Angel* (also known as the *Angel of Knives* and the *National Monument Against Violence & Aggression*). First installed outside Liverpool Cathedral in the UK on 29 November 2018, the sculpture stands 8 metres (27 feet) high and is made of more than 100,000 weapons voluntarily handed in to amnesty knife bins around the country in 2015/2016 and collected by 43 police forces. The project was part of a national campaign against knife-related offences.

Each one was disinfested and blunted before Bradley welded them onto a central steel structure of an angel. Families of those who had died in knife crimes engraved messages on some of the blades.

Since completion, it has been on a permanent tour of cities in the UK, including the fourth plinth in Trafalgar Square, London.

ALSO ON THIS DAY 1874: Welsh painter Francis Dodd born · **1924:** American painter Jane Freilicher born · **1928:** Azerbaijani painter Tahir Salahov born

30 NOVEMBER

The Crystal Palace in London burns down, 1936

So man is approaching a more complete fulfilment of that great and sacred mission which he has to perform in this world. His reason being created after the image of God, he has to use it to discover the laws by which the Almighty governs His creation, and, by making these laws his standard of action, to conquer nature to his use; himself a divine instrument.

Science discovers these laws of power, motion and transformation; industry applies them to raw matter, which the earth yields us in abundance, but which becomes valuable only by knowledge. Art teaches us the immutable laws of beauty and symmetry, and gives to our productions forms in accordance with them.

Gentlemen, the Exhibition of 1851 is to give us a true test and a living picture of the point of development at which the whole of mankind has arrived in this great task, and a new starting point from which all nations will be able to direct their further exertions.

I confidently hope that the first impression which the view of this vast collection will produce upon the spectator will be that of deep thankfulness to the Almighty for the blessings which He has bestowed upon us already here below; and the second, the conviction that they can only be realised in proportion to the help which we are prepared to render each other; therefore, only by peace, love and ready assistance, not only between individuals, but between the nations of the earth.

**Prince Albert, co-organizer of the 1851 Great Exhibition,
speech at a Mansion House banquet, London, 21 March 1849**

This is the end of an age

Winston Churchill, who witnessed the fire (attributed)

The vast Crystal Palace designed by English architect and gardener Joseph Paxton (1803–1865) was built in Hyde Park in London as the home for the 1851 Great Exhibition and then moved to Penge Common in south London in 1854 (*see also* 31 December). An innovative modular cast-iron and plate-glass structure, it gradually fell into disuse at the start of the 20th century and was completely destroyed by the fire on 30 November 1936, only a few days before Edward VIII abdicated.

ALSO ON THIS DAY 1508: Italian architect Andrea Palladio born (*see* 3 March) · **1876:** German archaeologist Heinrich Schliemann finds the golden funeral Mask of Agamemnon at Mycenae, Greece · **1953:** Death of French painter Francis Picabia

December

First Day Without Art, 1989

And in what sort of age – I thought – are artists living now? Are conditions favourable? Life is very multiple; full of 'movements', 'facts' and 'news'; with the limelight terribly turned on – and all this is adverse to the artist. Yet, leisure is abundant; the facilities for study great; Liberty is respected – more or less. But, there is one great reason why, in this age of ours, Art, it seems, must flourish. For, just as cross-breeding in Nature – if it be not too violent – often gives an extra vitality to the offspring, so does cross-breeding of philosophies make for vitality in Art.

I cannot help thinking that historians, looking back from the far future, will record this age as the Third Renaissance. We who are lost in it, working or looking on, can neither tell what we are doing, nor where standing; but we cannot help observing, that, just as in the Greek Renaissance, worn-out Pagan orthodoxy was penetrated by new philosophy; just as in the Italian Renaissance, Pagan philosophy, reasserting itself, fertilised again an already too inbred Christian creed; so now Orthodoxy fertilised by Science is producing a fresh and fuller conception of life – a love of Perfection, not for hope of reward, not for fear of punishment, but for Perfection's sake.

Slowly, under our feet, beneath our consciousness, is forming that new philosophy, and it is in times of new philosophies that Art, itself in essence always a discovery, must flourish. Those whose sacred suns and moons are ever in the past, tell us that our Art is going to the dogs; and it is, indeed, true that we are in confusion! The waters are broken, and every nerve and sinew of the artist is strained to discover his own safety. It is an age of stir and change, a season of new wine and old bottles. Yet, assuredly, in spite of breakages and waste, a wine worth the drinking is all the time being made.

English author John Galsworthy,
'Vague Thoughts on Art', *Fortnightly Review*, 1912

Day Without Art was established as part of the art activist organization Visual AIDS, which was set up to increase awareness of AIDS through exhibitions and events. It was created by Thomas Sokolowski (then Zimmerli Art Museum director at Rutgers University), Gary Garrels (senior curator of painting and sculpture, San Francisco Museum of Modern Art), Robert

Atkins (art historian) and William Olander (senior curator, New Museum of Contemporary Art, New York). Sokolowski said the impetus behind the project was that he and other friends in the creative art world, including curators and art handlers as well as artists, realized that if they all disappeared, there might actually be a day with no art.

The first Day Without Art was held on 1 December 1989 when museums closed for the day or temporarily removed artworks from galleries and replaced them with explanatory notes – among the works removed by the Metropolitan Museum of Art in New York have been Pablo Picasso's 1906 portrait *Gertrude Stein*, a 16th-century Nigerian pendant mask from the Edo peoples of the Court of Benin, an Egyptian *Horus Statue of Nectanebo II* (360–342 BC) and Julia Margaret Cameron's photograph of Philip Stanhope Worsley.

From its inception, the organizers have encouraged art galleries and museums in America and around the world to run events – including temporarily covering or removing works – that celebrate the lives of those who have died, to highlight AIDS and its damage to the world of art, and to educate people about HIV. It is held on the same date as World AIDS Day.

ALSO ON THIS DAY **1716:** French sculptor Étienne Falconet born · **1761:** French wax sculptor Marie Tussaud born · **1933:** Death of Finnish painter Pekka Halonen

2 DECEMBER

A photo of a llama in Times Square is published, 1957

Her photographs speak for her, down the years, establishing her as an artist with a painterly eye, who never condescended to her subjects but waited patiently for the moment when they would reveal themselves to her. She was an early pioneer of colour photography, and an accomplished technician. Although she was never a photojournalist, the range of her work was vast, from the ethnographic beauty of the studies she made of Iran on a journey there in 1956, to photographs of poverty in Gaza in 1960, to her portraits and coverage of fashion shows. Her approach was unsentimental and direct.

Sarah Crompton, 'The Quiet Brilliance of Magnum Photographer Inge Morath',
Observer, 23 November 2018

Austrian photographer Inge Morath (1923–2002) was one of the first female photographers at the Magnum photo agency. Her work covered a wide range of subject matter from documenting films such as *The Misfits* and *The Unforgiven* (during the filming of which she saved American actor Audie Murphy from drowning after seeing him in distress through her telephoto lens) to more surreal images such as those in her comic llama story 'High-paid llama in big city'. Published on 2 December 1957 in *Life* magazine, the image of 'Linda' the llama leaning out of a car window after coming home from an appearance on a television show ended up becoming one of her most iconic shots.

The story – about a collection of animals owned by Lorraine and Bernhard d'Essen who lived in a normal house in Manhattan, New York – appears as if Morath has snatched the shots off the cuff, but in fact her contact sheets indicated that she had been planning the shoot for some time, getting to know the family and animals first so that everybody would be relaxed for the moment when she photographed them in the street.

ALSO ON THIS DAY 1697: The new St Paul's Cathedral, London, opens (*see* 3 September) · **1859:** French painter Georges Seurat born · **1891:** German painter and printmaker Otto Dix born

3 DECEMBER

Pravda criticizes Western art, 1962

Art belongs to the people. It must have its deepest roots in the broad mass of workers. It must be understood and loved by them. It must be rooted in and grow with their feelings, thoughts and desires. It must arouse and develop the artist in them. Are we to give cake and sugar to a minority when the mass of workers and peasants still lack black bread? I mean that, not, as you might think, only in the literal sense of the word, but also figuratively. We must keep the workers and peasants always before our eyes. We must learn to reckon and to manage for them. Even in the sphere of art and culture.

Vladimir Lenin, as reported by Clara Zetkin in *Reminiscences of Lenin*, 1934

The idea that 'Art belongs to the people' was a key 20th-century concept in the USSR, but after the death of Soviet leader Joseph Stalin in 1953 there was a notable liberalization in the arts world despite no specific policy directives. In a reaction against this trend, the official Communist newspaper *Pravda* made its position very clear by emphasizing in an editorial on 3 December 1962 that the goal of artists should be Socialist Realism (*see* 2 August) and not 'all-forgiving liberalism' produced by what it called 'pseudo-innovators' obsessed with Western approaches to art. Abstractionism came in for particular criticism.

In 1977, the vast 'Art Belongs to the People' exhibition of Leningrad artists was held to celebrate the 60th anniversary of the October Revolution.

ALSO ON THIS DAY **1590:** Flemish painter Daniel Seghers born · **1919:** Death of French painter and sculptor Pierre-Auguste Renoir (*see* 26 August) · **1956:** Death of Russian sculptor and designer Alexander Rodchenko

4 DECEMBER

The Council of Trent decree on sacred images, 1563

...the images of Christ, of the Virgin Mother of God, and of the other saints, are to be had and retained particularly in temples, and that due honour and veneration are to be given them; not that any divinity, or virtue, is believed to be in them, on account of which they are to be worshipped; or that anything is to be asked of them; or, that trust is to be reposed in images, as was of old done by the Gentiles who placed their hope in idols; but because the honour which is shown them is referred to the prototypes which those images represent; in such wise that by the images which we kiss, and before which we uncover the head, and prostrate ourselves, we adore Christ; and we venerate the saints, whose similitude they bear: as, by the decrees of Councils, and especially of the second Synod of Nicaea, has been defined against the opponents of images.

And the bishops shall carefully teach this, that, by means of the histories of the mysteries of our Redemption, portrayed by paintings or other representations, the people is instructed, and confirmed in (the habit of) remembering, and continually revolving in mind the articles of faith; as also that great profit is derived from all sacred images, not only because the people are thereby admonished of the benefits and gifts bestowed upon them by Christ, but also because the miracles which God has performed by means of the saints, and their salutary examples, are set before the eyes of the faithful; that so they may give God thanks for those things; may order their own lives and manners in imitation of the saints; and may be excited to adore and love God, and to cultivate piety. But if any one shall teach, or entertain sentiments, contrary to these decrees; let him be anathema....

Moreover, in the invocation of saints, the veneration of relics and the sacred use of images, every superstition shall be removed, all filthy lucre be abolished; finally, all lasciviousness be avoided; in such wise that figures shall not be painted or adorned with a beauty exciting to lust; nor the celebration of the saints, and the visitation of relics be by any perverted into revellings and drunkenness; as if festivals are celebrated to the honour of the saints by luxury and wantonness.

In fine, let so great care and diligence be used herein by bishops, as that there be nothing seen that is disorderly, or that is unbecomingly or confusedly arranged, nothing that is profane, nothing indecorous, seeing that holiness becometh the house of God.

**Council of Trent, 25th session, decree 'On the Invocation,
Veneration and Relics of Saints, and on Sacred Images', 4 December 1563**

The Council of Trent was set up as one of the bulwarks of the Counter-Reformation and met for the final time between 1562 and 1563 to state and reinforce Catholic doctrine in key areas. The issue of what was suitable in religious art was a key area of debate with which the Council attempted to deal in this decree of 4 December 1563.

ALSO ON THIS DAY 1603: Death of Flemish painter Maerten de Vos · **1914:** Austrian painter and sculptor Rudolf Hausner born · **1920:** Portuguese painter and architect Nadir Afonso born

5 DECEMBER

Albert Namatjira's first solo exhibition opens in Australia, 1938

In this collection of water-color drawings the world that is always seeking fresh sensations is offered a completely new thing. The artist, Albert Namatjira (known popularly as Albert) is almost certainly the first of his race to rise to the dignity of an exhibition, even as he is assuredly the first to display, in European fashion, an outstanding talent in art. He is a pure-blood Australian aboriginal, a member of the great Arunta tribe which claimed, before the advent of the white man, the whole of that vast country now known as Central Australia.

Native art was accustomed to find expression in the representation of natural objects, painted or engraved, on the walls of caves and rock-shelters, and in the decoration of implements, weapons and utensils. So usual was this practice of decoration that it is a commonplace to find the most ordinary articles – shields, spear-throwers, boomerangs and their like – lavishly adorned, often in color, while sacred objects such as churinga and bull-roarers may be beautifully shaped and incised, and dilly-bags may display designs both useful and graceful, coupled with ornamentation of much appropriateness.

Now, breaking away from all tradition, Albert appears as the pioneer of a new art development.

**Australian author Robert Henderson Croll, introduction
in *Albert Namatjira: Central Australian Water Colours* catalogue, 1938**

Albert Namatjira (born Elea Namatjira, 1902–1959) was the first Aboriginal artist to successfully produce and exhibit a fusion of indigenous Australian and Western-style art. His detailed watercolour landscapes focused on sacred sites in the country's outback interior, featuring native flora such as white gum trees, and the effect of the absence or presence of water. His first solo exhibition in Melbourne in December 1938 was a landmark moment, selling out and catapulting him to national fame. Although he was awarded a limited form of Australian citizenship, at that time unavailable to Aboriginal people, he was convicted for supplying alcohol to another Aboriginal artist and sentenced to six months in prison, which caused a national scandal.

ALSO ON THIS DAY 1926: Death of French painter Claude Monet (*see* 13 November) · **1931:** Cathedral of Christ the Saviour, Moscow, is demolished (to be replaced by a Palace of the Soviets that was never finished) · **2006:** Audrey Hepburn's little black dress from the film *Breakfast at Tiffany's* is sold at auction in London for £467,200

Museum of Black Civilizations opens in Senegal, 2018

Keeping our cultures is what has saved African people from attempts made at making of them soulless people without a history. And if culture does link people together, it also stimulates progress.

Senegal President Macky Sall, speech at the Museum of Black Civilizations opening ceremony, 6 December 2018

The initial concept of creating a museum to celebrate African art and culture was suggested by Senegal's poet-president, Léopold Sédar Senghor (1906–2001), half a century before the doors finally opened and seven years after construction work began. In an address to the Ghanaian parliament in February 1961, he emphasized that it was crucial that the cultural values of all civilizations, in particular those 'seasoned with the salt of negritude' needed to be recognized.

The four-storey Museum of Black Civilizations in Dakar is built in a circular shape, inspired by the architecture of traditional southern Senegalese homes. It opened in December 2018 amid calls for the repatriation of objects and artworks held in European museums that were taken from African communities, in particular those in institutions in France, which exercised colonial rule until 1960.

The first exhibition was 'African Civilizations: Continuous Creation of Humanity', which looked at artistic creations from pre-history to the present day from the African diaspora, including work from artists from Mali, Burkina Faso, Cuba and Haiti.

ALSO ON THIS DAY 1912: The Nefertiti Bust is discovered by German archaeologist Ludwig Borchardt in Amarna, Egypt · **1998:** Death of French sculptor César Baldaccini · **1884:** Capstone is added to the Washington Monument, Washington DC, completing its construction

Maurizio Cattelan's installation is eaten, 2019

We regret to inform you that 'Comedian' will be removed from our Art Basel Miami Beach booth for the last day of the fair, Sunday, December 8th.

This morning, following recommendations, we removed the installation at 9 am. We want to thank the organizers of the fair for their help and continued support. Art Basel collaboratively worked with us to station guards and create uniform lines. However, the installation caused several uncontrollable crowd movements and the placement of the work on our booth compromised the safety of the artwork around us, including that of our neighbors. 'Comedian', with its simple composition, ultimately offered a complex reflection of ourselves. We would like to warmly thank all those who participated in this memorable adventure, as well as to our colleagues. We sincerely apologize to all the visitors of the fair who today will not be able to participate in 'Comedian'.

—

#cattelanbanana #artbaselmiamibeach #artbasel #mauriziocattelan #cattelan #perrotin

Galerie Perrotin, Instagram post, 8 December 2019

Comedian (2019) was an installation by Italian artist Maurizio Cattelan (b. 1960), consisting of a fresh banana bought from a Miami grocery shop and attached to a wall with duct tape. It sold at Art Basel Miami Beach on 6 December 2019 for $120,000 and made headlines in the international press, some of which remarked on the value placed on the work by wealthy collectors by quoting the comment made by the Lucille Bluth character in American television series *Arrested Development*: 'You're the one who charged his own brother for a Bluth frozen banana. I mean, it's one banana, Michael. What could it cost, ten dollars?'

On 7 December 2019, Georgian-born American artist David Datuna (b. 1974) upcycled the installation by pulling it off the wall, where it was displayed at the Galerie Perrotin booth in the Miami Beach Convention Center, and eating it, entitling this new intervention *Hungry Artist*. Unruffled, gallery director Lucien Terras pointed out: 'He did not destroy the art work. The banana is the idea.'

Cattelan's previous work included *America* (a solid gold lavatory, 2016), stolen from Blenheim Palace in the UK while on display in 2019.

ALSO ON THIS DAY **1680:** Death of Dutch painter Sir Peter Lely (Pieter van der Faes) · **1732:** The Royal Opera House opens in Covent Garden, London · **1899:** Death of Filipino painter and sculptor Juan Luna

8 DECEMBER

The Council of Europe adopts the Flag of Europe, 1955

The European flag is not only the symbol of the European Union, but also of Europe's unity and identity in a wider sense. The circle of gold stars represents solidarity and harmony between the peoples of Europe. The number of stars has nothing to do with the number of Member States. There are 12 stars because the number 12 is traditionally the symbol of perfection, completeness and unity. The flag therefore remains unchanged regardless of EU enlargements.... Thus the European flag and emblem represent both the Council of Europe and the European Union. It has now become the symbol par excellence of a united Europe and European identity....

Against the background of blue sky, 12 golden stars form a circle, representing the union of the peoples of Europe. The number of stars is fixed, 12 being the symbol of perfection and unity.... The circle is arranged so that the stars appear in the position of the hours on the face of a clock.... The colours of the emblem are Pantone Reflex Blue for the surface of the rectangle and Pantone Yellow for the stars.

'Graphics Guide to the European Emblem: Council of Europe, European Commission', European Union style guide, 2019

The European flag was co-designed by Paul Lévy (1910–2002), a former director of information at the Council of Europe, and Arsène Heitz (1908–1989), who worked in the council's postal service. Heitz submitted dozens of ideas to Lévy who then chose the current design, reworking it slightly. Heitz said the design was inspired by Revelation 12:1 in the Bible: 'And there appeared a great wonder in heaven; a woman clothed with the sun, and the moon under her feet, and upon her head a crown of twelve stars.' Other designs considered included a large green 'E' on a white background, and a yellow circle with a red cross on a blue background.

The flag was first unveiled on 13 December 1955, in Paris.

9 DECEMBER

Illustrator Jean de Brunhoff
is born, 1899

This is the time of year when even the bravest of us murmur to ourselves that we need a change. We probably do, and let us all joyfully take it. If we cannot buy a ticket to go adventuring we can perhaps buy a book and travel through its fresh, unexplored pages. For human staleness there is no remedy more magical in its results than a fine dose of foolishness. These two French books, written and illustrated by Jean de Brunhoff, are distinguished nonsense....

It is now time that the reviewer admits, rather reluctantly, that these books are intended, probably, only for children. Lucky youngsters, to have had their tastes so cleverly considered. The books have nice, stiff backbones so that they prop up perfectly if the reader prefers a seat on the nursery floor, and the covers are broad enough to hide behind if a bothering governess is near. The illustrations, done with that dashing simplicity which looks 'so easy' to those who have never tried to draw, are clear in color and explicit in theme. The story is related with such directness that even children who do not read French easily will not be too bewildered.

'*Babar fait un bon feu*
et prépare le déjeuner,'
and somehow we all feel invited.

Marguerite MacKellar Mitchell, review of *Histoire de Babar,
***le petit elephant* and *Le Voyage de Babar, Horn Book Magazine,* 1933**

French artist and writer Jean de Brunhoff (1899–1937), who created the *Babar the Elephant* illustrated stories, is regarded as a key innovator in the design of modern picture books starting with *Histoire de Babar* (The Story of Babar, 1931). Babar was in fact the invention of Brunhoff's wife Cécile who came up with the idea as a bedtime story for their children.

Brunhoff's colourfully detailed watercolour lithography made particular use of white space and was accompanied by cursive text, but the books also stood out because of their revolutionary oversize dimensions, which were used to their full advantage in double-page spreads.

In his preface to the first English translation in 1934, author A. A. Milne (*see* 14 October) wrote that even adults with no time for picture books would be fascinated by this one. Painter John Piper (*see* 10 November) described Brunhoff as 'Edward Lear's closest neighbour' and American fellow book illustrator Maurice Sendak commented that: 'Babar is at the very heart of my conception of what turns a picture book into a work of art.' After Brunhoff's early death, the Babar series was continued by his artist son Laurent (b. 1925).

The Alfred Jewel is first documented by William Musgrave, 1698

I enclose to you the figure of a curious piece of antiquity, lately found near Athelney in Somersetshire; the place where King Alfred built, as Milton affirms, a fortress: but according to William of Malmsbury, a monastery; in memory (as some have thought) of his deliverance, obscure retreat to that place, and concealment in it, from the Danes.

The substance is in the possession of Col. P of Fairfeild in the same county; by whose, permission, I had the sight of it. 'Tis of the same length and breadth with the figure: the work very fine; so as to make some men question its true age: but in all probability, it did belong to that great king, it is so well represented in the figure, that a short description will suffice.

The edge is thin, as far as the letters. The letters are on a plane rising obliquely. All within the inner pyramidal line is on a plane equidistant from the reverse. The representation (in that upper plane) seems to be of some person in a chair. It is in enamel, cover'd over with a crystal; which is secured in its place by the little leaves coming over its edges. In the reverse are flowers engraved. The whole piece may be of the weight of three guineas. The chrystal and enamel excepted, it is all of pure gold.

This, perhaps, was an amulet of King Alfred's.

Dr William Musgrave, letter to Dr Sloane, 10 December 1698,
in the *Philosophical Transactions of the Royal Society*, 1698

The 6-cm (2½-inch)-long Alfred Jewel that British physician Dr William Musgrave writes of in 1698 was discovered during ploughing in a field in North Petherton, Somerset, was given to the University of Oxford and is now on display in the city's Ashmolean Museum. Although certainly made during the reign of Alfred the Great – AELFRED MEC HEHT GEWYRCAN is inscribed on it ('Alfred ordered me made') – its function is still unclear, but it was most likely the headpiece of a wooden staff, or 'aestel', perhaps to point at words while reading. The image probably represents Christ or perhaps the figure of Sight, which also appears on the Fuller Brooch that dates from around the same time.

ALSO ON THIS DAY 1475: Death of Italian painter Paolo Uccello · **1768:** The Royal Academy in London is founded (*see* 25 April) · **1991:** Death of Austrian painter Greta Kempton

11 DECEMBER

The earliest-known figurative rock art discovery is announced, 2019

The images of therianthropes may represent the earliest evidence for our capacity to conceive of things that do not exist in the natural world, a basic concept that underpins modern religion. Therianthropes occur in the folklore or narrative fiction of almost every modern society and they are perceived as gods, spirits or ancestral beings in many religions worldwide. Sulawesi is now home to the oldest image of this kind – earlier even than the 'Lion-man' from Germany, a figurine of a lion-headed human, which, at 40,000 years old, was until now the oldest depiction of a therianthrope. Early Indonesians were creating art that may have expressed spiritual thinking about the special bond between humans and animals long before the first art was made in Europe, where it has often been assumed the roots of modern religious culture can be traced.

The painting found in a cave in Sulawesi, Indonesia, the findings of which were published in *Nature* on 11 December 2019, shows eight reddish-brown therianthropes – human-like figures with animal characteristics such as the heads of birds and reptiles – hunting two wild native warty pigs and four small buffalo known as anoas, using spears and ropes, perhaps as part of a game drive. The 4.5-metre (15-foot) images have been dated to more than 44,000 years old.

ALSO ON THIS DAY 1890: American painter Mark Tobey born · **1924:** American photographer Alfred Stieglitz and painter Georgia O'Keeffe marry (*see* 1 June) · **2015:** Death of Australian architect Ken Woolley

12 DECEMBER

Toku Shimomura
writes in her diary, 1941

I spent all day at home. Starting from today we were permitted to withdraw $100 from the bank. This was for our sustenance of life, we who are enemy to them. I deeply felt America's largeheartedness in dealing with us.

**Toku Shimomura, diary entry,
12 December 1941**

American artist Roger Shimomura (b. 1939) was inspired by the diary entry of his grandmother Toku to create his acrylic on canvas work, *Diary: December 12, 1941* (1980). A few days earlier on 7 December, Japanese planes had bombed Pearl Harbor and the bank accounts of Japanese Americans and Japanese citizens in the US had been frozen the following day. On 12 December, President Franklin D. Roosevelt (*see also* 12 April) revised the order and allowed up to a $100 a month to be withdrawn from bank accounts. A few months later, internment camps were set up and the infant Shimomura spent the next two years in the Minidoka camp in Idaho.

The work is his response to these events and specifically his grandmother's diary entry. It shows a young Toku in a kimono, sitting inside a traditional Japanese room instead of her actual American home, with tatami mats on the floor and rice-paper screen walls, writing her diary. The feel is of a Japanese ukiyo-e woodblock print.

Through the screens, the figure of Superman with his rippling cape stands in silhouette. His significance – representing the 'large-hearted American' – is unclear, perhaps guarding over Japanese Americans, or rather, keeping them under surveillance (as he did indeed in his comic book adventures during the war). The lattice work is reminiscent of the room dividers in the internment camps, pre-shadowing what will soon become of the family.

ALSO ON THIS DAY 1799: Russian painter Karl Bryullov born · **1863:** Norwegian painter Edvard Munch born (*see* 12 February) · **1928:** American painter Helen Frankenthaler born

13 DECEMBER

Peter the Great visits Jacob de Wilde's art collection, 1697

Alas! I have civilized my own subjects; I have conquered other nations; yet I have not been able to civilize or to conquer myself.

Peter the Great (attributed)

Between March 1697 and August 1698, Peter the Great, Tsar of Russia (1672–1725), undertook a long trip through western Europe known as the Grand Embassy. While its chief element was a diplomatic mission, Peter also used his time to acquaint himself with the cultural aspects of the countries he travelled through, and indeed his reign is notable for the way Western ideas were embraced and the arts in general were developed, from paying stipends to artists to taking a personal interest in all aspects of the architectural development of St Petersburg.

Peter was a keen collector of furniture, paintings, jewels and sculpture, and while he was in Amsterdam, on 13 December 1697 made time to visit a senior tax official and general collector for the Dutch Republic, Jacob de Wilde (1645–1721). De Wilde had collected enough objects – mainly statues, coins and scientific instruments – to set up his own museum behind his house. The meeting was documented in an engraving by his daughter Maria de Wilde (1682–1729), who became a successful engraver and playwright as an adult. The engraving showed the two men seated at a table in a book-lined room and was presented to the Tsar when he made a second visit in 1717. On Jacob's death, his collection was broken up but much of it is believed to have been bought by Peter.

Peter's devotion to the arts was recognized in archbishop and theologian Feofan Prokopovich's oration at the Tsar's funeral on 8 March 1725. He described him not only as a latter-day Solomon, but also as bringing to Russia a wide knowledge of inventions and craftwork previously unheard of in the country.

ALSO ON THIS DAY 1466: Death of Italian sculptor Donatello (Donato di Niccolò di Betto Bardi) · **1836:** German painter Franz von Lenbach born · **1871:** Canadian painter Emily Carr born

14 DECEMBER

Southey's assessment of William Hazlitt's portraits, 1805

Haslitt [*sic*], whom you saw at Paris, has been here; a man of real genius. He has made a very fine picture of Coleridge for Sir George Beaumont, which is said to be in Titian's manner; he has also painted Wordsworth, but so dismally, though Wordsworth's face is his idea of physiognomical perfection, that one of his friends, on seeing it, exclaimed, 'At the gallows – deeply affected by his deserved fate – yet determined to die like a man;' and if you saw the picture, you would admire the criticism. We have a neighbour here who also knows you – Wilkinson, a clergyman, who draws, if not with much genius, with great industry and most useful fidelity. I have learnt a good deal by examining his collection of etchings.

Robert Southey, letter to Richard Duppa, 14 December 1805

Before he became one of England's finest essayists and critics, William Hazlitt (1778–1830) worked as a painter, especially of portraits, and even exhibited

418

at the Royal Academy in 1802. He spent time copying works hanging in the Louvre in Paris, then returned to England and continued producing portraits including those of the Lakes poets William Wordsworth and Samuel Taylor Coleridge. His well-regarded 1804 portrait of his fellow essayist and poet Charles Lamb, depicted dressed as Spanish painter Diego Velázquez's *Philip IV of Spain*, is held by the National Portrait Gallery in London.

Fellow poet and mutual friend Robert Southey (1774–1843) had mixed feelings about his work, which he recounted to the writer Richard Duppa on 14 December 1805, and these were shared by others in the group, including Wordsworth's sister Dorothy. She described Hazlitt's portrait of Coleridge in a letter to Lady Beaumont as 'so dismal that I shrink from the sight of it'. Southey himself wrote to Coleridge in June the following year saying that the portrait 'looks as though you were on trial and certainly had stolen the horse'. Both paintings have not survived. Wordsworth wrote in a letter to Hazlitt's son, also William, that: 'At his desire, I sat to him but as he did not satisfy himself or my friends, the unfinished work was destroyed.'

ALSO ON THIS DAY 1785: Death of Italian engraver and painter Giovanni Cipriani · **1824:** French muralist Pierre de Chavannes born · **1866:** English painter and art critic Roger Fry born (*see* 12 June)

15 DECEMBER

The Glasgow School of Art opens its new Mackintosh building, 1909

When the School of Art was finished, we wondered if Mr Mackintosh felt forlorn or relieved at having this child of his imagination off his hands. Of course that would depend on whether it was a child of joy or sorrow to him, a prodigy or a freak. In our opinion – but, silence is the better part of discretion. There are, however, things which can be said about the child. The finest is, that it expresses what it professes to be. There are about it elements of mystery quite typical of the teaching of art, and it baffles the common man in the way all new art does, at the same time satisfying him, that though artists still study old masters, they are doing up to date work.

If Mr Mackintosh aimed at doing something bizarre, we would congratulate him on his success while condemning it on principle. But we think better of him, and it may be that Mackintoshian ideals are not to be expressed in the ordinary language of architecture. Let the public beware before they comment; like the writing of old on the wall, the meaning may be a horrid one when the right man arrives to translate it. The hackneyed anecdote about the man who thought the School of Art was a prison, is rather a compliment than otherwise; it recognises the serious expression of the building, for, notwithstanding the play of fancy (or is it humour) shown, the design is a serious effort – may be tragically so!

While the strength of Mr Mackintosh's architecture lies perhaps in its mystery, his system of decoration has its strength or weakness in its obviousness. His method is one of permutations and combinations applied to simple forms. This algebraical basis must account for the lack of romance in new art interiors. Coming fresh to the system, one finds interest in noticing that the details of a repeated ornamental motive are never the same, then it grows clear that the motive itself was selected in order that its internal arrangement might allow of endless different combinations, so that once the motive is selected an office boy or a trained cat can do the rest.

That some of these effects can be obtained economically is the advantage of the system; it is the advantage of his whole system. We do not mean to imply that the School of Art is a cheap building, but it is a plain building, and the interior is refreshingly free from the modern architect's ruination, machine-run mouldings. Above all things, it is an interesting building, and this is the next best to being beautiful.

Glasgow School of Art's new building was designed by Scottish architect Charles Rennie Mackintosh (1868–1928). In his speech at the official opening on 15 December 1909, politician and philanthropist Sir John Stirling Maxwell remarked that Mackintosh's work showed that it was possible to have a good building without covering it with expensive and ugly ornament. The building was destroyed by fires in 2014 and 2018.

ALSO ON THIS DAY 1610: Flemish painter David Teniers the Younger born · **1832:** French architect and engineer Gustave Eiffel born (*see* 31 March) · **2001:** Leaning Tower of Pisa is reopened after more than a decade of restoration work (*see* 9 August)

Sir John Tenniel sends out the first
Alice illustration proofs, 1864

The illustrating of the manuscript book gave him [Lewis Carroll] some trouble. He had to borrow a 'Natural History' from the Deanery to learn the correct shapes of some of the strange animals with which Alice conversed; the Mock Turtle he must have evolved out of his inner consciousness, for it is, I think, a species unknown to naturalists.... When he promised to write out 'Alice' for Miss Liddell he had no idea of publication; but his friend, Mr George Macdonald, to whom he had shown the story, persuaded him to submit it to a publisher. Messrs. Macmillan agreed to produce it, and as Mr Dodgson had not sufficient faith in his own artistic powers to venture to allow his illustrations to appear, it was necessary to find some artist who would undertake the work. By the advice of Tom Taylor he approached Mr Tenniel, who was fortunately well disposed, and on 5 April 1864, the final arrangements were made.

Stuart Dodgson Collingwood,
The Life and Letters of Lewis Carroll, **1898**

Realizing his *Alice's Adventures in Wonderland* required a more experienced illustrator, author Lewis Carroll (the pen name of Charles Dodgson; *see also* 6 July) turned to Sir John Tenniel (1820–1914), a mainstay of *Punch* magazine (*see* 27 November). After long negotiations, which started in late January 1864, Tenniel agreed to work on the project for a fee of £138. Carroll approved of his drawing of the white rabbit running away from Alice in October, then Tenniel sent him the first dozen proofs on 16 December. Six months later, Tenniel had finished all forty-two illustrations that appear in the book.

When Carroll began work on the sequel, *Through the Looking-Glass, and What Alice Found There* (1871), he again asked Tenniel to provide illustrations. Tenniel, who was much in demand, had found the process on the first book time-consuming and initially refused. It was Tenniel's last major book illustration work.

ALSO ON THIS DAY **1932:** English illustrator Quentin Blake born · **1937:** American painter Edward Ruscha born · **1946:** French designer Christian Dior founds his eponymous fashion house

Sir Henry Cole inspects the first Christmas card design, 1843

In the Evg Horsley came & brought his design for Christmas Cards.

Sir Henry Cole, diary entry, 17 December 1843

Just published. A Christmas Congratulation Card: or picture emblematical of Old English Festivity to Perpetuate kind recollections between Dear Friends.

Advertisement, *Athenaeum* magazine, 2 December 1843

Although German doctor Michael Maier sent a card at Christmas to King James I of England in 1611 with a greeting in the shape of a rose, the first commercially produced cards were created in 1843. They were the brainchild of Sir Henry Cole (1808–1882), the founding director of the Victoria and Albert Museum, a leading figure in postal reform and one of the organizers of the Great Exhibition of 1851 (*see* 30 November).

In 1843, Cole commissioned his friend the English painter and illustrator John Callcott Horsley (1817–1903; *see* 20 May) to come up with a greetings card to be sent at Christmas time. The card Horsley delivered on 17 December shows in the centre a multi-generational family toasting the person who is receiving the card (the children drinking wine was a controversial element, especially as Horsley was of a conservative disposition). They are flanked with scenes of poor people receiving charity in the form of food and clothes.

Cole had 2,050 cards printed and then hand-coloured. He used some himself and sold the rest for the steep price of a shilling each using the pseudonym 'Felix Summerly'. Fewer than two dozen are believed to have survived.

ALSO ON THIS DAY **1790:** Aztec sun stone sculpture uncovered in the Zócalo, Mexico City · **1934:** American painter Irving Petlin born · **2013:** Death of Latvian-Canadian photographer Fred Bruemmer

Frank Lloyd Wright
visits Bear Run, 1934

Wright introduced the western world to the concept of open-plan living; the plans of his houses flowed. His buildings connected to the outside world, blurring the distinctions between interior and exterior, landscape and architecture. Fallingwater went one step further: it made a dynamic and convincing connection between an uncompromisingly Modern architecture and a wild landscape.

Jonathan Glancey, 'The Folly of Fallingwater',
***Guardian*, 10 September 2001**

American architect Frank Lloyd Wright (1867–1959; *see also* 21 October 1959) designed the Fallingwater house in 1935 as a weekend retreat for businessman Edgar J. Kaufmann and his family, making a site visit in preparation on 18 December the previous year. Located in Fayette County, Pennsylvania, its iconic position above a waterfall in the Bear Run tributary was among various points of disagreement between architect and client, who had stated he wanted a view of the cascade from the house.

ALSO ON THIS DAY 1869: American painter Edward Willis Redfield born · **1879:** Swiss-German painter Paul Klee born · **2006:** Death of American animator Joseph Barbera

Kazimir Malevich's
Black Square goes on show, 1915

Only dull and powerless artists cover up their art with sincerity.

In art, truth is needed, but not sincerity.

These last artists [Supremacists] have thrown off the robes of the past and stepped outside of modern life and found new beauties.

And I say:

That no torture chambers of the academies will stand against the coming time.

**Kazimir Malevich, text in a leaflet distributed at the
'Last Futurist Exhibition of Paintings 0,10', Petrograd, Russia, 1915**

Shown for the first time at the 'Last Futurist Exhibition of Paintings 0, 10', which opened on 19 December in Petrograd (now St Petersburg), *Black Square* (1915) became the signature work of Russian abstract artist Kazimir Malevich (1879–1935). He also established the idea of Suprematism, a geometric-based abstract art that was created on his journey to find the 'zero' point in painting. He produced various versions of *Black Square*, although the pure black slab of the 1915 work has aged to include white cracks.

His later work *White on White* (1918) continued the theme with a slightly off-white square on a slightly off-white background. Malevich sometimes used a black square on his later paintings in place of a signature and his grave was marked by his colleagues, carrying flags with black squares, with a black square. Malevich's work did not find favour in Joseph Stalin's Russia (*see* 2 August), but became a sensation again when exhibited in the 1980s.

In 2015, art historians at the Tretyakov Gallery in Moscow analysed *Black Square* and found that beneath the black paint was a racist joke.

ALSO ON THIS DAY 1843: *A Christmas Carol* is first published featuring illustrations by English artist John Leech · **1851:** Death of English painter J. M. W. Turner (*see* 6 September) · **1914:** American animator Mel Shaw born

Death of painter
Grace Cossington Smith, 1984

I used to go out and sketch, make a drawing, not a very detailed one but just with the forms, and I'd put a little note as to the colour and then I came home and painted it in my studio. Afterwards, I wanted to paint from the thing itself and that is how I paint now, really, from the subject itself. My chief interest, I think, has always been colour, but not flat crude colour, it must be colour within colour, it has to shine; light must be in it, it is no good having heavy, dead colour.... I use squares in the way I paint, not from a conscious way but it came to me naturally because I feel in that way that light can be put into the colour, whereas just to put colour on to the surface in a flat way, I feel that it gives it a dead look.

**Grace Cossington Smith, interview recording
with oral historian Hazel de Berg, August 1965**

Bright colour, often built up in small square blocks, was central to the work of Australian modernist painter Grace Cossington Smith (1892–1984) whose *The Sock Knitter* (1915) is regarded as Australia's first post-Impressionist painting. The focus of much of her work was the city of Sydney, including aspects of smaller domestic suburban homes and restaurants (especially interiors full of light) as well as major landmarks such as Sydney Harbour Bridge (*The Bridge in Curve*, 1930). Cossington Smith's early work was built around sketches she made on trips to the city that provide accurate records of life in the early 20th century as well as major events such as the visit of the Prince of Wales in *The Prince* (1920).

ALSO ON THIS DAY 1629: Dutch painter Pieter de Hooch born · **1861:** Slovenian painter Ivana Kobilca born · **1922:** American land artist and sculptor Beverly Pepper born

US law introduces the first Medal of Honor, 1861

And be it further enacted, that the Secretary of the Navy be, and is hereby, authorized to cause two hundred 'medals of honor' to be prepared, with suitable emblematic devices, which shall be bestowed upon such petty officers, seamen, landsmen, and marines as shall most distinguish themselves by their gallantry in action and other seamanlike qualities during the present war, and that the sum of one thousand dollars be, and the same is hereby, appropriated out of any money in the Treasury, for the purpose of carrying this section into effect.

Resolution 82, An Act to further promote the Efficiency of the Navy, 21 December 1861

The first Medal of Honor – the USA's highest award to those in the military who have performed acts of bravery – was signed into law by President Abraham Lincoln (*see also* 9 March) on 21 December 1861 for the navy, followed by the army in 1862 and the air force in 1965. The first navy medal has barely changed since the Philadelphia firm of William Wilson & Sons produced the first design. On the front of an inverted five-pointed bronze star, Minerva (the Roman goddess of war, representing the USA) holds a bundle of rods (fasces) while beating off the figure of Discord (clutching writhing snakes) with her shield. On her head is an owl to indicate Wisdom. In the trefoils of the medal are oak (Strength) and laurel (Victory) leaves. Around them are thirty-four stars, the number of US states at the time. The words 'Personal Valor' are engraved on the reverse with space for the recipient's name. The medal is suspended from the flukes of an anchor.

ALSO ON THIS DAY 1815: French painter Thomas Couture born · **1937:** Premiere of the first full-length animated feature film, Walt Disney's *Snow White and the Seven Dwarfs* · **1959:** Death of Japanese ceramicist and painter Rosanjin (Kitaōji Fusajirō)

Chris Burden disappears
for three days, 1971

Burden said that his work is the 'acting out of an idea, the materialization of the idea'. The performances demonstrate this in their unencumbered actions that vehemently avoid any move towards symbolism.

David Zwirner gallery press release for 'Early Work' exhibition, 14 September–23 October 2004

American sculptor and performance artist Chris Burden (1946–2015) began his work *Disappearance Piece* on 22 December 1971 and finished on 24 December. No one knew where he had gone; in fact, he had simply checked into a motel where he said he did not feel like doing anything for three days because he had disappeared.

 .Among his other works were *Shoot* (1971), for which he asked a friend to shoot him in the arm with a rifle; *Five Day Locker Piece* (1971): he locked himself in a locker for five days; *B.C. Mexico* (1973): he kayaked to an isolated beach in Mexico and lived for eleven days on water; and *Honest Labor* (1979): he dug a big ditch.

ALSO ON THIS DAY 1554: Death of Italian painter Alessandro Bonvicino · **1943:** Death of English book illustrator Beatrix Potter (*see* 4 March) · **1960:** American painter Jean-Michel Basquiat born

Van Gogh cuts off his ear, 1888

I can assure you that a few days in the hospital were very interesting, and that one perhaps learns how to live from the sick. I hope that I've just had a simple artist's bout of craziness and then a lot of fever following a very considerable loss of blood, as an artery was severed. But my appetite came back immediately, my digestion is good, and the blood is recovering day by day, and likewise serenity is returning to my mind day by day.

Vincent van Gogh, letter to his brother Theo, 7 January 1889

One of the most famous episodes in art history is still the matter of much debate more than a century after it took place. This much is certain. On the night in question, Dutch painter Vincent van Gogh (1853–1890; *see also* 9 September) and his friend and housemate French artist Paul Gauguin (*see* 9 June) had an argument at their shared home in Arles in the south of France. Van Gogh threatened him with a razor, then gripped by one of his recurrent psychotic episodes, cut off most of his own left ear (not just his lobe as some contemporary accounts suggest).

Van Gogh then bandaged his wound and puzzlingly gave his ear, wrapped in paper, to a maid at a nearby brothel. The following day, he was found and taken to hospital where he was treated by a young doctor, Félix Rey. Even though the ear was tracked down, Rey did not try to reattach it as too much time had passed since its removal (instead it stayed in a jar full of alcohol in his office until it was stolen). So pleased was Van Gogh with his doctor that he painted a picture of him, the 1889 *Portrait of Doctor Félix Rey*, and gave it to him. Rey, however, was not keen on it and his mother even less so – she used it to repair a chicken coop, then gave it away. It is now in the Pushkin State Museum of Fine Arts in Moscow and valued at around $50 million.

What tipped Van Gogh over the edge? There is a suggestion that the argument with Gauguin may have been over money. Alternatively, it is argued that his behaviour was caused by the painter's discovery that his brother Theo van Gogh, an emotional shoulder to lean on as well as an important source of finance, had become engaged to be married. A more radical view suggests that it was in fact Gauguin who cut off the ear with his sword in a scuffle, with both men consequently agreeing never to reveal the truth.

ALSO ON THIS DAY 1908: Armenian-Canadian photographer Yousuf Karsh born · **1954:** Death of French sculptor René Iché · **1979:** Death of American art collector Peggy Guggenheim

Anders takes *Earthrise* photograph from Apollo 8, 1968

WILLIAM ANDERS: Oh my God, look at that picture over there! There's the Earth comin' up. Wow, is that pretty!

FRANK BORMAN: Hey don't take that, it's not scheduled.

ANDERS: You got a color film, Jim? Hand me a roll of color, quick, would you?

JIM LOVELL: Oh man, that's great.

ANDERS: Hurry.

LOVELL: Where is it?

ANDERS: Quick.

LOVELL: Down here?

ANDERS: Just grab me a color. A color exterior. Hurry up. Got one?

LOVELL: Yeah, I'm looking for one. C 368.

ANDERS: Anything. Quick.

LOVELL: Here.

ANDERS: Well, I think we missed it.

LOVELL: Hey, I got it right here.

ANDERS: Let me get it out this one, it's a lot clearer.

LOVELL: Bill, I got it framed, it's very clear right here!

LOVELL: Got it?

ANDERS: Yep.

LOVELL: Take several, take several of 'em! Here, give it to me!

ANDERS: Wait a minute, just let me get the right setting here now, just calm down.

LOVELL: Take...

ANDERS: Calm down, Lovell!

LOVELL: Well, I got it right – aw, that's a beautiful shot... Two-fifty at f/11.

ANDERS: OK.

LOVELL: Now vary – vary the exposure a little bit.

ANDERS: I did, I took two of 'em here.

LOVELL: You sure you got it now?

ANDERS: Yeah, we'll get – well, it'll come up again, I think.

**Conversation on board Apollo 8,
24 December 1968 (NASA transcript)**

As the Earth began to emerge above the lunar horizon on 24 December 1968, the first time any human had seen earthrise, American astronaut Bill Anders (b. 1933) reached for his Hasselblad 500EL camera and took a colour photograph. The image – a view of our planet's blue oceans in stark contrast to the grey of the moon and the black of space – has been hailed as a major contribution to the environmental movement and green politics.

ALSO ON THIS DAY **1734:** Spanish artist Diego Velázquez's painting *Las Meninas* is saved from a great fire at the Royal Alcázar of Madrid when it is thrown out of the window · **1810:** Danish painter Wilhelm Marstrand born · **1851:** Library of Congress, Washington DC, is badly damaged by fire

25 DECEMBER

Damien Hirst's spot work becomes the first art on Mars, 2003

Not in my wildest dreams would I have thought about making an artwork that would actually travel to the Red Planet. But the spot painting lends itself to this project and as an artist all the things you make you want to be useful on some level. It had to have as little weight as possible, so there are no dead cows strapped to the back of it.

Damien Hirst, press conference, 28 November 2003

English artist Damien Hirst (b. 1965; *see also* 1 March) produced one of his trademark spot works for the *Beagle 2* lander that touched down on the surface of Mars on Christmas Day 2003. The aim of the rows of different-coloured spots was to use them as an instrument calibration chart to help recalibrate scientific equipment on board *Beagle 2* in its new environment and assess the colour of the iron-rich landscape of the Red Planet.

The design is just 8 icm (3 inches) high and is made out of aluminium, weighing just under 26 ig (1 ioz) and looking a little like a small watercolour paintbox. It contains sixteen full or partial coloured dots made out of minerals including azurite (blue), molybdenum (yellow) and titanium oxide (white).

After briefly going on show at the White Cube gallery in London, it was attached to the exterior of the lander. Although *Beagle 2* landed, it failed to send signals back and was believed lost until 15 January 2015 when it was finally tracked down in reasonably good shape.

430

Hirst was confident that any Martians who came across his spot work would enjoy it. 'If they've got eyes,' he said, 'they'll love it.'

ALSO ON THIS DAY 1911: French-American sculptor and installation artist Louise Bourgeois born · **1952:** Death of American photographer Margrethe Mather · **1983:** Death of Catalan painter and sculptor Joan Miró

26 DECEMBER

The Battle of Trenton, which later inspires John Trumbull, 1776

When the conflict was ended, General Washington walked his horse over the field, to see that the wounded were properly attended to. Among them he observed an officer richly dressed in the hostile uniform, and upon inquiry, found that this was Col. Rahl, commanding officer of the enemy. He immediately called one of his aides-du-camp, Col. William Smith, and gave this memorable order: 'Smith, take charge of this gentleman; see him carefully and kindly conveyed to a house; call our best surgeons to his assistance, and let us save his life if possible.' Col. Rahl died in the afternoon, but the memory of this act should never die.

The magnanimous kindness displayed by Washington, on this occasion, offers a sublime example of true heroism, and well deserves to be imitated by all military men. The artist chose this subject, and composed the picture, for the express purpose of giving a lesson to all living and future soldiers in the service of his country, to show mercy and kindness to a fallen enemy – their enemy no longer when wounded and in their power.

**John Trumbull, *Catalogue of Paintings*,
for his exhibition at Yale College Gallery, 1835**

American painter John Trumbull (1756–1843) served in the American War of Independence, rising to become an aide-de-camp to George Washington and later chronicling key moments through a series of oil paintings, including *Surrender of Lord Cornwallis* and *The Death of General Mercer at the Battle of Princeton*, as well as *The Capture of the Hessians at Trenton*, which he had largely finished in 1786 but continued to work on until 1828. Inspired by the events of

26 December 1776, in this scene, Washington's troops have defeated enemy German soldiers on the morning of Boxing Day. Trumbull became known as 'The Painter of the Revolution'.

ALSO ON THIS DAY 1883: French painter Maurice Utrillo born · **1923:** American sculptor and painter Richard Artschwager born · **1968:** Death of American photojournalist Weegee (Arthur Fellig; *see* 9 October)

27 DECEMBER

Emerson lectures on the delights of art galleries, 1837

The mere passing through a gallery opens and educates the eye. The comparison of many forms drawn from the best thought and highest imagination of many cultivated painters enriches us by teaching the power of form. We have in sculpture and in painting now in the world more noble form than the eye ever saw in actual nature. Let me quote once more from Goethe. 'Today I was at the French Academy where stand together casts of the best statues of antiquity. In such presence man is more than man. We feel that the worthiest object wherewithal to busy us is the human from which we here behold in all its manifold lordliness. Yet who feels not at once at the first glance how insufficient his is? Though prepared, we stand mazed. I had endeavoured to unravel for myself in some measure proportion, anatomy, harmony of motion, yet now I was strongly impressed that the form at last comprises all conformity of limbs to a purpose, Proportion, Character and Beauty.'

Ralph Waldo Emerson, 'The Eye and the Ear' lecture,
Masonic Temple, Boston, 27 December 1837

As well as lecturing on art galleries, as in this lecture on 27 December 1837 that was fourth in a series on 'Human Culture', American lecturer and essayist Ralph Waldo Emerson (1803–1882) was also a firm adherent of transcendentalism. This 19th-century philosophy praised personal originality and invention as a means to self-improvement. He argued in his lectures that it was the duty of artists to provide inspiration via the beauty of their work so that those who viewed it could use it as a springboard to enhance their own intellectual being.

In a later 1841 essay for *Dial* magazine, the main organ of the transcendentalist movement, called simply 'Art' he wrote:

> There is higher work for Art than the arts. They are abortive births of an imperfect or vitiated instinct. Art is the need to create; but in its essence, immense and universal, it is impatient of working with lame or tied hands, and of making cripples and monsters, such as all pictures and statues are. Nothing less than the creation of man and nature is its end. A man should find in it an outlet for his whole energy. He may paint and carve only as long as he can do that. Art should exhilarate, and throw down the walls of circumstance on every side, awakening in the beholder the same sense of universal relation and power which the work evinced in the artist, and its highest effect is to make new artists.

ALSO ON THIS DAY **1864:** French painter René Hermann-Paul born · **1950:** Death of German painter and sculptor Max Beckmann · **2015:** Death of American painter Ellsworth Kelly

28 DECEMBER

Benjamin Haydon shows off
Christ's Entry into Jerusalem, 1817

On 28th December the immortal dinner came off in my painting-room, with *Jerusalem* towering up behind us as a background. Wordsworth was in fine cue, and we had a glorious set-to on Homer, Shakespeare, Milton and Virgil. Lamb got exceedingly merry and exquisitely witty; and his fun in the midst of Wordsworth's solemn intonations of oratory was like the sarcasm and wit of the fool in the intervals of Lear's passion. He made a speech and voted me absent, and made them drink my health. 'Now,' said Lamb, 'you old lake poet, you rascally poet, why do you call Voltaire dull?' We all defended Wordsworth, and affirmed there was a state of mind when Voltaire would be dull. 'Well,' said Lamb, 'here's Voltaire – the Messiah of the French nation, and a very proper one too.'

He then, in a strain of humour beyond description, abused me for putting Newton's head into my picture; 'a fellow,' said he, 'who believed nothing unless it was as clear as the three sides of a triangle.' And then he and Keats agreed he had destroyed all the poetry of the rainbow by reducing it to the prismatic colours. It was impossible to resist him, and we all drank 'Newton's health, and confusion to mathematics'. It was delightful to see the good humour of Wordsworth in giving in to all our frolics without affectation and laughing as heartily as the best of us.

Benjamin Haydon, autobiography (published posthumously in 1853)

English artist and diarist Benjamin Haydon (1786–1846; *see also* 11 July) was very pleased with his painting *Christ's Entry into Jerusalem* (1814–20), which was on view at the dinner he held on 28 December 1817 where poets William Wordsworth, John Keats and Charles Lamb were among his guests. He wrote four years later in his diary on 1 January:

> O God, let me not die in debt. Spare my eyes, invigorate my intellect, strengthen every faculty which thou has blessed me with, and supply me with those that thou hast not. Accept my deep gratitude for the triumphant success of 'Christ's entry into Jerusalem' and for its having advanced the public taste, Amen.

ALSO ON THIS DAY 1065: King Edward's first Westminster Abbey, London, is consecrated · **1882:** Danish painter and model Lili Elbe born · **1929:** Spanish painter Salvador Dalí is thrown out of his home by his father for captioning one of his paintings 'Sometimes, I spit for fun on my mother's portrait'

29 DECEMBER

Leonardo sketches the hanging of Bernardo di Bandino Baroncelli, 1479

A tan-coloured small cap, A doublet of black serge, A black jerkin lined, A blue coat lined with fur of foxes' breasts, and the collar of the jerkin covered with black and white stippled velvet, Bernardo di Bandino Baroncelli; black hose.

Leonardo da Vinci, text alongside sketch, 29 December 1479

Italian merchant Bernardo di Bandini Baroncelli (1420–1479) was a main player in the 1478 Pazzi Conspiracy, which attempted to oust the Medici family from their position as rulers of Florence by murdering brothers Lorenzo and Giuliano de' Medici. Although Guiliano was murdered, the plot failed catastrophically and those involved were either executed or banished from the city.

Baroncelli was among those executed, hanged at the Palazzo del Bargello on 29 December the following year after fleeing to and being extradited from Istanbul. Among those watching was artist Leonardo da Vinci (1452–1519; *see also* 28 September), who sketched the occasion and added in his mirror writing a description of what Baroncelli was wearing.

ALSO ON THIS DAY 1653: Dutch painter Johannes Vermeer enters the painters' guild in Delft · **1883:** William H. Vanderbilt opens the doors to his private art gallery · **1896:** Mexican painter David Siqueiros born

30 DECEMBER

Michelangelo's statue of Pope Julius II is pulled down, 1511

The Pope's anger being appeased, he blessed Michelangelo, who was loaded with gifts and promises, and ordered to prepare a bronze statue of the Pope, five braccia high, in a striking attitude of majesty, habited in rich vestments, and with determination and courage displayed in his countenance. This was placed in a niche above the S. Petronio gate.

It is said that while Michelangelo was engaged upon it Francia the painter came to see it, having heard much of him and his works, but seen none. He obtained the permission, and was amazed at Michelangelo's art. When asked what he thought of the figure, he replied that it was a fine cast and good material. Michelangelo, thinking that he had praised the bronze rather than the art, said: 'I am under the same obligation to Pope Julius, who gave it to me, as you are to those who provide your paints,' and in the presence of the nobles he angrily called him a blockhead. Meeting one day a son of Francia, who was said to be a very handsome youth, he said: 'Your father knows how to make living figures better than to paint them.' One of the nobles asked him which was the larger, the Pope's statue or a pair of oxen, and he replied, 'It depends upon the oxen, those of Bologna are certainly larger than our Florentine ones.'

Michelangelo finished the statue in clay before the Pope left for Rome; His Holiness went to see it, and the question was raised of what to put in the left hand, the right being held up with such a proud gesture that the Pope asked if it was giving a blessing or a curse. Michelangelo answered that he was admonishing the people of Bologna to be prudent. When he asked the Pope whether he should put a book in his left hand, the pontiff replied, 'Give me a sword; I am not a man of letters.' The Pope left 1,000 crowns wherewith to finish it in the bank of M. Antonmaria da Lignano. After sixteen months of hard work it was placed in front of the church of S. Petronio, as already related. It was destroyed by the Bentivogli, and the bronze sold to Duke Alfonso of Ferrara, who made a cannon of it, called the Julius, the head only being preserved, which is now in his wardrobe.

Giorgio Vasari, *Lives of the Most Eminent Painters,*
Sculptors and Architects, **1568**

Although Italian Renaissance artist Michelangelo (1475–1564) sculpted mostly in marble (*see* 21 May), he did also work in bronze, although very few examples have survived. The 3-metre (11-foot) statue of Pope Julius II that art historian Giorgio Vasari (1511–1574) mentions was erected on 21 February 1508, but when the rival Bentivogli family took control of Bologna in 1511, they encouraged an angry crowd of their followers to topple the statue and smash it up. The head, long since lost, apparently weighed 270 kg (600 lb). No images of the statue have survived.

ALSO ON THIS DAY **1724:** French painter Louis-Jean-François Lagrenée born · **1927:** Czech painter and sculptor Jan Kubíček born · **1941:** Death of Russian photographer and graphic designer Lazar Lissitzky

31 DECEMBER

A New Year's Eve party
is thrown inside a sculpture, 1853

Mr Waterhouse Hawkins requests the honour of ___ at dinner in the mould of the Iguanodon at the Crystal Palace on Saturday evening December the 31st at five o'clock 1853. An answer will oblige.

Soups: Mock Turtle; Julien; Hare
Fish: Cod and Oyster Sauce; Fillets of Whiting; Turbot a l'Hollandaise

Removes: Roast Turkey; Ham; Raised Pigeon Pie; Boiled Chicken and Celery Sauce

Entrées: Cotolettes de Moutonaux Tomates; Currie de Lapereaux au riz; Salmi de Perdrix; Mayonnaise de filets de Sole

Game: Pheasants; Woodcocks; Snipes

Sweets: Macedoine Jelly, Orange Jelly; Bavaroise; Charlotte Russe; French Pastry; Nougat a la Chantilly; Buisson de Meringue

Dessert: Grapes; Apples; Pears; Almonds and Raisins; French Plums; Pines; Filberts; Walnuts

Wines: Sherry; Madeira; Port; Moselle; Claret

Invitation and menu for Benjamin Waterhouse Hawkins's Crystal Palace dinner, 31 December 1853

When the Crystal Palace moved to Penge Common in south London after the success of the Great Exhibition (*see* 30 November), English artist and sculptor Benjamin Waterhouse Hawkins (1807–1894) was commissioned to make large model dinosaurs, which he did with the help of leading palaeontologist Sir Richard Owen, the naturalist who came up with the name 'dinosauria'.

Hawkins built the models out of cement on site. The largest were hollow, which gave him the idea for a marvellous public relations opportunity. On 31 December 1853, he held a dinner inside the mould of the biggest dinosaur, the Iguanodon (it was 9 metres/30 feet long from nose to tail), ahead of the unveiling of the sculptures the following year. He invited twenty-one scientists and friends to the eight-course meal within the back of the beast (only eleven could actually fit inside to eat; the others sat at a nearby table, which must have been a blow). Owen sat inside the skull at the head of the table, Hawkins in the centre. As the dinosaur was so high, a stage was erected to allow waiters to reach into the mould and serve the food. In PR terms it was a great success, featuring in write-ups in *Punch* magazine and the *Illustrated London News*, with accompanying drawings of the dinner.

The dinosaurs are still on show in London Borough of Bromley's Crystal Palace Park. Science has moved on since they were built and they are now believed to contain major inaccuracies, especially the Iguanodon.

ALSO ON THIS DAY 1869: French painter Henri Matisse born (*see* 17 October) · **1995:** American cartoonist Bill Watterson finishes his *Calvin and Hobbes* comic strip · **2007:** Death of Italian designer Ettore Sottsass

Sources and Credits

January

1 January: John Byng, *The Torrington Diaries: Containing the Tours Through England and Wales of the Hon. John Byng (later Fifth Viscount Torrington) Between the Years 1781 and 1794*, ed. John Beresford and Cyril Bruyn Andrews, London: Eyre & Spottiswoode, 1934–38. Rev. Richard Warner, *A Tour Through the Northern Counties of England and Borders of Scotland*, London: G. and J. Robinson, 1802.

2 January: 'Echoes of the Week' column, *Sunderland Echo*, 7 January 1895.

3 January: John Ruskin, *Praeterita: Outlines of Scenes and Thoughts Perhaps Worthy of Memory in My Past Life*, Sunnyside, Orpington: George Allen, 1885.

4 January: Guggenheim press release, 'First Comprehensive Exhibition of Artist On Kawara Opens at the Guggenheim Feb 6', 22 December 2014, https://www.guggenheim.org/press-release/first-comprehensive-exhibition-of-artist-on-kawara-opens-at-the-guggenheim-on-february-6.

5 January: Catalogue entry, quoted in *January 5–31, 1969* [exhibition catalogue], New York: Seth Siegelaub, 1969.

6 January: Brochure extract, quoted in 'Major Peirson is Avenged', War Memorials Archive Blog post, Imperial War Museums, 20 November 2008, https://ukniwm.wordpress.com/2008/11/20/major-peirson-is-avenged.

7 January: *Manchester Guardian*, 7 January 1928.

8 January: Eric Hebborn, 'The Language of Line' [unpublished], quoted in Dalya Alberge, 'Great Art Forger Continues to Ridicule Experts from Beyond the Grave', *Guardian*, 24 August 2015. Courtesy of Guardian News & Media Ltd.

9 January: William Dowsing, *The Journal of William Dowsing*, www.williamdowsing.org/journalnoindex.htm.

10 January: *Proceedings of the Zoological Society of London*, in *The London and Edinburgh Philosophical Magazine and Journal of Science*, vol. 12, 1838.

11 January: Charles Koczka, *Arts & Antiques*, November 1986, quoted in Janet Rapaport, 'Raider of the Lost Art', *Customs Today*, vol. 22, no. 2, Spring 1987.

12 January: Matthew Paris, *Matthew Paris's English History: From the Year 1235 to 1273*, vol. III, trans. Rev. John Allen Giles, London: Henry G. Bohn, 1854.

13 January: Gary Kemp, quoted in The Crown Estate press release, 27 March 2012. © Crown Copyright 2012.

14 January: Pliny the Elder, *The Natural History*, trans. John Bostock and H. T. Riley, London: Taylor and Francis, 1855.

15 January: Hans Sloane will, quoted in *Report from the Select Committee on British Museum*, London, 1836.

16 January: *Das Schwarze Korps*, 25 April 1940. Author's translation. *See* https://www.cgccomics.com/boards/topic/358479-superman-in-look-magazine/.

17 January: Athanasius, *St Athanasius: Select Works and Letters*, trans. H. Ellershaw, Select Library of Nicene and Post-Nicene Fathers in the Christian Church, eds P. Schaff and H. Wace, vol. IV, New York: The Christian Literature Company, 1892.

18 January: William Blake, quoted in Alexander Gilchrist, *Life of William Blake*, London: Macmillan & Co, 1863.

19 January: Marsden Hartley, quoted in Herschel Browning Chipp, *Theories of Modern Art: A Source Book by Artists and Critics*, Berkeley, CA: University of California Press, 1968.

20 January: Sir John Soane, *The Royal Academy Lectures*, ed. David Watkin, Cambridge, UK: Cambridge University Press, 2000.

21 January: Robert Henri, *The Art Spirit*, Philadelphia: J. B. Lippincott, 1923.

22 January: George Orwell, *Nineteen Eighty-Four*, London: Secker & Warburg, 1949. Apple Computer '1984' advert, dir. Ridley Scott, 1984.

23 January: *Ming History* (Míng Shǐ), quoted in Friedrich Hirth, *China and the Roman Orient: Researches into their Ancient and Mediaeval Relations as Represented in Old Chinese Records*, Leipzig: George Hirth, 1885.

24 January: Thomas Paine, *The Rights of Man*, London: J. S. Jordan, 1791. William

Shakespeare, *As You Like It*, in *Mr. William Shakespeare's Comedies, Histories, & Tragedies (First Folio)*, London: Edward Blount and William and Isaac Jaggard, 1623.

25 January: Michael Faraday, quoted in The Talbot Catalogue Raisonné, https://talbot.bodleian.ox.ac.uk/2016/01/29/25-january-1839-dame-nature-has-become-his-drawing-mistress. William Henry Fox Talbot, Document no. 3782, letter to William Jerdan, 30 January 1839, The Correspondence of William Henry Fox Talbot Project, http://foxtalbot.dmu.ac.uk/letters/transcriptDocnum.php?docnum=3782.

26 January: Benjamin Franklin, 'From Benjamin Franklin to Sarah Bache, 26 January 1784' [letter transcript], Founders Online, National Archives and Records Administration United States Federal Government, from *The Papers of Benjamin Franklin*, vol. 41, *September 16, 1783, through February 29, 1784*, ed. Ellen R. Cohn, New Haven and London: Yale University Press, 2014, https://founders.archives.gov/documents/Franklin/01-41-02-0327.

27 January: John James Audubon, quoted in Robert Buchanan (ed.), *The Life and Adventures of John James Audubon, the Naturalist*, London: Sampson Low, 1868.

28 January: Benvenuto Cellini, quoted in *The Life of Benvenuto Cellini, a Florentine Artist*, vol. II, trans. Thomas Nugent, London: Hunt and Clarke, 1828.

29 January: Edwin George Lutz, *Animated Cartoons*, New York: Charles Scribner's Sons, 1920.

30 January: Samuel Smiles, *The Life of Thomas Telford, Civil Engineer, With an Introductory History of Roads and Travelling in Great Britain*, London: John Murray, 1867.

31 January: Arthur Malkin, *The Gallery of Portraits: With Memoirs*, vol. III, London: Charles Knight, 1834.

February

1 February: William Morris, *The Decorative Arts, Their Relation to Modern Life and Progress: An Address Delivered Before the Trades' Guild of Learning*, London: Ellis and White, 1878.

2 February: William Morris, *The Collected Letters of William Morris: Volume II, 1881–1884*, ed. Norman Kelvin, Princeton, NJ: Princeton University Press, 2014.

3 February: Edward Lear diary entry [transcript], Edward Lear's Diaries [blog], leardiaries.wordpress.com/2009/02/03/thursday-3-february-1859.

4 February: Sir Walter Scott, letters quoted in John Gibson Lockhart, *Memoirs of the Life of Sir Walter Scott*, vol. V, Edinburgh: Robert Cadell, 1848.

5 February: F. T. Marinetti, quoted in *Exhibition of Works by the Italian Futurist Painters (with an Initial Manifesto of Futurism by F. T. Marinetti)* [exhibition catalogue], trans. unknown, London: Sackville Gallery, 1912.

6 February: Anon., *The Rise and Progress of the Present Taste in Planting Parks, Pleasure Grounds, Gardens*, London: C. Moran, 1767.

7 February: Girolamo Savonarola, quoted in Pasquale Villari, *Life and Times of Girolamo Savonarola*, vol. II, trans. Linda Villari, London: Unwin, 1888.

8 February: Caspar David Friedrich, quoted in Carl Gustav Carus, *Nine Letters on Landscape Painting: Written in the Years 1815–1824*, trans. David Britt, Los Angeles: Getty Publications, 2002. Author's translation.

9 February: Vincent van Gogh, Letter No. 850. Leo Jansen, Hans Luijten, Nienke Bakker (eds.) (2009), *Vincent van Gogh – The Letters*. Version: January 2020. Amsterdam & The Hague: Van Gogh Museum & Huygens ING. http://vangoghletters.org/en/let850.

10 February: Benjamin Day, US Patent, No. 214,493, filed 4 January 1878, https://patentimages.storage.googleapis.com/ec/57/9d/3eb454d181d979/US214493.pdf.

11 February: Monteiro Lobato, 'A propósito da exposição Malfatti', *O Estado de S. Paulo*, 20 December 1917. Author's translation.

12 February: Edvard Munch, quoted in Zuzanna Stanska, 'The Mysterious Road from Edvard Munch's *The Scream*', *Daily Art Magazine*, 12 December 2016, www.dailyartmagazine.com/the-mysterious-road-of-the-scream-by-edvard-munch/.

13 February: Thomas Eakins, quoted in Kathleen A. Foster, 'Thomas Eakins: Scenes from Modern Life', Public Broadcasting Service

(PBS), www.pbs.org/eakins/t_1886_
rumor.htm.

14 February: Valentine's Day card text, quoted
in Anna Maria Barry, 'A History of Valentine's
Day Celebrations – From Fertility Festivals
to the First Cards', BBC *HistoryExtra*, 2015,
www.historyextra.com/period/modern/
when-was-valentines-day-first-celebrated-
cards-history-saint-valentine/.

15 February: Unnamed staff reporter,
Reynolds News and Sunday Citizen newspaper,
2 December 1945.

16 February: Arthur Mace, 'A. C. Mace's
Account of the Opening of the Burial Chamber
of Tutankhamun on February 16, 1923', The
Griffith Institute, University of Oxford, http://
www.griffith.ox.ac.uk/discoveringTut/alt
-accounts/4maceope.html. © The Orr family.

17 February: Theodore Roosevelt, 'A Layman's
Views of an Art Exhibition', *Outlook*, no. 103,
29 March 1913.

18 February: Charles de Kay, *The Art Work
of Louis C. Tiffany*, New York: Doubleday,
Page & Co., 1914.

19 February: Edict, quoted in Charles Joseph
Hefele, *A History of the Councils of the Church,
from the Original Documents, Vol. 5: A.D. 626
to the Close of the Second Council of Nicea,
A.D. 787*, trans. William R. Clark, Edinburgh:
T. & T. Clark, 1896.

20 February: Ellen Terry, *The Story of My Life*,
London: Hutchinson, 1908.

21 February: Thomas Platter, *Thomas Platter's
Travels in England, 1599*, trans. Clare Williams,
London: Jonathan Cape, 1937.

22 February: Augustus Hare, *Walks in Rome*,
vol. 2, London: Daldy, Isbister & Co, 1875.

23 February: *Radio Times*, 20 February 1969.
© Immediate Media Co.

24 February: John Evelyn, *The Diary of John
Evelyn*, ed. William Bray, London: M. Walter
Dunne, 1901.

25 February: *If War Should Come*
[leaflet], Home Front: Thirsk, Thirk Museum,
www.thirskmuseum.org/homefront/
ifwarshouldcome_read.html.

26 February: William Sainsbury (ed.), *Original
Unpublished Papers Illustrative of the Life of Sir
Peter Paul Rubens as an Artist and a Diplomatist,
Preserved in H. M. State Paper Office*, London:
Bradbury & Evans, 1859.

27 February: Guillaume Apollinaire, quoted in
Vincent Gille, 'Des joies de toutes les couleurs',
Apollinaire critique d'art, Paris: Paris-Musees/
Gallimard, 1993. Author's translation.

28 February: Paul Nash, quoted in Claude
Colleer Abbott and Anthony Bertram (eds),
*Poet and Painter: Being the Correspondence
Between Gordon Bottomley and Paul Nash
1910–1946*, London: Oxford University Press,
1955.

29 February: James Weldon Johnson,
Lift Ev'ry Voice and Sing, International
Music Score Library Project, https://
imslp.org/wiki/Lift_Ev'ry_Voice_and_
Sing_(Johnson%2C_J._Rosamond).

March

1 March: Damien Hirst, quoted in Lynn
Barber, 'Bleeding Art', *Observer*, 20 April 2003,
https://www.theguardian.com/
artanddesign/2003/apr/20/
thesaatchigallery.art6. Courtesy of Guardian
News & Media Ltd.

2 March: Ebenezer Cooke, quoted in
*International Health Exhibition, London, 1884:
The Health Exhibition Literature: Vol XIV:
Conference on Education*, London: W. Clowes
& Sons, 1884.

3 March: Inigo Jones, quoted in Lily B.
Campbell, *Scenes and Machines on the English
Stage During the Renaissance: A Classical Revival*,
Cambridge, UK: Cambridge University Press,
1923.

4 March: Beatrix Potter, Beatrix Potter: The
Picture Letters, March 4, 1897, The Morgan
Library and Museum, New York, www.
themorgan.org/collections/works/potter/
letter/37.

5 March: Fidel Castro, 'Castro at Funeral for
Victims of Mar. 4 Ship Explosion: 03/07/1960',
Latin American Network Information Center,
Castro Speech Data Base, http://lanic.utexas.
edu/project/castro/db/1960/19600307-1.html.

6 March: Franklin D. Roosevelt, 'Our
Documents: Franklin Roosevelt's Annual
Address to Congress – the "Four Freedoms"',
FDR Presidential Library & Museum,
New York, http://docs.fdrlibrary.marist.edu/
od4frees.html.

7 March: António Guterres, quoted in United Nations press release, 6 March 2017, www.un.org/press/en/2017/sgsm18457.doc.htm.

8 March: Plaque inscription, quoted in J. Warburton, J. Whitelaw and Robert Walsh, *History of the City of Dublin from the Earliest Accounts to the Present Time*, vol. II, London: T. Cadell and W. Davies, 1818.

9 March: Abraham Lincoln, 'Address to the Wisconsin State Agricultural Society in Milwaukee, Wisconsin, September 30, 1859', *Transactions of the Wisconsin State Agricultural Society, 1858–1859*.

10 March: Mary Richardson, 'Miss Richardson's Statement', quoted in *The Times*, 11 March 1914.

11 March: Charlotte Brontë, quoted in Clement K. Shorter, *Charlotte Brontë and her Circle*, London: Hodder & Stoughton, 1896.

12 March: Cigarette packet sketch, *see* https://ukcomics.fandom.com/wiki/Ian_Chisholm_(1921-1981).

13 March: Monument inscription. Author's translation.

14 March: Queen Elizabeth I, quoted in Hayward Townshend's parliamentary journal for 1601.

15 March: National Gallery of Art, Washington DC, press release, 'Wyeth's Helga Pictures on View at National Gallery', 3 February 1987, www.nga.gov/content/dam/ngaweb/research/gallery-archives/PressReleases/1989-1980/1987/14A11_44670_19870424.pdf.

16 March: Elías García Martínez, quoted in Rocío Huerta, 'Restauradores profesionales tratarán de recuperar el eccehomo', *El País*, 22 August 2012. Author's translation.

17 March: Samuel Pepys, *The Diary of Samuel Pepys*, ed. Henry B. Wheatley, London: George Bell & Sons, 1893, www.pepysdiary.com/diary/1666/03/17/.

18 March: Natalia Sidlina interview, Mark Brown, 'First Picture Drawn in Space to Appear in Cosmonauts Show in London', *Guardian*, 31 August 2015. Courtesy of Guardian News & Media Ltd.

19 March: Louis Sullivan, quoted in Thomas E. Tallmadge, 'The Expiatory Temple of the Holy Family', *Western Architect*, XXXI, 1922.

George Orwell, *Homage to Catalonia*, London: Secker & Warburg, 1938.

20 March: Joseph Goebbels, *Tagebücher, Band 3: 1935–1939*, ed. Ralf Georg Reuth, Munich: Piper, 1992. Author's translation.

21 March: Empress Maria Feodorovna, reported in a letter to her sister Queen Alexandra, 1914, quoted in Geza von Habsburg, *Fabergé: Fantasies & Treasures*, London: Aurum Press, 1996.

22 March: Arnold Wright and Oskar Frankfurter, quoted in Wright (ed.), *Twentieth Century Impressions of Siam*, London: Lloyds Greater Britain Pub. Co., 1908.

23 March: Michelangelo, *Le Lettere di Michelangelo Buonarroti*, ed. Gaetano Milanesi, Florence: Le Monnier, 1875. Author's translation.

Giorgio Vasari, *Lives of the Most Eminent Painters, Sculptors & Architects*, trans. Gaston De Vere, London: Philip Lee Warner, 1915.

24 March: Havelock Ellis, *The Dance of Life*, Boston and New York: Houghton Mifflin Company, 1923.

25 March: Thomas Byerley, quoted in Sholto Percy and Reuben Percy, *The Percy Anecdotes*, London: J. Cumberland, 1826.

26 March: Amedeo Modigliani, quoted in Maurizio Bellandi, 'Modigliano e Livorno', Modigliani 1909, www.modigliani1909.com/modigliani_and_Livorno.html. Author's translation.

27 March: Charles Marion Russell letter, *see* Nicole Todd, 'Western Treasures: Illustrated Letters from Charles M. Russell', Buffalo Bill Center of the West, 27 October 2016, https://centerofthewest.org/2016/10/27/36195. Author's transcription.

28 March: Mary Berry, quoted in Sarah Burnage and Jason Edwards (eds), *The British School of Sculpture, c. 1760–1832*, Abingdon: Routledge, 2017.

29 March: Sima Qian, *Shiji*, quoted at Wikipedia, uncredited trans., https://en.wikipedia.org/wiki/Terracotta_Army Note 3. Original text at Chinese Text Project, https://ctext.org/pre-qin-and-han?filter=d270.

30 March: Jacques-Émile Blanche, *Correspondance Jacques-Émile Blanche-Maurice Denis (1901–1939)*, ed. Georges-Paul Collet, Geneva: Droz, 1989. Author's translation.

31 March: Gustave Eiffel, *Le Temps* newspaper, 14 February 1887. Author's translation.

April

1 April: *Saturday Evening Post*, 3 April 1943, quoted in Joyce K. Schiller, 'April Fool', Essays on Illustration, Rockwell Center for American Visual Studies, 1 April 2010, www.rockwell-center.org/essays-illustration/april-fool/.
2 April: Erik Satie, 'Bonjour Biqui, Bonjour!', 1893.
3 April: *Manchester Evening News*, 4 April 1913.
4 April: Charles Sanders Peirce, quoted in The Peirce Edition Project (ed.), *The Essential Peirce: Selected Philosophical Writings, Volume 2 (1893–1913)*, Bloomington, IN: Indiana University Press, 1998.
5 April: Sir Arthur Evans: report, in *The Annual of the British School at Athens*, London: Macmillan & Co, 1901; letter to his father, quoted in Leonard Cottrell, *The Bull of Minos*, New York: Rhinehart, 1958.
6 April: James Russel and Rev. Richard Russel, quoted in Jason Kelly, 'Letters from a Young Painter Abroad: James Russel in Rome, 1740–1763', in *The Annual Volume of the Walpole Society*, vol. 74, 2012.
7 April: Book of Funerals for the Parish of Santo Tomé, 1601–1614 [pub. in 1876], quoted in Albert F. Calvert and Catherine Gasquoine-Hartley, *El Greco: An Account of His Life and Works*, London: J. Lane, 1909.
8 April: Paul Carus, *The Venus of Milo: An Archeological Study of the Goddess of Womanhood*, Chicago and London: The Open House Publishing Company, 1916.
9 April: Sir Anthony Pigott and Sir Roderic Lyne, quoted in *The Iraq Inquiry*, 2016, https://webarchive.nationalarchives.gov.uk/20160202221446/http://www.iraqinquiry.org.uk/media/39120/091204pigott.pdf. Contains public sector information licensed under the Open Government Licence v3.0.
10 April: Jacob Roggeveen, quoted in Bolton Glanvill Corney (ed. and trans.), *The Voyage of Captain Don Felipe González to Easter Island, 1770–1*, Cambridge, UK: The Hakluyt Society, 1908.

11 April: Frederic Remington, Remington's Journal [selected entries from a transcript of original journal], Frederic Remington Art Museum, https://fredericremington.org/journal-c1388.php.
12 April: Lucy Mercer Rutherfurd [attrib.].
13 April: William Kent, quoted in Carol Blackett-Ord, 'Letters from William Kent to Burrell Massingberd from the Continent, 1712–1719', in *The Annual Volume of the Walpole Society*, vol. 63, 2001.
14 April: Plutarch, *Plutarch's Lives*, vol. 4, trans. Bernadotte Perrin, Cambridge, MA and London: Loeb, 1916.
15 April: Louis Leroy, 'L'Exposition des impressionnistes', *Le Charivari*, 25 April 1874. Author's translation.
16 April: John Ruskin: *The Diaries of John Ruskin: 1848–1873*, ed. Joan Evans and John Howard Whitehouse, Oxford: Clarendon Press, 1958; description of Flüelen painting, Ruskin, *Notes by Mr Ruskin on His Collection of Drawings by the Late J. M. W. Turner*, London: The Fine Art Society, 1878.
17 April: William Wordsworth, quoted in *The Complete Poetical Works of William Wordsworth*, ed. John Morley, London: Macmillan & Co, 1888.
18 April: Angelica Kauffman, quoted in J. E. Hodgson and F. A. Eaton, *The Royal Academy and Its Members 1768–1830*, London: John Murray, 1905.
19 April: Tarsila do Amaral, quoted in Edward Lucie-Smith, *Latin American Art of the 20th Century*, London: Thames & Hudson, 2004.
20 April: Agencies in Mexico City, 'Frida Kahlo's Great-niece Calls for Barbie Doll to be Redesigned', *Guardian*, 9 March 2018. Courtesy of Guardian News & Media Ltd.
21 April: Adamnan, *Life of Saint Columba, Founder of Hy*, ed. William Reeves, Edinburgh: Edmonston and Douglas, 1874.
22 April: Private William Hay, quoted in 'April 1915. The Ypres Salient. Battle of St Julien', 1/4th Battalion Alexandra, Princess of Wales's Own Yorkshire Regiment, http://4thyorks.yellowgrey.com/wp-content/uploads/004Bn1915.html.
23 April: *The Times*, 28 January 1926, https://www.thetimes.co.uk/archive/article/1926-01-28/9/6.html.

24 April: Henry Angelo, *Reminiscences of Henry Angelo, With Memoirs of His Late Father and Friends*, London: Henry Colburn, 1828.
25 April: Notice, quoted in *The Exhibition of the Royal Academy, MDCCLXIX (1769): The First* [exhibition catalogue], London: William Bunce, 1769.
26 April: Hermann Göring, quoted in Nuremberg Trial Proceedings Vol. 9, Thursday, 14 March 1946, The Avalan Project, Lillian Goldman Law Library, https://avalon.law.yale.edu/imt/03-14-46.asp.
27 April: Inigo Jones, sketchbook: quoted in Christy Anderson, 'Words Fail Me: Architectural Experience Beyond Language', in Jean-Philippe Garric, Frédérique Lemerle and Yves Pauwels (eds), *Architecture et théorie. L'héritage de la Renaissance*, Paris: Publications de l'Institut national d'histoire de l'art, 2012; marginalia, quoted in Edward Chaney, *The Evolution of the Grand Tour: Anglo-Italian Cultural Relations Since the Renaissance*, Abingdon: Routledge, 2000.
28 April: Margaret Thatcher, reported in Hansard, HC Deb vol. 974, col. 402, 21 November 1979. Contains public sector information licensed under the Open Government Licence v3.0.
29 April: Graffiti on the Berlin Wall.
30 April: Marysia Lewandowska, *It's About Time* [installation catalogue], 2019, http://marysialewandowska.com/its-about-time-58th-venice-biennale/.

May

1 May: Queen Victoria, quoted in 'William Wyon', The Royal Mint Museum Journal, www.royalmintmuseum.org.uk/journal/people/william-wyon.
2 May: Marcel Proust, quoted in sale lot details for original letter, '100 Book, Manuscripts, Documents and Objects from the Pierre Leroy Collection', Sotheby's, 2007, www.sothebys.com/fr/auctions/ecatalogue/2007/100-books-manuscripts-documents-and-objects-from-the-pierre-leroy-collection-pf7025/lot.86.html. Author's translation.
3 May: Edmonia Lewis, Letter from Edmonia Lewis, Rome, to Maria Weston Chapman, Digital Commonwealth, Massachusetts Collections Online, www.digitalcommonwealth.org/search/commonwealth:7s75f449r.
4 May: General Eisenhower, Memorandum from General Dwight D. Eisenhower regarding preservation of historical monuments in Europe, May 26, 1944, Eisenhower Library, https://www.eisenhowerlibrary.gov/sites/default/files/research/online-documents/monuments-men/033-006.pdf.
5 May: Virginia Woolf, *To the Lighthouse*, London: Hogarth Press, 1927.
6 May: Text in George Cruikshank's *Sales by Auction!*, 1819.
7 May: Codex Gigas, National Library of Sweden, http://ds.kb.se/codex-gigas/eng/Long/texter/excorsism/Translation-of-the-conjurations/.
8 May: Benjamin Haydon, *Neglected Genius: The Diaries of Benjamin Robert Haydon, 1808–1846*, ed. John Jolliffe, London: Hutchinson, 1990.
9 May: Samuel Pepys, *The Diary of Samuel Pepys*, ed. Henry B. Wheatley, London: George Bell & Sons, 1893.
10 May: Treasury minute, quoted in *The Literary Chronicle for the Year 1824*, London: Davidson.
11 May: Monument inscription, National Capital Commission, Commissioners Park, Ottawa, Canada.
12 May: Albrecht Dürer, quoted in Sir William Martin Conway, *Literary Remains of Albrecht Durer*, trans. Lina Eckenstein, Cambridge, UK: Cambridge University Press, 1889.
13 May: John Ruskin, letters quoted in E. T. Cook, *The Life of John Ruskin*, London: George Allen, 1911.
14 May: Inscription on Volaire painting, see *The Eruption of Vesuvius*, 1771, Art Institute of Chicago, https://www.artic.edu/artworks/57996/the-eruption-of-vesuvius. Author's translation.
15 May: Josiah Wedgwood, quoted in Eliza Meteyard, *Life of Josiah Wedgwood*, vol. I, London: Hurst and Blackett, 1865.
16 May: Guillaume Apollinaire, quoted in Jean-Paul Clébert, *Dictionnaire du surréalisme*, Chamalières: A.T.P. & Le Seuil, 1996. Author's translation.

17 May: Desmond Morris, quoted in Andrew Todd, 'Ape Artists of the 1950s', *Frieze*, no. 99, 6 May 2006, www.frieze.com/article/ape-artists-1950s.

18 May: Review of *The Works of James Gillray, the Caricaturist, with the History of his Life and Times*, ed. Thomas Wright, in *The Quarterly Review*, vol. 136, London: John Murray, 1874.

19 May: Georg Hegel, *The Logic of Hegel: Translated from the Encyclopaedia of the Philosophical Sciences*, trans. William Wallace, Oxford: Clarendon Press, 1892.

20 May: John Callcott Horsley, quoted in Alison Smith, *The Victorian Nude: Sexuality, Morality and Art*, Manchester, UK: Manchester University Press, 1996.

21 May: Giorgio Vasari, *Lives of the Most Eminent Painters, Sculptors & Architects*, trans. Gaston De Vere, London: Philip Lee Warner, 1915.

22 May: James McNeill Whistler, quoted in Whistler, *The Gentle Art of Making Enemies*, New York: John W. Lovell Company, 1890.

23 May: Arnold Bennett, quoted in Dominic Lee, 'Agnew Galleries WAR Exhibition 100 Years Ago – 23rd May 1918', 22 May 2018 [blog post], www.sirwilliamorpen.com/agnew-galleries-war-exhibition-100-years-ago-23rd-may-1918/.

24 May: T. E. Lawrence, quoted in *Men in Print: Essays in Literary Criticism by T. E. Lawrence*, ed. Prof. A. W. Lawrence, Leominster: Golden Cockerel Press, 1940.

25 May: Antoine-Claire Thibaudeau, *Histoire Générale de Napoléon Bonaparte*, Paris: Ponthieu et Comp, 1828. Author's translation.

26 May: Peter Blake, quoted in Charlotte Higgins, 'Peter Blake: It Was 37 Years Ago Today – and Sgt Pepper Cover Has Still Failed to Pay', *Guardian*, 3 June 2004, www.theguardian.com/uk/2004/jun/03/guardianhayfestival2004.arts. Courtesy of Guardian News & Media Ltd.

27 May: Charles Darwin, Letter no. 1688, Darwin Correspondence Project, https://www.darwinproject.ac.uk/letter/DCP-LETT-1688.xml.

28 May: Rosie Broadley, quoted in National Portrait Gallery, London, press release, 28 May 2015, https://artdaily.cc/news/78900/National-Portrait-Gallery-unveils-new-sculpture-of-inventor-of-the-World-Wide-Web#.X1jtDtZ7kcg.

29 May: Giovanni Baglione, *Le vite de' pittori, scultori, architetti, ed intagliatori*, Rome: Nella Stamperia d'Andrea Fei, 1642. Author's translation.

30 May: The Prince of Wales, 'A Speech by HRH the Prince of Wales at the 150th Anniversary of the Royal Institute of British Architects (RIBA), Royal Gala Evening at Hampton Court Palace', 30 May 1984, www.princeofwales.gov.uk/speech/speech-hrh-prince-wales-150th-anniversary-royal-institute-british-architects-riba-royal-gala.

31 May: St Helens Council, *Consultation Draft Creative St. Helens, Arts Strategy 2011–2016*, 21 September 2011, http://moderngov.sthelens.gov.uk/mgConvert2PDF.aspx?ID=10808.

June

1 June: Alfred Stieglitz, quoted in Sarah Greenough (ed.), *My Faraway One: Selected Letters of Georgia O'Keeffe and Alfred Stieglitz*, New Haven and London: Yale University Press, 2011.

2 June: Edward Gibbon, *The History of the Decline and Fall of the Roman Empire*, London: Strahan & Cadell, 1776–89.

3 June: Nicolas Poussin, quoted in Jean Duchesne, *Museum of Painting and Sculpture*, vol. V, London and Paris: Audot, 1829.

4 June: Adolf Zeigler, quoted in Neil Levi, '"Judge for Yourselves!" – The "Degenerate Art" Exhibition as Political Spectacle', *October*, Summer 1998.

5 June: Mary Cassatt [attrib.].

6 June: Supreme Headquarters of the Allied Expeditionary Force, Communique No. 1, 6 June 1944.

7 June: William Shakespeare, *Hamlet*, in *Mr. William Shakespeare's Comedies, Histories, & Tragedies (First Folio)*, London: Edward Blount and William and Isaac Jaggard, 1623.

8 June: Alexander Pushkin, quoted in *Poems by Alexander Pushkin*, trans. Ivan Panin, Boston: Cupples and Hurd, 1888.

9 June: Paul Gauguin, *Noa Noa*, Paris: Éditions de la Plume, 1901. Author's translation.

10 June: Émile Zola, *Correspondance: Lettres de Jeunesse*, Paris: Bibliotheque Charpentier, 1907. Author's translation.

11 June: Rev. Scott Trimmer, quoted in Walter Thornbury, *Life of J. M. W. Turner*, London: Hurst and Blackett, 1862.

12 June: Dinner menu, 'The Story of Omega Workshops' [menu card], Tate, www.tate.org.uk/art/art-terms/o/omega-workshops/story-omega-workshops.

13 June: Charles Dodgson, 'Lewis Carroll' diary 4, 1862–1864, Add MS 54343, British Library, www.bl.uk/manuscripts/Viewer.aspx?ref=add_ms_54343_fs001r.

14 June: William Carr, *University College History*, London: F. E. Robinson & Company, 1902.

15 June: Eadweard Muybridge [attrib.].

16 June: James Joyce, *Ulysses*, Paris: Shakespeare and Company, 1922.

17 June: Vincent van Gogh, Letter No. 627. Leo Jansen, Hans Luijten, Nienke Bakker (eds.) (2009), *Vincent van Gogh - The Letters*. Version: January 2020. Amsterdam & The Hague: Van Gogh Museum & Huygens ING. http://vangoghletters.org/en/let627.

18 June: Vincent van Gogh, Letter No. 782. Leo Jansen, Hans Luijten, Nienke Bakker (eds.) (2009), *Vincent van Gogh - The Letters*. Version: January 2020. Amsterdam & The Hague: Van Gogh Museum & Huygens ING. http://vangoghletters.org/en/let782.

19 June: Honoré Daumier caption, *Looking at a Manet Painting*, in 'Sketches from the Salon', *Le Charivari*, 19 June 1865; *see* metmuseum.org/art/collection/search/754576. Author's translation.

20 June: List of media used by Robert Rauschenberg on *First time Painting*, www.moma.org/audio/playlist/40/651.

21 June: John Evelyn, *The Diary of John Eveyln*, ed. William Bray, London: Walter Dunne, 1901.

22 June: Anna Rügerin's colophon, in Eike of Repgow, *Sachsenspiegel: Landrecht*, 1484; *see* https://commons.wikimedia.org/wiki/File:Anna-Rugerin-Colophon-Sachsenspeigel-1484.jpg.

23 June: Adolf Hitler telegram, 23 August 1944, *see* http://www.choltitz.de/bilderseiten/redentexte/truemmerfeldbefehl.htm. Author's translation.

24 June: Christo and Jeanne Claude, 'Wrapped Reichstag, Berlin 1971–95', https://christojeanneclaude.net/mobile/projects?p=wrapped-reichstag.

25 June: William Hogarth caption, *The Rake's Progress*, Plate 8, 1735.

26 June: 'Aims and Programme', quoted in Collection Overview, Collection of Cabaret Theatre Club and Cave of the Golden Calf Printed Ephemera, Archives at Yale, https://archives.yale.edu/repositories/2/resources/5731.

27 June: James McNeill Whistler, Letter 5189, 27 June 1892, University of Glasgow Library, Archives & Special Collections.

28 June: Sir Henry Newbolt, *The Building of Britain: A Series of Historical Paintings in St. Stephens Hall, Westminster*, London: T. Nelson, 1927.

29 June: Alfred Gilbert, *The Life and Work of Alfred Gilbert: Easter Art Annual*, ed. Joseph Hatton, London: *The Art Journal* Office, 1903.

30 June: Frédéric-Auguste Bartholdi, *The Statue of Liberty Enlightening the World* [fundraising pamphlet], New York: North American Review, 1885.

July

1 July: Students' note, quoted in 'The Beatles – A Day in the Life: July 1, 1968', Beatles Fab Four blog, Fab Four Store, https://www.fabfourstore.com/the-beatles-50-years-ago-today-november-12-1965-friday.

2 July: J. B. Henry Savigny and Alexander Corréard, *Narrative of a Voyage to Senegal in 1816*, London: Henry Colburn, 1818.

3 July: David Cameron, reported in Hansard, House of Commons Debate, vol. X, col. 1616, 10 April 2013. Contains Parliamentary information licensed under the Open Parliament Licence v3.0.

4 July: Henry David Thoreau, *Walden; or, Life in the Woods*, Boston: Ticknor and Fields, 1854.

5 July: D. H. Lawrence, quoted in *Life with a Capital L, D. H. Lawrence: Essays Chosen* *and Introduced by Geoff Dyer*, ed. Geoff Dyer, London: Penguin, 2019.

6 July: Charles Dodgson, quoted in 'Introduction', Art Owned by Charles Dodgson, The Lewis Carroll Society, lewiscarrollsociety.org.uk/ art-owned-by-charles-dodgson/.

7 July: Carmody Groarke, 7 July Memorial project statement, https://www. carmodygroarke.com/7-july-memorial/.

8 July: Nick Kimberley, *Guardian*, 21 October 2005. Courtesy of Guardian News & Media Ltd.

9 July: Advertisement, in *Alexandria Gazette*, vol. XCIX, no. 10, 12 January 1898.

10 July: Sir Joshua Reynolds, quoted in Charles Leslie and Tom Taylor, *Life and Times of Sir Joshua Reynolds: With Notices of Some of His Contemporaries*, London: John Murray, 1865.

11 July: Benjamin Haydon, *Neglected Genius: The Diaries of Benjamin Robert Haydon, 1808-1846*, ed. John Jolliffe, London: Hutchinson, 1990.

12 July: Anthony van Dyck note and sketch, in Lionel Cust, *A Description of the Sketch-book by Sir Anthony Van Dyck, Used by Him in Italy, 1621-1627*, London: George Bell & Sons, 1902.

13 July: Admiralty letter, quoted in '225 Years Ago: April–June 1772', *Cook's Log*, vol. 20, no. 2 (1997), Captain Cook Society, https:// www.captaincooksociety.com/home/ detail/225-years-ago-april-june-1772.

14 July: Smart Lethieullier, appendix in Andrew Ducarel, *Anglo-Norman Antiquities Considered*, London: J. Spilsbury, 1767.

15 July: 'The Work of Florence Wyman Ivins: A Class Room Exhibition', *The Metropolitan Museum of Art Bulletin*, vol. 16, 1921 [author unknown].

16 July: Arshile Gorky, quoted in Hayden Herrera, *Arshile Gorky: His Life and Work*, London: Bloomsbury, 2003.

17 July: John James Audubon: letter to Alexander Hill, quoted in Hindman sale lot details for original letter, 8 October 2020 auction; diary entry, quoted in Maria Audubon, *Audubon and his Journals*, New York: Charles Scribner's Sons, 1897.

18 July: Adolf Hitler, 'Hitler's Radio Speech about Degenerate Art', The Art and Popular Culture Encyclopedia, http:// artandpopularculture.com/Hitler%27s_radio_ speech_about_degenerate_art. Author's translation.

19 July: Apollo 11 transcript, quoted in NASA, 'Apollo 11 Spacecraft Commentary: July 16–24, 1969', Manned Spacecraft Center, Houston, at https://history.nasa.gov/alsj/ a11/a11transcript_pao.pdf.

20 July: Robert Smithson, 'A Provisional Theory of Nonsites', in *Robert Smithson: The Collected Writings*, ed. Jack Flam, Berkeley, CA: University of California Press, 1996.

21 July: Sir Thomas Browne, *Hydriotaphia*, London: Henry Brome, 1658.

22 July: Mark Twain, *A Tramp Abroad*, Hartford: American Publishing Company, 1880.

23 July: Judges' comment, quoted in 'The Man Booker Prize 2018 Longlist Announced', 23 July 2018, The Booker Prizes, https:// thebookerprizes.com/fiction/news/ man-booker-prize-2018-longlist-announced.

24 July: Field Marshal Lord Plumer, quoted in Gen. Sir Charles Harington, *Plumer of Messines*, London: John Murray, 1935.

25 July: Inventory extracts, quoted in J ohn Burnet, *Rembrandt and his Works*, London: David Bogue, 1849. Roger de Piles, *The Art of Painting and the Lives of the Painters*, trans. John Savage, London: Charles Marsh, 1706.

26 July: *Isle of Wight Observer*, 29 August 1874, quoted in 'Ryde Pier', Historic Ryde Society, http://historicrydesociety.com/history/ royal-victoria-arcade/ryde-pier/.

27 July: Martin Creed interview, Charlotte Higgins, 'Martin Creed: I Don't Know What Art Is', *Guardian*, 30 May 2012. Courtesy of Guardian News & Media Ltd.

28 July: Ohio State University, press release, 30 January 2017, https://news.osu.edu/ roy-lichtenstein-foundation- announces-the-creation-of-two-endowed- professorships-at-the-ohio-state- university/.

29 July: William Allingham, quoted in Arthur St John Adcock, *Famous Houses and Literary Shrines of London*, London: J. M. Dent & Sons, 1912.

30 July: Anna Klumpke, *Rosa Bonheur: Sa Vie Son Oeuvre*, Paris: Flammarion, 1908. Author's translation.

31 July: John Draper, 'On the Process of Daguerreotype, and Its Application to Taking Portraits from the Life', *The London, Edinburgh and Dublin Philosophical Magazine and Journal of Science*, vol. 17, no. 109, September 1840.

August

1 August: For a replica of the plaque, *see* https://airandspace.si.edu/collection-objects/plaque-memorial-apollo-15-fallen-astronauts-and-cosmonauts-reproduction.
2 August: Resolution, 23 April 1932 [transcript], History Faculty, Moscow State University, http://www.hist.msu.ru/ER/Etext/USSR/1932.htm. Author's translation.
3 August: Jim Bolger, 'Sky Tower Topping Off', 18 April 1997 [speech transcript], Beehive.govt.nz [New Zealand government website], https://www.beehive.govt.nz/speech/sky-tower-topping.
4 August: G. K. Chesterton, *The Everlasting Man*, London: Hodder & Stoughton, 1925.
5 August: Albrecht Dürer, *Dream Vision* [watercolour with text], *see* https://commons.wikimedia.org/wiki/File:Traumgesicht,_Albrecht_D%C3%BCrer_dokumentiert_einen_seiner_Albtr%C3%A4ume_(1525).jpg. Author's translation.
6 August: Pliny the Younger, *The Letters of the Younger Pliny, Book 4*, trans. John Benjamin Firth, London: W. Scott, 1900.
7 August: Sir Edward Sullivan, *The Book of Kells*, London: The Studio Ltd, 1920.
8 August: UK Government Department for Digital, Culture, Media & Sport and John Penrose, MP, '"And in the end…": the Abbey Road zebra crossing is "listed" by Tourism and Heritage Minister John Penrose', press release, 22 December 2010, www.gov.uk/government/news/and-in-the-end-the-abbey-road-zebra-crossing-is-listed-by-tourism-and-heritage-minister-john-penrose. Contains public sector information licensed under the Open Government Licence v3.0.
9 August: Giorgio Vasari, *Lives of the Most Eminent Painters, Sculptors & Architects*, trans. Gaston De Vere, London: Philip Lee Warner, 1915.
10 August: Paul Cézanne, *Cézanne: Correspondance*, ed. John Rewald, Paris: Éditions Grasset, 1978. Author's translation.
11 August: James McNeill Whistler, Letter 6606, 24 January 1892, University of Glasgow Library, Archives & Special Collections.
12 August: Howard Carter, Howard Carter's Excavation Diaries (Transcripts and Scans), 4th Season, September 28th 1925 to May 21st 1926, The Griffith Institute, University of Oxford, http://www.griffith.ox.ac.uk/discoveringTut/journals-and-diaries/season-4/journal.html. © The Griffith Institute, University of Oxford.
13 August: Dante Alighieri, *The Divine Comedy of Dante Alighieri*, trans. Henry Wadsworth Longfellow, Leipzig: Berhard Tauchnitz, 1867.
14 August: News Ticker, One Times Square, 14 August 1945.
15 August: Text on original Woodstock poster, author unknown, 1969.
16 August: Contract, quoted in Robert W. Carden (ed. and trans.), *Michelangelo: A Record of His Life as Told in His Own Letters and Papers*, London: Constable & Co, 1913.
17 August: Pliny the Elder, *The Natural History of Pliny, Book 35*, trans. John Bostock and Henry Riley, London: Henry G. Bohn, 1857.
18 August: Claude Monet letter, *see* André Buffet and Jean-Michel Peers, 'Les Jardins de Claude Monet', J. M. Peers de Nieuwburgh, Giverny Autrefois, https://www.pbase.com/image/122195798. Author's translation.
19 August: Memorial plaque inscription. Author's translation.
20 August: Käthe Kollwitz, quoted in Otto Nagel, *Käthe Kollwitz*, Dresden: Verlag der Kunst, 1971. Author's translation.
21 August: *New York Times*, 24 August 1911.
22 August: Piql press release, 'Edvard Munch's "Scream" stored in Arctic World Archive', 22 February 2018, https://www.piql.com/news/edvard-munchs-scream-stored-in-arctic-world-archive/.
23 August: Winston Churchill [attrib.].
24 August: Eugène Delacroix, *Journal de Eugène Delacroix*, Paris: Librairie Plon, 1893. Author's translation.
25 August: Richard Harding Davis, *New York Tribune*, 31 August 1914, quoted in John Avlon, Jesse Angelo and Errol Louis (eds), *Deadline*

Artists: Scandals, Tragedies & Triumphs, New York: Overview Press, 2012.

26 August: Ambroise Vollard, *La Vie & L'Oeuvre de Pierre-Auguste Renoir*, Paris: Chez Ambroise Vollard, 1919. Author's translation.

27 August: Albrecht Dürer, quoted in Moritz Thausing, *Albert Dürer: His Life and Works*, London: John Murray, 1882.

28 August: Fons Hickmann, artistic statement for *Bad News* newspaper, 2018, https://fonshickmann.com/work/wb_bad_news_newspaper/#.

29 August: Franklin D. Roosevelt, 'Annual Message to Congress', The American Presidency Project, https://www.presidency.ucsb.edu/documents/annual-message-congress-3. © The American Presidency Project.

30 August: Dante Gabriel Rossetti, quoted in William Michael Rossetti (ed.), *Dante Gabriel Rossetti: His Family Letters*, vol. 2, London: Ellis and Elvey, 1895.

31 August: Thomas Cobden-Sanderson, *The Journals of Thomas James Cobden-Sanderson 1879–1922*, London: Richard Cobden-Sanderson, 1926.

September

1 September: Eric Ravilious, quoted in Andy Williams (dir.), *Letters Home: Eric Ravilious*, 2019 [short film], YouTube (uploaded 11 May 2019), https://www.youtube.com/watch?v=HiTwUargweo.

2 September: Exhibition brochure, *The Imagery of Chess*, New York, 1944.

3 September: William Taswell, 'Autobiography and Anecdotes by William Taswell', ed. George Percy Elliott, in *The Camden Miscellany*, vol. 2, London: Camden Society, 1853.

4 September: William Hutton, *An History of Birmingham*, Birmingham: Wrightson & Webb, 1781.

5 September: *The Times*, 3 January 1915.

6 September: William Makepeace Thackeray, *Ballads and Miscellanies*, London: Smith Elder, 1899.

7 September: Guillaume Apollinaire, quoted in *Alcools*, Paris: Mercure de France, 1913. Author's translation.

8 September: Nicolas Poussin, quoted in Anthony Blunt (ed.), *Nicolas Poussin: Lettres et propos sur l'art*, Paris: Hermann, 1994. Author's translation.

9 September: Vincent van Gogh, Letter No. 677. Leo Jansen, Hans Luijten, Nienke Bakker (eds.) (2009), *Vincent van Gogh - The Letters*. Version: January 2020. Amsterdam & The Hague: Van Gogh Museum & Huygens ING. http://vangoghletters.org/en/let677.

10 September: Slogan text, quoted in 'Guernica: Testimony of War – The Spanish Pavilion', *Treasures of the World*, Public Broadcasting Service (PBS), www.pbs.org/treasuresoftheworld/guernica/glevel_1/3_pavilion.html.

11 September: Virgil, quoted in *The Works of Virgil*, trans. John Dryden, London: John Dryden and Jacob Tonson, 1697.

12 September: Pablo Picasso [attrib.].

13 September: John Addington Symonds, *The Life of Michelangelo Buonarroti*, London: J. C. Nimmo, 1893.

14 September: Gerard Baldwin Brown, *Rembrandt: A Study of His Life and Work*, London: Duckworth and Co, 1907.

15 September: Edmund Burke, *A Philosophical Enquiry into the Origin of Our Ideas of the Sublime and Beautiful*, London: R. and J. Dodsley, 1757.

16 September: Jane Austen, quoted in Sarah Chauncey Woolsey (ed.), *The Letters of Jane Austen: Selected from the Compilation of her Great Nephew, Edward, Lord Bradbourne*, Boston: Little, Brown and Company, 1908.

17 September: News report, 'She Wore Men's Clothes: On Walking Tour with Husband, Mrs Greve Explains – Police Let Couple Go', *New York Times*, 17 September 1910.

18 September: Advert, *Brighton Guardian*, 10 November 1841.

19 September: Scott Fahlman post, quoted in Fahlman, '"Joke" conversation in which the:-) was invented', Carnegie Mellon University School of Computer Science, 2002, www.cs.cmu.edu/~sef/Orig-Smiley.htm.

20 September: David Roberts, quoted in sale lot details for original letter, 13 November 2012, www.bonhams.com/auctions/20139/lot/45/.

21 September: *Radio Times*,
18 September 1980. © Immediate Media Co.
22 September: Violet Melnotte Wyatt, quoted
in Alexia Lazou, 'Opening of Duke of York's
Cinema, 1910', Royal Pavilion and Museums
Trust, Brighton & Hove, 22 September 2020,
https://closelook.brightonmuseums.org/tag/
mf000134.
Slogan, quoted in Anna Hayward,
'A Brief History', Duke of York's
Picturehouse 100 Project, Duke of York's
Cinema, http://dukeofyorkscinema.
co.uk/2010/06/a-brief-history/.
23 September: Joseph Farington, *The
Farington Diary, 1793–1821*, London:
Hutchinson, 1922.
24 September: Piet Mondrian, quoted
in Sophie Bowness, 'Mondrian in London:
Letters to Ben Nicholson and Barbara
Hepworth', *The Burlington Magazine*,
vol. 132, no. 1052, November 1990. Author's
translation.
25 September: UK Parliament, Speaker's
Advisory Committee for Works of
Art, 'Parliamentary Art Collection and
Links to the Transatlantic Slave Trade',
25 September 2020, https://www.
parliament.uk/globalassets/documents/
art/parliamentary-art-collection-and-links
-to-the-transatlantic-slave-trade-09.2020-
291kb-1.pdf. Contains Parliamentary
information licensed under the Open
Parliament Licence v3.0.
26 September: David Zwirner gallery press
release, 2013, https://www.davidzwirner.com/
exhibitions/gazing-ball/press-release.
27 September: Military Cross citation,
quoted in *Supplement to the Edinburgh
Gazette*, 20 June 1917, https://www.thegazette.
co.uk/Edinburgh/issue/13105/page/
1169.
28 September: Leonardo da Vinci, *The
Notebooks of Leonardo Da Vinci*, trans. Jean
Paul Richter, London: S. Low, Marston,
Searle & Rivington, 1880.
29 September: Hebrews 13:2, English
Standard Version.
30 September: Thomas Walker Arnold,
*Painting in Islam: A Study of the Place of Pictorial
Art in Muslim Culture*, Oxford: Clarendon Press,
1928.

October

1 October: Walter Crane, quoted in Arts &
Crafts Exhibition Society, *Catalogue of the First
Exhibition*, London: The New Gallery, 1888.
2 October: Beatrix Potter, quoted in 'Peter
Rabbit: The Tale of "The Tale"', Victoria and
Albert Museum, www.vam.ac.uk/articles/
peter-rabbit-the-tale-of-the-tale.
3 October: Theodore Roosevelt, quoted
in Rebecca Onion, 'In a Letter to His Son,
Teddy Roosevelt's Grinning Self-Portrait',
29 May 2013, The Vault [blog], *Slate*
[online magazine], https://slate.com/
human-interest/2013/05/teddy-roosevelt-
humorous-self-portrait-included-in-a-letter-
to-his-son-quentin.html. Original letter held
by the Gilder Lehrman Institute of American
History.
4 October: Franklin D. Roosevelt, quoted in
'Franklin D. Roosevelt', Mount Rushmore,
National Park Service, 7 April 2020, https://
www.nps.gov/moru/learn/historyculture/
franklin-d-roosevelt.htm.
5 October: Banksy, quoted in banksyfilm,
*Shredding the Girl and Balloon – The Director's
half cut* [video], YouTube (uploaded
17 October 2018), www.youtube.com/
watch?v=vxkwRNIZgdY.
6 October: Leonardo da Vinci, quoted in
The Notebooks of Leonardo da Vinci, trans.
Jean Paul Richter, London: S. Low, Marston,
Searle & Rivington, 1880.
7 October: Michelangelo, quoted in Robert
W. Carden (ed. and trans.), *Michelangelo:
A Record of His Life as Told in His Own Letters
and Papers*, London: Constable & Co, 1913.
8 October: Frédéric-Auguste Bartholdi,
sale lot details for the invitation and letter,
Raab Collection, https://www.raabcollection.
com/foreign-figures-autographs/
bartholdi-invitation.
9 October: *Hudson Register*, Hudson, NY,
10 October 1941.
10 October: *America* tagline, 1924; *see*
https://www.imdb.com/title/tt0014672/
taglines?ref_=tt_stry_tg.
11 October: National AIDS Memorial mission
statement, quoted in 'Our Focus', National
Aids Memorial, www.aidsmemorial.org/
the-memorial.

12 October: Arnold Bon, in Dirk van Bleyswijck, *Beschryvinge der stad Delft*, Delft: Arnold Bon, 1667. Author's translation.

13 October: Bible verses, King James Version.

14 October: *Aberdeen Journal*, 9 December 1926.

15 October: Grace Bedell, quoted in *The Collected Works of Abraham Lincoln*, ed. Roy P. Basler et al., Abraham Lincoln Association, 1953.
George P. A. Healy, *Reminiscences of a Portrait Painter*, Chicago: A. C. McClurg and Co., 1894.

16 October: Charles Robert Leslie, *Memoirs of the Life of John Constable*, London: James Carpenter, 1843.

17 October: Reported comment, quoted in Rhodri Marsden, '"Le Bateau", by Henri Matisse', *Independent*, 16 October 2015, https://www.independent.co.uk/ arts-entertainment/art/features/ le-bateau-henri-matisse-rhodri-marsden- s-interesting-objects-a6691981.html.

18 October: Robert the Monk's account of Pope Urban II's speech, quoted in Dana Munro (ed.), *Urban and the Crusaders*, Philadelphia: Dept. of History of the University of Pennsylvania, 1901.

19 October: Eunice Tietjens and Henry Ossawa Tanner, quoted in Naurice Frank Woods, Jr, *Henry Ossawa Tanner: Art, Faith, Race, and Legacy*, Abingdon: Routledge, 2018.

20 October: Press release, quoted in Titia Hulst (ed.), *A History of the Western Art Market: A Sourcebook of Writings on Artists, Dealers, and Markets*, Berkeley, CA: University of California Press, 2017.

21 October: Paula Modersohn-Becker: letter to her parents, quoted in Modersohn-Becker, *Briefe und Tagebuchblätter*, Berlin: Kurt Wolff Verlag, 1920. Author's translation; letter to her aunt, quoted in Modersohn-Becker, *The Letters and Journals*, ed. Arthur S. Wensinger (trans.), Carole Clew Hoey (trans.), Günter Busch and Liselotte von Reinken, Illinois: Northwestern University Press, 1998.

22 October: George Stanley, letter from G. F. G. Stanley, 1964, Library and Archives Canada/Alan B. Beddoe fonds/ e010964554–e010964557. © Government of Canada. Reproduced with the permission of Library and Archives Canada (2020).

23 October: Jervis McEntee: 23 October diary entry, 'Jervis McEntee Diaries', Smithsonian Archives of American Art, https://www. aaa.si.edu/collection-features/jervis- mcentee-diaries/diary-entry?date=18841023; second diary entry, quoted in George Sheldon, *American Painters: With Eighty-Three Examples of Their Work Engraved on Wood*, New York: D. Appleton & Co, 1879.

24 October: *Sydney Morning Herald*, 29 December 1915.

25 October: *Edmond de Belamy* auction details, Lot 363, Auction 16388, Prints & Multiples, Christie's, New York, 23–25 October 2018,www.christies.com/ lotfinder/Lot/edmond-de-belamy-from- la-famille-6166184-details.aspx.

26 October: Henry of Huntingdon, *Historia Anglorum*, London: Henry G. Bohn, 1853.

27 October: Egon Schiele, 139, Gedicht von Egon Schiele: Ein Selbstbild [poem document], Egon Schiele Autograph Database, http://www.schiele-dokumentation.at/objekt. php?id=139. Author's translation.

28 October: Édouard Manet, *Correspondance du siège de Paris et de la Commune 1870–1871*, ed. Samuel Rodary, Paris: L'Echoppe, 2014. Author's translation.

29 October: Caius Julius Caesar, *De Bello Gallico, Book VII*, trans. William MacDevitt, London: Everyman, 1915.

30 October: Abstract, quoted in Bernardo Palacios, Alfonso Rosario, Monica M. Wilhelmus, Sandra Zetina and Roberto Zenit, 'Pollock Avoided Hydrodynamic Instabilities to Paint with His Dripping Technique', *PLOS ONE*, 30 October 2019. © 2019 Palacios et al. under Creative Commons Attribution 4.0 International Public License.

31 October: Narendra Modi, quoted in Prime Minister's Office press release, 31 October 2018, Press Information Bureau Government of India, https://pib.gov.in/ PressReleasePage.aspx?PRID=1551402.

November

1 November: Giorgio Vasari, *Lives of the Most Eminent Painters, Sculptors & Architects*, trans.

Gaston De Vere, London: Philip Lee Warner, 1915.

2 November: Gerard Baldwin Brown, *Rembrandt: A Study of His Life and Work*, London: Duckworth and Co, 1907.

3 November: Vladimir Lenin, 'The Slogans and Organisation of Social-Democratic Work Inside and Outside the Duma', quoted in *Lenin Collected Works*, vol. 17, trans. Dora Cox, Moscow: Progress Publishers, 1974; *see* Marxists Internet Archive, https://www.marxists.org/archive/lenin/works/1911/dec/08.htm.

4 November: Giovanni Villani, quoted in Philip H. Wicksteed (ed.) and Rose E. Selfe (trans.), *Villani's Chronicle Being Selections from the First Nine Books of the Croniche Fiorentine of Giovanni Villani*, London: Archibald Constable & Co, 1906.

5 November: Benjamin Harris, *Domestick Intelligence*, no. 39, 18 November 1679, quoted in Brian Pugh, *Bonfire Night in Lewes*, London: MX Publishing, 2011.

6 November: Samuel Redgrave, *A Dictionary of Artists of the English School*, London: George Bell & Sons, 1878.

7 November: WAAC brief, quoted in 'The Secret Purpose of the War Artists Advisory Committee', Imperial War Museums, https://www.iwm.org.uk/history/the-secret-purpose-of-the-war-artists-advisory-committee.

8 November: Camille Claudel, quoted in Anne Rivière, *La Correspondance de Camille Claudel*, Angers: Musées d'Angers, 2015, https://en.calameo.com/read/00052689926911b4ffdbb. Author's translation.

9 November: Nazi letter regulations, *see* Old Letter Cover from the Natzweiler-Struthof Concentration Camp, 1944, Wikipedia, https://de.wikipedia.org/wiki/Datei:KZ_Natzweiler_H%C3%A4ftlingsbrief.JPG. Author's translation.

10 November: Robert Bridges, 'Septuagesima' quoted in *Poetical Works of Robert Bridges: Volume II*, London: Smith, Elder & Co, 1899, on *Pinner, via Bakerloo* [poster] by Nancy Smith, Underground Electric Railways Company Ltd, 1916, https://www.ltmuseum.co.uk/collections/collections-online/posters/item/1983-4-725.

11 November: Charlotte Mew poem, *Westminster Gazette*, 7 September 1919; *see* Poetry Foundation, https://www.poetryfoundation.org/poems/57272/the-cenotaph-56d23a9c7145a.

12 November: Buzz Aldrin, quoted in NASA, Gemini XII transcripts, Manned Spacecraft Center, Houston, https://historycollection.jsc.nasa.gov/JSCHistoryPortal/history/mission_trans/GT12_TEC.PDF. © NASA.

13 November: Louis Leroy, 'L'Exposition des impressionnistes', *Le Charivari*, 25 April 1874. Author's translation.

14 November: Mahatma Gandhi, Mathma [*sic*] Gandhi Address to WILPF Meeting in Geneva in 1931 [transcript], Women's International League for Peace and Freedom, https://www.peacewomen.org/content/mathma-gandhi-address-wilpf-meeting-geneva-1931.

15 November: Margaret Thatcher, reported in Hansard, HC Deb, vol 973, col 680W, 15 November 1979, https://api.parliament.uk/historic-hansard/written-answers/1979/nov/15/security. Contains Parliamentary information licensed under the Open Parliament Licence v3.0.

16 November: UK Treasure Act, 1996, https://www.legislation.gov.uk/ukpga/1996/24/section/1. Contains public sector information licensed under the Open Government Licence v3.0.

17 November: Oswald Wrigley speech, *Bury Guardian*, 29 April 1899, quoted in 'Bury Art Gallery and Public Library: Laying of the Foundation Stone April 1899', Bury Archives & Local History blog, 25 April 2019, https://buryculture.wordpress.com/2019/04/25/bury-art-gallery-and-public-library-laying-of-the-foundation-stone-april-1899/.

18 November: Raja Raja Varma, *The Diary of C. Raja Raja Varma, Brother of Raja Ravi Varma*, ed. Erwin Neumayer and Christine Schelberger, New Delhi: Oxford University Press, 2004.

19 November: Adrian Searle, *Guardian*, 12 November 2002. Courtesy of Guardian News & Media Ltd.

20 November: Georgia O'Keeffe, quoted in *Exhibition of Oils and Pastels* [exhibition catalogue], New York: An American Place, 1939. Copyright Georgia O'Keefe Museum.

21 November: Charles Dawson, quoted in Dawson and Arthur Smith Woodward, 'On the Discovery of a Palaeolithic Human Skull and Mandible in a Flint-bearing Gravel Overlying the Wealden (Hastings Beds) at Piltdown, Fletching (Sussex)', *Quarterly Journal of the Geological Society*, 1 March 1913, https://jgs.lyellcollection.org/content/69/1-4/117.

22 November: Eric Carle, quoted in The Eric Carle Museum of Picture Book Art 10th Anniversary press release, 17 October 2012. © 2020 The Eric Carle Museum of Picture Book Art.

23 November: UK Parliament, Early Day Motion, 'Rachel Whiteread's Sculpture at Grove Road, Bow', 25 November 1993, https://edm.parliament.uk/early-day-motion/10091. Contains Parliamentary information licensed under the Open Parliament Licence v3.0.

24 November: Jack Ruby, quoted in *Hearings Before the President's Commission on the Assassination of President Kennedy*, vol. V, Washington DC: United States Government Printing Office, 1964.

25 November: John Ruskin pamphlet, quoted in *The Works of John Ruskin*, ed. E. T. Cook and Alexander Wedderburn, London: George Allen, 1907.
Trial transcript, quoted in James McNeill Whistler, *The Gentle Art of Making Enemies*, New York: John W. Lovell Company, 1890.

26 November: Pontcysyllte Aqueduct inauguration plaque inscription.

27 November: Sir John Tenniel, *The Tempter*, *Punch* magazine, 27 November 1886; *see* https://www.metmuseum.org/art/collection/search/685296.

28 November: Alexander Gilchrist, *Life of William Blake*, London: Macmillan & Co, 1863.

29 November: Dr Sue Jones, quoted in 'Liverpool Cathedral Welcomes the Knife Angel', Liverpool Cathedral press release, 27 November 2018, https://www.liverpoolcathedral.org.uk/43/section.aspx/37/liverpool_cathedral_welcomes_the_knife_angel_27_11_2018.

30 November: Prince Albert, quoted in Theodore Martin, *The Life of His Royal Highness the Prince Consort*, vol. 2, New York: D. Appleton & Co, 1877. Winston Churchill [attrib.].

December

1 December: John Galsworthy, 'Vague Thoughts on Art', *Fortnightly Review*, February 1912.

2 December: Sarah Crompton, 'The Quiet Brilliance of Magnum Photographer Inge Morath', *Observer*, 23 November 2018. Courtesy of Guardian News & Media Ltd.

3 December: Vladimir Lenin, quoted in Clara Zetkin, *Reminiscences of Lenin*, New York: International Publishers, 1934.

4 December: Council of Trent decree, quoted in J. Waterworth (ed. and trans.), *The Canons and Decrees of the Sacred and Ecumenical Council of Trent*, London: C. Dolman, 1848.

5 December: Robert Henderson Croll, quoted in *Albert Namatjira: Central Australian Water Colours, 1938* [exhibition catalogue], Melbourne: Fine Art Society Gallery, 1938.

6 December: President Macky Sall, quoted in Aaron Ross, 'Senegal Opens New Art Museum Honoring Black Civilization', Reuters, 7 December 2018, https://www.reuters.com/article/us-africa-art/senegal-opens-new-art-museum-honoring-black-civilization-idUSKBN1O61JT.

7 December: Galerie Perrotin, Instagram post, 8 December 2019, https://www.instagram.com/p/B50RWWHlzRl/.

8 December: European Union Publications Office, 'Annex 1: Graphics Guide to the European Emblem: Council of Europe, European Commission', in *Europa Inter-institutional Style Guide*, updated August 2019, https://publications.europa.eu/code/en/en-5000100.htm.

9 December: Marguerite MacKellar Mitchell review, *Horn Book Magazine*, 9, no. 1, February 1933, quoted in 'Babar', Children's Literature Review, *Encyclopedia.com*, 12 January 2021, https://www.encyclopedia.com/people/history/south-asian-history-biographies/babar.

10 December: Dr William Musgrave, quoted in John Earle, *The Alfred Jewel: An Historical Essay*, Oxford: Clarendon Press, 1901.

11 December: Adam Brumm, quoted in Carley Rosengreen, 'Indonesian Cave Art Overturns Thinking on the Roots of Human Spirituality', Griffith University press release, 12 December 2019, https://news.griffith.edu.au/2019/12/12/indonesian-cave-art-overturns-thinking-on-the-roots-of-human-spirituality/.

12 December: Toku Shimomura, quoted in Smithsonian American Art Museum interview with Roger Shimomura, February 2012, https://s3.amazonaws.com/assets.saam.media/files/collections/search/artwork/researchNotes/1991.171.pdf via https://americanart.si.edu/artwork/diary-december-12-1941-32436. © Roger Shimomura.

13 December: Peter the Great [attrib.], quoted in Sholto Percy and Reuben Percy, *The Percy Anecdotes*, London: J. Cumberland, 1826.

14 December: Robert Southey, *Robert Southey: The Story of His Life Written in His Letters*, ed. John Dennis, Boston: Lothrop Company, 1887.

15 December: Magazine editorial, Anon., *The Vista: The Quarterly Magazine of the Glasgow School of Architecture Club*, 1, no. 4, Autumn 1909, quoted in M134 The Glasgow School of Art [Catalogue project entry], Mackintosh Architecture, University of Glasgow, https://www.mackintosh-architecture.gla.ac.uk/catalogue/browse/display/?rs=133&xml=des#s156des96a-back.

16 December: Stuart Dodgson Collingwood, *The Life and Letters of Lewis Carroll*, New York: Century Co, 1898.

17 December: Sir Henry Cole, quoted in 'The First Christmas Card', Victoria and Albert Museum, https://www.vam.ac.uk/articles/the-first-christmas-card. *Athenaeum* advert, see https://babel.hathitrust.org/cgi/pt?id=umn.31951001922942 4&view=1up&seq=1072&q1=%22 Christmas%20Congratulation%20Card%22.

18 December: Jonathan Glancey, 'The Folly of Fallingwater', *Guardian*, 10 September 2001. Courtesy of Guardian News & Media Ltd.

19 December: Kazimir Malevich leaflet, see http://www.k-malevich.ru/works/tom1/index7.html. Accessed November 2020. Author's translation.

20 December: Grace Cossington Smith interviewed by Hazel de Berg in the Hazel de Berg collection, 16 August 1965 [sound recording], TRC 1/122, National Library of Australia Archives.

21 December: 1861 US Act, Sec. 7, 'Public Acts of the Thirty-Seventh Congress of the United States', Library of Congress, https://www.loc.gov/law/help/statutes-at-large/37th-congress/session-2/c37s2ch1.pdf.

22 December: David Zwirner gallery 'Early Work' press release, 2004, https://www.davidzwirner.com/exhibitions/2004/early-work/press-release.

23 December: Vincent van Gogh, Letter No. 732. Leo Jansen, Hans Luijten, Nienke Bakker (eds.) (2009), *Vincent van Gogh - The Letters*. Version: January 2020. Amsterdam & The Hague: Van Gogh Museum & Huygens ING. http://vangoghletters.org/en/let732.

24 December: Apollo 8 conversation, quoted in NASA, 'Transcripts of *Earthrise: The 45th Anniversary*' [YouTube video, NASA Goddard, 20 December 2013], https://svs.gsfc.nasa.gov/vis/a000000/a004100/a004129/G2013-102_Earthrise_MASTER_youtube_hqTranscripts.html. © NASA.

25 December: Damien Hirst, press conference, 28 November 2003.

26 December: John Trumbull, *Catalogue of Paintings*, quoted in Trumbull, *Autobiography, Reminiscences and Letters of John Trumbull, from 1756 to 1841*, New Haven: Wiley and Putnam, 1841.

27 December: Ralph Waldo Emerson: lecture, quoted in *The Works of Ralph Waldo Emerson*, Boston and New York: Fireside Edition, 1909; 'Art' essay, in Emerson, *The Complete Works of Ralph Waldo Emerson, Volume II: Essays, First Series*, Boston: Jas. Monroe & Sons, 1841.

28 December: Benjamin Haydon: *The Autobiography and Memoirs of Benjamin Robert Haydon (1786–1846)*, ed. Tom Taylor, New York: Harcourt, Brace and Co, 1926; diary entry, quoted in *Neglected Genius: The Diaries of Benjamin Robert Haydon, 1808–1846*, ed. John Jolliffe, London: Hutchinson, 1990.

29 December: Leonardo da Vinci, quoted in *The Notebooks of Leonardo da Vinci*, trans. Jean Paul Richter, London: S. Low, Marston, Searle & Rivington, 1880.

30 December: Giorgio Vasari, *Lives of the Most Eminent Painters, Sculptors & Architects*, trans. Gaston De Vere, London: Philip Lee Warner, 1915.

31 December: Benjamin Waterhouse Hawkins, Dinner invitation and menu, Collection 803, Benjamin Waterhouse Hawkins Album, Academy of Natural Sciences of Drexel University, https://ansp.org/research/library/archives/0800-0899/hawkins803/.

Index